Thinking about Singapore's Tomorrow

WHY NOT?

Thinking about Singapore's Tomorrow

WHY NOT?

Editors

Margaret Thomas & Kanwaljit Soin

 **World Scientific**

NEW JERSEY · LONDON · SINGAPORE · BEIJING · SHANGHAI · HONG KONG · TAIPEI · CHENNAI · TOKYO

Published by

World Scientific Publishing Co. Pte. Ltd.
5 Toh Tuck Link, Singapore 596224
USA office: 27 Warren Street, Suite 401-402, Hackensack, NJ 07601
UK office: 57 Shelton Street, Covent Garden, London WC2H 9HE

British Library Cataloguing-in-Publication Data
A catalogue record for this book is available from the British Library.

Cover design courtesy of Cheng Puay Koon

WHY NOT?
Thinking About Singapore's Tomorrow

ISBN 978-981-12-9237-8 (hardcover)
ISBN 978-981-12-9279-8 (paperback)
ISBN 978-981-12-9238-5 (ebook for institutions)
ISBN 978-981-12-9239-2 (ebook for individuals)

For any available supplementary material, please visit
https://www.worldscientific.com/worldscibooks/10.1142/13819#t=suppl

Desk Editor: Sandhya Venkatesh

Typeset by Stallion Press
Email: enquiries@stallionpress.com

Printed in Singapore

This big book is about building a better future for women. Its authors represent the diversity they seek. Men, women, and ethnically and culturally diverse individuals cover themes that are wide-ranging and forward-looking. Academic, personal, lived experience, data-rich studies with policy recommendations – this is an essential resource for policy makers and for understanding women's lives.

CHAN HENG CHEE
Ambassador at Large and Chair, ISEAS-Yusof Ishak Institute

Kanwaljit and Margaret have put together a collection of essays from some of Singapore's most illustrious voices. With candid reflections and bold ideas, this anthology invites readers to imagine and advocate for a more inclusive, equitable Singapore.

BOO JUNFENG
Filmmaker

Just the list of authors would be enough of a reason to read this book: it represents the who's who of Singapore civil society. But beyond name recognition, the topics which are discussed are crucial if we are indeed bothered about Singapore's future. The book is as much a call for ordinary citizens as it is for the government to think deeply about issues which matter to us as a nation.

WALID JUMBLATT BIN ABDULLAH
Assistant Professor, School of Social Sciences,
Nanyang Technological University

It's a blockbuster of thought-provoking essays that offers personal, frank, and fresh views on many issues. There is so much to learn from the book.

CHRISTINE SUCHEN LIM
Award-winning writer and Cultural Medallion recipient

Why Not? is a thought-provoking, reflective, and ultimately hopeful volume of essays by people from all walks of life. Thoughtfully edited by Kanwaljit Soin and Margaret Thomas, this book invites us to come together to envision a more inclusive, equitable, and caring Singapore. As citizens of a young nation, it is our responsibility to build a national culture and identity that we can all be proud of. *Why Not?* reminds us that an intersectional approach to nation-building is essential if we are to create a future in which our children will not just survive but thrive.

KISHORE MAHBUBANI
Distinguished Fellow at Asia Research Institute and
author of Living the Asian Century

An energising read that showcases a mix of vital perspectives to an intriguing question - if our collective Singapore story were written with diversity in mind, what would change?

MICHELLE MARTIN
Broadcaster

An outstanding achievement — this collection of essays addresses crucial issues that must be actively confronted in working towards a better future for Singapore, among them gender equality, ageing, freedom to exercise choice, the right to dignity and respect; and brings together at the same time substantive works of scholarship, critical analysis, and personal reflection that are keenly informed and compellingly readable.

SHIRLEY CHEW
Professor, English Programme, Nanyang Technological University

Why Not? Thinking about Singapore's Tomorrow is a book that everyone should make time to read. It will get you thinking about issues like why diversity at the workplace is so important, what it is like to age in Singapore, why there is a need to redefine masculinity, and whether we are doing enough to educate our children about consent. These are just some of the complex but crucial topics discussed by the very capable contributors. No words are minced, no difficult questions avoided. And WHY NOT? Lasting change starts with education, and education means opening your mind to new ideas and different ways of looking at things. This book will do precisely that.

SHARUL CHANNA
Stand-up Comedian

As Singapore looks forward to celebrating 60 years of independence in 2025, this volume brings together a diverse range of authors to reflect on the society they envisage for Singapore in the years ahead. From academic analysis to personal reflection, from youthful hopes to experienced contemplation, this volume will offer insights and ideas for anyone who cares about how Singapore society evolves.

LILY KONG
President, Singapore Management University

One of my biggest issues with Singapore and the Crazy Rich Asians phenomenon is the stubborn reinforcement of both the myth and the bubble. The myth is, we're all obscenely wealthy. And the bubble is reserved exclusively for the obscenely wealthy minority who perpetuate the myth. This wonderful and vital new book — Why Not? — shatters both. In thinking about Singapore's tomorrow, the writers ask the most challenging questions, like why not demand more from a patriarchy that still rules from the boardroom to the bedroom? Why not demand fairness for the single mother, the domestic helper, and the migrant worker? As the proud son of a single mother, I admire anyone who speaks up for those overlooked, neglected, or pushed to the margins of society. The authors do all of this and so much more, leaving the reader to ponder the most hopeful question: why not dream of a kinder, happier, empathetic Singapore? Why not indeed.

NEIL HUMPHREYS
Author, Broadcaster, Journalist, Public Speaker

"Why Not?" is a playful challenge. Each writer invites you to see a norm they believe is 'not working' and proposes new norms that 'work' better. You may feel provoked into disagreement or have new convictions evoked in you. May you read and find a gem here that nudges you towards working with someone to create your preferred future for Singapore.

SHIAO-YIN KUIK
Executive Director, Common Ground Civic Centre & Consultancy

Contents

———✦⟨⟨✦⟩⟩✦———

Editors' Note

In 2015, we edited *Our Lives to Live: Putting a Woman's Face to Change in Singapore*. It was part of World Scientific's series marking Singapore's 50 years of independence and many of the essays, all written by women, had a historical slant.

In 2022, we decided it was time for another book. In the seven years since *Our Lives to Live*, much had happened globally and locally that affected women. The #MeToo movement that began in the United States in 2017 was encouraging women everywhere to speak up and take action about the sexual harassment and assault they had experienced.

In September 2020, Law and Home Affairs Minister K Shanmugam declared that if there was to be any hope of reducing the incidence of sexual violence, Singapore needed to embrace gender equality as a fundamental value. Children should be taught at a very young age about mutual respect and consent, he said.

His speech kicked off a year-long series of Conversations that involved thousands of people and that culminated with the publication in March 2022 of the White Paper on Singapore Women's

Development. The White Paper outlines a 10-year 25-point action plan to improve women's lives in Singapore.

Meanwhile, the Covid-19 pandemic had affected many lives and raised a host of questions about how we live and work, and the consequences of climate change were looming ever larger.

With so much having happened in seven years, we wondered what might lie ahead, and we decided this was something we should explore in a new book. We set out to get a bunch of women, and some feminist men, to write about what they would like to see take shape in Singapore in the years ahead, with gender equality as the underlying theme.

We listed the topics that should be covered, identified possible writers, and started contacting people. Not everyone we approached was able to join us in our project, and we had to drop a few topics. But we managed to pull together a diverse range of people who have produced the thoughtful and thought-provoking essays we wanted for the book. Some of the writers are old friends or acquaintances, others we tracked down after much research, and some we got to know through serendipitous chance encounters.

As the chapters began to take shape, we had the idea of using as chapter separators quotes by women in the Singapore Women's Hall of Fame. These quotes, pithy and pointed, add to the range of women's views and voices in this volume.

It took us a while to decide on the title. We had several working titles, then one day as we were tossing around ideas that got increasingly off the wall, we laughingly said 'Why not?' — and realised that was the title we needed. It signals a readiness to challenge convention, to explore new ideas, to open our minds to new approaches.

As with *Our Lives to Live*, the proceeds from sales of this book will be donated equally to three women's organisations: AWARE,

Singapore Women's Hall of Fame, and WINGS. For the editors and writers, this book is a labour of love. We put our minds to the task of envisioning our ideal Singapore because helping to bring about that future is important to us. We hope readers will find in the essays much food for thought about the society we should be shaping in Singapore.

Margaret Thomas and Kanwaljit Soin

"Whether openly or silently, I have always rebelled against attempts to define women. The lesson I have learned is to never let anyone or anything define you as that means ceding your choices to others and limiting yourself."

~ **Halimah Yacob, then Speaker of Parliament, at the National University of Singapore Commencement ceremony, July 2016**

Foreword

Halimah Yacob

Although Singapore started its life as an independent nation unexpectedly and inauspiciously in 1965, we are now a successful and vibrant nation that many other countries would like to emulate. The core values of multi-culturalism, meritocracy, and stewardship have been fundamental to Singapore's success, but it is the spirit and conviction of its people that is the bedrock of our nation. And half of the people of Singapore are women.

It has been rightly said that women hold up half the sky but, as in many other countries, for a long time this was not fully acknowledged in Singapore. In recent years, however, much has been done to recognise the role played by women in Singapore's development and to level the playing field so that women can realise their full potential and lead the lives they want.

I am grateful for the opportunities I have had to realise my potential and to serve Singapore in so many ways including, most recently, in its highest office. I hope that I have paved the way for other women, and that young girls will grow up knowing that whatever their current circumstances they can aspire to one day become the President or the Prime Minister of Singapore.

But for all the progress we have made, there are still entrenched societal attitudes that can limit and severely disadvantage women in many ways. There is, for example, still the expectation that women are responsible for caregiving, and there continues to be far too much violence against women and girls.

These are not women's issues. These are issues that affect all in our society, and we will only be able to find lasting solutions when there has been a mindset shift and attitudes have changed. The White Paper on Singapore Women's Development that was published in 2022 outlines the way ahead on this, and I am confident that we will in time achieve that shift in attitudes.

Nine years ago, when I was Speaker of Parliament, I contributed a chapter to the first book that Kanwaljit Soin and Margaret Thomas edited, *Our Lives to Live: Putting a Woman's Face to Change in Singapore*. In my chapter I argued the case for more women in Parliament because having women in the highest decision-making body of the nation changes perceptions about the role of men and women.

At that time, women made up about 24 per cent of parliamentarians; this has risen slightly to just under 30 per cent today. Then there was just one female full minister in the Cabinet; today there are three. So in nine years we have seen welcome progress in our political leadership. There has been similar progress in our corporate leadership. In 2018, women made up just 15 per cent of the boards of the top 100 listed companies; today the number is around 23 per cent.

So, the changes are taking place. But is the change happening fast enough? And are we heading in the right direction? What is the Singapore that Singaporeans want to see take shape over the next few decades, and how can we bring about gender equality as we shape our ideal society? How can women contribute effectively to this process so that their views are taken into account in the formulation of policies and programmes?

These are the questions that Kanwaljit and Margaret put to a diverse range of people, and the result is a collection of essays that will complement the government's *Forward Singapore* report published in 2023 following its consultation exercise to capture the shared values and aspirations of Singaporeans.

I am glad the editors brought together such a diverse group of writers — women and men, teenagers and octogenarians, academics, artists, journalists, educators, caregivers, activists, lawyers, doctors, and so many more. Their essays offer us much food for thought and discussion. Some of the ideas and ideals put forth may seem controversial, but they represent the perspectives and proposals from the different segments of our diverse society.

By listening objectively to the many voices in our society, discussing and debating robustly but rationally our different viewpoints, we deepen our understanding of the challenges and issues facing our society and how to collectively forge our way forward in a volatile and uncertain world.

HALIMAH YACOB, Chancellor of the Singapore University of Social Sciences, served as the eighth, and first female, President of Singapore from 2017 to 2023. Prior to that she was, from 2013, the first female Speaker of Parliament. After getting a law degree from the University of Singapore in 1978, she joined the National Trades Union Congress and headed the women's development secretariat and the legal services department before becoming NTUC's deputy secretary-general. She stood for election as a People's Action Party candidate in 2001 and was the first Malay woman to be elected an MP. Before becoming Speaker, Halimah served as minister of state in the Ministry of Social and Family Development. She was the first Singaporean to serve, from 1999 to 2011, on the Governing Body of the International Labour Organisation, a United Nations agency.

Review. Rewind. Revise.

"Singapore has achieved much since independence. But it must develop a 'soul' that will arouse citizens, at home and overseas, to feel immense pride to be a Singaporean. Citizens need to feel loved and cared for by their country just as they are expected to love and be loyal to their country."

~ Singapore Armed Forces trailblazer Koh Chai Hong, for The Lives of Women exhibition at the National Museum, Jan–Mar 2022

CHAPTER 1

Ordinary People Dream

— ⚬◦⟨◦⟩◦⚬ —

Teo You Yenn

What do ordinary people want from life?

Over the years, this question has weaved its way into my research projects. In some, I explicitly posed it in some form to respondents and addressed it directly in the process of data collection and report writing.[1] In others, I did not consciously and directly raise the issue, but it emerged anyway.[2] This simple question is the pulsating heart at the centre of conversations about work, marriage, parenting, family, children.

The question has a subtle presence in other aspects of my professional life as well. I hear it in students' comments and questions when I teach, notice its shadow when I am asked for advice about navigating academia, and encounter it when I discuss my research with a variety of audiences outside the university.

---

[1] See, for example, Ng *et al.* (2019); Ng *et al.* (2021); Teo (2011).

[2] See, for example, Teo (2018a); Teo (2022).

To say that this question emerges in these multiple sites is not to say that there is a singular or straightforward answer. Instead, it is to register that people from different backgrounds and at various points in the life course have hopes, aspirations, dreams. Precisely because of the diversity of our society, the shape and colour of 'hopes, aspirations, dreams' varies. Some people boldly list their wishes as timelines and goals — like coins to be picked up on a path; others pepper talk of ideals with constant loops back to realities — dreams tethered by a rope to a pole; yet others wonder if they are allowed to dream in daylight at all. Some think primarily in terms of individual goals; others speak mostly of what they wish for their children; and yet others think about friends, communities, society at large. To present this as different groups having different orientations is also not entirely precise because what emerges also depends on context: one-on-one conversations compel people to speak in individualistic terms but invitations to reflect broadly or conversations that happen in groups open up ruminations about Singapore society. Context matters in another, more profound way: what people want, how they think and talk about what they want, is also deeply shaped by how they relate to others, what they imagine as reasonable, realistic, or good to want given what society looks like and where they place within it. In other words, hopes, aspirations, dreams are not made up entirely in individual minds — their shapes and possibilities and boundaries are socially constructed and shared.

The editors of this book, Kanwaljit Soin and Margaret Thomas, invite us, writers and readers both, to contemplate an ideal society of the future. In imagining any ideal world — and let us use the word 'utopian' — the question must be asked: what do ordinary people want from life? If the imagined world is meant to house the same diverse population that exists in actuality, then it is crucial for us to also ask: *whose* ideal, *whose* utopia? In a context in which a single political party, the People's Action Party, has had monopoly in shaping answers to the question of what kind of society Singapore should be, it is especially urgent to consider these questions autonomously.

The notion of 'ordinary people' carries with it precisely some inclusion of both views as they differ and views where they coalesce, as well as the potential for imagining ourselves independent of how the state imagines us. Starting from this question in the imagination of a utopia is also important if we are interested in what Erik Olin Wright (2010) referred to as *real* utopias, ideals grounded by possibility:

> The idea of 'real utopias' embraces this tension between dreams and practice. It is grounded in the belief that what is pragmatically possible is not fixed independently of our imaginations, but is itself shaped by our visions. ...Nurturing clear-sighted understandings of what it would take to create social institutions free of oppression is part of creating a political will for radical social changes to reduce oppression. A vital belief in a utopian ideal may be necessary to motivate people to set off on the journey from the status quo in the first place, even though the actual destination may fall short of the utopian ideal. ...What we need, then, is "real utopias": utopian ideals that are grounded in the real potentials of humanity, utopian destinations that have accessible waystations, utopian designs of institutions that can inform our practical tasks of navigating a world of imperfect conditions for social change (6).

To bring about improvements to society, to bring about a better world, requires an understanding of existing realities, and then using those to stretch our imaginations to bring about better alternatives.

In this essay, I hope to show that it is precisely through listening to, making sense of, and taking seriously what ordinary people want that we can gain deeper understandings of the limitations and possibilities that structure our lives. And it is from there that we can consider alternative social arrangements wherein ideals — utopias — may serve the aspirations of a broad and diverse collective.

* * *

Over the past two decades, I have interviewed people who together make up the diversity of Singapore society: I met them at various points in the life course; they embody various ethnic or religious cultures; there are women and men, who relate to gender and sexuality in varied ways; they are single/married/widowed/divorced; they have had different experiences with education and hold a range of credentials; they have a variety of occupations, work different types of hours and make varying amounts of money; they live in different types of housing, within households of different configurations. Each research project had its specific goals and hence its unique questions, but I have had a longstanding interest in talking to people about everyday living — what time do you wake up, tell me about what a typical weekday is like? How did you decide where to buy your flat? What jobs have you worked in, and what was each one like? How are your co-workers and boss? How do you get from work to home? How often do you eat out? In your family, who cooks? When you say you must be home to supervise your children, what do you mean? What do your kids like to do, what are their personalities like, what do you hope for them when they grow up? When you stop working, how will you spend your time?

The responses and stories pile up. Pictures form of ordinary people going about their lives: the daily hum of work, sleep, eat, scroll, laugh, shout, chatter, quarrel; breakfast at the downstairs kopitiam and tonight whose turn to tabao dinner; the mundane packing of schoolbags bumping up against the conversation-hogging "PSLE Year"; peaceful me-time on the MRT pierced by frantic shower-dinner-nag-homework-pack (again with the schoolbag) bedtime routines; WhatsApp messages between mothers, teachers, grandparents, domestic workers forming webs of care that hold children's schedules together. In these daily acts of living, if you look closely, you see people seeking out meaning, making sense of who they are and who they want to be, thinking of themselves and contemplating loved ones, experiencing fear, frustration, and trepidation, feeling hope and wistfulness.

I won't lie — it is not always easy to spot the similarities. Every person's story can come to sound unique. But a job is a job and mine is to figure out patterns. Describing some of these patterns will help get to what I think we should know about what ordinary people are challenged by. This in turn can help us see what they want in life.

Patterns: Challenges
Quests for work-life balance

Parenting is busy. For those who work 'office hours', mornings are about getting everyone in the household ready for and travelling to school and work. Most of the day is spent at work, sometimes squeezing in an errand or a call home to check on the kids. Evenings are spent on household chores, supervising children with homework, bedtime routines.

The 'second shift' that sociologist Arlie Hochschild wrote about in 1989 remains relevant — it is still women more so than men who come home from jobs to this labour. In Singapore, for some middle- and upper-middle class households, some of this is transferred to migrant domestic workers, entrenching the tasks themselves as women's work. On the other hand, fatherhood deepens men's sense of duty and responsibility to be wage earners — upping the pressure to hold onto jobs, move up career ladders, or find additional sources of income through side hustles.

Weekends too are busy, particular for those with limited access to paid help — house cleaning and laundry, shopping for groceries and household items, visits with parents or other family members, bringing children to enrichment classes and tuition. Outings to parks and malls are squeezed into this schedule, but for many families, time for play and leisure is limited and unscheduled downtime rare.

With few exceptions, across class and ethnic lines, parents speak about this time in life — when jobs are demanding and children are young — as hectic and stressful. Time constraints, money pressures, having to be accountable to multiple parties, are each daily experiences. There is often a sense of life slightly off-kilter. Mothers in particular talk about profound feelings of guilt as they see themselves falling short both at work and at home.

Education as uneasy care labour

Paying attention to the norms around childhood and education in Singapore today, we can further specify the challenges of work-life balance as well as the gendered nature of care labour.

Significant chunks of parents' time are spent on educated-related issues. I use 'issues' here purposefully. It is not just that parents spend time teaching children how to read or calculate, but that they engage in a whole host of other tasks — surf online forums to find out which primary schools they have good odds of getting into and how to improve those odds; tap on networks to figure out suitable tuition centres or tuition teachers; coordinate with teachers and tutors the tasks and strategies for improving children's performance; bring children to and from classes and wait while they are in them;

re-learn how to do mathematics homework from parent chatgroups or school-run workshops; sit with, check, nag, scold, coax, threaten, bribe children.

Most of these, in most households and within the larger culture, is gendered labour — marked as women's domain. Even for those with the means to pay for help, or in households where fathers are involved in caregiving, some tasks seem tethered to motherhood. Mothers are the ones re-arranging work schedules and career goals, often realigning their identities and self-worth in the process. They are the ones forming information networks and running parent volunteer groups. Mothers are whom teachers and tutors call when children act up. Mothers are even the ones using their "own money" to pay for tuition or enrichment in cases where fathers "do not believe in tuition". Built into ideals of contemporary Singaporean motherhood is the duty of supporting children in their schooling. Are women bringing this on themselves? Sometimes their husbands say so and sometimes they themselves think so. An image of water flowing is useful here. These are beliefs, practices, habits, common sense that flow through society in complex ways — repeatedly enacted by women, men, teachers, grandparents, co-workers, children; sometimes informal and uncoordinated, other times guided by procedures, policies, rules; not without resistance or contradiction but nonetheless ending up affirming, like so many grooves deep and shallow, narrow and wide, mothers' work in children's education. Regardless of what individual women want, motherhood in Singapore today entails, as an interviewee told me when explaining what she is suspending her aspirations for: "be decent mother, go through PSLE".

There are few things a social scientist can say so unequivocally: no parent enjoys these tasks. They take up time and sap energy, generate parent-child or marital tension and conflict, cost money, and leave parents feeling uneasy. The texture of the unease is instructive: on a regular basis, parents talk about children's educational progress as problems requiring dutiful intervention. A child is not reading and writing yet; they are not keeping up in maths; they regularly forget to do their homework; their Mother Tongue is very weak; they are already in Primary 5 but not studying hard enough, et cetera. Children are regularly framed — through parent-teacher conferences, chat groups and online forums, marking rubrics and grading curves, numerous conversations comparing results — as lacking, problematic, always with room for improvement. Parents are compelled to view their kids through this 'problem' lens. Missing or difficult to sustain is a sense of awe at children's growth, a sense of joy around learning, and a feeling of security that one expects *should* accompany handing over one's child to a 'world-class education system'.

Contrary to popular discourses around *kiasu* parents or Tiger mums, the driving forces fuelling parental anxiety and intervention, for most parents, have to do with fears of being left out or behind rather than drive and ambition for getting ahead. The aspirations are not centred on cultivating great talents but on 'average is good enough'. It is a 'how to avoid...' orientation and not a 'how to become...' sensibility. This is substantively different from the stereotype of parents as competitive, ambitious, striving for upward mobility. It is a negative rather than an upbeat posture, with emotional registers hovering at angst, frustration, or resignation. In interview after interview, parents lamented and sighed: childhood should not be like this. They "feel sorry" for their kids; they worry about the pressures and stresses children today face and the mental health problems that seem common; they are not convinced this is the right way to push their children but do it because "no choice". Parents hope their children can make it through — somehow "find their passion" and eventually have "good jobs" that allow them to be "independent". Despite all the time spent in schools — every one ostensibly a good one — they do not seem to have much faith that schools will guide students toward these goals, only that credentials are a precondition to these ends. Some parents, indeed, go a step further and wonder aloud if the focus on tests and exams are preparing children appropriately for a rapidly changing world.

In Singapore today, parents see the steering of children through a tough education journey as their major duty. I have been astonished to hear the many stories of their investment in and commitment to the process. I am struck to see that it is an uneasy existence: leisure sacrificed, money spent, emotions and relationships characterised by contradictions and tensions, ambivalence and fear.

Matthias Doepke and Fabrizio Zilibotti (2019), in a study investigating the links between economic conditions and parenting practices, found that societies with higher levels of income and wealth inequality also tend to be societies where parents put a great deal of private investment into education. When people experience high costs of living and when they see unequal lives resulting from different educational trajectories and credentials, these shape their parenting decisions. Viewing Singaporean parents and their education practices through this lens, we are compelled to look to forces that shape individual behaviours from the outside in.

Basic needs through the life course

The unease I have just described can be de-particularised — that is, separated from the specific experiences of mothers/parents and considered instead from the perspective of other ordinary Singaporeans and across the life course. This helps us see more clearly what we overlook if we narrowly prejudge that the problem is to do with "parents' mindsets". What *are* parents so concerned about that drives them to spend money, time, and energy on children's education? That their children can live good lives — where they can meet their needs, have some semblance of security, be fulfilled, contribute to society. This aspiration is not limited to parents, nor only on behalf of children. At multiple points in the life course, people aspire to these for themselves and their loved ones.

According to a wide range of people across the life course, these are basic needs: housing, food, clothing; opportunities to education, employment, work-life balance, healthcare; a sense of belonging, respect, security, and independence; choices to participate in social activities, and the freedom to engage in one's cultural and religious practices.[3] At different times in life, priorities shift: older persons are slightly more concerned than younger ones about healthcare and slightly less preoccupied about work-life balance, for example. How needs are met also vary. Young children may attend birthday parties and working adults go out to meals with friends, and both these activities meet their needs for social belonging. Across variations of age, occupation, education level, gender, ethnicity and religion, the entire list of needs matter for living a life of dignity. Everyone wants to live a life of dignity.

Talking and listening to people about their lives over the years, I hear worries about rising living costs, job insecurities and the attendant risks of insufficient income for meeting these needs. Ordinary people recognise that Singaporeans live in a relatively wealthy and peaceful country and some talk about feeling lucky and grateful for this. Nonetheless, they are also deeply aware that things are expensive and that there are challenges to meeting needs. This is a sentiment that looks different from different perspectives: older

---

[3] For how we ascertained basic needs through focus group discussions, see Ng *et al.* (2019).

people worry about falling sick and burdening their children with healthcare costs. Working adults worry about not making enough to support dependent children/parents and save for their own retirements. Younger adults wonder if they will be able to live independently, including whether they can afford HDB flats of their own. Everyone but the wealthiest understands that they must work consistently and over many years to meet their needs; no one thinks there is anywhere a free lunch.

Understandably, ordinary people are most aware of and concerned about their own circumstances — their idiosyncratic pains and struggles, the well-being of their own families. But it is worth pointing out that there is also significant awareness and concern about inequalities in society more broadly. People recognise that the challenges of everyday living are not experienced evenly across society. They care that people have unequal access to things. While talking to a group of young people about basic needs, for example, my research collaborators and I listened to them articulate the importance of university degrees for securing good jobs. They insisted that we should include the cost of university in basic needs budgets while also pointing out that not all young people can qualify for university because of earlier inequalities in access to tuition and other resources. They expressed these views not with jadedness or cynicism but with a sense that things *should* be fairer. Including university fees in basic needs budgets are a way of redressing unfairness — for these youth, no one who qualifies for university should be deprived of that opportunity due to inability to pay.

In sum, the broader expressions of need and anxieties I have heard over the years suggest that here is an uneasiness that is not limited to people who are parents. In addition, the unease is both narrow and wide: fear for the self, certainly, but also uneasiness about where society is.

Patterns: Human needs

What do ordinary people want from life? Having seen some common challenges, let's circle back to this question.

In a diverse society, there are varying tastes and preferences, disparate belief systems and practices. Different objects, relationships, and activities hold meaning for people. As I have also indicated, each of us morphs as we move through the life course. To think 'what ordinary people want', as I said I would at the beginning of the essay, and to do this while respecting diverse aspirations and orientations, we must contemplate things at a general level. That is, we should consider the broad principles and values anchoring most people's relationship to needs; to think, in other words, expansively and broadly about what people want, without falling into traps of narrow prescription or social engineering.

Three interlocking principles illustrate what I have learnt from ordinary people about human needs. The three pinciples are social belonging and respect; choice and autonomy; ethical agency.

People want to belong and to be respected. Belonging comes from being able to partake in social life. This encompasses a wide range of human activities and social spaces: the workplace and the labour market, community activities, family and friendship networks, schooling and education, religious and cultural gatherings, virtual spaces of public and political discourse, et cetera. Most people are embedded in some groups and networks, and they care to be in step with the norms of the social groups they are a part of. Indeed, one's place in social groups is continuously enacted and negotiated through shared practices and beliefs with others in that group. Belonging, in other words, is not a static state but a continuous work-in-progress, with the risk of exclusion always built in. Children's embeddedness in relationships with their classmates, for example, is daily enacted by their sharing of experiences and knowledge of certain toys, games, TV shows, Tik Tok phenomena, et cetera, as well as their participation in activities considered 'normal' in a given time and place — tuition, enrichment activities, school trips, hanging out after school. Exclusion happens when, in a sustained manner — over time and across situations — a kid is unable to partake in what their peers generally do.

Respect is a crucial component of one's membership in a social world. Belonging is genuinely achieved when one is respected by others in one's circles. This is predicated on entering into relationships as an equal; more precisely, in fact, respect is given and received when people abide by the many unspoken rules of social contracts. Most relationships are guided by relational roles such as student-teacher, parent-child, and senior-junior. To maintain these ties, different things are expected of people in different positions. For example, an older member of a family would not be expected to give a very large *ang bao* at a wedding but their standing in the community would be affected if they showed up empty-handed. Respect, then, has to be continuously forged. This is not to indicate that it is quid pro quo or difficult strategic work — most of what we do in social life is habitual and effortless and certainly human relations are not all instrumental. But 'give and take' — that easygoing phrase we use to describe relationships — is exactly that: give *and* take, not give and give or take and take.

The importance of social belonging and respect, and the conditions and continuous work necessary for securing them, is especially salient when people experience being on the edge of attaining belonging and respect. One interesting and perhaps unobvious example comes from women who quit their jobs to take care of children. Women as mothers often pay attention to how their children are keeping in step with peers, sometimes putting aside their own dreams to make sure children do not fall too out of step where education is concerned. In the process, their own needs of belonging and respect may fray. Despite the backdrop of social scripts about 'motherly love' or 'sacrifice' or essentialist beliefs about women's nature as caregivers, it turns out quitting wage work to care for children is not an easy transition. It is not social esteem that awaits. Women's access to belonging and respect come under challenge. My interviewees described losing common ground with co-workers and other employed friends, going through periods of loneliness, and feeling out of step with society. They lament no longer being able to talk to ex-colleagues and knowing only things like "Daiso which product is good to wash toilets". This is not simply one set of knowledge swapped out for another, but the loss of belonging and respect that accompanies losing more highly valued knowledge. Although most women who make decisions to cut back on wage work to care for children make peace with their decisions, this takes time, effort to build up alternative social communities (of other full-time mothers). The loss of social standing from the loss of income never goes away entirely.

Paying closer attention to money and its meaning, we see also that what's at stake are people's needs for choice and autonomy. What are choice and autonomy and how can they be thought of as general needs (i.e. shared by all humans)? These are needs to make decisions, to exercise one's will, to have some control over what one wants to do and how one wants to live. It is rarely unlimited; indeed, people do not demand unfettered choice. Instead, when ordinary people express this need, they refer to wanting *some* degree of autonomy and independence, *some* degree of being able to choose from *some* options. What is the relationship between money and choice? Not having access to money can limit one's choices: about clothing, food and nutrition, exercise and healthcare, social activities, and education. Some of these can seem trivial and inconsequential, and yet have long-term consequences on well-being. Having insufficient money to accept one invitation to eat out with friends may not seem like a big deal, but persistent inability to 'choose' to participate can mean being left out of future invitations and activities. Not having enough money to 'choose' to give children tuition and enrichment, over the long run, may result in narrowing their future prospects relative to their peers.

What is the relationship between money, choice, and gender? Looking closely at women who have no independent income, we see that money shapes relationships. Women speak of the discomfort of having to ask husbands for money, of 'choosing' to cut down on their own needs when they no longer have income. Conversely, women who have independent earnings speak of being able to 'choose' to spend more on children's activities or things, of being able to treat friends to meals, of being able to more freely give their parents money or contribute to their religious groups — *without having to ask for permission*. Having these options, and the capacity to exercise them, brings a sense of worth and dignity. In general, relationships in which all parties have choice are relationships that are voluntary and free, rather than obligatory and captive.[4] When people articulate needs for choice and autonomy, they mean this in a wide range of areas — material objects, practices and life paths, relationships.

Finally, it is worth drawing attention to the notion of *ethical* agency. Being able to do the 'right' thing matters to ordinary people. 'Choices' are of course often about pedantic things that hold little moral weight — choosing what clothes to wear or what to eat for lunch on an ordinary day, for example, do not usually mean very

---

[4] For a thought-provoking and insightful account of this, see Partanen (2017).

much. There are many human actions, however, that people feel *should* be guided by values — some judgement about what is right or wrong, good or bad. When talking about parenting, for example, people invoked "values" — the importance of having values; values they want to teach their kids; and the "good persons" with "right values" they hope their children will become. Wanting to do what is right, to show and teach their children the 'right' values, is something parents want to be able to do — the kind of ethical agency they need and want.

Ethical agency is not easy to exercise. Take enrichment and tuition as a ubiquitous part of parental decisions and practice in Singapore today. This is an interesting example because it is a site of ethical tension — where parents feel that what they are doing is not exactly right from a certain perspective, and yet a duty from another angle. They feel they should be supervising homework, nagging at their kids, putting them in tuition, but they also feel that doing these things takes away the joy of learning, stress their children out, and undermine other values they want their kids to learn. The unease I refer to earlier stems from the troubling of one's ethical agency. Embedded in this is the lack of agency to do something according to one's sense of right and wrong.

Ethical agency should not be thought of as merely an individual capacity or quality. It is something one truly has only when one's choices and values, when exercised, are also *legible* to others in the larger social context. That is, it is not good enough to say that people can do whatever they want, can go ahead and exercise their own values even if against the grain ("no one is stopping you", "it's up to the individual"). True ethical agency is possible only when those choices, those values, that life, have a dignified space to exist — acknowledged with respect if not empathy — within a society. What is legibility? It is the acknowledgement or recognition by others. It is about one's life having a place in the stories told about a society; it is living a life imaginable to others; it is being a social actor worthy and comprehensible within the vocabularies and frames that contain imagined communities of 'nation', or 'country', or 'city', or 'we the citizens'. It is, as the philosopher Judith Butler put it, to be 'grievable' — considered worth defending and potentially worth grieving over if lost (Butler 2020, 2009).

Butler's account of 'precarity' typically draws our attention to those who are cast completely outside of 'grievability' — the queer subject, the transient migrant subject, the refugee, the racialised other. These are persons, or rather categories, stripped of personhood — with incomprehensible 'lifestyles' or 'cultures'; with no standing in history or stories told in half-truths; lives unvalued in profound material ways as witnessed when lives lost go ungrieved. If we suspend our belief that these are 'minority issues', there is a larger lesson we can draw about the social schema we all reside in: in which life is organised around hierarchies in human worth; in which there are systematic mechanisms marking some people for exclusion. Butler reminds us that legibility — the acknowledgement or recognition by others — is central to our capacity to live as humans with agency.

Ethical agency, then, is the ability to exercise some will, make some choices, have some degree of control over one's life, while *also* socially belonging. It entails being regarded with respect as a human equal by others in society, to have one's moral choices be recognised as legitimate and worthy.

* * *

How can people live the lives they want? Now that I have laid claims about what people want from life, another, more precise, way to ask the question is this: what conditions enable people to encounter social belonging and respect, to have capacities to exercise choice, autonomy, and ethical agency?

Enabling conditions: Principles

Let us consider the mothers I interviewed.

First, we must acknowledge and embrace that women do not all have the same preferences. This is the case even when we narrow our focus to mothers. That is the point of thinking in terms of *choices*, *autonomy*, *ethical agency*, instead of specific arrangements of work and care. Some mothers prefer to take time off when their children are born and then return to work when babies are old enough to be cared for by others. Some would like to spend more years primarily caring for young children. Some women value what they do at work and prefer not to give it up after children. At present, many mothers have limited options — they continue to work because they would otherwise have no income for their families; they quit their jobs because their children have no other caregivers; they fold down their own aspirations because there is otherwise insufficient time to supervise their children. They do all this in response to some combination of policies, familial constraints, and social norms. To exercise choice and agency, women need real options that span a range of possibilities, which allow for more alignment between preferences and practices. We can call these *options* only if they are *all* rewarded with dignity and meeting of material needs, and insofar as opportunity costs — particularly regarding security, social belonging, and respect — of some were not much more than others.

It is important to underscore that although choices appear to be taken in singular instances of time, the need for choice and agency in life is a continuous one. Options have to be regarded for their long-term consequences, including how they affect choice and agency later on. Again, this is not to suggest that people should have endless open doors available to them throughout life; no reasonable person expects this. Instead, it is to highlight that many women are offered 'choices' that may look alright at one point but are actually problematic over the long term. The 'choice' of quitting one's job at age 29 has to be considered not just for what it does at that point — for example, free up one's time to care for a baby; instead, we must also recognise that this looks like a quite different sort of choice if at age 36, this same person — still relatively young — encounters difficulties getting a job, pursuing a career, attaining financial independence and security.

In principle, then, social conditions can be said to be enabling if they have these qualities: some range of options that speak to variant preferences and needs; these options are each valued, recognised, and rewarded; they cannot be punishing either in the short- or long-term.

To this list, I will also add that options must be accessible to everyone, not only women, not just the university-educated, and not just the high-income. The current situation of inequality — where some women's choices are valorised and valued while other women's choices are judged and frowned upon; where men have one set of choices and women have another[5] — must be disrupted through breaking the connection between class background and gender on the one hand and options on the other. If, as I have argued, the true realisation of ethical agency depends on social recognition, this can only come about when all choices are respected *and* when *everyone's* choices are respected.

---

[5] For detailed descriptions, see "Work-life balance should not be class privilege" and "I want my children better than me" in *This is What Inequality Looks Like* (Teo 2018), and Teo (2018b, 2016, 2013b).

How will a range of options be made accessible to all mothers, in ways that do not simply mean the displacement of care labour from some women (with more money and power) to other women (with less)? Care labour must be valued differently than it currently is. We have to re-draw the balance sheet between wage work/income on the one side and the tasks associated with the care of children (or the elderly and disabled) on the other. To consider how, it is worthwhile reiterating a point feminist scholars have been making for a long time. Labour designated only to women tends to be undervalued labour — dismissed as unskilled, trivial, inconsequential. On the other hand, labour monopolised by men tends to be valorised as more difficult, serious, consequential. For care to be valued differently in society, the tethering of care labour to women and the gendering of care as 'feminine' need to be disrupted. The juxtaposition of care as secondary or inferior to employment/money/career — where these are to an extent gendered 'masculine' — has to be dislodged as well. Put more concretely, both men and women must be able to freely partake in both care labour and wage work. The right to work and the right to care should not be limited to one group or the other. That is the only way to de-gender both — to bring into being and hence into imaginations that these are human activities and everyone can do both or either. Simultaneously, precisely because the current organisation of care labour today is essentially a gendered displacement — from mothers to female domestic workers, female childcare teachers, female nannies — that also builds upon and extends class inequalities, we cannot neglect attending to how paid care work is recognised and caregivers compensated for their labour. For care work to be valued differently, it also must be paid for differently — not merely with 'appreciation' and 'gratitude' but also with fair wages and work conditions.

These are not issues that can be resolved at the individual level. Individuals cannot alter the conditions that reproduce gender or class inequalities and dynamics. Absent of a range of options, individuals take the ones typically accessible to their gender and class. Doing so tends to reify existing gendered and classed patterns. This occurs even though many women today want to have wage work while raising children and some men want to be more present as caregivers than their own fathers were.

Enabling conditions: Principles X policies

Policies can pave the way for shifting conditions to better match various aspirations and needs. We know this from a large body of international research, from which we can distill some ideas of best practices.[6] What sorts of policies enable the combination of work and care for parents? What kinds of policies can shift care labour away from being only women's work? What types of policies are necessary to enable parents across class backgrounds to combine employment and parental duties?

First, policies must address both work conditions and care infrastructure. These include, for example, parental leave throughout childhood; wage replacement (i.e. leave has to be paid) for all types of workers (full- or part-time; permanent or contract); protection of workers against excessive work hours, irregular schedules, and unfair dismissal; high quality care institutions and affordable paid care services accessible to all children throughout the childhood years.

Second, policies must pay special attention to addressing gender and class inequalities and not presume that these will magically resolve on their own. Paternity and maternity leaves need to be

---

[6] See, for example, Ochiai (2009); Gornick and Meyers (2009); Saraceno (2011); Keck and Saraceno (2013); Le Bihan, Knijn, and Martin (2014); Peng (2018).

relatively balanced so that parents, particularly at the beginning of parenthood and early in their careers, do not get entrenched in gendered patterns of care and gendered patterns of employment. Anti-discrimination measures need to be in place to ensure that women and/or low-wage workers who are parents are not discriminated against at the workplace. Regulations around paid time-off, maximum work hours, living wages and benefits, and rights to negotiation over work schedules are especially important for ensuring that the job conditions of part-time and contract workers, including low-wage workers, enable people to both maintain employment and have family lives. The improvement of work-life harmony for parents should not be subsidised by paid caregivers. Given the expansion of this sector, not just for care of the young but also the elderly, attention must be given to improving wages and work conditions here.

One can look at policies in Singapore today and claim they check all the boxes. But form is not content and the proof of a pudding is in the eating. We know box-checking is inadequate because we see these interconnected empirical realities. There is the persistence of gender and class patterns and inequalities in the workplace and the home; the spectacular failure of four decades of pro-natalist policies to reverse low fertility trends; and, as I have described in my work over the years and in this essay, the unease and frustrations experienced by ordinary people as they live their lives.

Perhaps we need to look at the policy approaches I described above from a different angle. Without implying that specifics are unimportant, the puzzle of why a case can check all boxes and yet not actually be effective in meeting its goals (I'm assuming the goals of pro-natalist policies is to increase fertility) may be better answered by a think on fundamental values. The policy approaches listed above, which exist to different degrees in different places and is nowhere perfect, rests on a few key principles. First, rights — people have them, states have obligations to respect them, and dignified lives depend on having a confluence of rights. For example, people have parental rights to care (and children have rights to be cared for) as well as worker rights to decent work. Second, inequalities are not natural phenomena. Mitigating inequalities requires understanding sites and mechanisms of unequal treatment and access, and then targeted solutions to redress past and present injustices, including those that have become systematised in institutional practices. Third, how care needs are resolved have consequences for societal well-being — how well or poorly children, the elderly, and the disabled are cared for, how caregivers carry out their care duties, have effects on economy, society, polity. Care is an important social function and affects everyone at some point in their life course, but it has limited commercial value. It therefore requires public investment and coordination and must be conceived as a public good. Finally, running through these three principles is the belief regarding what members of society owe each other — a sense that society is held together by ties of mutual obligations.[7]

Contrast the list to the principles that the Singapore Government has been articulating explicitly and embedding in its approach to social policies for several decades: self-reliance; family as the first line of support; many helping hands.[8] It is in many ways directly oppositional. No one has a 'right' to anything — you have something if you or your family can acquire it through your own participation in the market. Inequalities are natural outcomes (of unequal capacities/talents/hard work, or more vaguely, 'globalisation') and

---

[7] Numerous thinkers, across disciplines, help us think about how people can live well together in society and the value of mutual obligations. See, for example, Ackerman, Alstott, and Van Parijs (2006); Somers (2008); Low and Yeoh (2014); Ferguson (2015); Banerjee and Duflo (2019); George (2020); Sandel (2020); Shafik (2021).

[8] For an articulation and defense of this approach, see Lim (2007).

are problems for society only at its extremes. Then, the 'many helping hands' of 'community' (i.e. non-profits/charities) step in before the state intervenes as a last resort. In this schema, there is little room for recognising interdependencies and contemplating shared fates (of childhood, old age, illness) among the people who inhabit a society, no sense that pooled resources can serve the collective well-being and benefit people at different points in their life course. In fact, what is implied is that tapping on public resources is parasitical, damaging behaviour that should be avoided as well as discouraged. 'Personal responsibility' trumps 'mutual obligations'.

Although we usually see the principles as applying to 'welfare' narrowly conceived (i.e. poverty relief), the Singapore state has been faithful to them more generally, and certainly on issues of care. Foreign domestic workers were the initial policy solution, put forth in the late 1970s, and for a long time the main answer the state had to offer to meet care needs. This set the tone for relegating care problems to individual women, as well as naturalising in care relations and arrangements, intersecting gender, class, and racial hierarchies and inequalities.[9] A 'market' and demand-supply dynamics of a specific sort were set up through regulations: on the supply side, the workers must be women, only from certain countries and hence ethno-national backgrounds; the workers are permanently transient — with no rights to citizenship or family unification; they are required to reside at their workplace and with limited protections on job scope and work hours. On the demand side, the 'market' was also deeply managed in ways that perpetuate different options along gender and class lines: only households above certain income levels can hire domestic workers; women are the default employers; costs are differentially state-supported through taxes/reliefs depending on

---

[9] See Teo and Piper (2009); Teo (2013a); Tan (2023).

alignment with the state's vision of ideal family structure. To understand how all this could have solidified patterns, we should also note what did *not* happen. Between the 1970s and through the 2000s, even as the care gap problem grew in intensity as more women entered the workforce, the Singapore state was slow to invest in care institutions and reticent in regulating work to respond to the changing profile and needs of the workforce. This was a length of time sufficient to entrench beliefs and habits around domestic and care labour. The result is unsurprising: housework and care labour are, in practice and therefore also in people's minds, low-status, feminine labour. Men have not stepped up in the domestic sphere in the ways women have stepped up in the earning sphere. Women, including those who can afford paid care, remain responsible for resolving care needs, and this impedes their workplace advancements. Importantly, the issue of reconciling work and care, although widely shared and a consequence of significant social transformations, is a private problem to be sorted out by individual families and usually by 'the woman'. If this was not enough to entrench care labour as women's work, the significant expansion of maternity leave in tandem with the snail's pace movement on paternity leave over these same decades sealed the gap between mothers' and fathers' abilities to care as well as their capacities to pursue wage work.[10]

What do ordinary people want? Choice and autonomy, belonging and respect, ethical agency. The current policy regime does not

---

[10] The Singapore state made a major turn toward pro-natalist policies in 2004. Among other schemes, paid maternity leave of 12 weeks was introduced (this increased to 16 weeks in 2008). Paternity leave was not mandated and three days was a recommendation. It took nine more years, in 2013, for a one-week paid paternity leave to be introduced and another four years, in 2017, for it to be increased to two weeks. A full decade after paternity leave was first mandated, in 2023, the government announced that paternity leave would be increased to four weeks beginning in 2024, but the additional two weeks are voluntary rather than mandated (for employers) in the immediate term. This summary does not capture the state's very specific views of who should be having children, how many, and when. To see the full genesis of turns from anti-natalism to pro-natalism, and the state's attempts at implementing its imaginations of gender, class, and race as it relates to the population, see Chapter 3 of Teo (2011).

adequately enable these. Above all, the discussion in this section suggests that enabling conditions cannot be created merely by tinkering on the edges of programmes and schemes. What we need is reorientation of the principles embedded in policies — away from an individualistic and market-focused ethos and toward values of equality and mutual care.

Where is 'there' and how will we travel?

The well-being of specific groups, such as mothers or parents, is not separate from the well-being of others in society. Moreover, social groups have porous boundaries because each human has multiple social roles that evolve over time — no one is *just* a parent, or *just* an employer, or *just* someone's child. We should not accept wholesale the rhetoric that we are fighting over a finite pie, or that one group's well-being must come at cost to another's.

As Nancy Folbre and Paula England (1999) have argued, children should be conceived as public goods. Their wellbeing or lack thereof — as educated persons, persons who contribute to society in social, economic, political ways — affects everyone. When we take collective responsibility for children, we invest in our shared futures. The principles we enact through public policy — universal childcare and public education, for example — have the potential for building a civic-political culture in which children understand that they benefit from public resources and are obliged to contribute as they become adults. This is less likely when the upbringing of children is primarily constructed and experienced as individual family investments and private hustles in service of individual success.

Each of us are multifaceted social actors — with the potential to contribute to society in various ways over the life course. To the extent that some of us take on caregiving roles during certain times in life, this does not negate other roles we can play before, during, or after this period. Mothers or parents or caregivers more generally, when adequately supported and enabled, can continue to be workers and colleagues, volunteers and neighbours, artists and creatives, civic actors. A society needs to have people doing things — building community ties, generating ideas for problems, innovating and creating things — in order to deal with the many challenges of our times and to thrive. Enabling everyone access to choice and agency, preventing people from getting trapped in narrow duties and stuck on pathways, is crucial for drawing out the full potential of our population and in turn building a vibrant and dynamic economy, polity, society.

The needs for care are universal to the human condition. Even if some do not ever have people they need to care for (highly unlikely), most eventually need care. Even if some do not have children, every adult today was once a child who was cared for. The devaluing of care, seen from this perspective, diminishes us as humans. It is, or can be, affirming to recognise this fundamental interdependence that exists between humans.

The expansion of options, widely accessible, can enable everyone to live flourishing lives, in which we can exercise choice, ethical agency, while counting on social belonging and respect. To bring about such a society, we must imagine it is possible to expand rather than contract the space of flourishing lives for everyone. We should nurture shared norms and habits for recognising and valorising interdependencies and mutual obligations. This will of course not be easy. Conflicts in a diverse society are inevitable, and not every interest can be served in every instance. Moreover, no society gets to begin with a clean slate and ours already has deep grooves of inequalities. Hence, apart from imagining 'where' we hope to go — what ideals are worth having — we must also consider how we will travel toward there.

Social policies and institutions can ossify over time. The ones we have in Singapore today come from a strong-handed state, composed by a relatively narrow elite, with firm beliefs about what family, society, polity, and citizenry, should look like and how each should behave. It is a state that has historically had a monopoly on decision-making and resource allocation, with great capacity for delivering its vision with efficiency, and deep commitment to a handful of principles. In insisting on narrow definitions of gender and family, and offering narrow parameters for work and care, these increasingly do not serve the diverse range of ordinary people's hopes and dreams. Citizens have a right and duty to participate in the process of pushing for policies and institutions that better serve our evolving needs.

How people will come together to speak to one another and forge new ideas and consensus, without the heavy hand of state coordination or constraint, is a major challenge to overcome.

Artists, journalists, activists, teachers, social workers, academics can make ourselves useful and worthy of our titles/vocations. Creating spaces for diverse voices and dialogue and critical thinking, in the context of this strong-state environment, is a contribution, even if it does not immediately change policies or norms. It is key to think of this process in expansive and creative ways. Work that happens in different spaces, engages the participation of a variety of persons and groups, occurs in different physical or virtual mediums and across languages, and embraces a range of foci and agendas.

The significance of people coming together goes beyond generating ideas or knowledge — it also involves cultivating relational ties, the building of trust and solidarity, the development of strategies and practices to bring about change. For ordinary people to meaningfully partake in social reform, we need to build some collective voices and some mechanisms for them to be heard. Spaces, dialogues, gatherings matter then in at least two ways: first, until we have regular reminders and vocabularies for perceiving that we each are part of a larger reality, that we exist alongside others both similar and different from us, we are stuck thinking of ourselves as individuals and acting as such. Continual and regular processes of forging consensus on difficult issues is necessary for bringing into being, not just as concept but as ontological reality, 'ordinary people', 'social body', 'society'. Second, to be heard by social actors whose decisions have strong and durable effects — politicians, policy makers, corporate leaders, stewards of institutions — this social body must have ways to communicate its positions. It is ultimately through collective action and amplified voices that people can move decision-makers to see problems differently and make different decisions.

What do ordinary people want? This is a question that deserves continuous contemplation, by everyone who lives in Singapore today, on many different occasions. Over the years, in interview encounters and focus group discussions and meetings and Q&As, this is to me a question that reveals what already is and what still could be. To ask and attempt to answer this question is, I believe, how we can bring into existence an ideal Singapore that serves many different needs and the needs of many.

TEO YOU YENN is an Associate Professor in Sociology at Nanyang Technological University. Her research is on poverty and inequality, governance and policy, gender and class inequalities. Ongoing projects focus on care/welfare regimes and minimum income standards. She is the author of Neoliberal Morality in Singapore: How Family Policies Make State and Society *(Routledge, 2011) and* This is What Inequality Looks Like *(Ethos Books, 2018). She has been a member and volunteer at AWARE since 2004, and is a founding editor of AcademiaSG, which promotes Singapore scholarship and public discourse. More information about her work can be found at https:// teoyouyenn.sg*

References

Ackerman, Bruce, Anne Alstott, and Philippe Van Parijs, eds. 2006. *Redesigning Distribution: Basic Income and Stakeholder Grants as Cornerstones for an Egalitarian Capitalism.* London and New York: Verso.

Banerjee, Abhijit V. and Esther Duflo. 2019. *Good Economics for Hard Times: Better Answers to our Biggest Problems.* UK: Penguin Random House.

Butler, Judith. 2009. "Performativity, precarity and sexual politics". *AIBR-Revista de Antropologia Iberoamericana* 4 (3):321.

Butler, Judith. 2020. *The Force of Nonviolence: An Ethico-Political Bind.* London: New York: Verso.

Doepke, Matthias and Fabrizio Zilibotti. 2019. *Love, Money & Parenting: How Economics Explains the Way We Raise Our Kids.* Princeton, NJ: Princeton University Press.

England, Paula and Nancy Folbre. 1999. "Who should pay for the kids?" *Annals of the American Academy of Political and Social Science* 563 (1):194–207.

Ferguson, James. 2015. *Give a Man a Fish: Reflections on the New Politics of Distribution*. Durham and London: Duke University Press.

George, Cherian. 2020. *Air-Conditioned Nation Revisited: Essays on Singapore Politics*. Singapore: Ethos Books.

Gornick, Janet C. and Marcia K. Meyers. 2009. "Institutions that Support Gender Equality in Parenthood and Employment". In *Gender Equality: Transforming family divisions of labor*, edited by Janet C. Gornick, Marcia K. Meyers and Erik Olin Wright, pp 3–64. London: Verso.

Keck, Wolfgang and Chiara Saraceno. 2013. "The impact of different social-policy frameworks on social inequalities among women in the European Union: The labour-market participation of mothers". *Social Politics: International Studies in Gender, State & Society* 20 (3):297–328.

Le Bihan, Blanche, Trudie Knijn and Claude Martin, eds. 2014. *Work and Care under Pressure: Care Arrangements across Europe*. Amsterdam: Amsterdam University Press.

Lim, Xiuhui. 2007. "Security with Self-Reliance: The Argument for the Singapore Model". Civil Service College, *Ethos* Issue 3, accessed 1 May 2023. https://www.csc.gov.sg/articles/security-with-self-reliance-the-argument-for-the-singapore-model.

Low, Donald and Lam Keong Yeoh. 2014. "Beware the Inequality Trap". In *Hard Choices: Challenging the Singapore Consensus*, edited by Donald Low and Sudhir Vadaketh, pp 113–119. Singapore: NUS Press.

Ng, Kok Hoe, You Yenn Teo, Yu Wei Neo, Ad Maulod and Yi-Ting Ting. 2019. "What Older People Need in Singapore: A Household Budgets Study". Singapore.

Ng, Kok Hoe, You Yenn Teo, Yu Wei Neo, Ad Maulod and Yee Lok Wong. 2021. "What People Need in Singapore: A Household Budgets Study". Singapore.

Ochiai, Emiko. 2009. "Care Diamonds and Welfare Regimes in East and South-East Asian Societies: Bridging Family and Welfare Sociology". *International Journal of Japanese Sociology* 18 (1):60–78.

Partanen, Anu. 2017. *The Nordic Theory of Everything: In Search of a Better Life*. New York; London; Toronto; Sydney: HarperCollins.

Peng, Ito. 2018. "Culture, Institution and Diverse Approaches to Care and Care Work in East Asia". *Current Sociology* 66 (4):643–659.

Sandel, Michael J. 2020. *The Tyranny of Merit: What's Become of the Common Good?* UK: Penguin Random House.

Saraceno, Chiara. 2011. "Childcare Needs and Childcare Policies: A Multidimensional Issue". *Current Sociology* 59 (1):78–96.

Shafik, Minouche. 2021. *What We Owe Each Other: A New Social Contract.* Princeton N.J.: Princeton University Press.

Somers, Margaret R. 2008. *Genealogies of Citizenship: Markets, Statelessness, and the Right to Have Rights.* Cambridge, UK; New York: Cambridge University Press.

Tan, Shih Joo. 2023. "When the Home Is Also the Workplace: Women Migrant Domestic Workers' Experiences with the 'live-in' Policy in Singapore and Hong Kong". *Anti-Trafficking Review* 20:75–91.

Teo, You Yenn. 2018a. *This is What Inequality Looks Like.* Singapore: Ethos Books.

Teo, Youyenn. 2011. *Neoliberal Morality in Singapore: How Family Policies Make State and Society.* London and New York: Routledge.

Teo, Youyenn. 2013a. "Support for Deserving Families: Inventing the Anti-welfare Familialist State in Singapore". *Social Politics: International Studies in Gender, State & Society* 20 (3):387–406.

Teo, Youyenn. 2013b. "Women hold up the Anti-welfare Regime: How Social Policies Produce Social Differentiation in Singapore". In *The Global Political Economy of the Household in Asia*, edited by Juanita Elias and Samanthi Gunawardana, 15–27. Houndmills, Basingstoke, Hampshire; New York: Palgrave Macmillan.

Teo, Youyenn. 2016. "Not Everyone has 'Maids': Class Differentials in the Elusive Quest for Work-life Balance".

Teo, Youyenn. 2018b. "Falling Short: Class and the Performance of the Familial". In *Family and Population Change in Singapore: A Unique Case in the Global Family Changes*, edited by Wei-Jun Jean Yeung and Shu Hu, pp 96–111. London: Routledge.

Teo, Youyenn. 2022. "Education as Care Labor: Expanding our Lens on the Work-life Balance Problem". *Current Sociology* 71(7): 1181–382.

Teo, Youyenn and Nicola Piper. 2009. "Foreigners in our Homes: Linking Migration and Family Policies in Singapore". *Population, Space and Place* 15 (2):147–159.

Wright, Erik Olin. 2010. *Envisioning Real Utopias*. London: Verso.

"Change is constant, and the pace of change is really accelerating. So I think the ability to keep an open mind, willingness to explore new ideas, the importance of having the right values is absolutely critical."

~ Corporate leader Chua Sock Koong, speaking at the Human Capital Leadership Institute, February 2021

CHAPTER 2

Time to Sacrifice the Sacred Cows of Conventional Economics

Audrey Chin

We can no longer deny it. The world as we know it is unravelling. Inequality of access to resources has become extreme. Livelihoods are at risk from climate change, environmental degradation, job threatening technological developments, ongoing trade and hot wars. Society is fragmenting, fuelled in part by misinformation on social media. It has become increasingly difficult to achieve rules and values-based consensus both between and within nations. As individuals, we seem to be suffering from a loss of meaning and self.

As an illustration of these problems with the environment, inequality, and personal wellbeing, Otto Scharmer's 2018 book *The Essentials of Theory U*,[1] states that we are currently consuming

---

[1] Claus Otto Scharmer, *The Essentials of Theory U*. London: Blackwells, 2018; Read also: Joanna Macy & Chris Johnstone, *Active Hope*. San Francisco: New World Library, 2022; and Martin-Brehm Christensen *et al.*, *Survival of the Richest, How We Must Tax the Super-Rich Now to Fight Inequality*. Oxford, UK: Oxfam, 2023.

1.5 times the regenerative capacity of the earth; the net wealth of the poorer half of the 3.8 billion people of the world just equals the wealth of the eight richest people; and 800,000 people died by suicide that year, one every 40 seconds.

Our Singapore is not immune to these pressures. The government has noted that there is an uneasy road ahead into our seventh decade of Independence. Abroad, there are challenges from uncertain geopolitics, global financial and economic volatility, and climate change. At home we face rapid ageing, limited land/labour/carbon, inequality and frictional social mobility. In response, Forward SG[2] has been presented as a new strategy to meet these challenges.

However, we must do more than the strategies proposed by Forward SG. The familiar global economic system on which our political economy is based seems less coherent and functional than previously imagined. Business within the usual framework will not work. If we are to survive and thrive in a more humane and environmentally conscious political economy, we must kill some of the sacred cows underpinning the economic thinking that drives our political economy.

The sacred cows and their alternatives
Economics — A value-free science?

Our theoretical frames determine how we view issues, and hence our engagement with economic policy. Simply defined, an economy is a system of inter-related production and consumption activities that ultimately determine the allocation of resources within that network of relationships. The study of economics is the study of

---

[2] *Forward SG: An Overview*, 2023.

scarcity and its implications for the allocation and use of resources to provide goods and services to promote the growth of welfare over time.

Narratives derived from the predominant neo-classical school of economics suggest it is a positive science free from any value judgements, with axioms determined by the analysis of economic data using sophisticated statistical models. Moreover, as most schools of economics deem markets to be the most efficient means to arrive at an optimal allocation of resources to produce and distribute goods and services, market prices may be taken as a given. Policy intervention should only happen at the margins, when informational asymmetries, transactions costs, market psychology or human emotions cause market inefficiencies.

Within this frame of reference, public policy responses will be seen as value neutral. They will not be a subject of political discussion. A mind frame that economic analysis is value-free limits the discussion of economic policy. We focus only on ways, means and efficacy. Politics and values/philosophy are left on the sidelines. Yet economic destinations are value judgements, as are judgements on what is efficacious, and what means are acceptable.

Moreover, in the age of large-scale multinationals, growing asset and income inequality between countries and among individuals, free markets are not the level playing field pre-supposed by economic theory. In fact, markets privilege wealthier, more networked, and more informed participants. Market prices may be manipulated by market participants, psychological factors and government policies, distorting markets' ability to channel resources efficiently. We cannot arrive at economic utopia until we reframe the study of economics and present it as the messy dirty exercise that it is.

In the infancy of this discipline, the subject was labelled the study of the political economy. Indeed, the basic degree for aspiring public servants and politicians at Oxford University is the PPE, the degree in Philosophy, Politics and Economics.

It is time to remove that 'value-free' description from introductory economics courses everywhere.

As for ourselves in Singapore, let's not use the moniker 'don't be political' to shut down discussions about policy proposals. Giving space to dialogue and well-intentioned contestation is essential for coming to consensus about the allocation of scarce resources. Experiments in participatory budgeting, whereby citizens vote on budgets for some projects, may be useful.

GDP growth — not the best measure of our best eforts

The publicity material for Forward SG, Singapore's policy approach to our oncoming challenges, prioritises a successful, strong and growing economy as the first of three strategic initiatives. The second and third are developing as a fairer, more just and more equal society, and to deepen our sense of solidarity and unity.

In Singapore, a convenient measure of economic health is GDP growth. This indicator is also used to calibrate the incentive bonuses of politicians and government servants. However, the measure has limitations. It is not the best measure of our best efforts.

GDP (Gross Domestic Product) is the presumed value of an economy's total production of goods and services. It can be estimated by summing the value-added at each stage of production; the expenditure of final consumers; or the income of employees, the gross operating surplus of private entrepreneurs, companies and non-profits, rentals and imputed rentals, and production and import taxes paid to the government. However, only market exchanges measurable in monetary terms can be counted. No regard is paid to the actual benefit or cost of these monetary exchanges to individual and societal well-being.

Consider how increases in property transactions might lead to rising income for property agents, rising profits for developers and a supposedly 'virtuous cycle' of rising property investment. This would contribute to positive GDP growth whether measured by the consumption or income methods. However, the negative impact of such property dynamics being funded by inflows of black money from money launderers would not be measured; nor would the impact of rising private property prices on public housing affordability.

If Forward SG is concerned about economic strength, then we must go beyond GDP growth to monitor economic diversity and balance. If we are also concerned about fairness, justice, equality, unity, and solidarity, then let's explicitly incorporate these indicators into our monitoring and remuneration systems. Indeed, as corporations are doing now, we should incorporate a 360-degree wellness monitoring system into our governmental feedback systems.

To start, let us explicitly incorporate more granular measures of how well we are doing with inequality:

- The proportion of population in each income and age quintile, the gender, race, educational attainment, health, employment status, incarceration and addiction, and support needs of these groups and the gaps between these groups various quintiles; also, and more significantly, the progress we are making in narrowing these gaps.
- Our objective coefficients and global rankings on the <u>GINI coefficients</u>[3] of income and wealth.

---

[3] Ha-Joon Chang, *Economics, The Users' Guide*. UK: Penguin, 2014. GINI coefficients compare the area encompassed by a society's actual income-distribution curve against a hypothetical equal income distribution curve, with the difference between the two areas as the measure of inequality.

These indicators are already available in our various ministries and only need to be aggregated and incorporated into an overall 360-degree monitoring system.

As a next step, let's seriously study recent attempts at measuring overall happiness, well-being and ecological sustainability. Let's begin to consider the following:

- Subjective judgements on life satisfaction as reflected in Gallup's World Happiness Poll
- The objective multi-factor indicators of income, jobs, community life and work life balance.
- Our actual and relative ranking on the OECD's Better Life Index,[4] and how changes in this index are related to our own GDP growth.

If we are serious about equality, justice, and individual and community well-being, let us begin to seriously monitor indicators of these in our feedback and reward systems.

Monetisation — not the answer to everything

Not all valuable exchanges take place in markets. Not all costs are accounted for. Household and care work have value. Clean air, green spaces and light are other goods which everyone uses but no one owns. The loss of leisure due to long commutes and on-line work, rising marginalisation and loss of self-esteem due to social inequality, family breakdowns as migrant workers travel to provide cheap labour in more developed countries, are costs which individuals, corporates and societies bear. Yet nowhere are they included in national, corporate, or household accounts.

---

[4] The OECD Better Life Index is an aggregate of individuals' subjective judgements of life satisfaction as well as objective multi-factor indicators of income, jobs, community life and work-life balance.

There have been attempts to valorise these goods in dollar terms, or to turn them into property value of which can be determined in markets, for example, in carbon emission exchanges. However, it appears some exchanges are beyond monetisation, for example: care given by beloved family members during illness, the psychic benefits of 'forest-bathing' or breathing in unpolluted air, rest time free of sound pollution, walking home on crime-free streets, affordable public housing, the networking advantages of having a national oil-company owned by the government.

Indeed, it appears that removing the market mechanism from certain exchanges may lead to more optimal outcomes, as evidenced by the quality of blood obtained by donation rather than purchase, the better attendance of volunteers than employees in social enterprises, the ability of non-profit models to support the arts.

For care services, we would need a multi-pronged approach involving provision of more services (perhaps by adequately paid providers working at subsidised and regulated non-profits), publicly funded subsidies and respite services for at-home caretakers, and a networked referral system to connect the entire support network.

For resources used in common like public land and water, we can reconsider the role of market pricing and instead just charge production costs for the use of the land and water. In the property sector, why not let the public sector lead instead of referencing private sector pricing. Why not release leasehold land at 0 cost and value only the built-up areas. After all the land reverts to the nation once the leases are up. Imagine the impact on overall costs once the base land price falls.

For recreational land and heritage buildings, we might allow citizens to vote on the priority they would give to these various 'goods' as exercises in participatory democracy.

What matters is not to automatically apply the notion of market efficiency and $ valorisation to every social policy endeavour. Instead, we should consider other means of prioritising and supporting what are essential invaluable experiences and assets.

Who pays? Sharing but not sparing

We will need to pay for all the Forward SG initiatives. This will be best done by ensuring tax equity. Here, we should do away with our fear that higher taxes will drive out good business. A survey of the Scandinavian countries with much higher tax regimes suggests this may not always be the case. Other factors like the skill of the workforce, the ease of doing business, the availability of good infrastructure, a clean environment, and educational facilities also contribute to our attractiveness as a site for business.

Lower is not better. Instead, one simple concept should apply: Everyone should pay their share.

In Singapore, government expenditure is funded by taxes, charges, a share of the investment returns from our reserves, and capitalisation of nationally significant infrastructure. According to estimates[5] for the 2023 budget, 2/3 of our estimated expenditure of S$123 billion will be funded by GST and personal income tax (S$35 bn), corporate income tax (S$24 bn), net investment returns (S$23.5 bn), stamp duty and asset (primarily property) taxes (S$11 bn), and vehicle quota and motoring taxes (S$6.42 bn). In the non-governmental sector, the Commissioner of Charity's annual report shows charities received slightly below S$3 bn between 2015 and 2020, of which S$1 bn were tax-deductible donations.

---

[5] Table 1.1, *Budget for FY 2023, Revenue and Expenditure Estimates*. See also *Commissioner of Charities Annual Report 2022*, Ministry of Finance, *Economic Survey of Singapore* (2013, 2021).

Looked at another way, the general public funds roughly 27 per cent of expenditure; those owning, buying and selling property and cars support another 14 per cent; companies' contribute 20 per cent; and an additional 19 per cent comes from the returns from our national savings.

Companies could do more. Profits have increased from around 50 per cent of national income in the years 1990–2009 to 57 per cent of national income in 2021. Our labour share of income has dropped to 36.6 per cent from the average of 42 per cent in the 1990–2009 period. Yet, the share of companies' contribution to expenditure is still less than that of the general public.

We could increase our taxes on gambling, liquor, cigarettes and other unhealthy goods. There should be greater tax incentives for donations to social enterprises. Taxes on financial sector transactions have hitherto been neglected. Capital inflows and capital gains from financial trading should all come under IRAS scrutiny. In addition to being a revenue raising mechanism, such a tax will allow the authorities to monitor financial transactions and add friction to sometimes too-volatile financial markets. We are already a very low tax regime globally. We have room to share a little more, and sparing fewer of those who can afford to pay.

My economic utopia

This is what I would like to be free of in my economic utopia:

- The notion that economics is a value-free science
- Mind frames that use only GDP growth as a measure of societal health
- The belief that everything has value only when monetisable and monetised

- The notion that higher taxes are detrimental to economic growth.

And this is what I would like to see:

- An acceptance that we must dialogue over economic policy goals and priorities
- The practice of participatory budgeting and prioritisation to foster that dialogue
- The incorporation of more granular measures of societal equality and wellness into our current economic monitoring and feedback systems
- The acceptance that some goods/services/experiences are invaluable and must be protected because they are 'goods' in themselves and perhaps should not be $-valorised
- Finally, a greater willingness to create an equitable tax regime where we truly share and do not inequitably spare.

AUDREY CHIN'S work explores the intersections between society, gender, and faith. She is a Fellow of the Iowa International Writing Program and has been nominated for the Dayton Literary Peace Prize and shortlisted for the Singapore Literature Prize. A financial practitioner and a life member of AWARE, she helped to develop the organisation's Financial Intelligence Training Programme. She is a Christian.

"By 2050, I would like to see women of all ages in Singapore fully empowered in society and in the workforce, proving to be economic and social game-changers. There will be no more gender wage gap and corporations will embrace care work as part of their business models. There will be new pension systems and health care portability to reflect the changing nature of work in the digital economy and to support young women to succeed in the cyber world. Older women can live with respect and dignity, fully cared for after contributing so much to society and to their families."

~ Global champion of women's rights Noeleen Heyzer, for The Lives of Women exhibition at the National Museum, Jan–Mar 2022

CHAPTER 3

Transformative and Inclusive Boards: A Vision for the Future

⚬⊙⚬

Su-Yen Wong

Prelude: My diversity journey

Disruption. Decisions. Diversity. This essay touches on these dimensions. But first, why does this matter to me?

In the heart of the Pacific Northwest, where drizzles are persistent and the air carries the scent of pine, I found my world view both challenged and infinitely expanded. As a young Singaporean who had grown up reciting the national pledge "regardless of race, language, or religion", I believed I understood diversity. However, as I ventured 13,000 km from home to attend university, and flanked by peers whose homelands spanned the globe, I was struck by a profound realisation: my understanding of diversity was barely in its infancy.

Living, studying, and working alongside students from countries I had only read about till that time — including Brazil, China,

Germany, Japan, Nepal, South Africa, Sweden, and of course the United States — I discovered the myriad realities that shape our collective experience.

It was here, amid the cacophony of languages and the kaleidoscope of cultures, that I truly grasped the power of diverse lenses. It was a revelation to see the world through their eyes — a spectrum of perspectives that my prior experience could not possibly capture. And I understood, viscerally, that someone else's reality, whilst different from mine, was equally valid. Not more, not less.

It was not a seamless journey; we grappled with the friction of our differences in language, religion, socio-economic backgrounds, and cultural norms, and we wrestled to find harmony. Yet, I reflect on those days as the crucible that forged my commitment to diversity — a cornerstone I have since carried into every aspect of my professional life.

The dream: An inspired future through inclusive boardrooms

I have a dream. Not born of idle fantasy as the ABBA song goes, but of a clear-eyed vision for what we in Singapore can achieve together. My conviction is that as leaders charged with steering our companies and organisations, board directors play a critical role in refreshing the social compact for the future of Singapore.

In this dream, our boardrooms are drivers of innovation and champions of inclusion. They are places where the voices of veterans blend with the fresh perspectives of those who are younger; where the rich experiences of directors are sought, regardless of gender, ethnicity, functional expertise, or geographic background; where every decision is weighed not just on scales of profit, but on broader measures of progress and purpose.

In this dream, the boardroom represents a circle of trust, a gathering of diverse individuals committed to steering our enterprises towards sustainable success. Each member brings a slice of the wider world into our discussions, ensuring that when we act, we do so with wisdom, empathy, and foresight. Beyond our role as directors of the organisations we serve, we are integral to shaping the way forward for Singapore.

The reality: The current state of board diversity

As of December 2023, I have served as an independent director for 14 years on the boards of a variety of organisations based in Asia, Australia, and North America. The organisations have spanned a full range of complexity and ownership structures, including multi-billion dollar listed companies, small cap companies, government-linked companies, publicly-listed and privately-held family firms, startups, private-equity held companies, social enterprises, non-profit organisations, and statutory boards.

Some of these boards have been highly focused on long-term strategic issues and ambitious transformation agendas. Some have had to attend to short-term crises. Some have placed a strong emphasis on embedding Environment, Social, and Governance (ESG) goals within the business, while others are just commencing their ESG journey.

Suffice to say I have also had a front row seat to a wide gamut of board cultures and have witnessed a broad spectrum of ways by which boards are formed. On several boards I have been the sole female director, while on others I have been the youngest. Each board is unique in its composition, and its norms.

Differences notwithstanding, on the whole, there has been an increased emphasis on gender diversity, as the data indicates. As of June 2023, according to statistics from the Council for Board Diversity, women's participation on the boards of the top 100 primary-listed companies on the Singapore Exchange (SGX) stood at 22.7 per cent, reflecting a consistent upward trend from 15.2 per cent as of the end of 2018. Meanwhile the top 100 institutions of a public character (IPCs) and statutory boards saw women holding 29.5 per cent and 32 per cent of directorships, respectively.

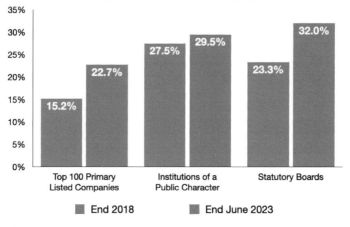

Percentage of Women on Singapore Boards

Source: Women's Representation on Boards, Council for Board Diversity

When we look at data across all Singapore listed companies, the picture similarly shows progress, albeit at a slower rate. The Singapore Directorship Report produced by the Singapore Institute of Directors is considered an industry benchmark for matters related to boards and directors of Singapore-listed entities.

According to the 2023 Report — which was released in October 2023 and reflects information from corporate filings and annual reports of 650 firms listed on the SGX — of the total number of 4,051 board seats analysed, 14.9 per cent or 603 were occupied by women. This reflects a steady upward trajectory since 2014 when the figure was 8.3 per cent, but there is clearly still a long road ahead.

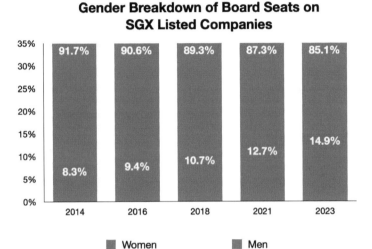

Gender Breakdown of Board Seats on SGX Listed Companies

Source: 2023 Singapore Directorship Report, Singapore Institute of Directors

Furthermore, it does strike me as anachronistic that in 2023, there remain 41.5 per cent of Singapore-listed companies that did not have a single female director on their boards. Yes, this has improved since 2014 when the figure stood at 56.1 per cent, but it is hardly a statistic to gloat over!

Shifting to another dimension of diversity, nearly 60 per cent of Independent Directors on Singapore-listed firms are over 61 years old. While there is immense value in accumulated experience, there is also a need to complement the Baby Boomer voices in the boardroom with Gen X and Gen Y perspectives to reflect a broad spectrum of life experiences, technological and workforce acumen.

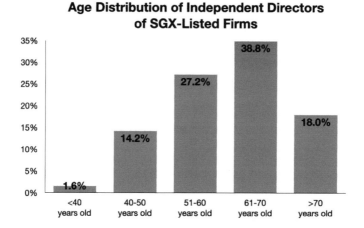

Source: 2023 Singapore Directorship Report, Singapore Institute of Directors

Diversity also needs to extend beyond physical attributes such as gender and age. In fact, a diverse board will optimally reflect multiple dimensions of diversity. For example, the Singapore Board Diversity Index developed by WTW in partnership with SID analyses board diversity across eight attributes: gender, age, tenure, board independence, cultural ethnicity, international experience, domain/functional expertise, and industry expertise.

The 2020 Index revealed that among companies with a primary listing on the Singapore Exchange, only 4 per cent of board directors bring Technology domain expertise, just 3 per cent have Public Relations or Marketing expertise, and a mere 1 per cent have professional HR expertise.

In summary, catalyzed by the concerted efforts of various stakeholders, Singapore's boardrooms have been experiencing a gradual but definitive shift towards diversity, at least from a gender perspective.

So, what's missing?

The following boardroom dialogue which I was privy to (albeit disguised and abbreviated) illustrates the point.

Nominating Committee Chair: One of our directors is retiring at the next AGM.

Director A: We need to bring in a female director.

Director B: Hmm… do you know Ms. T? She's a partner at XYZ Law Firm.

Director A: Yes, I've come across her. She did some work for one of my other boards.

Director B: Our AGM is in four months, so we need to move quickly!

Nominating Committee Chair: Perhaps each of us could surface a few names? We can arrange for the NC to meet them.

This is of course a caricature, but it effectively highlights the need for action in four areas:

1. Strategic Alignment: There is an opportunity to tighten the linkage between organisational strategy and board composition. The starting point for nominations discussions should be an articulation of the organisation's direction for the future.

2. Board Renewal Processes: Boards and Nominating Committees can do more to ensure proactive succession planning. Leaving it to the eleventh hour will likely deprive the board from accessing as rich a slate of candidates as it should. Furthermore, while it is human nature to consider people within our immediate network, it is critical to expand the universe of candidates under consideration.

3. Holistic Approach to Diversity: Consideration of gender equality together with other critical dimensions of diversity such as age, ethnicity, geographic exposure, and functional expertise would enrich boardroom discussions, and improve the quality of decision-making.

4. Culture Change: Overcoming entrenched perceptions around board qualifications and embracing a more inclusive view of what constitutes valuable board contribution would enable organisations to better mitigate risk and adapt to changing business environments.

The best boards from a nominations perspective first ask, "where are we headed?" and "what do we need?" before jumping into "who do we know?" While the current state of board diversity in Singapore is marked by notable progress and forward momentum, there is room for boards in Singapore to improve representation of all voices and drive positive outcomes for all.

A 4-P model for the future

In order to realise the dream of boards that drive innovation, champion inclusion, and create value for all stakeholders; that make decisions which combat biases by leveraging a breadth of perspectives; that help steward organisations which are aligned with the future Singapore we want to see; I posit a "4-P Model" that can help to close the aforementioned gaps.

4-P MODEL FOR TRANSFORMATIVE AND INCLUSIVE BOARDS

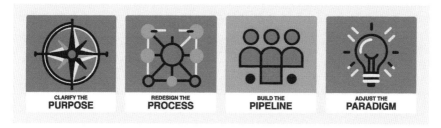

| CLARIFY THE **PURPOSE** | REDESIGN THE **PROCESS** | BUILD THE **PIPELINE** | ADJUST THE **PARADIGM** |

1. Clarify the PURPOSE

In curating a board that is fit for purpose, the starting point must necessarily be definition of that purpose. As Milton Friedman shareholder primacy arguments give way to consideration of stakeholders including customers, employees, suppliers, partners, community, and shareholders, board directors need to ensure the organisation's mission is aligned with the broader societal good.

To do so, directors must lead by asking profound existential questions: Why does the organisation exist? What is our vision? Whom do we serve? They must then weave the answers into the very fabric of their governance structure.

The concept of social welfare has been intertwined with the activities of businesses for centuries, often reflecting the cultural and ethical norms of the times.

In classical Greece and Rome, wealthy individuals, including business owners, were expected to fund public works, games, or festivals, which, while boosting their status, also supported public welfare. During the Middle Ages in Europe, the Catholic Church played a significant role in dictating social responsibility. Guilds, which were associations of artisans or merchants, often took on responsibilities such as caring for their sick members and supporting the poor.

During the Islamic Golden Age, commerce was encouraged, with a strong emphasis on social justice. The concept of Zakat, one of the Five Pillars of Islam, required merchants to donate a portion of their wealth to those in need. In China, Confucian ideals promoted ethical behavior and benevolence in business dealings. In feudal Japan, the concept of "shonindo" or "The Way of the Merchant" reflecting a spirit of co-operation and mutual support, emerged during the Edo period.

More recently, businesses as wide-ranging as Cadbury, Unilever, Ford Motor Company, Tata Group, Patagonia, and, closer to home, Eu Yan Sang and OCBC, were founded with the principle that social progress and development are integral to their growth and success.

Case Vignettes

Cadbury: The British chocolate company, founded in the 19th century, is known for its Quaker principles. The Cadbury family did not just build a factory; they also built an entire community called Bournville for their workers, providing quality housing, recreational facilities, and gardens, believing that a contented workforce would be more productive.

Ford Motor Company: Henry Ford famously introduced the $5-a-day wage for his workers, which was about double the average auto worker's wage at the time. He believed that paying workers more would enable them to afford the cars they produced, thus expanding his market. Ford also invested in education and training for his workforce.

Eu Yan Sang: Eu Kong opened his first shop in Gopeng to provide herbal remedies as an alternative to opium, which was widespread among the Chinese labourers in Malaya. This initiative was born out of concern for the well-being of his community and demonstrated a commitment to healthcare and social responsibility.

OCBC: The three banks that merged to form OCBC were initially established to serve the financial needs of the local Chinese community, which were not adequately addressed by foreign banks. The merger during the Great Depression was a strategic move to consolidate resources and ensure the community had continued access to financial services during tough economic times.

In relative terms, the majority of recorded human history has seen businesses as integral parts of their societies, with expectations to contribute positively. The more modern focus on businesses as purely profit-driven entities is a relatively recent development, mostly associated with the period of industrial capitalism. However, we are currently in an era where the pendulum is swinging back towards integrating social contribution into business practices and making companies more accountable to their stakeholders.

Looking ahead, it is likely that businesses will be expected to continue strengthening their link to society more broadly, especially as consumers and investors increasingly favour companies with strong social and environmental records. In fact, the current trend towards sustainability and social responsibility may be seen as a re-emergence of historical norms adapted to contemporary global challenges.

This suggests that a company's value will be measured not just by its financial performance, but equally by its contribution to the greater good. This reflects an evolving cultural expectation that businesses must be active participants in building a better society for all. Businesses are expected not only to avoid harm but also to actively do good.

The next chapter of the Singapore story will require corporates and community organisations alike to rethink their purpose, then define and implement strategies that are aligned with that purpose. This in turn necessitates high-performing boards comprising directors that bring the knowledge, skills and attributes required to steer the organisation forward.

Such boards do not come about by chance and happenstance. They need to be purposefully curated through a rigorous process, supported by a robust pipeline, with the benefit of a reframed paradigm.

2. Redesign the PROCESS

The board nomination process has seen significant changes with the implementation — effective January 2022 — by Singapore Exchange Regulation (SGX RegCo) of the 9-year rule for independent directors of listed companies. This has led to a decrease in long-serving independent directors and has opened up opportunities for new appointments.

In a similar vein, the revised code of governance for charities stipulates a 10-year board term limit for all Institutions of a Public Character (IPCs) and large non-IPC charities with gross annual receipts or expenditure of $10 million or more. This is likewise intended to encourage board renewal and succession planning.

Such regulatory shifts are crucial to catalysing fresh perspectives in boardrooms. At the same time, what ultimately matters is how the spirit of the rule is adhered to. For example, there have been instances in various parts of the world where companies have faced criticism for appointing female directors primarily to meet quotas, without consideration to their qualifications. This of course gives rise to a broader concern about tokenism, where women are appointed to board positions more for symbolic value than for their actual input or influence.

SGX RegCo has in fact signaled the desire to see real change and renewal across the directorship landscape rather than a game of musical chairs. This will take deliberate action on the part of boards and Nominating Committees as the default is often to reach out to people who are known quantities. This is, however, a mistake, as research demonstrates.

Ronald Burt is an American sociologist and Professor at the University of Chicago School of Business. He coined the term "structural hole" to refer to the social gap between two groups. Structural holes are everywhere. When they occur within an organisation, executives commonly speak of the groups as "silos". Sales and Engineering are a classic example of two groups whose members traditionally interact with their peers rather than across groups.

He conducted a study at Raytheon, a large U.S. electronics company and military contractor, that involved several hundred managers. As part of the study, he asked each manager to propose ideas to improve Raytheon's business operations. He also asked each of them who they had consulted with in the process. Then he had two Raytheon executives independently rate the quality of the ideas.

As it turns out, the best suggestions consistently came from managers who discussed ideas outside their regular work group. Too often, Professor Burt said, the managers discussed their ideas with colleagues already in their informal discussion network. Instead, he said, they should have had discussions outside their typical contacts.

Professor Burt's research reinforces the point that diversity yields better ideas. Beyond that, it highlights the importance of breaking out of the structural holes we find ourselves in. It takes deliberate effort to be exposed to people and ideas that we do not already know.

According to the most recent Singapore Board of Directors Survey which was published by the Singapore Institute of Directors (SID) at the end of 2022, the proportion of companies that identify potential non-executive directors through executive search firms and SID's board appointment services stands at a mere 27 per cent and 21 per cent of respondents, respectively. While this is a marked increase from 17 per cent and 8 per cent in 2019, to put things in perspective, a whopping 96 per cent of respondents source applicants through personal contacts.

Taken together with the analysis of Interlocking Directorships in the Singapore Directorship Report published by the Singapore Institute of Directors at the end of 2023, this further underscores the tendency for boards to tap their close contacts rather than engaging in an impartial process for board appointments. Note: Interlocking directorships refer to situations where the same individuals serve as members of boards of two or more firms. In total, 114 Firms (representing 17.5 per cent of the firms analysed) have director interlocks.

Transformative and inclusive boards require that directors demand a more intellectually rigorous nominating process. This starts with clarity around the organisation's purpose and strategy for the future. The next step in the process is to be intentional about the competencies required to guide the company, and finally to complement the board's networks with candidates that are sourced independently.

A strategic approach to board composition will enable Nominating Committees to ascertain the skills required to propel the organisation forward. And a candidate sourcing process that draws on external sources such as executive search firms and SID's board appointment services will help boards break out of structural holes.

3. Build the PIPELINE

According to research conducted by EY on Asia-Pacific Board Priorities, the crux of the challenge confronting board directors is the need to create clarity amid ambiguity.

Directors are dealing with uncertain geopolitical and economic conditions, including supply chain disruption, rising costs, and inflation. They are grappling with changing demographics and expectations, particularly as they relate to the workforce and consumer base. There is heightened focus on climate-related risks. Lastly, generative AI (Artificial Intelligence) and digital disruption loom large.

These factors point to an urgent need for a broader palette of skillsets in the boardroom than in the past. Thus, when we talk about building the pipeline of directors, it requires not only that boards bring on historically under-represented populations such as women, and younger directors. Increasingly, it is about ensuring that directors have the ability to address a full gamut of emerging and complex issues.

There are two ways to bring about this shift in board capabilities. The first is by enhancing the skills and capabilities of current board members to encompass the domains that are essential for future-ready boards. The second is to develop a pipeline of board-ready candidates that bring knowledge of contemporary boardroom challenges. In the future, we may expect to see more directors with backgrounds that include geopolitics, technology, sustainability, human capital, and communications, for example.

Taking human capital as an example, if people are indeed an organisation's greatest asset, boards need to level up their human capital quotient as a matter of urgency. And believing you know about human capital is not the same as having professional HR experience on the board. Similarly, with the rise of new technologies, including generative AI, that threaten to upend business models, the workforce, and society, professional digital experience on the board will help organisations navigate disruption and mitigate risk.

Building a robust and diverse pipeline of future-ready board directors will require concerted effort from a multitude of agents:

Board Directors and Chairs set the tone and lead by example, embodying the principles of diversity and inclusion. They need to challenge and change outdated mindsets through public discourse and corporate policy. Current directors also play a significant role in mentoring and sponsoring aspiring directors.

Nominating Committees and Chairs are gatekeepers of board composition, tasked with the critical role of identifying and selecting diverse talent. They need to ensure rigor and objectivity in the nominations process and seek candidate slates that are truly diverse. Considering directors who are accredited by the Singapore Institute of Directors will raise professional standards for the board and help mitigate risk for the organisation.

Aspiring Directors need to proactively seek opportunities to hone their skills and contribute fresh perspectives. They need to recognise that board directorship is a profession unto itself and commit to uplifting standards of governance by staying current and relevant.

The Singapore Institute of Directors provides education and resources and plays a key role in developing a diverse array of candidates holistically for board roles. For example, SID's Competency Model (see diagram) reflects eight competencies that directors need to exhibit in the boardroom.

The first edition of SID's Board Readiness Programme which is based on this competency model was launched in July 2023 in collaboration with the Singapore Computer Society Women in Tech Chapter. By expanding the talent pool of board-ready women leaders with a background or expertise in technology, the intent is to simultaneously increase board diversity in terms of gender and functional expertise.

Regulators create the frameworks within which diversity can thrive. They play a vital role in encouraging and facilitating the entry of new talent into the boardroom.

Media are the storytellers who amplify the successes and encourage public discourse around board diversity.

Slowly but surely, the resolute efforts across the entire governance ecosystem are yielding results. Among the top 100 listed companies in Singapore, a record 47 per cent of board appointments in 2022 went to first-time directors. Women accounted for 45 per cent of these first-time appointments, demonstrating an expansion of the talent pool and a shift towards more inclusive boards. Across all listed companies, we see a similar pattern. In 2022, 24.5 per cent of newly appointed independent directors were women, as compared to 21.2 per cent the year prior.

Companies such as Singapore Post, DBS, and SingTel have demonstrated that opening doors to first-time female directors can bridge new gaps and bring innovation to the boardroom. These exemplars demonstrate the value of looking beyond conventional pools for board candidates.

These are but early steps. Building a diverse pipeline of board-ready candidates will require deliberate efforts and ongoing commitment by all stakeholders.

4. Adjust the PARADIGM

The rise in the appointment of first-time directors suggests there is a greater openness in Singapore's boardrooms to consider candidates from a broader range of backgrounds. Yet, there remains more work ahead to change mindsets around diversity.

Two prevalent narratives support the case for board diversity, and in particular, gender diversity. The first narrative references studies that have shown a correlation between diverse boards and better financial performance. That being said, correlation should never be confused with causation — organisations with a history of success understand the need to continually innovate and adapt, and thus may be more open to bringing in a diverse slate of directors, rather than the other way around.

The second narrative revolves around diversity being the 'right thing to do'. Its central assertion is that providing equal opportunities for all, regardless of gender, race, ethnicity, or other characteristics, is inherently the right approach for any society committed to equality and respect for individual merit. It aligns with broader societal movements towards inclusivity and reflects the belief that organisations should model the principles of the diverse communities they serve.

While both arguments have their merits (as well as their detractors), the most compelling factor for me is that diversity improves the quality of our decisions. This is a paradigm shift.

Joseph Luft and Harrington Ingham developed the Johari Window in 1955, as a result of their research on group dynamics at the University of California, Los Angeles. The four-quadrant framework (so named by combining "Jo" from Joseph and "Hari" from Harrington) presents our 'Open', 'Hidden', 'Blind', and 'Unknown' selves. The 'Blind Spot' quadrant represents aspects that we are not aware of, but others are.

Diversity can play a key role in addressing these blind spots. By interacting with a diverse group of people, individuals can gain insights and feedback from different perspectives, which can illuminate aspects of their thoughts, behaviours, or attitudes that they were previously unaware of.

The field of behavioural economics, decision science, and human judgment is well-established and Nobel Prize winner Professor Daniel Kahneman's insights into cognitive biases are often applied to discussions about the benefits of diversity in decision-making contexts. Diverse groups are thought to counteract some of the biases he has identified, such as group-think, confirmation bias, hindsight bias, and loss aversion.

Organisational psychologist Professor Adam Grant argues that group-think occurs when the desire for harmony and cohesiveness results in a lack of diversity, individuality, and creativity. As a counterbalance to the tendency to stick with the mainstream, he advocates actively seeking people that do not necessarily agree with us.

In his book *Originals: How Non-Conformists Move the World*, Adam Grant reveals that great creators seek the broadest perspectives, rather than necessarily being the deepest experts. "The more expertise and experience people gain, the more entrenched they become in a particular way of viewing the world. As we gain knowledge about a domain, we become prisoners of our prototypes," Grant explains.

One of the most prevalent biases in board decision-making is the overconfidence effect, where experts may hold their beliefs with undue conviction, overlooking the need to question the supporting evidence. Good decision-making requires primary knowledge as well as metacognitive competence, such as an awareness of limitations, biases, and the need for good process.

Research conducted by Professor Anil Gaba from INSEAD further sheds light on how cognitive biases can specifically affect boardroom decisions. He points out that the nature of board roles often requires directors to use heuristics, which are mental shortcuts that allow for quick information processing. While generally useful, these shortcuts can sometimes lead to incorrect assessments, with potentially negative consequences. Recognising these biases is increasingly acknowledged as fundamental to the work of boards.

By seeking disconfirming evidence and employing diverse viewpoints as anchors for discussion, boards can challenge biases and reduce cognitive distortions. This approach ultimately fosters better boardroom deliberation, enhancing collective intelligence and decision quality.

Regardless of organisation type or ownership structure, boards in Singapore need to be prepared to meet the challenges of a VUCA (volatile, uncertain, complex, and ambiguous) and BANI (brittle, anxious, nonlinear, and incomprehensible) operating environment.

As board directors, we have a responsibility to make the best decisions possible, particularly in the face of conflicting or missing information. The research on decision science demonstrates compellingly that diversity in the boardroom is not just a matter of fulfilling quotas or creating a positive image — it has a practical impact on the quality of decision-making, particularly in the face of disruption and complexity. It is time for a paradigm shift.

The call to action: Leaving a legacy for the future

The late Minister Mentor Lee Kuan Yew once said that leaders must have a sense of reality of what is possible. However, it is not only about being realistic. He said, "You must be able to soar above reality and say, this is also possible."

History demonstrates that changing the default trajectory takes bold action. We as board directors of this generation have the opportunity to craft legacies. This is our promise for the future, where diversity is not an objective but the norm; where boards assume a pivotal role in empowering organisations, individuals, and society to not merely survive but thrive.

To aspiring Directors, particularly those from under-represented populations — be it gender, ethnicity, or functional background — your voices at the table matter. That seat, however, is not an entitlement. It is about charting your course and embarking on your directorship journey.

You can earn a seat at the boardroom table by:

- Investing in your directorship journey and highlighting your commitment to excellence and ethical stewardship
- Crafting a professional identity and becoming an SID Accredited Director
- Keeping in mind that long-term, systemic change is an endurance race

To my fellow Board Directors, Nominating Committee Chairs, and Board Chairs, our commitment to board diversity must go beyond setting and reaching numerical targets. It's about ensuring that boards are not just diverse in appearance but in thought and action as well. It's about embracing differing perspectives and making better decisions in the face of uncertainty.

We can shape the contours of directorship in Singapore by:

- Refreshing our purpose to contribute to a thriving society
- Drawing on external sources to identify potential non-executive directors
- Insisting on a slate of candidates that represents multiple dimensions of diversity, including gender
- Fostering an inclusive board culture that enables us to draw strength from differences

Let us confront Disruption by enriching the quality of the Decisions we make in the boardroom, and harnessing the tangible value that Diversity contributes.

Let us lead with clarity of Purpose, commit to an enhanced nominations Process, build a robust Pipeline of board candidates, and shift the Paradigm.

I have a dream. It's a dream where every decision made within the hallowed confines of our boardrooms contributes to a future where business and society advance in harmony, where every stride we take in our corporate journey leaves a footprint of positive impact.

Let us dream together. And let us take concrete action so that the organisations we helm contribute to shaping the way forward for a stronger Singapore.

WONG SU-YEN is an experienced chairperson and independent director who has served on the Boards of multiple public, private, and not-for-profit organisations in Australia, Asia, and the United States. She was the first female Chairperson of the Singapore Institute of Directors (2020–2023) and is one of 24 women featured in Women on Board: Making a Difference. *With over three decades of experience across Asia and North America, she has helped some of the world's largest, most innovative, and complex organisations navigate the intersection of technology, strategy, and people. She is Adjunct Associate Professor of Leadership at the National University of Singapore Business School, and member of the Executive Education Faculty at Duke University. She is a professional speaker who engages audiences globally on leadership, transformation, and the future of work, and is a published author of an Amazon Bestseller —* Unleash Your Voice: Powerful Public Speaking for Every Woman. *She is an avid adventure traveller and has ventured to some of the world's most remote locations, including Antarctica and Timbuktu.*

"Women have the qualities we need to make the world a better place. A world driven by compassion and care rather than machismo and might; a world shaped by cooperation and collaboration rather than conflict and aggression. We need many more women in leadership positions in Singapore — and in the world — so that it is these qualities that will prevail."

~ Trailblazing Golden Girl of swimming Pat Chan, for The Lives of Women exhibition at the National Museum, Jan–Mar 2022

CHAPTER 4

Women Leadership in Singapore Business, Politics, and the Community: The Next Bound

Lin Suling

There is a world where women leaders have unquestionably achieved parity with men.

Sometimes, this place takes the form of a multiverse, where a mother must cross all of space and time to save her daughter and restore peace and stability to the conscious world, even if this entails spending all of eternity in purgatory.

In another dimension, gender equality is found in the figure of a grieving daughter at the helm of one of the most technologically advanced nations. Our young heroine overcomes her demons and responds valiantly with conviction in a time of crisis as her country comes under attack by an unknown force.

In 2023, both the Oscar-winning film Everything, Everywhere, All at Once and the Marvel blockbuster Black Panther: Wakanda

Forever have propelled visions of gender equality forward, by leaning into the heroism of their female icons and painting a picture of what women leadership can achieve.

Film has long furnished inspiration for a bolder and better world and, in this case, one that celebrates the gender that holds up half the sky, recognising that everyone benefits when the talents of strong women can be drawn on.

The bigger question is whether reality can catch up.

Progress for women leadership in politics, business and the community

Here in Singapore, there is arguably no better time to be a woman. We have women breaking barriers and getting cracking on the most pressing issues facing society. There is a palpable sense women are hitting senior ranks and pinnacle roles at a steady clip.

Today, one in three seats in Parliament is held by a woman. We have three full female ministers — Grace Fu, Josephine Teo, and Indranee Rajah. Halimah Yacob, as the first woman head of state, actively advocated for workers, the less fortunate, and people with disabilities in her time as President.

We are also seeing a record number of women appointed to boards on Singapore Exchange listed companies, statutory boards and Institutions of Public Character (IPCs) in 2023. The goal set by the Council for Board Diversity of having the top 100 largest listed firms achieve a share of 30 percent female representation on boards by 2030 — the critical mass needed for firms to reap the full benefits of gender diversity — looks within reach.

But with only 51 percent of boards at the top 100 IPCs, 46 percent of statutory boards and 26 percent of the top 100 listed companies meeting this benchmark in Singapore, there is room for improvement.

New rules by SGX imposing term limits for independent directors and mandatory remuneration disclosure should go some way to narrowing this gap.

But we can go further to achieve a vision of gender equality. Instead of satisficing minimal standards, we can afford to be more ambitious in Singapore and focus our minds on setting long-term goals, build on the progress forged by those who have paved the way forward and strengthen the needed scaffolding.

In Business: Informing occupational choices, eliminating work-life conflict

In business, we should seek to eliminate talk of quotas for board representation and executive roles because we have reached a stage where we are brimming with women corporate leaders and have a strong pipeline in middle-to-senior management positions.

Phrases like "she was the first woman to lead a regional HQ for a tech firm" would vanish because it is no longer unusual to see a woman there.

But the challenge to those goals lies in two key hurdles impeding career progression for women and exacerbating the gender pay gap, disincentivising advancement altogether.

First, much of Singapore's 16.3 per cent gender pay gap can be explained by gendered distribution across and within occupations: more men are found in higher-paying sectors like tech, banking and medicine and they progress to higher positions on average compared to women.

To tackle this, profiling female role models in those industries early on in schools can help shift mindsets and showcase a wide spectrum of career options for young girls at the point where they decide which educational route and field of specialisation to pursue.

This can be part of an annual Careers Day at the primary school level, something that schools like St Hilda's Primary, my alma mater, already practise, which featured women social entrepreneurs, bankers and scientists.

Targetted career scaffolding when women enter the workforce and through the course of their careers can also help groom cohorts of aspiring women leaders to encourage more to continue on their route of progression. Gender parity remains elusive at entry- and mid-level management roles — a gap McKinsey refers to as the broken rung on the leadership ladder — even though men and women enter the workforce in equal measure.

This is not an argument to do more but to focus efforts more surgically. While women mentorship and leadership development programmes have mushroomed in Singapore in recent years, a 2010 *Harvard Business Review* study showed sponsorship programmes — involving advocacy for advancement and practised in global firms like Deutsche Bank, Unilever and IBM Europe proved comparatively more effective in moving women up the chain.

The creation of sponsorship programmes with suitably powerful and senior sponsors have the additional benefits of equipping women with advice and coaching to develop their leadership style while connecting them to stepping-stone opportunities and enhancing their visibility to corporate C-suites and boards. These help high-potential women "stay the course", according to a 2016 McKinsey study, and fight the tendency to shift from line roles with profit and loss responsibilities to supporting staff functions perceived as less demanding as they grow their families and move up their organisations' hierarchies.

Women with leadership potential and suitably long working experiences of eight to 15 years — a juncture where many might become "stuck" — can be identified and paired with influential sponsors in the same organisation or sector.

Such sponsorships build on a first wave of complementary women mentorship initiatives by the Singapore Council of Women's Organisations (SCWO) BoardAgender programme and the Singapore Institute of Directors' board membership matching services.

Second, even after the gender pay gap has been adjusted for factors impacting occupational differences, the remaining six percent has been attributed by a study by the Manpower Ministry and the National University of Singapore to differences between the genders in their average job level, work experience and caregiving responsibilities. This is where interventions to tackle work-life conflict and build family -riendly workplaces can help more stay at work.

Singapore is in a strong position to make greater gains on this front. The growth of childcare and elderly care facilities to take the load off caregivers who are largely female, and the adoption of flexible work arrangements, accelerated by the pandemic, has helped more high-potential women stay employed and focused on their jobs.

But much of the pay gap difference here still remains unexplained. Increased transparency can shed light on when women slow down in their career and why, while improving corporate governance. Building on new Singapore Exchange Listing Rules requiring listed companies to maintain a board diversity target, plans and timelines, companies should also be made to disclose aggregate plans for talent development and leadership succession within the middle- to senior management band, including their gender and pay gap in roles of similar seniority.

Far from being a witch-hunt, such efforts might create better understanding of the impediments to women in reaching their leadership potential and shed light on best practices worth emulating. Citibank, for example, achieved its representation goal of 40 percent women at the assistant vice president to managing director levels in 2021, three years after setting this objective. They accomplished this through a mix of inclusive hiring practices, proactive recruitment efforts to source for mid-career hires and a four-month talent development programme involving 14,000 women.

High-profile surveys like Statistica's annual Best Employers in Singapore ranking, which currently allows employees to rate their companies on various aspects of their jobs, work environment and reputation could also highlight scores for family life-conflict and perceptions of gender diversity.

In Politics: Strengthening the women's movement, enhancing political representation

In the political arena, Singapore should see more women hold leadership roles in front bench, political parties and Parliament. We have made significant headway since 1984 where not a single woman was in Parliament. Women have won a third of seats, and Parliament has had a woman Speaker and Leader of the House.

At some point, Singapore could see a female Defence Minister not by virtue of tokenism or political pressure but because women in politics have strong geopolitical experience and exposure; they understand the strategic calculations needed to maintain Singapore's strong deterrence and commitment to National Service.

If political leadership continues to draw from public service technocrats, the track record augurs well. Singapore has already seen its first female brigadier-general BG Gan Siow Huang, currently Minister of State for Manpower and Education. The Deputy Secretary roles in administration and policy in the Defence Ministry have been filled by at least three women in the last 20 years. Middle and senior management roles in the policy, national service and finance departments in the Ministry of Defence today also have a good measure of women.

The problem is less one of insufficient women with the needed capabilities and experience than that of outdated norms quick to cast judgement on women in politics as somehow less capable. In such scenarios, the best way to break the barrier is to simply have some visible representation and let the results speak for themselves to shift mindsets and shape public opinion.

Meaning to say also that in the same fashion where soft aspirational targets have been set for women representation on boards in the world of business to achieve gender equality, a similar argument could be made for better female representation in politics.

Even so, this objective sits awkwardly for two reasons. First, enhancing women's political representation can be tricky if political parties championing gender diversity in leadership appoint more women to play identity politics. This would be counterproductive to the goal of promoting women's issues as one that benefits the whole of society.

Second, increasing female numerical representation in public life does not guarantee greater women political empowerment, much of which relies on prevailing institutions, practices and norms.

Instead, the best proxy of women empowerment in politics may be that of the strength of civic organisations that continue to put women's issues on the national agenda.

Here in Singapore particularly, it is civil society organisations like SCWO and AWARE that have taken the lead to advance a myriad women's issues, spanning board directorship, sexual assault, coercive control, challenges around caregiving, and fairness in the workplace. They have provided thought leadership and grassroots activism to catalyse policy and legislative changes. Funding the development of leaders in these organisations, as well as their research capacities that shed light on the challenges faced by women leaders, could go some way to strengthen women's issues.

Another idea is to institutionalise a permanent Nominated Member of Parliament (NMP) for women's issues to ensure diverse women's issues are heard in the political process. Dr Kanwaljit Soin's tenure in that role in the 1990s attracted public attention to the issue of domestic violence against women when she introduced a Private Member's Bill on family violence, with many recommendations subsequently incorporated into amendments to the Women's Charter the year after. But there has not been a women's issues NMP since.

This approach of a women's issues NMP also has the additional benefit of addressing gender equality and other factors exacerbating social exclusion — across age, race and class.

In the community: Supporting social innovation, creating virtuous communities

In the community, women leaders in Singapore play critical roles spearheading collaborative efforts to solve complex problems. Nowhere is this clearer than in the community health sector, where women leaders pioneering research, pushing for practical and new models of care, and galvanising community resources have made a sum difference.

Take these three examples: First, Dr. Angelique Chan, who serves as Executive Director of the Duke-NUS Centre for Ageing Research and Education and Director of non-profit Tsao Foundation's Ageing Research Initiative. Her research work on a wide spectrum of ageing issues have shed light on dementia, loneliness and integrated care models, influenced healthcare policy development, and led to innovative programmes.

Second, Jaga Me's Kuan Ling Ling and Homage's Gillian Tee, pioneers of a digital home care platform matching volunteers and professionals with nursing experience to the elderly and patients requiring help transitioning from the hospital to home. Their social enterprises have benefitted many seniors and provided respite care and advanced practical solutions to caregiving for an ageing population.

Third, Mary Ann Tsao, chairwoman and founding director of Tsao Foundation. Her philanthropy has pushed the envelope of the community-based care model which has seen the launch of a Community for Successful Ageing at Whampoa, and sought to shift mindsets over longevity and ageing.

Taken together, their collective efforts to tackle eldercare and ageing from academic, social entrepreneurship and philanthropy lenses have enriched Singapore's approach to eldercare with transformative ideas, at a time when the country is nearing "super aged" status, with one in four citizens aged 65 and above come 2030.

Imagine if other sectors had the same critical mass of female entrepreneurs, researchers and philanthropists catalysing community resources to solve the big issues.

So how can we ensure there are women leaders equally at the forefront of community development in Singapore? We must accelerate women's representation in community leadership goals in two ways.

First, we must strengthen women's professional associations, many of which are driven by volunteers but can achieve more with full-time staff and a dedicated executive director. Although the aim must be for such organisations to be financed through services rendered discussed in this chapter, funding from the government might be needed to kickstart their professionalisation.

In recent years, professional networks, like the Singapore Business Federation's Singapore Women Entrepreneurs Network and the BoardAgender Mentorship Programme for Aspiring Women Directors, have been established, focused on building a community of aspiring women leaders with shared goals and common challenges.

But they have the potential to achieve more with greater support and wider networks of supportive businesses. In the U.S., well-funded women's professional associations have aided in leadership development by helping women work directly with and observe other women leaders in action, gain confidence in their skills and receive support from others to take on leadership roles, according to a 2023 *Human Resource Development Quarterly* journal.

Second, we must double down on efforts to celebrate the achievements of women community leaders, that help to role model success and tackle stubborn biases that harm the development of women leadership.

The Singapore Women's Hall of Fame launched by the SCWO in 2014 has showcased women who have made an impact in Singapore as community leaders, changemakers, and barrier breakers, to great effect. Greater visibility through representation in popular culture, the arts and other media may inspire the next wave of community women leaders to step forward.

Looking to the future: Adopting an inclusive approach

Amid this discussion on female leadership, two concerns stand out. First, the discourse calling for more women leadership around the world is often seen in zero-sum terms, as if proponents are pushing for some sort of special dispensation or some type of affirmative action to equalise outcomes for both genders.

This cannot be further from the truth. Diversity in leadership — whether gender, race, or class — provides more varied perspectives and strengthens organisational decision-making. Pushing to see more women in positions where they can make a difference is grounded on this belief.

A second issue around women leadership concerns doubts over whether the style of leadership by women truly differs from male leadership. Admittedly, the scholarship on this is sparse but among the global research conducted, U.S. business academic Susan R. Madsen's research illuminates what female leaders have in common: Men are more strategic and their leadership journey follows a linear pathway, whereas the road women take tends to be more experimental and emergent, which is why they are inclined to take a more hands-on approach to truly understand the people they lead and the fields they're thrusted in.

But the track record regarding women involvement in leadership teams is clear. Groundbreaking research by McKinsey in 2008 measuring company performance on every possible metric — profit-making, innovation and accountability — show firms with three or more women in top management positions outperformed those without such representation. These same companies scored 48 percent higher profits and 1.7 times the growth in stock price.

In the boardroom, McKinsey also found that female members temper the risk-taking inclinations of their fellow members, by challenging assumptions, identifying blindspots and prodding boards to make longer-term and less aggressive investment and acquisition decisions.

I remain optimistic of Singapore's prospects for women leaders. As a country that broke ground to recognise the importance of protecting women's rights and enshrine these in the Women's Charter in 1961, we are continuing from a strong position. The real question is the size of our ambitions in wanting to see more women faces in leadership roles and whether there is shared societal zeal to do this work.

The answer should come easy. Every day and in most fields, women already make significant contributions: Whether in the home as mothers, wives, daughters, sisters; in the community as researchers, social entrepreneurs and philanthropists; or in running companies and organisations in business and politics.

Imagine the potential we can unleash if women can take on more positions of leadership here.

LIN SULING is Opinion Editor at The Straits Times. *Prior to that, she spent the last five years in the CNA (Channel NewsAsia) digital newsroom as founding editor of the Commentary and Podcast sections. She also has a background in public service, having served at the Ministry of Defence, the Ministry of Finance and the Pioneer Generation Office for almost a decade. Suling has also served on the Singapore Council of Women's Organisation's BoardAgender 2022 Mentorship Programme for Aspiring Women Directors.*

"I hope homemaking, undertaken by choice by either men or women, will be included as a GDP indicator matched by an appropriate level of State funding. Homemaking, which women have contributed to phenomenally, has not been accorded the economic recognition it deserves. I would like to see it becoming a productive asset to be valued."

~ Corporate social responsibility champion Claire Chiang, for The Lives of Women exhibition at the National Museum, Jan–Mar 2022

Chapter 5

Want to Shift Mindsets? Put a Value to Household Work

Euston Quah & Tan Jun Rui

Home labour is often taken for granted due to its unpaid (or lowly paid) and loosely monitored nature in the absence of a formal work environment. However, the amount and value of time used to provide the day-to-day services of cooking, cleaning, shopping, child-rearing and the myriad other chores that are demanded by households is clearly not insignificant. It represents a very substantial portion of the total productive time available to members of a household and to a society. Thus, an accounting of its worth commensurate with wages earned from other employment is an issue of increasing practical importance.

The adequacy of the GDP as a measure of economic growth and performance has always been questioned. One of its main criticisms is that it understates economic welfare through the omission of non-market productive activity, of which household work forms a large portion. Excluding paid domestic maids, the services provided by informal caregivers or housewives are welfare-improving. Faced with an ageing society, a quarter of Singaporeans is expected to be a senior citizen by 2030, implying that more caregiving services would be needed in the near future.

Additionally, if the time and effort spent by caregivers or housewives on children improves their discipline, then it yields positive spin-offs to society. For example, a caring mother who spends valuable time educating her children may improve their skills and future work attributes. A stable home environment makes for a more secure society, and children from such homes are less likely to commit crime.

Discussions on the contribution of household production centre mainly on two issues: the amount that is produced, and the economic value attributable to the time necessary to produce it. A market for household production clearly exists due to the demand for homemakers and caregivers and supply of women who are willing to be either part-time or full-time homemakers. If left solely to market forces, household production may be underproduced and the economic contribution of housewives may be underestimated and not given its due recognition.

How can valuing household production alleviate gender inequality?

In 2020, the Singapore Government declared that gender equality should be a fundamental value. Much has been discussed about the cultural, social, and structural domains with regards to gender equality. Balancing family responsibilities and flexible work arrangements are among the key aspects that warrant attention, which allude to the often-overlooked importance of household production.

Singaporean females generally earn lower market wages than males — a 26 percent difference in average mean monthly earnings in 2021, according to the *Singapore Yearbook of Manpower Statistics*

2022. Women's home productivity as measured strictly by the services or output that can be produced at home per unit time is commonly perceived as generally higher than that of men. Therefore, women tend to specialise in housework and men in market work to their increased common benefit and cost minimisation. Both partners are contributors to a household even though the act of one appears in cash flows and the other, in non-pecuniary household production, does not. This division of labour is said to enable the household to maximise their total real income with the husband and wife specialising in complementary activities. However, such an arrangement may be detrimental to the wife, for the following reasons.

Firstly, the opportunity costs of giving up one's career and being a homemaker have been increasing over the years. Being more qualified with an improvement in female literacy rates and amount of education attained over the years has seen more women being employed and actively seeking market work in Singapore.

Based on the proportion of employed residents by gender, it appears that although Singaporean females spend less time in the market compared to men, this divergence has narrowed over time. For Singaporean females, as per the findings of the collaborative study by Ipsos and United Women Singapore in 2021, household production comes with greater perceived trade-offs to their career opportunities and quality of life as compared to men.

Secondly, while household responsibilities are typically shared between both spouses in a marriage, women are more likely to take on cleaning, cooking, and caregiver roles that are more demanding in time commitment with less flexibility in scheduling. It may not be the case that women are inherently better at homemaking rather than men, but rather it may be the product of the age-long tradition of housewives' homemaking skills being imparted from their own mothers. However, the pressure of conforming to societal expectations means that there is much inertia in the shifting of such household responsibilities from housewives to husbands that are traditionally associated with the female gender.

According to the Ministry of Manpower's (MOM) findings in 2021, most females (23.9 per cent) outside the labour force did not work because of housework responsibilities, while 14.3 per cent of them prioritised care for their family members and relatives over work. This is a stark contrast to males' reasons for not working, whereby only about 3.7 per cent did not work because of housework and caregiving reasons combined.

Knowing the value of household work helps household members come to optimal decisions on the allocation of time between work in the market and work at home. Once members of a family understand the economic value of their contribution to housework, this value can be used to decide whether these contributions are comparable, less than or exceed wages that they could have earned or are earning in the market. This provides a more meaningful estimate of how much women and men are willing to trade off market work and leisure time for time spent on household production activities.

Home labour is work and the home is essentially considered a workplace. One may also argue that just like wage labour, housework is also generally performed out of love, duty and responsibility for the family's well-being. Therefore, knowing the value of household production may help to reduce gender discrimination and stereotypes to promote a more equal allocation of home labour between both spouses. For example, the husband knowing that he contributes less to the household than his wife may feel more inclined to take on some of the home labour burden for a more equitable overall contribution if the cost of attempting to earn higher market wages is too high.

In the long run, such knowledge will hopefully facilitate acceptance of a family structure whereby men contribute more to non-market household labour and women to market work as a new gender norm rather than a deviation from the norm.

In short, valuing household production will move society closer to achieving the key milestones of the White Paper on Singapore's Women's Development in the areas of equal opportunities in the workplace, recognition and support for caregivers as well as mindset shifts.

Labour force participation and the economy

The need for the measurement and valuation of housework lies not only in a desire to provide a better estimate of the total economic production for an economy and understanding how it affects the labour supply of women, but also in providing a better basis for growth calculations and for international comparisons of national income.

The value of household production derived for an economy and disaggregated by age of household members, size of household, income and other household characteristics would be useful guidelines for policymakers in the event of a desire to influence the labour force participation rate of men and women in either direction—that is, from non-market to market and vice-versa. In short, this leads to a better understanding of a country's labour supply. This, in turn, will allow policymakers to come up with a better formulation of marginal income tax rates and observed changes in taxable revenue. For example, some empirical studies have shown that married women working outside the home react negatively to higher levels of taxation by reducing their paid market hours and increasing their time devoted to home production.

The information that married women's market labour supply reacts positively to net marginal earnings gives rise to several pertinent questions: what is the magnitude of the loss in welfare associated with increases in income taxation of married women to the household? How large is the withdrawal or injection of married women from or to the market following changes in marginal tax rates? Is it likely that the tax system influences the provision of home goods and services, marriage patterns, and fertility behaviour? This is particularly important for Singapore because of its constant low fertility rate (all-time low of 1.05 children per female in 2022).

It has been argued that because national income accounts include both income and consumption which are, in effect, welfare estimates, the GDP statistic can be taken to be an indicator of welfare. But because the GDP includes, among other things, market goods and services that make no obvious contribution to individual economic well-being (e.g. police firearms, anti-pollution equipment) and excludes items which contribute to economic welfare (e.g. leisure, household services), the GDP statistic, as it is argued, is a flawed index of a country's economic welfare.

High or low growth rates as reflected in a country's GDP may also be inaccurate as they ignore changes in the household economy. To the extent that home production is not measured in conventional income accounts and to the degree that the household output omitted changes over time, then both the quantity and total output are mismeasured.

During economic recoveries, the fall in household production growth indicates women exiting the household to enter the market sector, thus reducing the strains on a growing economy by relaxing the labour constraint. When more women enter the workforce to do paid work, GDP will rise, and the economy will be said to have grown. But that growth is overestimated since it comes only as a transfer of unpaid women's work at home to paid women's work in the market. This is because the labour force participation rate of women has been increasing over time. aWith increasing commercialisation of housework activities, it is possible that the total production of goods and services over time may not have changed by much.

Similarly, in periods of economic downturns, falling growth rates may not be indicative of the real state of the economy, as women may have returned to their households and now generate increased home production, where the high household sector growth helped to reduce the fall in combined GDP growth.

Legal uses

Another practical benefit lies in deriving the value of housework in legal cases involving compensation for accident victims whose family would suffer from the loss of household services normally provided by the injured victim. Such a loss is equivalent to losing part of a family's real income. Understanding the value of household work would help victims be compensated adequately without making the family worse off.

Singapore's highest court considers the value of household production in a marriage when determining the division of matrimonial assets. However, because much of what goes on within households is unrecorded, such indirect and intangible contributions are likely to be estimated based on mostly self-reported qualitative claims and crudely quantified in the derivation of a 'scoring ratio' between both spouses.

By assigning a wage to home production that can be justifiably negotiated just like paid labour, this would empower women by effectively enforcing a less arbitrary marital contract between homemakers and their spouses. The values elicited would allow policymakers to better disentangle the value-producing labour component from the act of love or familial obligation and duty component.

In matrimonial property settlements and in divorce proceedings, information on the value of the contribution made by the spouse who does household work — whether in caregiving, cooking, cleaning, marketing, or doing the laundry — would go a long way in establishing a more equitable balance of respective spousal contribution in adjudication and litigation.

Welfare consequence

By ignoring the non-market household economy, a measure of income distribution based only on market income is obviously deficient. As a measure of economic well-being, the value of household work should be imputed for supplementing social security designs, understanding poverty issues and for general happiness studies.

In setting the poverty line level and a measure of welfare, a rather unacceptable proposition may arise that two households with similar characteristics — size of household, location of house, number of children, type of house, etc. — and earning the same money income are equally poor or rich when one household has a full-time homemaker and the other does not. Moreover, it is not only income but also time which is a finite resource that affects well-being. A poverty line should be multidimensional in the sense that it includes the monetary value of the time deficit that homemakers face after spending time on personal maintenance, unpaid care work and employment activities. If a measure of the income and time distribution could be improved by knowledge of an estimate of the value of household produced goods and services not included in household money income, then a better measure of the distribution of economic welfare could be devised for policy purposes.

It can be argued that husbands already compensate their wives for household labour indiscriminately such as via CPF contributions and other monetary allowances. The same may apply to employers since employers pay according to the productivity of workers, and that the housewife freeing up housework time for the husband can be said to make him more productive indirectly.

However, suppose that society is willing to pay housewives and informal caregivers for their role in maintaining a liveable society. An aggregate estimate of the economic value of household production would allow for more accurate knowledge on say, how financial support for informal caregivers such as Singapore's Home Caregiving Grant or the Seniors' Mobility and Enabling Fund should be enhanced.

Ways to value household production

One commonly used method to value household production is to estimate the foregone wages the homemaker spouse could have earned had he or she worked in the labour market instead of spending time at home. This is known as the opportunity cost method. But this leads to questionable issues of housework value being higher for a housewife who is a qualified medical doctor, than for another who is a secretary.

Another method is to consider how much it would cost to hire a replacement worker, such as a domestic maid, to provide similar household services. This method has two variants: one is a generalised replacement worker, and the other, cost incurred by a team of specialised replacement workers.

The value derived from the former is deemed to be inadequate because there are clearly many household services which a replacement worker would not be able to provide, such as tutoring small children and home budgeting and planning. Using the second variant involves estimating the cost of hiring a tutor, driver, cook, cleaner and so on. But this is arguably an overestimation since a housewife is essentially a general worker, and not a specialist one.

A novel method that I first proposed in 1993 is to marry the two variants of the replacement cost, such that the major component of housework is replaced by hiring a maid, while the additional work done by the housewife and not by the maid is separately estimated.

The latter would include replacement cost by hiring a kindergarten teacher as tutor and the wages earned by a manager of a small firm comprising four to six workers since running a household can be comparable to running a small firm.

This method also proposes to correct the efficiency differences in time use for housework between the homemaker and the replacement worker such that if a maid, for example, is more efficient than a housewife in terms of time taken to do housework, then the dollar value estimated for household production would be reduced by the efficiency factor. However, the issue of quality differences in the work done remains.

The contingent evaluation method has been used, with growing success, to value other non-market goods and seems an appropriate approach to value household production as well. For example, the method could involve posing alternative contingencies to households in terms of whether they would rather pay specific amounts to reduce the time given over to household tasks or to keep the money and do the work themselves.

The theoretical presumption is that one would not expect households to be willing to pay more than their own marginal opportunity cost of household production nor more than what they expect to gain from having additional hours to home production. At most, it might be expected that households are willing to pay an amount equal to their own cost of production or up to their marginal benefit from having the additional hours.

The difference between the mean values of the households' total willingness to pay for household production and their total opportunity cost would give a measure of the amount of welfare enjoyed by households from having household production.

Effect of the pandemic on household production

The Covid-19 pandemic has raised interesting questions on the value of time. Time spent at home versus time spent in the office; time spent travelling to work; leisure and recreation time; time spent in treatment and hospitalisation; time spent on volunteer work; and time spent on household production.

During the pandemic, many workers, both male and female, spent more time working from home than in the office. MOM noted that 49 per cent of workers overall and more than 70 per cent of employed residents in the services and education industries in Singapore worked from home as of mid-2020.

During the circuit breaker period, offices and retail shops were mostly closed with forced work-from-home arrangements. If traditionally foregone market wages were used as a proxy measure for the value of household production, this value would be less than the full wage rates. As the time devoted to household production increases involuntarily because of reduced options in alternative uses of time including market-work time and outdoor leisure, the value of time per hour would likely be valued less compared with pre-circuit breaker days.

A study based on the American Time Use Survey found a substantial time allocation from paid work to home production for less-educated married women with children in the U.S. during the peak of the pandemic. Based on the specialist replacement cost method, it was found that the increased value of monthly home production had partially offset the fall in GDP during that period by 9.1 per cent.

Would this involuntary and indirect increase in time spent in the household exacerbate or alleviate gender inequality? A study in Japan found a more equitable allocation of housework and childcare among both spouses accompanied by more neutral gender attitudes during the Covid-19 period. This is likely due to prolonged work-from-home arrangements, whereby spending more time at home has alerted husbands that their non-market contribution is needed.

With more members of the household working from home and the shift to home-based learning, more household chores might have been inadvertently produced which could reduce the homemaker's efficiency. For instance, having to eat lunch at home might have required more dishes to be washed and more cleaning of the house as more people were spending more time at home. Childcare centres were forced to close temporarily, which necessitated parents to take on the role themselves if hiring domestic helpers was not an option.

A study commissioned by The *Straits Times* in 2022 found that Singaporeans spending longer hours on paid work during the pandemic could be partly attributed to the allocation of some working time at their own discretion to care for their family members. Despite the flexibility of working arrangements, a study in India found that with the convergence of employment and household responsibilities, it could have become harder for employed women to draw the line between paid and unpaid work, as well as leisure. Consequently, housewives might have had less quality time to focus on the development of their professional and personal growth, which are important for both their material and non-material well-being.

Unemployed women or full-time homemakers might have become more self-conscious about their own abilities and lack of tangible income contribution when other members of the household were doing paid work at home but they were not. This might have created greater familial pressure for these group of women to shoulder a greater burden of household chores.

Bottom line

Feminists have traditionally championed for market work to be as accessible to women just as it has been for men. This might have led to the unintended side effect of women having less time for not only leisure but also household production activities as they engage in market work. This has implications for society and the economy.

The value of household production should carry more weight. This is because it is no less important than the value of paid work and should be appropriately accounted for in the economic output of a nation. Estimates of the value of household production should be compiled periodically and weighed against the economic growth statistics provided by national income accounts. Such estimates should also be adjusted in the event of exogenous shocks which distort the value of time. In this way, society may know to what extent GDP growth can be attributable to increased labour force participation of women, or for that matter, homemakers; and policies can be designed to influence this labour force participation rate.

Attention should not only be paid to our caregiving needs but also to the needs of caregivers, given the many compromises that they must make to paid work and leisure that have competing usage for time. It is important that society recognises these trade-offs and reduces the psychological costs of women who feel that they are confined to the role of household production out of necessity or that they are more responsible for it than men.

Accounting for the value of household production using cost and benefit methodologies, while imperfect, will still be useful to facilitate an economic and legal recognition of the value of household production. This will help the government design policies such as paternal leave, flexible working arrangements and social security benefits for both genders more prudently and fairly.

EUSTON QUAH is Albert Winsemius Chair Professor of Economics at the Nanyang Technological University, with research interests in Cost-Benefit Analysis and Environmental Economics. He has published over 100 papers in journals, and lead opinion articles in media. Widely cited, his internationally known book on Cost-Benefit Analysis *with E. J. Mishan published by Routledge, UK is now in its 6th edition, 2021. The Asian edition of his* Principles of Economics *with Gregory Mankiw is now a 3rd edition Cengage published book, 2021. Professor Quah is also the only person who headed both the economics departments at the National University of Singapore, and at the Nanyang Technological University.*

TAN JUN RUI is a researcher in the Economic Growth Centre at Nanyang Technological University. His current projects include the study of Singapore's living standards and sustainability strategies. As second author, he has contributed to several opinion articles in media about the analysing of contemporary issues from an economics perspective.

References

Chauhan, P. 2021. "Gendering COVID-19: Impact of the Pandemic on Women's Burden of Unpaid Work in India". *Gender Issues* 38:395–419. https://doi.org/10.1007/s12147-020-09269-w.

Fang, C. S. 27 Sep 2022. "S'pore's population ageing rapidly: Nearly 1 in 5 citizens is 65 years and older". *The Straits Times.*

Hara, H. and D. Kawaguchi. 2022. "A Positive Outcome of COVID-19? The Effects of Work from Home on Gender Attitudes and Household Production". Bank of Japan Working Paper Series.

Ipsos. 2021. "Unpaid Work: A Study on the Behaviours and Attitudes towards Household and Domestic Caring Responsibilities in Singapore".

Khazanah Research Institute (2019). *Time to Care: Gender Inequality, Unpaid Care Work and Time Use Survey.* Kuala Lumpur, Malaysia.

Leukhina, O. & Z. Yu. 9 December 2021. "Home production activity during the COVID-19 shutdown: St. Louis Fed". *Saint Louis Fed Eagle.* Retrieved 1 March 2023, from https://www.stlouisfed.org/publications/regional-economist/third-quarter-2020/home-production-activity-covid-19.

Ministry of Manpower. 2021. "Labour Force in Singapore 2021". Manpower Research and Statistics Department.

Ministry of Manpower. 2022. Average mean monthly earnings per employee in Singapore from 2012 to 2021, by gender [Data]. Singapore Yearbook of Manpower Statistics.

Ministry of Manpower. 12 November 2021. "Are Singaporeans working more remotely?" Article: Impact of COVID-19: Remote Working in Singapore. Retrieved 1 March 2023, from https://stats.mom.gov.sg/Pages/Impact-of-COVID-19-Remote-Working-in-Singapore.aspx.

Ministry of Social and Family Development. 2022. White Paper on Singapore Women's Development.

Ng, A. 24 February 2023. "Singapore's total fertility rate drops to historic low of 1.05". CNA. Retrieved 1 March 2023, from https://www.channelnewsasia.com/singapore/singapore-total-fertility-rate-population-births-ageing-parents-children-3301846.

Quah, E. & D. Lee. 1987. "Economics of Marriage". In *Economics: Sense or Nonsense.* Singapore: Longman.

Quah, E. 1987. "Valuing family household production: a contingent evaluation approach". *Applied Economics* 19(7): 875–889. DOI: 10.1080/00036848700000035.

Quah, E. 1993. *Economics and Home Production.* Athenaeum Press Ltd.

Quah, E. 2004 "Measuring Relative Efficiency in Household Production". In *Household Economics and the Asian Family* edited by by E. Quah & D. Lee. Singapore: Eastern Universities Press, Marshall Cavendish.

Quah, E. 20 May 2006. "Time to Take Stock of Housewives' Economic Worth". *The Straits Times*.

Quah, E. 2007, 16 March 2007. "The Quagmire of Calculating the Value of Housework". *The Straits Times*.

Quah, E. 29 May 2018. "The value of unpaid housework". *The Straits Times*.

Quah, E. 1 Oct 2020. "A guide to valuing time spent and saved during the pandemic". *The Straits Times*.

Quah, E. and S.H.Lim. 2008. "Household production as a moderator in Singapore's economic development". In *Social Policy in Post-industrial Singapore*, edited by K.F. Lian & C.K. Tong. Brill.

Silbaugh, K. B. 1996. "Turning Labor into Love: Housework and the Law". *Law Review* 1, 91 Northwestern University.

Singapore Department of Statistics. 2022. "Elderly, Youth and Gender Profile [Data]". Last updated: 3/10/2022.

Tan, O. B. 3 Oct 2021. "Why a housewife's contributions can be worth millions in Singapore". *The Straits Times*.

Yang, C. 24 Jan 2022. "Overworked in S'pore: Study shows one in two logs extra hours since Covid-19 pandemic started". *The Straits Times*.

"By 2050 blocks of vertical farms run by the latest technology supply 80% of the nation's food and medicinal herbs. People walk and cycle under beautiful forests of trees everywhere. The nation depends on green energy totally. Singapore is the top exporter of air-con jackets to the rest of the world. People wear these jackets during extreme temperatures."

~ Award-winning novelist Suchen Christine Lim, for The Lives of Women exhibition at the National Museum, Jan–Mar 2022

CHAPTER 6

In My Singapore Galaxy

Cheng Puay Koon

I was taken aback when my usually taciturn little gang at the dinner table all started speaking up right after I told them about Margie's assignment (for me). This one-off exuberance put me in a spot because I realised then that both my teenage daughters and their father do have many thoughts about what they wish their Singapore could be although we've talked about (almost) everything else but. Now, I had to actually rope them in to help me build the illustrated Singapore utopia that was Margie's assignment for me. As suspected, having them participate in this assignment really complicated matters.

Firstly, half the family still sleep with cuddly creatures on their beds and the other half grew up in a now-unimaginable era before the existence of mobile phones and the Internet. More importantly, we are all starkly different in personality, temperament, priorities, and life-views. How then will we be able to share a similar dream, a single vision of a perfect Singapore?

I held onto those disparate, passionate, thoughtful words that were spewed across the dinner table that evening… and stewed over them. They followed me the entire month I spent travelling, bothered me at work, and distressed me when I played. They made my heart full, and heavy. I wanted so much to show my girls that what they wish for isn't entirely impossible. I had to make these thoughts into pictures. But how to?

I was immersed in Tomihiko Morimi's *The Tatami Galaxy* (translated by Emily Balistrieri). The book was originally written in Japanese in 2004 and later made into an anime. The parallel realities described in the novel fascinated me, very much the way Paul Auster's *4321* (published in 2017) did. I was intrigued by these loopy tales of how an entire life story can change, or not, each time the protagonist makes a different, innocuous decision at some seemingly insignificant juncture in life.

What flummoxed me was not the anticipated butterfly effect of small actions with their dramatic and divergent outcomes but the quiet, unpredictable 'or nots' that sometimes happen. How can I show that the unbearable exasperation of nothing happening is sometimes also okay? Because when nothing happens in one Singapore, something else happens in another. And another.

Quite suddenly, just like that, I knew what to do. So I took out my pencil, and drew.

IN MY
SINGAPORE GALAXY,
THERE ARE
NO BORDERS.

WE READ STORIES,
EACH ONE A LESSON
ON EMPATHY.

CHILDREN PLAY,
ADULTS TOO.

AND WE ALWAYS
SLEEP ENOUGH.

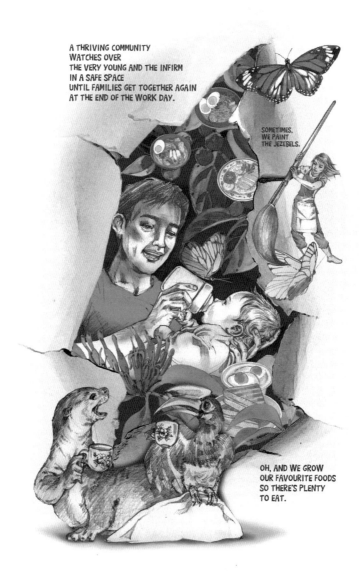

THERE ARE NO PENALTIES FOR LIVING A LONG TIME
AND YOU CAN PRETTY MUCH CONTINUE DOING
WHAT YOU WANT TO DO,
AND WHAT YOU'RE PROBABLY ALREADY VERY GOOD AT,
FOR AS LONG AS YOU WANT.

IN MY SINGAPORE GALAXY,
STORIES BEGIN WITH AN END
AND END WITH A BEGINNING
SO ANYWHERE IS A GOOD PLACE
TO TELL A STORY.

CHENG PUAY KOON *is proprietor of a busy caterpillar hotel who sends off a few dozen fluttering guests every season. She also habitually rescues baby guppies and stalks olive-backed sunbirds in their nests. After a long-ago stint doing various things at various newsrooms, where she also designed a brand-new newspaper, she decided to settle on drawing for a living. She has since illustrated more than a hundred books of different genres. She happily draws for magazines, the Singapore Zoo, the Ministry of Education, Changi Airport Group and is thrilled to be a research and conservation artist of the Singapore Botanic Gardens.*

Regardless of Race, Language, or Religion

"As Singapore engages the complexities of a globalised world, we will continue to bump up against diverse cultures and peoples. Our human tendency is to align with the beliefs and behaviours of our preferred social groups. We avoid chronic ambiguity and fear differences because we perceive them as threats to our way of life. I hope that by 2050, we live in the conviction that plurality of perspectives and voices offer keen insight into how we could live more authentically and meaningfully, and we embrace ambiguity, risk, and uncertainty as levers to pull toward a multifaceted, inclusive, and sustainable Singapore."

~ Pioneering police officer Florence Chua Siew Lian, for The Lives of Women exhibition at the National Museum, Jan–Mar 2022

CHAPTER 7

The Maze and Minefield of CMIO Multiculturalism

⁗⊷⊶⊷⁗

Lai Ah Eng

Much has occurred and been discussed and debated about multiculturalism in many parts of the world, including Singapore. This will continue as massive migrations lead to super-diversities involving peoples, goods and ideas which interact in all sorts of ways, and add on to the layers and details of history and culture, complexifying their meanings in each unique context. Almost everywhere, multiculturalism promises both celebrations and challenges for individuals, communities and nation-states.

Elsewhere (Lai, 2017), I have characterised living with Singapore's CMIO (Chinese, Malay, Indian, Others) multiculturalism as at once wandering both in a wondrous maze and a risky minefield along a

---

Note: This essay has many observations, ideas and reflections drawn from a variety of sources over several decades of my research, teaching, lived everyday experiences, and participation in social activities and communities. Some of them have been published as research books and chapters and as short articles in newspapers and popular books, while others have been articulated in talks and panel discussions and as comments, opinions and musings in social media.

road always under construction. It is a maze of diverse cultural range, multifaceted celebratory aspects, and limitless combinations and exchanges, and a minefield of complexities, challenges, tensions, and conflicts. In such mazes and minefields, one can easily get confused and lost, encounter misunderstanding and misjudgement, and experience uncertainty and anxiety.

In recent years, we appear to be wandering in a minefield of overt racist incidents, casual racism, micro-aggressions and the like, with vehement counter responses of calling out, answering back, exposes of racial bullying and victimisation and the like. However, the underlying causes of recent incidents is not new. What is happening is that both incidents and the questioning of their underlying assumptions and causes are now openly aired. Such openness is aided by social media, where previously "race" (also "religion") have been considered out of bounds for public discourse by the state.

Multiculturalism (broadly encompassing race, culture and religion) as one of Singapore's founding nation-state principles does not mean it is only a state ideology and state imposition and therefore can be outrightly rejected for any underlying political motives of divide and rule or control. Rather, I see multiculturalism as a constant and complex reality of Singapore life with historical and social origins and dynamic forces at work. It is at once a maze and a minefield because of its inherent diversities, differences, dilemmas and difficulties. That engenders enjoyable spontaneous moments yet requires careful and considered navigation living within it.

In this essay, I examine some core areas and recent developments in Singapore's multiculturalism: structural inequalities, racism and discrimination; culture and its many fields of identity, change, heterogeneity, hybridity and heritage; and immigration, integration and citizenship. In parts, I focus on some Chinese majority members' responses, as majority-minority relations are affected. Other important dimensions — the sharing of common living spaces and religion — are mentioned briefly. Overall, I point out their implications on CMIO multiculturalism and ask what cohesive multiculturalism then means amidst the many differences, disconnects and divides. The hope of this essay is to inform, advance and guide us, both as individuals and as members of society and humanity, to better understand, face and construct in progressive ways the maze-minefield filled road of multiculturalism.

But first, a brief clarification of "race" in Singapore as it is prone to much misunderstanding, ignorance and loose usage. There is the often-made allegation, especially by judgemental visitors and newcomers, that Singaporeans are obsessed with "race" or are "racists".

Discourses on multiculturalism in Singapore

Discourses on race and multiculturalism in Singapore have evolved in the fields of scholarship, public policy and administration, and public life.

Race and culture in scholarship

One main take from scholarship is the overlap of race, ethnicity and ethnic culture, in place of the original focus on biological race (and racial ideology of [white] superiority) which by now has been clearly rejected. The racial ideology of superiority came with imperialism and (white) British colonial rule, while the overlaps of race and ethnicity/ethnic cultures have historical (also contemporary) roots in the migrations and settlements of culturally distinct categories of peoples mainly from the Southeast Asian regions, China, India,

Middle East and Europe. Closely related to the latter is a second main take from academia — of cultural knowledge, exchanges, fusions, hybridities and new formations. Here is a fascinating body of knowledge that keeps growing as more is unearthed, understood and (re)interpreted. A third is that of structural and ideological realities about race/ethnicity and its intersections with other main dimensions of social life — class, gender, religion — and some of the tensions and conflicts arising from these intersections. Critical race theory in recent years has led to one focus on majority Chinese privilege and the implied oppression of ethnic minorities in majority-minority relations. This is akin to white privilege and coloured peoples' oppression in the United States where critical race theory first originated.

Race in public policy and administration

"Race" in public policy and administration is inherited from British colonial rule but uncritically continued in categorisations of ethnic populations, applications and assumptions or perceptions, and from which serious problems have arisen. Official references to CMIO as races and cultures interchangeably have their roots not only in their historical antecedents but also in present state ideology and administration.

Race and culture in public cultures

"Race" and "culture" in public life are perhaps the most diverse and complex, given the wide range of practices, lived realities, experiences and perceptions. This is further complicated by structural and intersectional dimensions and by identity politics. People refer to "race" when they often mean "culture" and to "racism" that has become a convenient and popular term to use when they actually mean ethnocentrism, ethnic discrimination, prejudice and stereotyping. The reference to race and culture interchangeably is often loose.

Overall, it may be truer to say that any "obsession" is not with race but with ethnic culture in Singapore. In the important conceptual overlap of race with ethnicity and culture, it is vital to have contextual understanding of their referencing, especially with regard to inequality and prejudice. Racism is often about ethnocentrism and prejudice, sometimes with skin colour added to the tone. It should also be noted that people hold multiple identities and invoke them accordingly to situation and context. Ethnic cultural identity may also vie with other identities and values, such as religious ones, in a culturally diverse world.

CMIO: Racism, discrimination and privilege
Racism and discrimination

In my research work on multiculturalism, I have found some aspects of equality but have also often encountered evidences and responses such as "What multiculturalism? The Chinese are the majority everywhere", "There is ethnic discrimination and racism" and "Singapore is becoming Chinapore".

The end of empire and its ideology of racial superiority was replaced by the principle of equality for all in many new nation-states. CMIO multiculturalism as a founding principle of the Singapore nation-state with a large Chinese majority population promises equality for all, the protection of minorities and separate but equal representation of ethnic groups in the management of majority-minority relations. Yet, this ethnic-based approach has been blamed for racism's prevalence and divisiveness. Deeply entrenched in government systems, the ethnic framework has permeated every major field and level, affecting mindsets, policy-planning, resource allocation, political representation, population profiling, public housing, education and the like. For example, educational performance by ethnicity is highlighted regularly and ethnic quotas in public housing integration policy to prevent ethnic enclave formation is implemented even for rental housing. This ethnicised mindset, when applied irrespective of context and relevance and to the exclusion of other criteria particularly class, has major consequences on the conceptualisation, analysis and solution of problems.

The focus on ethnic groups has the effect of tending towards strong cultural explanations, easily falling back on cultural stereotypes and reinforcing them. For example, there are the common and still prevalent stereotypes of the hardworking Chinese and lazy Malays, which are supposed to represent ethnic cultural capital and deficit respectively. It further leads to the seeking of cultural solutions presumed best provided by their ethnic groups, hence the ethnic self-help organisations' existence. This ethnic-cultural approach tends to be biased in selection, singling out Malays and other minorities for their supposed cultural propensities in problems. How else to explain ethnic profiling, such as the identification of drug offenders as mainly Malays, but not gambling addiction and patronage of underage prostitutes by the vast majority of whom are Chinese men? The singling out of Malays is particularly ignominious, with roots in history and prejudice — the 'lazy native' world view and an ethnic division of labour during colonial rule — now sustained by structural inequalities, policies and ethnicised approaches. The resultant reality is one in which Malays disproportionately constitute the poor in Singapore and are more affected by problems such as unemployment, homelessness and educational difficulties but the dominant view is that they have only themselves to blame.

Privilege, Chinese privilege and prejudice/racism

Institutionalised racism has its rationale based on claims of 'objective' fact and reality or simplistic comparisons by ethnicity. It disclaims bigotry and lacks historical and sociological understanding as to why, for instance, Malay numbers are high in drug addiction or Chinese predominate in gambling addiction, but will consistently only highlight the Malay proportions. Some among the Chinese majority population are likely not to see the ethnic profiling of Malays, the 'ability to speak Mandarin' requirement for jobs, or speaking in Mandarin for work matters in the presence of non-Chinese speaking colleagues, as racist, discriminatory or insensitive, but simply going by a numerical "majority" count or as simply being practical. That minority members encounter job discrimination due to 'race' and language (the top two complaints received by the Tripartite Alliance for Fair Employment [TAFEP]) escapes them. For those Chinese with a strong ethnicised cultural approach, it is about themselves possessing superior, powerful or numerical majority cultural values, resources and knowledge. This can be further reinforced when some members of minorities on the receiving end internalise such racism and display negative self-perceptions of inadequacy, stigmatisation, marginalisation and fatalism.

The simplistic use of a numerical majority argument can skew outcomes and result in poor judgement and unfairness. Take, for example, the recent political argument that the majority Chinese are not ready for an Indian Prime Minister. How true is this or is it just an assertion in majoritarian politics? Even if true, why are some Chinese not ready for a minority race Prime Minister and when might they ever be? And why is this ethnicised perspective among some Chinese allowed to rule over a matter of national interest? Should race or proven professional experience and competency be the main criteria in the selection of a Prime Minister? It is rather telling that the strong claim that Singaporeans of all ethnic backgrounds are ready for an Indian Prime Minister was circulating in social media when the issue came up. It also requires a visionary rather than a pragmatic political leadership to say "no" to ethnic background and "yes" to competency in the requirements for this top job.[1]

It is thus not surprising that Chinese privilege has surfaced as an issue and explanation for racism against minorities in recent years. According to this explanation, privilege — the unequal access to power, resources, benefits and advantages in overt and covert ways and which excludes others from this access — are accorded to Chinese members of society within systems and structures and in everyday life. This exclusion is often supported with a conscious or unconscious ideology of supposed Chinese cultural traits which are valued as superior or better over others, especially in a pragmatic-economistic orientated development.

Privilege and any Chinese ethnic privilege need historical and social understanding as to how it came about. At the same time, it cannot be separated from class and other deep social inequalities which also exist. References to the rich Chinese towkay, Crazy Rich Asians, the rich and famous — the "rich" parts inevitably surface as a chief indicator of class and social standing. Historically, it was not just Chinese privilege that led some to become rich towkays. Privileged colonials, Chinese and Arabs who could manipulate race,

---

[1] As an important aside, there was a claim that the Chinese sacrificed much for the sake of nation-building, especially in giving up common dialects and Mandarin language-based education in favour of the English language. It is obvious that across the board, many populations irrespective of ethnic community sacrificed much, be this their languages and dialects and their homes in massive resettlement. The many nostalgic Facebook pages dedicated to former villages and schools attest to this.

ethnicity and culture for their class power ruled over thousands of indentured Indians, Chinese and Javanese labourers. Privilege therefore needs a careful recognition of the contextual intersections of ethnicity with class. Indeed, race and class as intersections of reality have largely been the main framework of understanding and analysis and serves better than a predominantly ethnicised lens that focuses on privilege and race among the Chinese majority. "Chinese privilege" alone cannot be the dominant lens or dimension for understanding inequality and prejudice. It runs the risk of a racialised/ethnicised view without clarity of context.

The focus on Chinese privilege has also led to the automatic inclusion of all Chinese individuals and groups under it. This is a grossly over-simplified view in which every Chinese runs the risk of being viewed a bigot, racist or oppressor of minorities just because he/she is a majority group member. This view is obviously unacceptable as there are various subgroups and individuals within any ethnic group. Nor can every Chinese access privileges just by belonging to the Chinese majority. Again, the "rich", "poor" or "middling" categories inevitably surface and show up the intersections between race and class (and for that matter in any group, Chinese or others). It would be more accurate to say privileges exist within and across groups but that there are more Chinese who enjoy privileges because of sheer class and numbers. It can also be simplistic, unfair and divisive when "Chinese privilege" is bandied about loosely.

Any outright denial that privileges among Chinese exist would be dishonest and Chinese individuals confronting it need to search honestly. Privilege among Chinese definitely exists and results in structures, practices and acts of discrimination, stereotyping and exclusion, conscious or otherwise. These need to be called out whenever they occur. It also requires a constant call to Chinese majority members and organised groups with a Chinese majority to be aware, sensitive and to end stereotyping and discrimination. In principle, majority groups with access to power must always look out for inequalities and unfairness and address them for the protection and equal status of minorities.

Culture, cultural identity and identity politics

Central to CMIO multiculturalism is ethnic culture and identity, with their symbolism, expressions and politics that have waxed and waned over the years. Such expressions and politics have recently emerged, both within and between groups/various stakeholders, over cultural and religious items and events, examples being food, wearing of *hijab* and Thaipusam. Among some Chinese, new ethnic identity expressions and claims have surfaced that may impact Singapore's multiculturalism, given the Chinese majority population.

Chinese identity claims

Since the mid-2010s, articles have regularly circulated on the Internet which are pro-China, admiring of a rising China and appeal to a sense of belonging to a shared Chinese civilisational heritage and ethnic culture among all Chinese including the Chinese diaspora the world over. Some of these articles might still be understandable or acceptable within limits if not for their being framed in chauvinistic terms,[2] and mostly within a binary, dichotomised and polarised China/Chinese versus the West/USA frame in which an underdog China is now rising but up against the usual bullying West.

---

[2] Earlier, around 2012, Malay hero Hang Tuah (of the 15th century Malaccan royal court) had been the subject of an urban legend claiming that he was actually of Chinese descent. Another story (undated, based on my recollection) claimed that it was a Chinese cook, from Admiral Zheng He's entourage to the Malacca sultan's court, who cleverly concocted the satay dish out of whatever ingredients available when asked by the sultan to show his culinary skills. Satay is associated with Malay culinary origin.

Some Chinese Singaporeans have been drawn into this renewed Chinese identity and pro-China trend. A 2022 poll conducted by Pew Research Center showed a high 67 per cent of Singaporean respondents expressing a positive view of China, in contrast to respondents in other Southeast Asian countries. In the China versus West frame, some Chinese-Singaporeans not only take on as their own (Chinese) burden China's past humiliation by bullying Western imperialist powers (the Opium Wars are the most cited), they also express strong anti-West and even racist anti-White sentiments (white-bashing syndrome?). They also embrace, with Chinese ethnic and nationalistic pride, a rising China as their own rise as part of a global Chinese community.[3] They reassert their Chinese identity, culture, heritage and ancestral ties with China (with some even equating ancestral land with motherland). In this frame, almost nothing about China can be wrong, while almost everything about the U.S. and the West is bad or wrong. Chinese imperialism old and new or violation of human rights is not mentioned; only Western and U.S. imperialism is highlighted. Politically for some, the orderliness of (Chinese) one-party authoritarian rule is preferred over the chaos of (Western) democracy.

Chinese Singaporeans are characterised by cultural, religious and political heterogeneity. The pro-China or China-inclined among the older Chinese population and recent immigrants from China may be understandable. But how to explain today's born and bred in Singapore Chinese-Singaporeans, including the English-educated Chinese, Chinese Peranakan and the well-travelled and cosmopolitan, embracing this binary, polarised and divisive view on the side of

---

[3] When the Chinese company Huawei's CFO Meng Wanchou (under house arrest in Vancouver in 2018 and the U.S. sought to extradite her on bank and wire fraud charges) was released and returned to China in 2021, the videos showing the rapturous nationalistic welcome home was circulated and cheered by some Chinese-Singaporeans. A friend was advised by her father to give her newborn a "very Chinese" sounding name because "China is rising". Or that the U.S. is depicted as the "The Evil Empire" and bound for self-destruction.

China and being Chinese? Personal extended family ties or vested economic interests in China, strong sentiments against historical injustices of Western imperialism and pro-China stances in the present tensions between China and the U.S. certainly exist, but my own theory about why some older Chinese-Singaporeans turn to China and Chinese identity is a psychological one — the loss of prestige, status and meaning of life in retirement and old age. The turn to a readily available and long and strong civilisational Chinese history and heritage provides meaning, identity and some certainty, in contrast to the unknown and fearsome worlds of ageing (which comes with frailness and illness) or the immensity of a vague and unfamiliar "common humanity" (which comes with distant geographical and difficult intercultural dimensions). The convenience of being Chinese in a binary analysis avoids the intellectual demands of understanding complexities of history and geopolitics and of objectivity and perspective about one's place and position in all this.

How might this reassertion of Chinese cultural identity and pro-China stances affect us as individuals and multicultural Singapore society, such as in the navigation of identities in personal relations and social ties? Anecdotal evidence suggests that differences and tensions between family members and friends over "being Chinese" and "Chineseness" have led to strained exchanges or avoidances. At the societal level, there can be distrust within Singapore's multicultural society when some Chinese majority members turn pro-China or assert their Chinese identity especially in the present contexts of a rising China and growing superpower rivalry in the larger Southeast Asian region. We do not know the real extent of these tendencies and how they will further develop. But for the individual with a Chinese background, the choice should not be to prove Chineseness or to assert Chinese identity in opportunistic advantage of cultural affinity with a rising China. The choice is to be cognizant of what being of Chinese background is and where one belongs in Singapore's multicultural society and a superdiverse world. Unfortunately for Chinese Singaporeans in today's geopolitical context, Chinese ethnicity can be a "burden" due to historical and contemporary ties with China, a Chinese state that defines Chineseness globally and ethno-nationalistic education in China (Chong, 2022).

The choice is also not just for Chinese Singaporeans alone to make. As members of a multicultural nation-state, all citizens need to objectively clarify what it means to be living in a nation-state caught in superpower geopolitics without sliding into binary, polarised and even racialised and ethnicised positions. It behoves us to remain independent and universal in our values, recognise and applaud whichever country contributes to world peace and progress, view historical trauma and humiliation in perspective, and reject superiority, chauvinism and racism from whichever source. We can also fall back on our Singaporean multicultural sensibilities to navigate the world sensitively, confidently and fairly.

Culture, change, heterogeneity, hybridity, heritage

The separateness of ethnic cultures in CMIO multiculturalism tends to assume homogeneity among members within a group. It also shapes expectations for conformity and that one should manifest some core features and markers of ethnic identity, such as language. It does not easily allow for the acceptance of cultural change nor intercultural exchanges and new cultural creations.

Yet, culture and context is constantly changing even if imperceptibly so. There are always individuals and groups that will differ or breakaway from "tradition" depending on the contextual processes at hand. The loss of traditional cultural heritage is often lamented, while the gain of new cultural forms that may eventually also become heritage can be initially resisted or criticised. Western pop music and culture were seen as "decadent" and "culturally polluting" by the state and certain Chinese populations during Singapore's early nation-building years. Cross-cultural marriages are still unacceptable to some parents even as their rates have increased drastically.

Heterogeneity and hybridity

In reality, multiculturalism in the past and present has long enabled and recognised the amazing mixtures, fusions and hybrids over long periods of exchanges and interactions. Cuisines are the most easily influenced, which also explains why Singapore's foodscapes are so dynamic. In dress as another example, the kebaya, currently put up as a joint nomination by five Southeast Asia countries (Singapore, Brunei, Indonesia, Malaysia and Thailand) to be added to the UNESCO Representative List of the Intangible Cultural Heritage of Humanity, captures the wide range of cultural inputs and influences in its long evolution. Intermarriages are more complicated but have always happened anyway. Their offspring, cultural diversities and intercultural dimensions over generations visibly attest to how this very human phenomenon overcomes and copes with differences and comes up with new "creations". The offspring of Indian and Chinese parents are now openly acknowledged as "Chindian" and joked about being "kopi susu" (coffee with milk colour) in skin tone, where previously such a marriage union could likely be rejected, even the marrying child disowned (probably by a Chinese parent who preferred light skins and high status) and their children viewed as "half-breeds".

The references to "Chinese banana" (Chinese yellow on the outside, white Westernised on the inside), "Indian coconut" (Indian dark brown on the outside, white Westernised on the inside), "chap cheng" (mixed breed, used by Chinese on Eurasians and Chinese Peranakans), "OCBC" (orang Cina bukan Cina — Chinese but not Chinese, applied to Chinese Peranakans), "Mat Salleh" (a Westerner or a Westerner behaving like a Malay), "Mat Salleh Celup" (Malays who behave like Westerners/whites), "Angmoh" (red haired white people) and other labels and names can be neutral, derogatory, stereotypical, ethnocentric, even racist, depending on context of usage. But they also capture the cultural mix and hybrid cultures already present in many individuals but which may be frowned upon by conformist others.

Westernisation

One other component of the cultural mix common in most of these labels but not normally associated with CMIO multiculturalism is being "Westernised". It speaks to the vast contexts and complexities of being colonised or subjugated under Western imperialism or influenced by Western values and cultures. This "Westernisation" is beyond substantive discussion here. Suffice to point out that a wide spectrum about being Westernised exists today, ranging from the most to the least at both ends and a huge maze of intercultural combinations in between.[4] Individuals labelled as above embody some of these combinations. Their histories and lived experiences about cultural fusions and tensions, like in intermarriages, tell much about the individual's pursuit of well-being and happiness across cultural boundaries. They also reveal much about Singapore's multiculturalism within the C, M, I and O components, such as among Eurasians (who reject being classified as Os) whose histories span centuries in the larger region.

---

[4] Similarly, political views about Westernisation range from the most "anti" to the most "pro", with further complications of individualism, secularism and liberalism associated with it such as by some religious Christian and Muslim groups.

Being open to new creations in cultural change is as much a conscious decision as that of what to retain of tradition. In today's multicultural Singapore and hyper-diverse world, one progressive way to deal with cultural change is to embrace it. While some are largely still within their ethnic containers and communities, another reality in Singapore's multiculturalism is about cultural hybridity, intercultural exchange and heterogeneity. Shared heritages or mixed heritages and multicultural pride is as much part of the picture as is ethnic exclusivity and ethnic pride. Nor are they necessarily mutually exclusive; their combination is possible and for the individual to choose.

Heritage

Singapore's cultural diversities and hybridities further point to the significances and meanings of cultural life and heritage through which the sense and essence of belonging and community are regularly experienced and revivified. The celebratory and heritage aspects of Singapore's multiculturalism speak of a diversity that did not come about overnight; it developed bit by bit and layer by layer over time and generations and is still evolving, and to be appreciated in their historical and social significance.

But here again the maze can also a minefield. Cultural politics, such as over heritage, space or memory, may lurk beneath celebrations and erupt unexpectedly. Even peaceful and enjoyable processes of food hybridisation may have politics simmering 'in the pot', such as when origins and shared heritages are unacknowledged or contested. For example, are *sambal belacan* and *sarong kebaya* Peranakan or Malay or Peranakan with Malay or Southeast Asian roots? Backed by the promotional powers of museums, tourism and donorship, Chinese Peranakan culture with its cuisines, costumes, patois and *pantuns* now passes off as a distinct culture. This pleases Peranakans and fascinates tourists but the understated recognition of Malay and Southeast Asian roots, hybridisation and shared heritages upset others because it marginalizes their origins and contributions. The revamped Peranakan Museum tries to be inclusive of what constitutes Peranakan, but some say the scope is now "too broad".

Heritage items and issues may be raised unexpectedly in the future in the new politics of heritage and culture in Singapore's multiculturalism. While challenging to navigate, knowing historical origins and contexts, acknowledging roots and evolution, and accepting shared heritages are ways of facing the future progressively.

Immigration and integration

The above discussion on intercultural exchange further leads to several important local-immigrant and intercultural issues raised by immigration and their implications on multicultural integration, cohesion and citizenship.

The tremendous scale, speed and intensity of recent immigration since 2000 have enlarged and complicated the maze and minefield of Singapore's diversity and multiculturalism profoundly. Singapore's population has nearly doubled to 5.98 million in 2023, from 5.31 million (2012), 4.028 million (2000) and 3.047 million (1990), with the increase due mainly to the new citizen, permanent resident and foreign worker populations under the government's immigration policy to sustain economic growth and to address declining fertility and an ageing population. The majority of immigrants and migrant workers are Chinese-Malaysian, People's Republic of China (PRC) Chinese, Indians and "expatriates" who fall into two broad categories — skilled 'foreign talent' on employment passes and 'migrant workers' on work permits — that receive highly differential prospects of permanent settlement and permanent transience respectively.

Immigration related issues have arisen quickly since 2010 and show up to be extremely complex and controversial. Among these, several stand out: immigration policy itself, economic competition and foreign talent, migrant workers' employment and living conditions, immigrants' adjustments and settlement, ethnic and cultural identities, and belonging and citizenship. They reveal significant economic, social and cultural diversities, differences, disconnects, tensions and divides between locals and immigrants, often along intertwining ethnic, nationality and class lines. It is important to unpack their complexities beyond the simple broad categories of "immigrant" and "local", as common or simplistic notions associated with each have led to easy binary and polarised "pro-immigrant" versus "anti-immigrant" sentiments, the "us versus them" mentality and mutual blame without advancing our view and approach.

Locals and foreigners, locals versus foreigners

Locals have long been criticised for their treatment of unskilled foreign workers. Employers are criticised for flouting employment laws, abuse, exploitation and disrespect of workers' human rights; and ordinary Singaporeans are criticised for intolerance, prejudice, and racism particularly towards darker-skinned migrant workers, and xenophobia particularly towards PRC Chinese and lately towards Indians both who have immigrated in massive numbers.

Locals on their part have been raising economic and social issues such as depressed wages, soaring housing prices, high costs of living and over-stretched public facilities linked to immigration, discrimination in favour of 'foreign talent' and unfair competition in high-stakes education such as through university places and scholarships allocated to foreign students. Locals also complain about some immigrants' anti-social behaviour and their disregard for local norms, as well as question the loyalty of internationally mobile immigrants who obtain citizenship and permanent residence for self-vested 'strategic' reasons. Some citizens feel overwhelmed and displaced in their sense of familiarity, place and social order that they have established over time and generations prior to the arrival of immigrants. Some controversial behaviour by individual immigrants which upset or affected locals (see, Lai and Mathews, 2015) have further served as landmark lightning rods that convey on-line resentment against massive immigration. In general, issues and sentiments about immigration are raised by Singaporeans of diverse class and ethnic backgrounds. Malays additionally express unhappiness over the large influx of PRC Chinese which they see as further Sinification of an already Chinese-majority and Chinese-dominant Singapore.

The Covid-19 pandemic (2020–22) affected the entire population but saw soaring infection rates among the estimated 370,000 male migrant workers living in crowded mass accommodation especially dormitories. Their sheer numbers required massive mobilisation efforts to trace, contain and reduce infections — this threw into sharp focus their harsh living and working conditions and the underlying inequalities and indignities many of which have long been raised especially by dedicated NGOs. Among Singaporeans' responses to these massive infections were some xenophobic comments of the "go home" and "don't go near them they might infect us" kind in social media. However, in the main, there has been tremendous outpouring of sympathy and humanitarian aid to provide relocated and locked down workers with food and living essentials, and psychological support by individuals, organisations, schools, businesses and civil society groups such as Transient

Workers Count Too, HOME, Welcome in My Backyard, Covid-19 Migrant Support Coalition, It's Raining Raincoats, and Project Chulia Street. These responses debunk the stereotype of locals as xenophobic and racist, and reveal their humane and compassionate sides in a time of crisis.

"Foreign talent" (estimated at 378,000 in June 2020) first tapped to supplement Singapore's workforce in 1988 has remained contentious throughout. Several significant issues have arisen (Lai, 2023): employment discrimination against locals in the professional, managerial, executive and technical (PMET) categories in various industries, especially services (financial, employment agencies and academia); insider networks and hiring by own nationality; too many foreign workers in some sectors; job advertisements for hiring of foreigners; exclusionary and condescending behaviour by expatriates; and displacement of local incumbents from their jobs and nepotistic practices by foreign companies. Additionally, complaints by locals are against all nationalities while there are some complaints by foreigners about locals, such as about name-calling and calls to "go home". Much of locals' grievances above has remained, with half of all cases handled by MOM between 2014 to 2018 linked to nationality and many cases raised to TAFEP by whistle-blowers.[5]

How to look at both sides and many sides

Racism and cultural issues have been consistently raised in public discourses on immigration and local-immigrant disconnects.One strong depiction by critics that has emerged about the immigration

---

[5] See, for example, Diversity and Inclusion in Asia Network, 2012, for issues over definition, insider networking, discrimination, leadership and cultural biases.

landscape is that Singaporeans are xenophobic, racist and anti-immigrant.

Methodologically, it is vital to consider both locals' and immigrants' experiences and views in two broad respective spectrums as both groups and subgroups are different. On the part of locals, these can range from the racist and xenophobic at one end to the most welcoming at the other. Similarly, the range can be from the racist and prejudiced to the strongly "I love Singapore" among immigrants. However, a popular approach tends to be highly selective of negative traits or to refer to the extreme negative ends of both spectrums, posing them in a "us versus them" world view.

Claims of racism, inferior/superior mentalities, culturally biased/flawed attitudes and the "you take away jobs" or "we have skills and outlooks you don't have" type appear in the negative extremes within each spectrum, further reinforced by highly selected negative experiences, confirmation bias and scapegoating. In reality, both locals and immigrants can be the best towards each other — appreciative, compassionate, respectful — or the worst — racist, prejudiced and biased. Each has a whole spectrum of views and experiences that range from the most positive to the most negative about each other, with many qualified ones in-between. (Here, it should be noted that methodologically, it is much easier to research on vocal locals, especially xenophobic and racist comments openly voiced in local social media, while it is more difficult to access expatriates' and immigrants' views.)

Anxieties, racism, xenophobia, cultural misassumptions
Local anxieties and responses over immigration

Locals' anxieties over immigration and their questioning of policy and its consequences can easily be confused as being "anti-immigrant" if read superficially[6] and with preconceived binary notions of "pro" or "anti" immigrant. However, a more objective unpacking of locals' sentiments and other issues would show a more complex picture and corroborate locals' strong feelings against the consequences of rapid and massive immigration. Broadly, locals' sentiments can be grouped around three areas: immigration policy's rationale, numbers in immigration flows and sources; economic issues around definitions of talent, recruitment practices and wage levels; and social and cultural impacts of immigration on ethnic and cultural identities, rights and responsibilities.[7] Taken together, these are mainly anxieties about being disadvantaged or set back by economic competition and social citizenship. Such sentiments, calling out biased hiring and calling for a more calibrated immigration policy should not be simplistically read as being inherently xenophobic or anti-immigrant. Indeed, the clarification made by locals (see Lai, 2023) is that they are not against immigration but for controlled immigration and review of immigration policy's excessive openness.

Locals, like immigrants, are diverse in their responses to immigration, and the "anti-immigrant" and "xenophobic" labels should not be carelessly used but applied only to known categories such as netizens indulging in hate speech on the Internet. Unlike elsewhere, there have not been any major acts of provocation and violence arising from divides and tensions between locals and immigrants. Nor has there been any coherent political or nationalistic extremist ideology against immigrants or organised efforts calling for an end to immigration and the exclusion or expulsion of

---

[6] For example, the well-known "cook a pot of curry" event in response to what was perceived by locals as a poor mediation outcome over cooking curry smells between two neighbours, one a local and the other an immigrant, was reported as an anti-immigration protest (see Lai and Mathew, 2015).

[7] One other contentious issue is National Service (and reservist training). As this is compulsory for local male citizens and involves a long period away from higher education or work as well as some safety issues, the strategic avoidance of National Service by sons of Permanent Residents upon completion of school negatively affects locals' perceptions of Permanent Residents and immigrants.

immigrants. On the contrary, there are strong ground practices of multiculturalism and prevailing codes of civility including hospitality, tolerance and conflict avoidance, for convivial social interaction and maintenance of social order. These have been based on local cultures honed through generations of intergroup relations, but which are now tested as massive immigration disrupts, destabilises and complicates the more gradual processes of multiculturalism already in place.

Cultural knowledge and (mis)assumptions

Immigrants need to understand Singapore society in more contextualised terms, such as its position in Southeast Asia and local diversities. This means learning more about local and regional histories, cultures and norms, as Singapore and the region have a diverse range of peoples, cultures and histories preceding new immigrants' arrival.

The idea that Singapore is an immigrant society has regularly surfaced in the face of massive immigration, but is at best true only to a limited extent and needs much qualification. Malays consider themselves indigenous while Singaporeans of other ethnicities with backgrounds of earlier immigrant generations should be viewed as having distinct local or even Southeast Asian histories, cultures and identities. Cultural similarities between locals and immigrants should not be assumed, imagined or exaggerated under a broader ethnic identity,[8] such as by some PRC Chinese under "Chinese-ness"

---

[8] Other aspects of immigration that might impact Singapore multiculturalism pertain to immigration of Chinese-Malaysians from Malaysia who form the largest immigrant population, which can only be briefly outlined here. Chinese-Malaysian migration to Singapore has deep and extensive historical and contemporary roots. Singapore's official approach to immigration from Malaysia is that it is a "traditional" source and assumes cultural similarities that make for ease of integration. Singapore as a nearby/border economy has become the largest diaspora destination country for emigration by mainly Chinese Malaysians for economic mobility and alternatives in the face of pro-bumiputra policies and economic uncertainties in Malaysia. Little is known about how their "diasporic unbelonging" (Koh, 2014) affect their relationship with locals, local Malays and engagement with Singapore's multiculturalism.

or "Chinese diaspora" or who even see Singapore as a "province" of China. That some PRC Chinese do not seem to understand local Chinese Singaporeans' diversity well probably stems from their strong ethnic identities as Han Chinese as well as tales heard about Chinese-majority Singapore.

Furthermore, for recent immigrants from India and China, their official classification under the same ethnic categories as local ethnic Indians and Chinese is a misfit that is based on false or weak assumptions of common cultural identities. The official CMIO ethnic classification system — already heavily criticised for its assumptions of homogeneity and fixity of group identity — shows up to be even weaker in its assumptions when Chinese and Indian immigrants are included, and can lead to misplaced judgements and expectations of common values and behaviour and relatively problem-free cultural integration.

Some common examples come to mind. In cultural practices, local Indians' continued traditional practice of Thaipusam is judged as "barbaric" by some newer Indian citizens who think they have undergone social reform in India. On the other hand, locals balk at the idea of caste that some Indian immigrants still hold on to and practise in Singapore. Among PRC Chinese immigrants used to strong ethnic markers of Chinese identity, many hold assumptions and expectations of cultural similarities with Chinese Singaporeans. Imagine their initial shocks over differences and diversities, such as of Anglophile Chinese of the English-speaking "yellow banana" or Chinese Peranakan variety, Chinese-Singlish and lower standards of Mandarin. Local Chinese Singaporeans also hold certain stereotypes about PRC Chinese immigrants, including that of coarseness of poorer migrant workers, scheming husband-stealers and gold-diggers. Cultural superiority and inferiority complexes are held by some on both sides, mostly over language as identity marker, and expectations of being Chinese.

Mutual understandings

The extensive and quick pace of change brought about by massive immigration had had significant challenging effects on both immigrants and locals. Mutual understandings, adjustments and interactions in gradual and sensitive ways are therefore needed, and the rules of civility-hospitality and open-mindedness without quick judgement apply equally to all.

The considerations and processes that immigrants go through in arriving at their "big decision" to work and settle in Singapore and their adjustments over time require better understanding from the locals. For higher-skilled immigrants who have chosen to come to Singapore for strategic purposes, there might be some truth in the perception that they see the country as a mere stepping stone although they might not admit to it. However, this does not diminish their contributions and often unappreciated difficulties that they bear in their decision to settle in the new country. The sense of attachment to more than one place for the first generation is also to be expected and understood. The same call for empathy can also be extended to immigrants' residential clustering and support networks. The speculation that they will necessarily be disloyal and leave in time of crisis is yet to be supported by evidence and should not be too readily accepted.

What is also crucial for locals' understanding and expectations of immigrant issues lies in the big difference between the first and subsequent generations. My study (Lai, 2023) shows that some children of immigrants perceived themselves as Singaporeans as they have lived their formative years in Singapore and undergone experiences in its key institutions of school and national service (for males) as well as in ordinary everyday social and community life. They also do not relate to India or China as their parents do, and their choice to be in Singapore is an important factor in their parents' decisions to sink roots, become citizens themselves and to make adjustments, including mindset changes, expectations and participation in local life. Through this inter-generational change over time, some of the perceptions, prejudices and stereotypes of Singapore and Singaporeans or cultural rigidities held by their parents may also gradually wither away.

Immigrants, on the other hand, need to understand why locals are anxious or resentful of their presence. This requires them to see beyond their personal considerations and contributions. The issues of economic competition should also be understood beyond their personal qualifications, experiences, interests and rights. An important understanding is that Singapore is not merely a globalising city but also a small nation-state with citizens who also have rights. Seen from this perspective, locals' concern over economic conditions on home grounds ought to be understandable, as many immigrants themselves have similar concerns in their home countries and have migrated to Singapore/Asia mainly because of unemployment and job uncertainties in their countries of origin. The fact that Singapore does not have enough talent (in terms of numbers due to the small population or skills sets) should not become an interpretation that Singaporeans are not as talented as foreigners. For locals, the rights and stakes of citizenship reasonably extend to expectations of fair employment opportunities and fair wages, all the more in the context of intense competition and growing inequality amidst globalisation and open immigration. The call for a balance between costs (wages), quality, and "Singaporean first" or "Singapore core" is a reasonable one.

Massive immigration within Singapore's intensely competitive environment has brought about unprecedented dimensions of inequality and unfairness and introduced new dimensions of culturally divisive politics. How immigration and population policies, citizens' and immigrants' concerns and interests, economic growth and distribution issues are addressed will affect the conduciveness or adversity of conditions for local-immigrant relations and Singapore multiculturalism. For healthy and cohesive multiculturalism to prevail and to ensure extremes do not take root, immigration needs to be carefully managed. Here, two principles ought to be remembered. One is that immigrants, once they are allowed to enter Singapore, are entitled to decent and dignified treatment. The other is that Singapore is not merely a convenient global city for people to flow in and out but a country where citizenship and belonging is what is meaningful, rightful and at the heart of it. The minefield that massive immigration has created is challenging to navigate as both locals and immigrants claim rights and responsibilities.

Immigration is here to stay and immigration and integration issues in economic, social and cultural terms will continue to exist with some controversy, disconnects, tensions and misalignment. However, these should not be allowed to run too deep, pervasive or become long lasting. All parties at the individual, group and societal levels need to be cognizant of this and to work towards their mitigation and solution and towards positive social interactions. Only then can work-life, citizenship and belonging in a cohesive local-global multicultural Singapore be meaningful and fruitful for all.

Religious issues

In Singapore that is one of the world's most diverse religion-wise, the realms of culture and religion often overlap and intersect. Issues arising warrant an entire discussion but is out of the scope of this essay. Suffice here to outline some main ones: extremist, literalist, absolutist and exclusivist interpretations of texts and religious teachings; proselytisation and conversion strategies by some religious groups; conservative trends in evangelical Christianity and Islam, some of which are imports from elsewhere; mutual anxieties, ignorance and distrust of each other, such as between some Christians and Muslims and between some religionists and secularists; association of Western liberalism and secularism with godlessness, immorality and LBGTQ rights; association of some local religious practices with Satanic, paganistic and infidel beliefs; growing religiosity among some and "no religion" among others; and a secular state that maintains a tightrope balance in managing issues, such as the allocation of public spaces for religious sites, the wearing of *hijab* (headscarves) by Muslim women in public services, and religious objections to homosexuality and same sex marriages.

The blanket approach to keep religion out of a secular public sphere is problematic when the vast majority of Singaporeans profess having a religion. It would be more reasonable and nuanced to decide when and how religion and secularism can interact civilly and cooperatively and how to navigate and accommodate differences. The larger complex and everchanging religious landscape requires understanding, acceptance and appreciation of its diversity, and complex dialogue, negotiation, management and resolution of issues.

Shared living spaces

Shared living spaces in public housing for 85 per cent of Singapore's population warrants a last but not least reminder of what matters especially in everyday life multiculturalism. Mundane everyday life is usually taken for granted and regarded as insignificant, yet requires regular reminders of rules and considerations for shared living, and of how to maintain the civic social order that has evolved over decades. My earlier work (Lai, 1995) traced resettlement from mainly ethnic enclaves and clusters to more multicultural HDB estates under massive resettlement. I discussed some features of ethnic interaction and accommodation: in everyday life (friendly chatting, neigbouring in which mutual look out, help and gift offering take place, and children playing with familiar others as part of socialising in a cohesive environment); and on different cultural occasions (understanding, appreciation, mediation of disputes over noise, music, cultural practices and use of common spaces). Accommodation and acceptance did not emerge overnight but developed as local community over time. My study also showed an overwhelming preference for multi-ethnic living but with a qualification that there be a minimum pool of co-ethnics for familiarity and belonging.

The examples from my research thirty years ago are still valid today. Ethnic boundaries remain part of the residential community's public and cultural life and most residents have come to accept and respect them as aspects of their multicultural environment. However, tensions are likely to recur every now and then. Here, the approaches in navigating boundaries and managing disputes that have evolved over time to become norms — expectations of civil behaviour by residents, HDB rules, use of mediators' negotiation skills and personal intercultural knowledge — are crucial. In light of massive movements of residents, concentrations of newer citizens and young residents, every new housing estate, new generation and new resident needs to be socialised and reminded about navigating diversity with civility, competency, and sensitivity. Gong banging to retaliate against a neighbour's praying is unacceptable and not a solution. At the policy level, the rationale and assumption of the HDB policy of ethnic integration through ethnic quotas implemented in 1989 — fear of enclaving and racial rioting — need to be carefully and regularly reassessed.

Living with CMIO multiculturalism and beyond

I write in a time of flux in which disconnects and divides threaten multiculturalism and cohesion. A main concern today is that racism, notorious for entrenching inequality which in turn exacerbates it, will get worse with growing inequalities. So how can we address divisions and issues towards their reduction and solution and towards equality and cohesiveness?

Equality in citizenship is a core principle in multiculturalism. As such, there must be fair and just treatment for all and this must be perceived to be so. At the state level, the Government must take the lead in not ethnicising socio-economic problems and in addressing structural inequalities as national problems. Issues should be addressed for what they are — as social and national issues. Specific ethnic dimensions can still be included where they are judged significant and relevant, such as in intersections with class, and in context and appropriate to the issue at hand.

Some aspects of CMIO multiculturalism will be with us that are worthy of keeping, such as ethnic heritages, while others are to be ended quickly or erased over time. But clearly, living with and building a cohesive multiculturalism is to say "no" to racism and prejudice, "yes" to equality, justice, respect. The opening up of discussion is overdue and needs to go beyond current dominant cultural frameworks and interpretations. Public discourses on race will/should continue even though uncomfortable and stressful.

A cohesive multiculturalism is not without problems and issues but these should not be too many, too deep and too overwhelming as to be divisive and polarising. A cohesive multiculturalism involves strong bonds and stakeholdership in which society's members, irrespective of cultural differences, must feel they belong to it, have a stake in it and are involved in its development. It also involves civil negotiation for a citizenship that must be seen to embrace and manage differences in an equal and fair manner. There should be many effective ways — through institutions, mechanisms and attitudes — to reduce or eliminate problems. The minimum conditions of tolerance without abuse and maximum conditions of inclusion, exchange and appreciation should apply.

In general, dealing with cultural diversity issues requires necessary mediation, negotiation and resolution skills and processes. Showing and practising the values of fairness, reasonableness, respect, justice and equality when coming up with an acceptable approach or solutions to a conflict is essential. Developing intercultural intelligence, awareness and skills is crucial to navigate potentially tense inter-cultural issues. Beyond more conflict prevention, these also contribute to lasting and meaningful peace-building and cultural understanding and appreciation in both real and cyber spaces.

While living with its dominant ethnic structures, we also need to go beyond CMIO multiculturalism to acknowledge and embrace intersections, hybridities, new formations, common values and common humanity. Some common humanity and common values are already found in our multicultural interactions when living together — sharing common spaces, community, compromise, acceptance and appreciation of diversity, mutual help, neighbourliness, friendliness and compassion. Indeed, these ties and norms that bind and the principles of justice, equality and respect are today's values of a common human tribe that supercedes a particularistic ethnic or religious kin/tribe.

There are so many minefields in Singapore's multiculturalism that it can seem overwhelming. In reality, even as the road is long and always under construction, many concrete areas and stretches can be treaded on and steps taken to create a cohesive multiculturalism with positivity, passion and responsibility. Safe and brave spaces can be created and expanded, bridges and crossings built. Navigation requires both group and individual efforts, grounded in knowledge, awareness, competences and skills. Both spontaneous action and deliberate policy are required.

For the individual, roles in this navigation are important and many, and require many qualities: independent critical thought, reflection and action; open-mindedness, objectivity and reasonableness; not to be easily influenced by group think, ability to seek clarity and perspective, judge sensitively and speak up wisely; co-create effectively; participate in dialogue and exchange in good faith and in civil, friendly, cooperative ways; going beyond the pragmatic to be imaginative and visionary about the future. Individuals can be at the forefront of many thoughts, words and deeds in roles in everyday life or in movements and activism. For example, countering strong stereotyping among family members at home, writing against xenophobia in social media, exchanging views at interfaith dialogues or sharing stories of intercultural experiences and incidents. Discrimination and prejudice especially need to be called out and their basis questioned against the shared values of a common humanity and the principles of equality, justice and respect. It is always good and necessary for individuals as well as groups to call out the "truth" (narratives of what happened), the "bad" (reflectively with a view of what is good to learn from it) and the "good" (such as the friendships and the kind helpful acts in everyday life and specific moments). Intercultural alliances and networks can be formed as powerful mechanisms that can unite peoples across diversities, differences, and affiliations based on their shared humanity and common values; promote understanding, competences and appreciation in cultural interaction and exchanges; inspire people to work, live and play together; and respond positively and responsibly to challenging issues and developments.

It is obvious I cannot live without diversity. I can put up with some problems and issues. But I would like a cohesive community where the values of respect, equality, fairness and compassion are the norm and I can participate in it in progressive ways and to overcome problems.

LAI Ah-Eng has accumulated some valuable experiences and memories in her adult life as researcher, instructor, writer, community organiser, friend and parent. Her background training in Economics, Development Studies and Social Anthropology has enabled her to work and contribute both professionally and socially. She has published books, chapters and articles on women, family, ethnicity, religion, multiculturalism and heritage in her work career. In social life, she has contributed her ideas and energies in various committees and groups pertaining to women, family, ethnicity, religion and heritage. Now, she teaches as an Adjunct Senior Fellow at the National University of Singapore, writes, comments, and supports charities and good causes (welfare homes, migrant workers, refugees, environment). In between these activities, she does adventure travelling, singing, photography and nature walks.

References

Chong, Ian. 2020. "The Burden of Ethnicity: Chinese Communities in Singapore and Their Relations with China". In *Navigating Differences: Integration in Singapore*, edited by Terence Chong. Singapore: ISEAS Publishing.

Diversity and Inclusion in Asia Network (DIAN). 2012. "Adopting an Asian Lens to Talent Development, Report 2012: Asian "Gaps" in Diversity

Issues in Business Corporations Operating in Asia". Report presented at Seminar (Post-Conference) on Cultural Diversity, Conference on Fair Employment Practices, organised by the Tripartite Alliance for Fair Employment (TAFEP).

Koh, Sin Yee. 2014. "Diasporic 'Unbelonging' to Malaysia and Singapore: Second-Generation Malaysian-Chinese Migrants in Singapore". In *The Age of Asian Migration: Continuity, Diversity, and Susceptibility,* edited by Y.W. Chan, D. Haines & J.H.X. Lee. Newcastle-upon-Tyne: Cambridge Scholars Publishing.

Lai, Ah Eng. 1995. *Meanings of Multiethnicity: A Case-Study of Ethnicity and Ethnic Relations in Singapore.* Kuala Lumpur: Oxford University Press.

Lai, Ah Eng and Mathew Mathews. 2016. "Navigating Disconnects and Divides in Singapore's Cultural Diversity". In *Managing Diversity in Singapore: Policies and Prospects*, edited by Mathew Mathews and Chiang Wai Fong. London: Imperial College Press and Singapore: Institute of Policy Studies.

Lai, Ah Eng. 2017. "Maze and Minefield: Reflections on Multiculturalism in Singapore". In *Living with Myths in Singapore,* edited by Loh Kah Seng, P.J. Thum and Jack Chia. Singapore: Ethos Books.

Lai, Ah Eng. 2023. "Viewing Ourselves and Others: Differences, Disconnects and Divides Amongst Locals and Immigrants in Singapore". In *Immigrant Integration in Contemporary Singapore* edited by Mathew Mathews & Melvin Tay. Singapore: World Scientific Publishing. https://www. worldscientific.com/do/10.1142/do.13176-writeup/full/.

Siow, Maria and Joseph Sipalan. 23 July 2022. "Why do Singapore and Malaysia have a more favourable view of China than the US?" *South China Morning Post.*

"The greatness of a nation depends on the quality of its people. It is a society where everyone is equal regardless of gender or race or religion. Where a person is considered for his or her abilities and for his or her character. Fairness and equality goes with justice and right order and unless these exist we continue to struggle in life and not live our lives."

~ Foster mother extraordinaire Indranee Elizabeth Nadisen, for The Lives of Women exhibition at the National Museum, Jan–Mar 2022

CHAPTER 8

The Multiracial Society I Want to See in Singapore

Mysara Aljaru

When I was in primary school, my English teacher made us keep an exercise book where we would write prompts that were almost like diary entries. One of the assignments had us sharing what our dreams were, and I remember very enthusiastically writing that I wanted to be a journalist or a writer. All you had to do was to work hard and you could be what you wanted. You believed that the possibilities were endless!

As an adult now, I can say that I have achieved most of my dreams. However, over the years I grew to realise that the reality was not as simple as nine-year-old Mysara thought. The future does have its limits — especially when you're a minority woman in your country.

When I get asked on panels what my ideal Singapore is, it is, I confess, quite the question for me to answer. It's easy to fall into the default template: a Singapore that isn't just equal but pushes for equity for all its citizens — regardless of race, language and religion.

Turning 30, I wish for a Singapore where everyone gets to live through their childlike enthusiasm of life without a worry. Where dreams are possible without us stopping and doubting ourselves, worried that we're not good enough because of our skin colour or we're inferior simply because we look different from the majority.

An ideal Singapore is a Singapore where we are loved sincerely, and where we get to love ourselves unconditionally.

To reach that ideal, we must be brave. And we must be brave to acknowledge that we're not perfect. That there is still quite a distance to go before we reach that shiny, beautiful, equal country that everyone seems to talk about.

* * *

I can't quite place the moment when I realised that being a minority meant things were different for me. Very much like the moment when, as girls, we realise that there are different standards being imposed on us compared to our brothers or men, there comes a time when, as a member of a minority ethnic group, you realise there are different standards and experiences for you in your own country.

Discussions on race and racism in Singapore aren't new, but there is a need to push the discourse forward. In this essay I raise some points that I think need to be discussed — such as shifting narratives with transparent data and research, understanding intersectionality, and seeing us as knowledge producers and not just subjects.

Shifting the narratives with transparent data and research

Once in a car ride, my driver started asking the usual questions — what I was working as and if I was married. Upon hearing I was single, he responded by saying that it was probably hard for me to find a good Malay guy, because in his view, "most Malay men are drug addicts". He even proceeded to say that "most Malay women also take drugs".

Sentiments such as these are a reflection of how racialised policies have failed the marginalised. We regularly see headlines such as "48 per cent of drug offenders held last year were Malay"[1] in the mainstream media, creating an unconscious bias towards the community. When campaigns such as "Dadah itu Haram (Drugs are forbidden)" are created, the reason for drug abuse cases in the community is framed as being related to religion (or the lack of religion) and shifts attention away from the underlying socio-economic issues of the community.

Such narratives and campaigns reproduce a cultural deficit perspective, where individuals from a certain group are seen as inferior and unable to achieve due to their cultural backgrounds. This cultural deficit perspective presents the problem as something linked to the community's culture instead of issues like underdevelopment, which are tied to socio-economic and other structural inequalities, as well as historical factors.

Policies addressing such issues need to shift from a culturalist lens that simplifies the issue too much. Politician Fadli Fawzi, a Workers' Party candidate in 2020, has suggested more data transparency as data can be manipulated to frame marginalised communities a certain way. This need for transparent data can be applied across all socio-economic issues marginalised communities face, such as crime, health, and housing.

Shifting the narratives goes hand-in-hand with ensuring research is free from personal bias and does not reproduce such sentiments. For example, research on health and Malay women, often done by majority

---

[1]   This was from a *Straits Times* article in November 2012.
[2]   See S.A. Goh *et al.* (2022), "Multi-level determinants of breast cancer screening among Malay-Muslim women in Singapore: A sequential mixed-methods study". *BMC Womens Health* 22(1):383.

race women, tends to revolve around religious beliefs and frames Malay Muslim women as fatalists, while ignoring socio-economic issues. This is despite the fact that poverty and access to healthcare are crucial elements in understanding health issues in minority communities.

When people assume Malays are fatalists and ignore the socioeconomic issues that may prevent them from seeking medical attention, they're ignoring the needs of Malay women who may need some help, whether financial or otherwise, in order to see a doctor. The stereotyping continues even though research has shown that fatalistic beliefs also exist amongst Chinese women.

For example, the authors of "*Multi-level determinants of breast cancer screening among Malay-Muslim women in Singapore: A sequential mixed-methods study*" noted the lack of data on breast cancer screening behaviour specific to the Malay community. They added: "Therefore, specific insights about this community are often underpowered and inconclusive. For instance, Straughan and Seow found fatalism, a belief that some health issues are beyond human control, to be associated with mammography uptake in a survey among predominantly Chinese respondents (84.3%). However the same authors also reported that Malay women were less fatalistic in a separate study therefore leaving the relationship of fatalism and mammography uptake in this community inconclusive."

Understanding intersectionality

In 2022, a local fashion designer was called out for her remarks at an online panel. When asked why the cheongsam was a recurring theme in her work, she said Chinese women had "progressed significantly faster and further as compared to their Malay and Indian counterparts".

She explained that Chinese women were the "first Asian women to shake hands with men" and that they were also quick to adopt

Western dressing such as miniskirts. She then asked if Malay and Indian women "were allowed by their husbands or fathers to dress a certain way, go out and work, to perform certain duties".

Not only was she stereotyping women by their ethnicity, but she was also linking the idea of progress to men and Western ideals, and she was pitting women against each other. Such statements erase the agency Indian and Malay women have, their history of fighting for rights, and harms women by assuming Chinese men do not uphold any form of patriarchy.

Commenting on the episode in RICE Media, Delfina Utomo made a point relatable to many minority women: "Some days, I think we can't change what people want to believe and say about elitism, privilege, and racism. Other days I wonder if the onus is on us to educate and change their minds."

What does intersectionality mean, and how do race and gender come into play?

In the West, the conversation about racial privilege and feminism has long included a debate about the relationship between black/brown women and white women. Writers such as Luvvie Ajayi and Ruby Hamad have talked about 'White Women tears', where attempts by minority women to call out racism by white women result in them being called aggressors — so white women do not have to hold themselves responsible.

Ruby writes in an op-ed: "As I look back over my adult life a pattern emerges. Often, when I have attempted to speak to or confront a white woman about something she has said or done that has impacted me adversely, I am met with tearful denials and indignant accusations that I am hurting her. My confidence diminished and second-guessing myself, I either flare up in frustration at not being heard (which only seems to prove her point) or I back down immediately, apologising and consoling the very person causing me harm."

We hear the word 'intersectionality' being thrown about — feminism that considers the interconnected nature of various systems of oppression, including those related to race, gender, class, sexuality, and ability. Being an intersectional feminist, especially in a multi-racial country like Singapore, means recognising that racism and sexism are interconnected.

It means recognising that different ethnic groups may have different experiences of gender and oppression. Simply put, Malay and Indian women face another layer of oppression, and sometimes this oppression may come from Chinese women who may uphold stereotypes and racist ideologies themselves.

Allyship, not saviour complex

The idea of intersectionality is growing in civil society and activist circles. It requires an understanding of the different privileges that exist amongst such circles in the first place. In the movement to achieve equity, there is a need to step back and understand the difference between speaking up and speaking on behalf of minority women and other marginalised groups.

Stories are important but what is equally important is ensuring that the stories are used with care — that minority and marginalised groups are not merely being used as subjects. This means letting them speak for themselves. It means handing the resources that you have to them so they can pave the way ahead for themselves.

The AWARE Power Fund is an example of how resources can be shared amongst groups. In 2017, Singapore's leading feminist organisation AWARE (Association of Women for Action and Research) launched the Power Fund to provide financial and capacity-building support for emerging organisations and new initiatives of established organisations that work with marginalised women and girls.

The beneficiary organisations planned and organised their own activities and sessions, with AWARE simply providing support in the form of meeting space and mentorship and some financial aid. This approach meant the beneficiary organisations had a seat at the table and were the key decision makers. It allowed them to grow organically. Minority and marginalised women were positioned as the experts and knowledge producers, and not merely the subjects for majority-led movements and campaigns.

Relooking definitions and relearning history, with care

In creating space where equity is practised, we need to re-examine definitions and re-learn history. What is 'success' for example? Are we defining it within the conforms of a racist and capitalist society? We need to understand that the demands and needs of the majority women do not always equal the needs and demands of minority and most marginalised women.

This effort can start with something as simple as taking a fresh look at our history. Are we forgetting the narratives of minority women who have actively contributed to society? We might be familiar with the stories of those who have had political power, but what about the others? There needs to be a constant re-looking and checking to see who has been left behind, and how the systems have been structured to leave them behind in the first place.

As civil rights activist and feminist Audre Lorde once said: "I am not free while any woman is unfree, even when her shackles are very different from my own."

* * *

As I grow older, I no longer want a colour-blind society. I want to live in a society where diversity is encouraged and appreciated, where my culture is seen as beautiful and not as a burden to others.

I want to see the future generations have that same glimmer of hope that I had when I was young, the belief that the world offers endless possibilities, without it disappearing as they grow up and replaced by uncertainty, worry, and frustration.

I want the future generations of brown women and kids to be able to love themselves unconditionally.

MYSARA ALJARU (she/her) is a lens-based practitioner, writer, and researcher. Mysara was previously a journalist and documentary producer and has also worked with various research institutions. She has showcased and performed at Objectifs, The Substation, ArtScience Museum, and Singapore Art Week 2022. Her works look at state narratives forming across race, class, and gender. She is also co-editor of Brown is Redacted, an anthology that looks into minority experiences.

"Everything in life is transient. Only charity is real and enduring. When you give, you receive. Charity is the best antidote to bad karma."

~ Abbess and charity-worker Ho Yuen Hoe in an interview with The Straits Times, February 2004

CHAPTER 9

Is There Space for Faith-based Values in the Modern World?

Stefanie Yuen Thio

I am 54, a wife, a mother, and an established corporate lawyer. I am also a committed Christian.

This is a book about women in Singapore in the years ahead, and this chapter is on how Singaporeans with religious beliefs engage. Is there a space for faith-based values in the modern world or will we have to compartmentalise our convictions? I make a living grappling with principles and structuring win-win solutions, using words as my tools, but this is the hardest thing I have ever had to write.

First, let me introduce myself.

For work, I run a law firm and a busy legal practice. For interest, I often contribute opinion pieces to the local press on issues that catch my eye — gender equality in Singapore, the fate of girls in the aftermath of the U.S. pullout from Afghanistan, how our country needs to respond to the challenges of a post-Covid world. I am also an occasional commentator in the BBC Business Matters radio programme where I provide a Singapore perspective on breaking news. To assuage moral guilt for my unmerited success, I do community service, including recently establishing a new non-profit championing women called SHE (SG Her Empowerment).

I am perceived as the outspoken, pull-no-punches female lawyer, and was named a LinkedIn Top Voice for Singapore in its inaugural list, for my forthright opinions on current affairs. During Covid lockdowns, when news media reported that karaoke lounges were using their new food & beverage licences to conduct vice activities, I cheekily wondered– in a post that went viral — whether the "B" in "F&B" stood for blowjob, and the "F" referred to something other than food.

I sound like a strident and opinionated feminist. But that is only one side of the story.

The other is this: I am just as much a cliched oriental woman. Married straight out of university, I adopted my husband's surname and moved into his family home where I still live. Twenty-six years ago, I joined the Thio family business when my mother-in-law set up TSMP Law Corporation. I did everything from advising clients on IPOs, to buying office stationery. One time, when the water mains burst, I spent the night solitarily mopping the floor, afraid to impose on anyone else because I felt it was my duty. I am the good wife, in both Chinese and Christian tradition: when I took my marriage vows, to the horrified amusement of my friends, I even promised to "obey".

Finally, and most importantly, I am a Christian. My faith is my bulwark. It provides the moral compass by which I live and the values by which I judge myself. When I — so often — fall short, my belief in a God of second chances is what keeps me trying to be better.

I am a product of the Singapore I grew up in. We had a prescient Prime Minister who understood that women should be treated as equals, and that if our economy was to have any chance, both sexes needed to be in the workforce. As a result, I received as good an education and the same job opportunities as my male counterparts. Multi-racial and multi-faith acceptance meant I could grow up practising my religion while being respectful of others' moral codes.

The Singapore of today

But the economic backwater that was the Singapore of my youth is no longer our reality. Our success as an international financial centre and regional legal hub has made us the new wealth and business base for people from all over the world, an influx only magnified by the continuing U.S.-China tensions. Becoming an overseas headquarters, and not just a minor corporate outpost, means that Singapore's laws and policies receive more attention from today's ESG-focused companies. Expanding the melting pot of people adds a broader spectrum of beliefs into the mix. Singapore's hyper Internet connectivity (we have one of the world's highest digital penetration rates) has increased our speed and access to mind-sets prevalent offshore, especially among the youth. A Singapore teen is more likely to be exercised over *#MeToo* issues in the U.S .than subconscious gender biases in our own society.

Because of this, our nation will not be able to develop its own norms in a more organic way based on its citizens' privately held belief systems, but must contend with the calm and clamourous extremes of the larger world. The Singapore of tomorrow has to work out a new compact for various cultures to coexist harmoniously.

Faith in the world of the woke

Clearly, the more liberal mindsets prevalent in some parts of the world today are at odds with the dogma of, among other religions, the church, most clearly in the attitudes towards alternative sexual orientations.

Debate on the issue really took off in 2009 when the AWARE Saga blew up.

A group of Christians had come into leadership positions in the non-government organisation known as Association of Women for Action & Research (AWARE). They did this legally through election at the Annual General Meeting. What followed has become social sector history. It had been said that AWARE, hired to give sexuality education in schools, were espousing pro-gay views. The "new guard" wanted to put a stop to this to prevent school children in Singapore — unbeknownst to their parents — being taught principles those parents did not agree with. The old guard at AWARE promptly rose in furious and organised response and threw out the newcomers in a hastily convened and (to put it mildly) boisterous general meeting, attended by thousands.

The AWARE saga galvanised Singapore society. The middle ground which had, prior to this issue hitting the front page of The *Straits Times*, not given much thought to gay rights, was confronted with taking a stand. An early fault line was drawn. At the same time, Pink Dot SG, a not-for-profit pro-LGBTQ movement that organises a large annual event to celebrate gay pride, was born when the government allowed citizens to hold demonstrations in Hong Lim Park without a public licence in 2008. Its attendance numbers continue to rise and its supporters increase.

For many Christians, myself included, hitherto living in a happy social compact of "don't ask, don't tell" with their gay neighbours, this forced the issue. Whatever we want to teach our children, what should be our response at a public policy level? A renewed spotlight has since been directed at this: in 2022, the government repealed

Section 377A of the Penal Code and decriminalised male homosexual intercourse, reigniting debate.

I don't think the principal concern over repeal is whether consenting male adults should be allowed to engage in sex. I don't believe that Singaporeans want a country whose laws take from the teachings of one faith — that would make us a theocracy.

Conservatives' greater fear is that repeal will be the pebble that starts an avalanche, hurtling our community into a future where traditional or religion-based values — or indeed any values that are not "woke" — would be derided, their champions aggressively cancelled, and the new generation bullied into accepting liberal principles not our own. Their worry is that this is the start of a slippery slope towards a liberal agenda not reflecting the values of the community. In part, this was born of what was reportedly happening in the liberal West, where school and church leadership were prevented from imparting their religious teachings. Whether this was a serious and imminent threat to Singapore is uncertain, but the fear was real.

And perhaps, looking at world developments in the ensuing 15 years, it was legitimate. Take cancel culture. In today's digitally connected world, individuals expressing views that are not aligned with certain vocal segments of society are subject to harassment which can spill over into real life. In the Christian context, conservative parents are reporting that their school-aged children are under pressure to adopt liberal views, including wearing gay pride colours. Some churchgoers may feel that they have no choice but to draw a battle line by opposing repeal.

Perhaps there is a different way to look at this.

Singapore should build a community based on the values of its people. At the same time, no group should be able to impose their views on others, whether through laws or any kind of bullying or harassment. As a multi-racial society, our communities should be free to advocate for their convictions, including on social and family issues, so long as the discussion is respectful and recognises another's right to disagree. Underpinning this is the principle that individuals must be treated with equal respect.

Given the contentious and polarised views today, it would be useful to start with some open conversations, and commit to a genuine engagement. Let us not dance around the real reason we oppose repeal and address the elephant in the room that is cancel culture and the tyranny of the "woke".

The conversation might begin with an admission where each side has fallen short. Having pinned my colours to the Christian mast, let me begin with this: I think the church's casual assurance that we will "love the sinner but hate the sin" rings hollow if we don't take the time to genuinely engage with those of alternative sexual orientations. It is also morally lazy.

We need to rebuild trust, and trust needs to extend to the information we draw from. In the past decade, we have seen the rise of fake news. Using misinformation to influence outcomes (as alleged in the 2016 U.S. Presidential election) is what troll farms, largely run by black hat governments, have been using as a form of warfare. Social media's targeted posts can amplify echo chambers. Factions on both extremes thus mistrust mainstream media. Strengthening the independence and objectivity — both perceived and real — of Singapore's news outlets will contribute to an orderly and informed discourse.

If Singaporeans can begin, and commit to continuing, such an open and respectful engagement, we can build the Singapore we want. Yes, there will be areas of intractable disagreement — gay marriage, same-sex adoption, increasingly complex issues around alternative sexual orientation. Those don't align with the teachings of the Bible. But neither do sharp business practices, failing to care for the less privileged, and sanctimonious know-it-all*ism*. We have to get used to our society having ever increasing elements that don't accord with our personal beliefs, without impeding Singaporeans' ability to practise their faiths respectfully, which includes articulating their convictions.

How any group engages on difficult issues is critical. If right-wing Christians make gay rights their defining battle, they will risk being labelled a one-issue lobby. What could come across as a bigoted position — if we do not honestly and holistically address all the issues at play — will discredit us on engagement in other matters. This is also important because our young people, already so influenced by foreign opinion, may simply adopt those external positions if we do not have a landing on our own community values developed through engagement. Given the extreme divergence of views internationally, the fissures in our society will only deepen.

I started writing this article by asking myself if it is possible to be a Christian in the world of tomorrow; if my religious beliefs are too divergent from the Zeitgeist. The more I struggle with this, the less I believe I have the answers. And I pen this piece trembling in the fear that one day I will read it and realise I got it wrong.

But I battle with yet another internal conflict: the Jesus of the Bible was interested in personal transformation, Christians extending love and compassion to their community, and the church being a beacon of light in a troubled world. Drawing a bright line on the single issue of gay rights may hamper Christians' ability to fulfil those commandments which are so core to what they are called to do. To love our neighbour, we first need to see them and acknowledge their place in society. So maybe let's start there.

STEFANIE YUEN THIO is a wife, a mother, an established corporate lawyer, and a committed Christian. She often contributes opinion pieces to the local press on issues that catch her eye. She is also an occasional commentator in the BBC Business Matters radio programme where she provides a Singapore perspective on breaking news. To assuage moral guilt for what she considers her unmerited success, she does community service, including recently establishing a new non-profit championing women called SHE (SG Her Empowerment).

"One shouldn't be trapped where one is historically at the moment... every individual has more than one strength; one should detach, identify these strengths and see where they can be best utilised. It's a big leap of faith to move on, but it's about empowering the self."

~ Pioneering diplomat Jayalekshmi Mohideen, in an interview with The Business Times, March 2001

CHAPTER 10

The Promise of Islamic Feminism as Religion-based Advocacy for Gender Justice and Equality

Mohamed Imran Mohamed Taib & Nurul Fadiah Johari

Women's rights have been at the forefront of contemporary debates in modern society within the last two centuries. Women's rights constitute a global revolution in thinking, otherwise known as feminism. Feminism itself emerged as a social movement that, at its basic core ideal, represents a call for *equal worth and opportunities* between men and women, and a challenge *against patriarchy* in all its manifestations.

Stanford University historian, Estelle B. Freedman (2002) identifies the global consciousness towards feminism as being located within two corresponding features of modern society: the rise of market economies and the expansion of democratic systems.[1]

---

[1] Estelle B. Freedman, *No Turning Back: The History of Feminism and the Future of Women.* New York: Ballantine Books, 2002, pp. 1–2.

These two aspects had disrupted the idea of women as dependents of men, hence calling for the equal worth of women as social, economic, and political contributors in the current world-system. This requires the expansion of rights in all spheres of life, ranging from equal opportunities in education to management of domestic affairs and political suffrage.

The emergence of feminism as a modern phenomenon would also naturally affect Muslim societies. In fact, the call for women's emancipation was one of the defining features of early modern reform of Muslim societies. Unlike the later essentialist critique by secular feminism that religion hampers efforts to realise women's rights in Muslim societies, the emergence of feminism in the Muslim experience is rooted in *religious consciousness*. In fact, this religious consciousness can be traced to the pre-modern period.[2] A similar case could be argued within the context of Western feminism where those who spoke for themselves and for their sex, as Margaret Walters (2005) argued, "did so within a religious framework and in religious terms."[3]

It is this religious basis for feminism, Muslim or otherwise, that is often missed in many writings. Within the Muslim context, to ignore this aspect would play into two camps that are detrimental to Muslim societies. The first is what has been described as "liberal White feminism" that employed the trope of the Muslim women in need of saving from "Islam". As Lila Abu-Lughod (2013) demonstrated, this trope has been used to demonise Muslim cultures and justify political interventions — often with atrocious humanitarian

---

[2] For example, the philosopher Ibn Rushd (Averroes, d. 1198) rejects the idea that women are naturally inferior to men. Women can hold their own in a war, and nothing rules out the possibility of them becoming philosophers and rulers. He believes that the low social status of women in a society was because of them not being taught in human virtues, hence narrowing, and nullifying their capabilities. This situation, in fact, will impoverish the city even more. (See, Ralph Lerner, tr. *Averroes on Plato's Republic*. Ithaca and London: Cornell University Press, 1974.)

[3] Margaret Walters, *Feminism: A Very Short Introduction*. Oxford. England: Oxford University Press, 2005.

consequences — of Muslim societies, ranging from foreign political interferences to outright military invasions.[4]

The second is the trope of feminism as an alien ideology — often of the corrupt enemy, the West — to destroy Islam. This trope is often upheld by Islamist movements that seek to capture social and political power in Muslim societies to implement what they view as Islamic exceptionalism in terms of how to order and govern society, including gender relations.

This paper posits that between these two camps, there has been the exciting emergence and expansion of what is best described as "Islamic feminism". As a movement, Islamic feminism adopts an ontological position that Islam per se is not the source of oppression, although as a religion, Islam has been used to oppress and deny women's human rights. For Islamic feminists, the root problem lies within patriarchy, which informs the way religion has been taught, understood, and interpreted. Ultimately, Islamic feminists understand Islam as a dynamic religion that can be subjected to multiple ways of understanding and interpretations. Hence, much of the work of Islamic feminism is about reclaiming Islam from patriarchal interpretations and positioning Islam as a foundation in the struggle for gender equality and gender justice.

The emergence and rise of Islamic feminism

The rise of Islamic feminism could be traced to the late 19th century, particularly in Egypt. It corresponds with the awakening of Muslim subjects under colonial rule. Among the earliest proponents of women's rights was the Al-Azhar don, Shaykh Rifa'a al-Tahtawi (d. 1873). Said to have set the foundations for Arab renaissance

---

[4] Lila Abu-Lughod, *Do Muslim Women Need Saving?* Cambridge, Mass.: : Harvard University Press, 2013.

(*nahdah*) — the "liberal age of Arabic thought", as described by the historian Albert Hourani (1962) — al-Tahtawi promoted women's education as early as the 1830s when he was a member of the Educational Council of Egypt.

A school textbook which he wrote in his later years, called *Al murshid al-amin lil-banat wa'l-banin* (The Honest Guide for Girls and Boys), promoted nascent ideas on gender equality, namely that girls should be educated as much as boys, and on equal footing. Hence, the differences between women and men pertain to their biological features and not intelligence. Al-Tahtawi also believed that harmonious marriages and good upbringing of children required the education of women. In addition, women ought to be given opportunities, albeit within their capabilities, to take up similar occupations as men. On polygamy, although he did not prohibit it, he did assert that Islam allows it only if the husband can do justice between his wives — a point taken up by later writers to virtually forbid polygamy.[5]

Al-Tahtawi's reformist position on women was followed by another towering figure of the Al-Azhar fraternity, Shaykh Muhammad 'Abduh (d. 1905). In 1899, 'Abduh became the Grand Mufti of Egypt, arguably the most respected position for a religious scholar in the Sunni world. Among his notable reforms were issuing fatwas (religious edicts) that 1) promoted monogamy and allowing polygamy only when the first wife is barren, and 2) making it a legal requirement for a man who wanted to divorce his wife to state his case to judge and abide by the judges' verdict and advice.[6]

'Abduh's fatwas issued in Egypt had a great influence in the emergence of Muslim reformism in other parts of the Muslim world,

---

[5] Albert Hourani, *Arabic Thought in the Liberal Age 1798–1939*. Cambridge, Mass.: Cambridge University Press, 2009, pp. 77–78.

[6] Kinda AlSamara (2018), "Muhammad 'Abduh: Islam and New Urbanity in the Nineteenth-Century Arab World". *Australian Journal of Islamic Studies* 3(1): 63–79.

including Southeast Asian Malay society. Being a cosmopolitan trading centre and a major port for connecting pilgrims and students in the region with the Middle East, Singapore played a critical role in the transmission of reformist ideas on women. This could be seen in the Kaum Muda (Young Faction) movement fronted by figures such as Syed Sheikh al-Hady (d. 1934), Sheikh Tahir Jalaluddin (d. 1956) and Haji Abbas Taha (d. 1950). Between 1906 to 1908, the movement established a progressive magazine called *Al-Imam*, which, among others, advocated for the education of Malay girls, much to the chagrin of the traditionalist ulama faction.[7]

Syed Sheik Al-Hady, the most prominent of the Kaum Muda faction, was much inspired by 'Abduh's brand of reformism. In 1930, he translated a key text on women's emancipation written by the Egyptian Qasim Amin (d. 1908). Amin was a student of 'Abduh and his *Tahrir al-Mar'ah* (Liberation of Women), written in 1899, was considered as a pioneering call for women's rights in modern Muslim society. His critique against patriarchy was carefully constructed to challenge what he considered as tradition and social conventions, rather than Islam. For Amin, God's law demands "life and progress" rather than "immobility and inflexibility". He wrote:

> "Some people will say that today I am publishing heresy. To these people I will respond: yes, I have come up with a heresy, but the heresy is not against Islam. It is against our traditions and social dealings, where the demand for perfection is extolled. Why should a Muslim believe that his traditions cannot be changed or replaced by new ones, and that it is his duty to preserve them forever? Why does he drag this

---

[7] Abu Bakar Hamzah, *Al-Imam: Its Role in Malay Society, 1905–1908*. Kuala Lumpur: Pustaka Antara, 1991.

belief along to his work, even though he and his traditions are a part of the universe, falling at all times under the laws of change?"[8]

Qasim Amin — along with religious scholars such as Tahtawi and 'Abduh — were the intellectual progenitors of Islamic feminism. The fact that they were male indicates that Islamic feminism, though critical of male privilege, has no baggage with men and recognises the need for both men and women to work together in the struggle against patriarchy that affects all. This has been a key feature of Islamic feminism that adopts three key concepts: *musawah* (equality), *'adalah* (justice) and *mubadalah* (reciprocity) as the epistemic lens for gender justice.

Today, the intellectual and religious foundations of Islamic feminism could be found across scholarships developed by a loose global network of both female and male scholars, such as Fatima Mernissi, Riffat Hassan, Aziza El-Hibri, Ziba Mir-Hosseini, Nawal El-Saadawi, Leila Ahmed, Amina Wadud, Asma Barlas, Kecia Ali, Zainah Anwar, Musdah Mulia, Nur Rofiah, Lies Marcos-Natsir, Lily Zakiah Munir, Asma Lamrabet, Tahir Haddad, Fazlur Rahman, Khaled Abou El-Fadl, Abdullahi An-Na'im, Farid Esack, Asghar Ali Engineer, Nasr Hamid Abu-Zayd, Abdulaziz Sachedina, Masdar F. Masudi, Nasaruddin Umar, Husein Muhammad, Faqihuddin Abdul Qodir, Adis Duderija and more.

One important aspect among the cited scholars above is their adoption of multi-disciplinary approaches in tackling the problem of patriarchy. Though these scholars are engaging primarily with the inherited body of knowledge from the Islamic tradition, they are nonetheless not averse to adopting critical social sciences

---

[8] Qasim Amin, *The Liberation of Women and The New Woman*. Tr. by Samiha Sidhom Peterson. Cairo, Egypt: The American University in Cairo Press, 2005, pp. 4–5.

including the best of secular feminist studies located in the Western context. But key to their hermeneutical approach is contextualisation.

The resulting synthesis therefore can be said to be the third way between Western secular feminism and anti-feminist Islamism. Islamic feminism, therefore, is both critical and creative. It represents a progressive vision of Islam that is best described in the popular adage among Indonesian reformist movements: *al-muhafadzhoh ʻala qadim al-shalih wa al-akhdzhu bi al-jadid al-aslah* (preserving the good from the old and taking what is better from the new).

It must be noted here that although Islamic feminism draws inspiration from early Islam, it does not adopt an apologetic approach to women's issues. This is unlike some modernist Muslims who engage in *apologia* by extolling rhetorical statements such as "Prophet Muhammad was a feminist" and "Islam does not need women's rights because Islam has granted these rights from the beginning". Such statements are often attempts to avoid engaging in real issues affecting Muslim women in the complex modern world. By dismissing attempts to engage in reforms, apologists often find themselves in the same camp as Islamists who engage in Islamic exceptionalism through the utopian notion of a "perfect Islam".

Prophet Muhammad was not a feminist in the sense that his movement in the 7th century was not solely focused on instituting gender equality. But it will not be wrong to say that in seeding humanistic values for mercy and justice centred around the concept of *tauhid* (monotheism), he sets in motion a reformist vision towards the ideal state of full humanity for women. Essentially, Islam is a liberation movement with the Prophet emphasising a preferential option for the marginalised and oppressed.

In this sense, women were counted alongside the poor, orphans and slaves whose rights cannot be ignored. Hence, modern Islamic feminism drew inspiration from the values of the founding moments of Islam while acknowledging that it was not fully realised during the Prophetic period. In fact, the progressive vision of the Prophet was subverted as Islam regressed into a patriarchal mode as social hierarchy hardened through the subsequent consolidation of male privilege among the political and religious elites.

Islamic feminists therefore do not reject the view that Islam does contain the seeds of gender equality and justice. But Islamic feminists do not see Islam, in its development and human interpretations of it, as "perfect" but rather as a dynamic force that is constantly evolving towards perfection. Islamic feminists view Islam as a constant movement towards universal values of humanity as intended by God. For example, drawing from the Prophet granting partial inheritance to women (as revealed in the Qur'an) at a time where women did not inherit anything at all, Muslims today ought to struggle for equal inheritance for male and female as embodied in the spirit of the Prophetic idea of full humanity of both men and women.

Islamic feminists recognise the fact that social conditions were not ripe for equality to be realised fully during the early Islamic period. It may still be a struggle in today's context. But one thing that sets apart Islamic feminists from their conservative counterparts is the rejection of the "natural order" of male superiority over women, which is often tied to the concepts of "*qiwamah*" (that generally denotes a husband's authority over his wife) and "*wilayah*" (that generally denote male jurisdiction over women).[9] It is this gendered idea that continues to sustain the view that women must always be subordinated to men, and hence privileges men in all spheres of life from the family to social, political, and economic aspects.

---

[9] On the concepts of "qiwamah" and "wilayah", see Ziba Mir-Hosseini, Mulki Al-Sharmani and Jana Rumminger, eds. *Men in Charge? Rethinking Authority in Muslim Legal Tradition*. London, England: Oneworld Academic, 2015.,

Islamic feminist movements

What we described above may not do justice to the range and spectrum of Islamic feminism as a broad and globalised movement within Muslim societies. Nonetheless, it is important to acknowledge several key movers that have given shape to it. While there are many important Islamic feminist movements in different parts of the world, we shall highlight three that can be considered as pioneering, ground-breaking and impactful respectively: 1) Sisters in Islam in Malaysia, 2) the global Musawah movement, and 3) Indonesian Women Ulama Congress (KUPI).

Sisters in Islam, Malaysia

Sisters in Islam (SIS) is primarily a non-governmental organisation (NGO) that was established in 1993 in Malaysia as SIS Forum Berhad, although the group had existed informally as a study circle in the 1980s. While there were several other Muslim women organisations then, SIS was the first to approach Muslim women's issues from the liberal perspectives of justice, equality, freedom and dignity within a democratic nation-state. The eight founding members were multinational, comprising five Malaysians, an American, an Australian, and a Singaporean. As an Islamic feminist organisation, SIS sought to engage with feminist interpretations of the primary sources of Islam (Qur'an and Hadith) alongside constitutional and human rights principles.

One of the defining features of SIS' approach to reforming Islamic law is to clarify the difference between *shari'a* (lit., the way) as divine will and *fiqh* (lit., the understanding) as human effort to make sense of the concepts and purposes of God's Law. According to Basarudin (2016), SIS' work has been about "producing and transmitting Islamic knowledge that accounts for women's experiences and lived realities, as well as shifting cultural and political landscapes of communities of Muslims".[10]

For challenging traditional interpretations of Islam that are seen as patriarchal, SIS had to contend with public campaigns to discredit its legitimacy as an Islamic organisation. These campaigns were led by the government religious authority, JAKIM, as well as the Islamist political party, PAS, and several conservative Muslim NGOs. In 2014, SIS was mentioned in a fatwa by the Selangor Islamic Religious Council (MAIS) as promoting deviant ideas, namely "liberalism" and "pluralism" and hence to be declared as an unlawful organisation.

In challenging the fatwa, including the jurisdiction of the Syariah Court over SIS, which is registered as a company, SIS was drawn into a long court battle that is still unfolding. In March 2023, the Malaysian Court of Appeal upheld the High Court's decision that the civil courts have no jurisdiction to judge on the case brought against the fatwa, and that SIS should instead head to the Syariah courts to challenge the fatwa. This puts SIS in a precarious situation as they face the possibility of having to be deregistered, books confiscated and banned, and their online presence restricted or blocked.

Musawah

While SIS may face sanctions in Malaysia, it had successfully led the formation of a global initiative called Musawah. As recounted by Ziba Mir-Hosseini (2022), it was Zainah Anwar of SIS that catalysed the formation of Musawah by "bringing together a diverse group of activists and scholars from a range of countries to discuss

---

[10] Azza Basarudin, *Humanizing the Sacred: Sisters in Islam and the Struggle for Gender Justice in Malaysia*. Seattle, WA:: University of Washington Press, 2015, p. 4.

Islamic Family Law Reform" in 2007 in Istanbul.[11] During this meeting, a planning committee was formed to develop the conceptual framework for a new movement for the reform of Muslim family laws and practices along the principle of "musawah" or equality.

In 2009, Musawah was launched in Kuala Lumpur. Two hundred scholars, activists, policy makers, lawyers, and journalists from over 45 countries attended this momentous event. The organisation describes itself as a "global movement for equality and justice in the Muslim family, which advances human rights for women in Muslim contexts, in both their public and private lives".[12] In many ways, Musawah is similar to SIS' advocacy and calls for reform of Muslim family law on issues such as marriage, polygamy, divorce, inheritance, custody and guardianship. What was significant was the collaborative efforts by a range of Muslim scholars competent in classical Islamic jurisprudence (*fiqh*) and modern laws to develop the framework for actions for reform.

In terms of methodology, Musawah adopts a similar approach as SIS where *shari'a* (God's Law) is not synonymous with *fiqh*, which is the human understanding of the divine law. Hence, legal rulings or *ahkam* (sing. *hukum*) that were extracted from the sacred sources (Qur'an and Hadith), are "human, temporal and local" and not absolute and permanent. In addition, legal rulings can be categorised into *'ibadat* (ritual/devotional acts) and *mu'amalat* (social/contractual acts). The former regulate relations between the human and God, and jurists would argue that there is a limited scope for rationalisation, explanation and change. But the *mu'amalat* is human to human relations and therefore is open to rational considerations and social factors, which must conform to values such as fairness, compassion

---

[11] Ziba Mir-Hosseini, *Journeys Toward Gender Equality in Islam*. London, England: Oneworld Academic, 2022, p. 10.

[12] See the website, www.musawah.org.

and justice. Issues concerning women and gender belong to this category and hence have latitudes for change and reform.

Indonesian Women Ulama Congress (KUPI)

While equality or *musawah* has been a key feature of Islamic feminism, critics often equivocate this principle with *identicality*. Hence, detractors of Islamic feminism often argued that equality ignores biological differences between the male and female sex and hence, creates an unnatural state and chaos in gender relations. This criticism has been taken up by Islamic feminists in Indonesia in particular, who developed a response through the principle of *mubadalah* or reciprocity. This principle was initially developed and applied by reformist ulama working with a feminist NGO, Fahmina Institute, which then became the defining methodology of Kongres Ulama Perempuan Indonesia (KUPI/Indonesian Women Ulama Congress).

KUPI is the culmination of almost three decades of engagements by the ulama with reformist ideas on gender. Unlike Malaysia, these engagements had been deep and thorough, particularly within the framework of classical Islamic traditions, by both the ulama and lay activists alike. Islamic feminism in Indonesia could be said to have taken roots in the 1990s when "Islam and feminism converged and proliferated".[13] The convergence could be attributed to the changing consciousness brought by the weakening of patriarchal norms in society. This corresponded with several legal reforms that ended discriminatory practices against women. As a result, egalitarian mental frameworks entered the discursive sphere, leading to the willingness of knowledge producers to rethink several inherited

---

[13] Etin Anwar, *A Genealogy of Islamic Feminism: Pattern and Change in Indonesia.* London; New York: Routledge, 2018, p. 23.

discourses that were patriarchal and sexist in nature, including those derived from the religious traditions.

One example is the study group known as Forum Kajian Kitab Kuning (FK3/Classical Scriptural Studies Forum), helmed by a prominent ulama Masdar F. Masudi and organised by the central leadership of Nahdlatul Ulama (NU) in the late 1980s. One of the outcomes was the publication of *Wajah Baru Relasi Suami Istri*, which is a critique of misogynistic traditions found in the popular *kitab* (religious text) on the rights of husbands and the duties of wives, called *Uqud al-Lujain fi bayan huquq al-zawjain*. Written by a prominent 19th century ulama, Shaykh Nawawi al-Banteni (d. 1897), this *kitab* was used throughout Indonesian *pesantren* (Islamic boarding schools), hence shaping the traditionalist but patriarchal views towards women.

One definitive feature of Indonesian discourse on Islamic feminism — exemplified by KUPI's methodological framework known as *mubadalah* (reciprocity) — is its insistence on theological before legal reforms. Starting from the ontological assertion that any form of unequal relations could lead to injustices, the *mubadalah* framework critiques the dichotomous view of male superiority vis-a-vis female inferiority and how the latter's worthiness is measured in relation to male benefits. This is the root of stigmatisation towards women.

For example, when men's actions bring harm or violence towards women, the fault lies with women and therefore it is the women who must take measures to protect themselves or for other men to protect the women. Such stigmatisation could lead to further marginalisation, subordination, coercion and double burden on women. Viewed from this perspective, the *mubadalah* framework sees gender oppression as equally affecting men. This is because such unequal relations are based on the premise of the strong dominating the weak, which means that the stronger male could dominate the weaker male and while men dominate over women, the stronger women would dominate over their weaker kind.

As a theological approach, *mubadalah* views gender relations through the lens of reciprocity, which means: 1) both genders are equally responsible in protecting the good and preventing harm, 2) strength in any form should not be a reason to oppress another person, and 3) the stronger persons — male or female — are equally responsible to ensure that the weaker ones in society are treated with dignity. This reciprocity is based on the Islamic principle of *tauhid* or monotheism where only God is supreme while humans are created equal in status and dignity.

According to Nur Rofiah, a female theologian and Qur'anic scholar, *tauhid* "had brought a new lens towards status, position, responsibility and worthiness of both male and female".[14] Firstly, in accordance with the Qur'an, the female was not created from the male (Q.4:1); instead, they were created biologically from the same source (Q.23:12-14). Secondly, man is not the primary being while woman is not a secondary being. Both are primary beings tasked as the stewards of earth (*khalifah fil 'ard*) while in front of God, both are secondary beings as the created. Thirdly, women do not exist in order to serve men. Instead both are required to serve God and be of benefit to each other equally. Fourthly, there is no absolute obedience and duty of the woman towards the man, and both must obey God and cooperate to fulfil their duties to do good. Fifthly, the human qualities of the male and female are not determined by their sex but their piety that is measured by their contributions to humanity.

* * *

What we observed thus far is that Islamic feminism as exemplified by the movements mentioned above are rooted in Islam as a faith

---

[14] Nur Rofiah, "Prolog: Qira'ah Mubadalah sebagai Syarat Tafsir Agama Adil Gender", in Faqihuddin Abdul Kodir *Qira'ah Mubadalah: Tafsir Progresif untuk Keadilan Gender dalam Islam*. Yogyakarta: IRCiSoD, 2019, p. 32.

determined by the sacred texts (Qur'an and Hadith). Where Islamic feminism departs from patriarchal forms of Islam is their interpretations of these source-texts as well as their critical evaluation of traditions located in a context where gender relations were viewed through a hierarchical lens, i.e. female as the weaker sex, hence to be subordinated by the male, while her religious duties to God are tied to serving men and her obedience to the male authority in domestic as well as public affairs.

In positioning Islamic feminism as a theological as well as legal reformist movement of the modern world, it is also marked by a changing consciousness towards the ethical, as discussed in the scholarship of prominent theologian, jurist and legal professor, Khaled Abou El Fadl.[15] This is also strengthened by Indonesian gender scholar, Etin Anwar's observations on Islamic feminism's ethical approach towards Islam that 1) locates the oppressive sites toward women using Islamic feminist analysis, 2) strategically addresses specific women's needs and concerns, 3) proposes relevant solutions, and (4) simultaneously draws on Islamic values that empower women and centre their agency.[16] It will be apt therefore to say that Islamic feminism is the most well developed reformist discourse of the modern period, and hence, presents the greatest lesson for other faith-based progressive movements dealing with modern challenges and the burden of traditions.

The challenge of religious conservatism

Despite the advancements made by Muslim feminists to further the cause of gender equality and justice, it could be argued that the discourse on feminism within Islam is still relatively marginal within

---

[15] Khaled Abou El Fadl *Speaking in God's Name: Islamic Law, Authority and Women.* Oxford, U.K.: Oneworld Academic, 2001.

[16] Etin Anwar *A Genealogy of Islamic Feminism: Pattern and Change in Indonesia.* op. cit.; p. 251.

the broader Muslim community. There has been a lot of backlash against the push for gender justice, notably by the proponents of the Islamisation of society, otherwise known as "Islamists".[17]

What we see now is the rising conservatism and authoritarianism in Muslim societies, which is also patriarchal and misogynist in nature. It further entrenches patriarchal and conservative norms through social media and popular culture as well, which means that Islamists are no longer on the fringes of society, but are gaining mainstream clout and legitimacy. Observably, the Islamist movement in the region is dynamic and fluid, and it has gained further traction due to the development of regional networks and endorsement by political and community elites.

This version of Islam and the drive to Islamise society, in relation to gender norms, reduces women to their bodies (i.e. both sexual and reproductive functions) and is about the reassertion of male control over women, both in the public and domestic spheres. It is more apt therefore to draw parallels on this with the wider emergence of what the German political thinker, Susanne Kaiser (2022) termed as "political masculinity". In other words, what we are seeing, particularly with the rise of assertive right wing populism and hardline fundamentalism that inform conservative movements everywhere, are common reactions to the present global situation.

Kaiser opined that radical economic changes brought by neoliberalism have primarily affected men. It is not merely a matter of men losing their jobs. It is men expecting secure jobs while believing that they are entitled to be the breadwinner, head of the household and unquestioned decision maker. Hence, slogans like

---

[17] While the term may be contested and be referred to a wide spectrum of movements that seek to implement Islamic supremacy and rule, we refer to "Islamists" as social and/or political actors who 1) assert the supremacy of Islam over all other "non- or unIslamic" systems in society, 2) view Islam in an exclusivist, monolithic and absolutist manner, and 3) seek to impose, coerce or persuade others to adopt and submit to this form of Islam as a matter of obedience to God's will and power that is not distinguished from theirs.

"make it great again" and "take back control" reveal a gendered feeling of losing control.[18] This is the authoritarian backlash that is also found in anti-feminist movements within Muslim societies. They expressed themselves through peddling narratives that are predominantly about dictating the women's attire, especially the *hijab*, and reasserting male authority over women in highly gendered and segregated spaces.

Even in a relatively secular Singapore, we observe the same preoccupation with women's attire, such as the public campaigning for nurses to wear the *hijab* at the workplace. While it can be viewed through the lens of human rights and the freedom of religion, the largely male proponents of the *hijab* speak of it as a matter of absolute religious obligation. What is not noted however, is that the overwhelming pressure placed on Muslim women to don the *hijab* reduced the *hijab* issue to a matter of religious obligation versus the decision to work. It was as though women had to choose between wearing the *hijab* or keeping their jobs (and in some cases, to choose between attending religious or secular schools), when historically, the *hijab* has never been made an obligation to the extent that it is done now.[19]

It can be argued that given the increasingly dual-income nature of Singaporean households now, there is a greater understanding of the need for women to participate in the labour force. It is accepted as necessary, even though it is often still argued that women's economic contribution is secondary and that it is more of a charity rather than the women's shared responsibility in the household. In the patriarchal Muslim society, Islamic discourse is used to further entrench the male breadwinner and head of the household model,

---

[18] Susanne Kaiser, *Political Masculinity*. New York: Polity, 2022.,

[19] See for example the nuanced views offered by Indonesian Qur'an scholar, M. Quraish Shihab in his book, *Jilbab, Pakaian Wanita Muslimah: Pandangan Ulama Masa Lalu dan Cendekiawan Kontemporer*. Ciputat, Tangerang: Lentera Hati, 2004.

the presumption of women's inherent domesticity and the subservience of women's unpaid care work to men's paid work. Women are also expected to seek permission from their fathers or spouses to go to work. The preoccupation with the *hijab* can thus be seen as a last bastion of control over women, given the socioeconomic realities which necessitate women's economic participation and contribution.

The drive to further entrench a patriarchal and authoritarian version of Islam also entails the demonisation of feminism and the so-called "liberal Muslims".[20] According to Jumblatt (2021), one key characteristic of liberal Muslims is their challenging of "uncritical adherence to traditions found in the Islamic corpus of knowledge" and calling for "a fundamental rethinking of certain issues". This is especially true, according to him, "in the domain of gender and sexuality" where they "question injunctions which they [liberal Muslims] deem to be not in line with the Islamic spirit and principle of equality".[21]

Despite how ideas such as freedom and equality could be constructed from within the Islamic traditions as done by the ulama and activists in SIS, Musawah and KUPI, they are nonetheless seen as threatening to the kind of Islam understood by the conservative Muslim public. As mentioned earlier, state instruments such as fatwas have been used to pressure a ban on Muslim gender justice

---

[20] We note the highly contentious use of the term "liberal" to refer to a range of Muslim scholars and activists who offer a reformist view of Islam that is critical of traditions while finding compatibilities between Islam and modern ideas, such as the separation of state and religion (secularism), equality of religions before the state (pluralism), democracy, and gender equality. Many of these ideas, according to liberal Muslims, are not entirely modern but could be found within Islam. Liberal Muslims therefore put an emphasis on the values of freedom, tolerance, and equality. Democracy and human rights are also the main focus of liberal Muslims' social and political activism. Sometimes, liberal Muslims are also described as "progressive Muslims". The authors of this essay contend that there is a difference between the two, although there are many similarities between them — which is a subject best discussed in another paper.

[21] Walid Jumblatt Abdullah, *Islam in a Secular State: Muslim Activism in Singapore*. Amsterdam: Amsterdam University Press, 2021, p. 163.

movements such as Sisters In Islam in Malaysia. It also comes with the spread of prejudicial views and hate speeches targeting Islamic feminists and liberal Muslims. Some common observable tropes are: Islamic feminists are "destroying Islam from within". The anti-liberal Muslim propaganda has become increasingly more mainstream, as it is spread through both social and mainstream media by Muslim elites and organisations.[22]

In Singapore, efforts have been made to censure and demonise Muslims who are labelled as "liberal". These include escalating complaints to religious authorities, the Islamic Religious Council of Singapore (MUIS) or calling for the ban of foreign speakers who are deemed as "liberal" from entering Singapore. Public talks have also been organised to warn the public of this "threat" of the liberal Muslims, which includes the so-called "dangers of feminism".

The response by WALI in Singapore

In Singapore, Islamic feminism is a late phenomenon, with very few proponents. A small experiment, however, emerged in 2010 with the formation of a working group that called itself Not-Just-Inheritance (NJI), which was later renamed WALI, an acronym for Women and Law in Islam. NJI/WALI was a synergy between several social activists from the secular feminist organisation AWARE with a loose network of self-identified progressive Muslims called "The Reading Group (RG)". The core members include lawyers, academics and professionals.

While the initial years of NJI was focusing on the unjust consequences of the application of *faraid* (inheritance) law that favoured the male and agnatic beneficiaries as coded into AMLA

---

[22] For a discussion on the mainstreaming of anti-liberal Islam prejudice in Singapore and the region, see Nurul Fadiah Johari, "Fearing the Enemy Within: A Study of Intra-Muslim Prejudice among Singaporean Muslims", Academic Exercise, National University of Singapore, 2017.

(Administration of Muslim Law Act)'s Sections 60, 111 and 112, members soon realised that this was related to a host of other issues, including 1) the lack of awareness of the basic distinctions between the divine law (*shari'a*), Islamic jurisprudence (*fiqh*), and *Syariah* as codified state laws introduced during the colonial period that mirrored the British common law, 2) the absence of critical engagements with emerging fields of Islamic feminism and reforms made in other countries, and 3) how a conservative interpretation of Islamic law in AMLA was also holding back the government of Singapore's full adoption of CEDAW (Convention on the Elimination of all Forms of Discrimination Against Women), particularly over Articles 2 and 16, which the government argued might not be consistent with AMLA.

Hence, NJI was renamed WALI and embarked on public education efforts that introduced and informed Muslims on Islamic feminism, the problems of patriarchy, and the rights of Muslim women within Singapore's legal system on family law matters such as marriage, divorce, child custody, and inheritance.

Between 2010 to 2017, WALI organised talks, seminars and workshops. Several members of WALI also participated in regional and international conferences and training on Muslim gender issues in Cairo, Zanzibar, Kuala Lumpur and Jakarta. Two landmark programmes were organised in Singapore. In 2012, a seminar called "Rethinking the Muslim Marriage Contract" was organised with the support of AWARE, the Department of Malay Studies at the National University of Singapore (NUS), the Faculty of Arts and Social Sciences Religion Cluster at NUS, and Leftwrite Center.

The seminar's publicity attracted considerable backlash from the conservative Muslim public who urged the authorities to step in to ban the seminar because the presenters included prominent "liberal

Muslim" scholars, namely Indonesian feminist *kiyai* (religious leader), Husein Muhammad and Iranian-born then University of London's professorial research associate, Dr Ziba Mir-Hosseini. Several days before the seminar, the organisers received a call from the police inquiring about the event, which indicated a report had been made. The seminar proceeded with no incident.

With the support of AWARE's GEC (Gender Equality is Our Culture) project grant, WALI organised another landmark programme in 2014. A two-day training workshop called "Harmonious Family in Islam" was conducted for Singapore gender activists to empower them with the tools of Islamic feminism in understanding family laws, tackling gender-based violence, and how to unpack the male bias in Arabic language and interpretations of the Qur'an. The workshop was primarily conducted by two of Indonesia's leading scholars on gender, Imam Nakha'i (currently the Commissioner of Indonesia's National Commission on Violence Against Women/ KOMNAS Perempuan) and Dr Nur Rofiah (lecturer at the Institute of Qur'anic Studies/PTQI, Jakarta). WALI's contributions to further the cause of gender justice in the Singaporean Muslim community were recognised through the Gender Equality award given by AWARE in 2017.

Notably, the GEC grant by AWARE was pivotal in sparking interest on gender equality issues among young Muslims. Several initiatives emerged as a result of the foundations laid by WALI. These include Penawar (a religious trauma support group for women), and Beyond the Hijab (a blog for Muslim women to share their experiences and challenges on a variety of themes). In 2018, members of Beyond the Hijab launched a book titled *Growing Up Perempuan* that was published by AWARE. The book was met with mixed reactions. The rawness of the depictions of several Muslim women's experiences growing up within the conservative Muslim setting of Singapore had drawn sympathy as well as unhappiness. Unfortunately, it was largely met with silence within the Muslim leadership who were probably uncomfortable that such a sensitive topic was made public.

Given the insurmountable task facing feminist Muslims, some of the younger activists have turned to the online space within the last decade. This was facilitated by the rise of social media and platforms that are less regulated and hence, allowing a more democratic exchange of ideas that challenge the dominant narratives on Muslim women. Observably, there are now online spaces for queer Muslims as well, to develop a sense of belonging in an environment that is still very intolerant and sometimes hostile towards them.

Given the current socio-religious climate, it is still very difficult for feminist Muslims to conduct activities like knowledge sharing and capacity-building workshops in mainstream spaces such as mosques or community centres. There also has not been much support for Islamic feminism by community leaders, which thus further embolden the conservative and patriarchal voices to assert their so-called "mainstream-ness" and push away any attempt at reforms that could strengthen gender equality or empower women within the context of the Malay/Muslim community.

It is within this context that the call for gender justice and development of Islamic feminism is more important now than ever. It is also tied to the greater struggle against rising religious conservatism and authoritarianism which seek to erase the rich diversity within Islamic traditions and the religious freedom that Muslims as citizens should be able to enjoy like any other. The struggles of Islamic feminists must therefore be seen within the larger contestations within Islam as the faith confronts societal changes and the evolving needs of a modern and globalised world.

Conclusion

We have shown that Islamic feminism offers a vision for Muslims who want to remain faithful to Islam but feel that the gap between the values espoused by Islam and reality of oppression and marginalisation of women in Muslim societies, needs to be addressed. It is our position that religion does not hamper efforts to achieve gender equality. Instead, religion can be a source of inspiration as it did in the founding moments of Islam, although we acknowledge that a lot more needs to be done to fully realise its vision.

According to Badran, "Religion from the very start has been integral to the feminisms that Muslim women have constructed, both explicitly and implicitly"[23] and this paper has shown how this might augur well for the future as Muslim women and men reclaim the spaces that have been ceded to patriarchy in the name of Islam.

However, given the challenges posed by the rise of conservative forces that want to perpetuate and entrench a patriarchal vision for Muslim society, we argue for the need to support the development of Islamic feminism in Singapore and the region. Here, we conclude by way of proposing a few broad strategies to continue the momentum that has already been set over the past 20 years.

Firstly, there is a need to recognise the need for a regional feminist network. Such a network may plug the gaps in resources and develop a shared pool of experts and expertise. Such a network, in some ways, has been forged where members of WALI had frequent contacts with their regional counterparts such as SIS and a range of ulama, public intellectuals and activists across Indonesia. However, the network must also look into the broader need to seed progressive ideas on Islam beyond gender issues.

---

[23] Margot Badran, *Feminism and Islam: Secular and Religious Convergences.* Oxford, England: Oneworld, 2009, p. 2.

Ultimately, we recognise that the challenges facing gender equality are tied to the absence or weakness of democratic institutions and ethos within society. Since 2020, SIS has developed a project to understand and counter religious conservatism through workshops and seminars that involve participants from Singapore and Indonesia. Such efforts should continue as part of capacity-building that can widen the spheres of actions for Islamic feminists and progressive activists.

In addition, it is important to recognise the importance of community-building that exists to provide not only critical alternatives through discursive efforts but also spaces where Muslims who disagree or do not fit into the Islamist narrative can foster a sense of belonging. This will empower more Muslims to develop an Islamic identity that is independent of the kind that is promoted by Islamists, and to confidently articulate a vision of Islam that challenges the authoritarian Islamist version. It is about taking spaces away from the control of Islamists so as to provide a more humanistic and just vision of Islam.

Secondly, there is a need to develop a vision of gender equality inspired by and in engagement with the religious traditions. One of the main criticisms against feminism in Muslim society is that it is an import from the West and alien to Islam. Others would argue that Muslims do not need feminism because gender justice for women was already established and perfected during the Prophetic period in 7th century Arabia. Muslim feminists should take these criticisms seriously and show the rootedness of Islamic feminism within the traditions.

However, what Muslim feminists can offer is not just a re-engagement with the Islamic traditions, but an understanding of contemporary contexts and problems faced by women. Therefore, part of the development of Islamic feminism is to build on the corpus of Islamic knowledge and to make Islamic feminism a living part of that corpus as well, through contemporary knowledge. This will challenge the pronouncements made by Islamists that Islamic traditions have all the solutions to present-day problems. It is important to acknowledge the work of gender justice as promoted by Muslim scholars who are trained in the traditional as well as the modern sciences.

This must be complemented by a synergy of perspectives from contemporary social sciences, including the adoption of a gender lens and sensitisation for key influencers in society. Muslim feminists therefore must also address the false dichotomy between the "religious versus secular" knowledge and the assumption that only those who are trained in the traditional Islamic sciences get to speak on issues concerning Muslims. There has to be more dialogues and engagements between Muslim scholars and activists who come from a diverse range of disciplines so as to properly develop a discourse on gender that is rooted in tradition and which also critically understands the complexities of contemporary issues.

Last but not least, there is a need to ground Islamic knowledge and values with lived realities. Islamic feminism therefore must go beyond the theoretical and be able to address contemporary problems faced by Muslim women in all areas beyond the religious. In this article, we acknowledge the importance of the work done by SIS, Musawah and KUPI in trying to develop Islamic paradigms that are grounded in the lived realities of Muslim women.

This means that Islamic feminism is not just a discursive endeavour that is focused on theories and abstract knowledge, but it is aimed to address concrete problems through the Islamic traditions as a source of values and inspiration. For instance, KUPI is committing itself towards ending child marriages and SIS commits a lot of its efforts in tackling domestic violence through their TeleNisa programme.

* * *

There are many layers to the work of Muslim feminists. Aside from providing critical and gender-just perspectives of Islam and advocating for legal and policy changes, the work also includes bringing about solutions to real world problems and building communities. In this regard, it is thus crucial that Islamic feminism is multi-faceted and also class conscious in its approach towards advocating for gender justice. The development of Islamic feminism in Muslim society therefore deserves closer attention for anyone who is interested to see a more just and equal world where women are not the subordinates of men and that both sexes are equally contributing and capable partners in making this world a better place for all.

Mohamed Imran Mohamed Taib is an independent researcher, writer, and consultant. He is the founding director of Dialogue Centre and editor of Progresif.net. He writes on issues of religion and society, and has commentaries published in various dailies, book chapters and journals. He is co-editor of a book compilation of critical essays on Malay society, titled Budi Kritik *(Ethos Books, 2019; expanded edition with Math Paper Press, 2020) with Nurul Fadiah Johari.*

Nurul Fadiah Johari is currently working as a research associate at the National University of Singapore. Her current research interests include sociology of religion, social inequalities and critical discourses on mental health. She has written articles and book chapters for Singaporean publications in both English and Malay on topics concerning religion, gender and mental health.

References

Abdul Qodir, Faqihuddin. 2019. *Qira'ah Mubadalah: Tafsir Progresif untuk Keadilan Gender dalam Islam.* Yogyakarta: IRCiSoD.

Abdul Qodir, Faqihuddin. 2022. *Metodologi Fatwa KUPI: Pokok-Pokok Pikiran Keagamaan Kongres Ulama Perempuan.* Cirebon: KUPI.

Abou El Fadl, Khaled. 2001. *Speaking in God's Name: Islamic Law, Authority and Women.* Oxford, U.K.: Oneworld Academic.

Abu-Lughod, Lila. 2013. *Do Muslim Women Need Saving?* Cambridge, Mass.: Harvard University Press.

AlSamara, Kinda. 2018. "Muhammad 'Abduh: Islam and New Urbanity in the Nineteenth-Century Arab World". *Australian Journal of Islamic Studies* 3(1): 63–79.

Amin, Qasim. 2005 (1899). *The Liberation of Women and The New Woman.* Tr. by Samiha Sidhom Peterson. Cairo, Egypt: The American University in Cairo Press.

Anwar, Etin. 2018. *A Genealogy of Islamic Feminism: Pattern and Change in Indonesia.* London: Routledge.

Aslan, Ednan, Marcia Hermansen and Elif Medeni, eds. 2013. *Muslima Theology: The Voices of Muslim Women Theologians.* Frankfurt am Main: Peter Lang.

Badran, Margot. 2009. *Feminism and Islam: Secular and Religious Convergences.* Oxford, England: Oneworld.

Basarudin, Azza. 2015. *Humanizing the Sacred: Sisters in Islam and the Struggle for Gender Justice in Malaysia.* Seattle, WA: University of Washington Press.

Freedman, Estelle B. 2002. *No Turning Back: The History of Feminism and the Future of Women.* New York: Ballantine Books.

Hamzah, Abu Bakar. 1991. *Al-Imam: Its Role in Malay Society, 1905–1908.* Kuala Lumpur: Pustaka Antara.

Hourani, Albert. 2009, r.1962. *Arabic Thought in the Liberal Age 1798–1939.* Cambridge, Mass.: CambridgeUniversity Press.

Johari, Nurul Fadiah. 2017. "Fearing the Enemy Within: A Study of Intra-Muslim Prejudice among Singaporean Muslims". Academic Exercise. Singapore: National University of Singapore.

Jumblatt Abdullah, Walid. 2021. *Islam in a Secular State: Muslim Activism in Singapore*. Amsterdam: Amsterdam University Press.

Kaiser, Susanne. 2022. *Political Masculinity*. New York: Polity.

Ralph Lerner, tr. 1974, *Averroes on Plato's Republic*. Ithaca: Cornell University Press.

Mir-Hosseini, Ziba. 2022. *Journeys Toward Gender Equality in Islam*. London, England: Oneworld.

Mir-Hosseini, Ziba, Mulki Al-Sharmani and Jana Rumminger, eds. (2015). *Men in Charge? Rethinking Authority in Muslim Legal Tradition*. London, England: Oneworld Academic.

Mulia, Musdah. 2005. *Muslimah Reformis: Perempuan Pembaru Keagamaan*. Bandung: Mizan.

Walters, Margaret. 2005. *Feminism: A Very Short Introduction*. Oxford, England: Oxford University Press.

Learning to Chart
their Own Paths

"A teacher who is not an inquirer nor a problem-solver is hardly likely to provide the right intellectual climate for his pupils to ask constructive questions or develop critical ability."

~ Pioneering educator Ruth Wong, cited in SingTeach,
National Institute of Education, July/August 2010

CHAPTER 11

A Future School Where Children Can Enjoy Learning

Kho Ee Moi

For more than a decade, Singapore has been ranked among the world's top performing education systems, with its students consistently scoring higher than the OECD average in the Program for International Student Assessment (PISA) which measures students' knowledge and skills in reading, mathematics, and science. The 2022 PISA results for Singapore showed that compared to the OECD average, more Singapore students performed at the highest levels of proficiency (Level 5 or 6) in at least one subject and similarly, a greater number of students attained a minimum proficiency level (Level 2 or higher) in all three subjects. (OECD, 2023)

While we can be proud of our system, we should also be aware that all is not rosy as the drive to maintain this ranking comes at a cost. The pressure of sustaining academic excellence has affected both educators and students. There is a high attrition rate among teachers and the average length of service of primary and secondary school teachers is between five and nine years. (Hirschmann, 2022)

The pressure for students to perform well academically has also caused many of them to be enrolled in after-school learning or tuition centres. Instead of being able to relax after school, students are subjected to even more 'enrichment' or 'remedial' classes. It is no wonder that a study conducted by the National University of Singapore in collaboration with the Ministry of Education and Institute of Mental Health reported that one in three youths in Singapore indicated that they had experienced mental health symptoms such as sadness, anxiety, and loneliness and one in six had externalised their mental health symptoms in ways such as rule-breaking and aggression (Ang, 2022).

An issue of concern is the high incidence of bullying in school. The 2018 PISA factsheet indicated that 26 per cent of Singapore students reported being bullied a few times a month. This is higher than the average of 23 per cent across the other OECD countries (OECD 2019). The 2022 PISA study found that 15 per cent of girls in Singapore reported being bullied, compared with the OECD average for girls of 20 per cent. But the percentage of Singapore boys who reported bullying, at 26 per cent, was higher than the OECD average of 21 per cent.

The 2018 report noted that frequently bullied students were more likely to have skipped school. Students who received greater support from parents and whose schools have a safer and better disciplinary climate were more likely to value attending school.

Recently, while reading about the purpose of education, I came across this excerpt from Ken & Kate Robinson:

"Learning is the process of acquiring new skills and understanding. Education is an organized system of learning. Training is a type of education that is focused on learning

specific skills. A school is a community of learners: a group that comes together to learn with and from each other. It is vital that we differentiate these terms: children love to learn, they do it naturally; many have a hard time with education, and some have big problems with school." (Robinson & Robinson, 2022)

The differentiated definitions of the concepts of education, training, and school was enlightening. But what drew my attention was the statement that "children love to learn …many have a hard time with education, and some have big problems with school".

It is such a sad contrast that children naturally love to learn but some have big problems with school — the very agency through which organised learning takes place. When I reflect on my children's and my own school experiences, I begin to appreciate the truth of that statement. School was never always enjoyable. There were many days when I dreaded going to school and my self-esteem was often at rock bottom because there was only one measure of success and that was my academic performance determined by standardised pen and paper tests.

But getting a good educational qualification is crucial for many reasons and despite the high level of stress in Singapore schools, most children will need to be enrolled in the public school system. How then do we improve the system so that our children can enjoy attending and learning in school? What would an ideal school look like and how can we achieve this ideal? Here are some of my daydreams on this subject.

School organisation

The ideal school will provide elementary to post-secondary education for children from the ages of approximately six to eighteen. Students from age 6 to 12 will attend elementary school and then move on to secondary (age 13 to 16) and then to post-secondary school (age 17–18). These are just approximate ages for the different school levels as movement between the levels will be rather fluid, depending on the interest, knowledge and skill levels of the students. For example, a student who is 12 years old and shows interest and ability to take on higher level studies will be encouraged to do so.

It will be a full day school from 8:30am to about 5:30pm with a half hour recess at mid-morning and a one-and-a-half-hour break for lunch and siesta. The hours may seem long, but the afternoon hours will be spent on committee work, going out for field investigations, or project work and discussions, engaging in activities in the community, consultation with teachers or other co-curricular activities.

Having a full-day school will eliminate the need for after-school care for elementary level students as well as supplementary tuition which many parents in Singapore seem to feel is a need for their children. Onerous, mundane homework that focuses only on memory work or drilling will not be assigned. School will end at about the time most parents leave the office, so children will be home at approximately the same time as their parents. The goal is that parents and children will be able to have relaxed and meaningful family time when they are home.

Lessons are one hour long but there will be short breaks of about 10 minutes between lessons. These breaks are important for students to consolidate, reflect on what they have just learned, rest or move to the next class. Class size is kept small, with a maximum of 15 students, so that teachers can give sufficient attention to and track the progress of each learner in the class. Every class that has special needs students will have, besides the main instructor, a special needs educator in the room to help them. Students meet in Form classes at the start of the day and then move to their respective special interest classes according to their interest. These special interest classes may be organised by subject area or interdisciplinary areas. Students have free choice of what they want to study.

School vision, climate & culture

The school envisions graduates who are global citizens, knowledgeable, competent, confident, and compassionate and who will contribute towards improving society and the world at large. Students are valued as individuals with potential to learn and achieve and not viewed as digits that will increase the school's position in ranking lists.

The school climate is safe, warm, and inclusive. Staff and students in the school are secure in the knowledge that school is a safe place in which to work and study. Students will recognise that this is a place where they are accepted and can be themselves. It is also a place where they can develop a secure identity and positive self-esteem as well as discover their strengths. A recent study by the National University of Singapore found that about one in three youths in Singapore has reported having mental health symptoms such as anxiety and loneliness. The same study asserted that positive self-image and building relationships are important factors for healthy mental well-being (Ang, 2022) Thus, self-confidence, self-esteem, strong relationships and acceptance are important in the culture of this ideal school.

There is also a culture of respect for all and zero tolerance of any acts of prejudices of race, religion, socio-economic status, gender, sexuality, and disability. Bullying, violence and discrimination will not be tolerated. School personnel have open minds and are careful not to stereotype children by race, gender, faith, nationality, or any other attribute. In this way, children are not boxed in by adults' conception of how they should act and what they should learn. Care will be taken to ensure that there is no gender discrimination or gender stereotyping in the school. Girls and boys will be treated equally and there will be no gender differentiated curriculum. For example, boys and girls alike will learn STEM (science, technology, engineering and mathematics) subjects as well as home economics. Leadership opportunities will be offered equally to students irrespective of their gender.

The school will take steps to ensure that children from less privileged homes will not be disadvantaged. Research has shown that socio-economic status (SES) has a direct impact on children's achievement in school. Children of lower SES have lower academic performance than their higher SES peers. A NUS study on the impact of family SES on young children's academic performance revealed a significant achievement gap among preschool children aged 3 to 6 (Yeung & Chen, 2023). Family income and parental education had a significant impact on these young children.

It is thus important to mediate the effects of SES and family environment to close the achievement gap. Equity rather than equality will be practised in the ideal school, and children from lower income families will be provided with the necessary economic, social, and cultural capital to ensure that they are not disadvantaged by the lack of finances. In this way, the school will ensure a more level playing field so that the government-espoused principle of meritocracy can be more effectively realised.

Minimal school rules

School rules will be discussed with and voted on by students and regularly reviewed. Currently, many schools have rules that focus on external manifestations of discipline such as conformity with the school's dress code. Over time, there have been many changes in the rules about the appropriate length of hair and skirt and how they should be worn. For example, in the 1980s, girls were not allowed to wear their hair long. There were a number of cases of girls' hair being cut to appropriate lengths because they had flouted the school rule that hair length should not reach below the collar. In the 1990s, schools discouraged girls from sporting very short boyish crops out of fear that they would not appear feminine. Boys, on the other hand, had to keep their hair cut short and above the collar.

This obsessive focus on dress codes is the result of the fear that the distinctions between masculinity and femininity would be blurred and reflects the conservative gender ideologies of the school leadership. In my ideal school, Singapore society has progressed to the point where hair length for both male and females is no longer an issue. We should not impose a conservative idea of masculinity or femininity on children but allow them to construct a healthy and positive identity of their own, one that allows them to aspire to greatness and not be confined within restrictive social norms and expectations. Thus, school rules, I feel, should not obsess on outward physical appearance other than to stress on cleanliness and neatness. The school rules in my ideal school will be kept to a minimum, with emphasis on virtues such as punctuality, respect, and care and concern for others.

Discipline in the school will be managed by a student committee with teachers as mentors. There are clear and transparent consequences of misbehaviour and breaches of school rules and students are made aware of these. The discipline committee will discuss misdemeanours and decide on disciplinary actions to be taken. There will be no public caning or corporal punishment of any sort. Currently caning of boys is allowed albeit with strict guidelines on how it is to be carried out. Caning, I feel, does not achieve any corrective purpose but may, in fact, send an unintended message that violence is justifiable. It may not even be effective as a deterrent as, after a while, some boys begin to see being caned as a badge of honour. That boys and not girls can be caned also communicates an implicit message that girls are weaker, boys are tougher and therefore can be caned. This misconception needs to be eradicated.

Counselling and Reflective Practice are more humane and effective approaches to correcting misbehaviour. Everyone makes mistakes and reflecting on these mistakes is integral to learning and changing behaviour. Children respond more to care and genuine concern from teachers, peers, and other adults than to stern and impersonal punishment. There is a lot more value in helping students to reflect on the reasons for their poor choices of action and thinking about how they can make better choices. It will help students learn to regulate their emotions and impulses a lot better than caning ever can.

Curriculum and pedagogy

A social constructivist approach to teaching and learning is advocated. This approach views learning as a collaborative process which takes place in response to environmental stimuli. Hence, social interaction and collaboration are important facets of instruction in the classroom.

In the ideal classroom, the curriculum is child-centred, arising from students' own curiosity so that they become explorers and problem solvers in finding out answers to their questions. Meaningful play and practical applied learning for students to internalise new learning are incorporated. I once watched a video of a physics teacher demonstrating the principles of centrifugal force to a group of young children. It was a simple demonstration, but it fascinated the children and demonstrated so clearly how centrifugal force works.

Lessons like these are far more effective than the usual teacher talk. Teachers act as facilitators of learning rather than founts of knowledge and wisdom and they use a blended approach and multimodal ways to facilitate learning. Advanced technology such as virtual reality (VR) and artificial intelligence (AI) will be carefully and meaningfully harnessed to enhance student learning. For example, VR can be used to bring students to the past to understand the conditions of people in that society and time period. Regarding the use of AI such as ChatGPT, teachers will need to evaluate the potential of such technologies and teach students to ethically use these tools to enhance their learning.

So what should children learn in school? This is a very challenging and often contested issue. At the elementary school level, the 3Rs — reading, writing, and arithmetic — are fundamental knowledge and skills. Children need to be well grounded in literacy and numeracy to be able to learn, communicate, and function efficiently when they grow up. Besides the 3Rs, elementary school children should be exposed to as wide a range of fields of knowledge as possible. They should be able to learn in fun ways about science, be introduced to basic scientific inquiry, learn about mathematics through games and puzzles, be exposed to the literary arts and drama, learn about the social sciences and acquire sound physical and mental health practices.

At the secondary and post-secondary levels, students may begin to deepen their knowledge and competencies in their areas of interest and aptitude. They should be given the freedom to choose their areas of study and learn them at the level that they are capable of. Having said that, there are vital knowledge, skills and attributes needed to prepare children for the 21st century and to enable them to successfully navigate through an increasingly volatile, uncertain, complex, and ambiguous (VUCA) world. The Singapore Ministry of Education (MOE) has developed a framework of 21st Century Competencies (21CC) and student outcomes which include Core Values, Social-Emotional Competencies, and Competencies for a

Globalised World (MOE, 2022). This framework, I feel, is very valuable in guiding the construction of curriculum in schools.

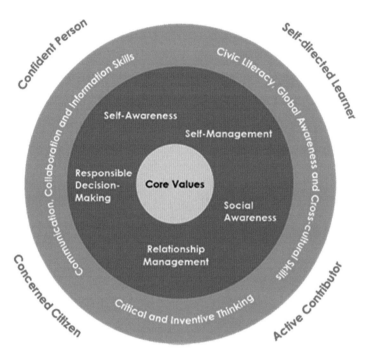

Source: https://www.moe.gov.sg/education-in-sg/21st-century-competencies

The core values and dispositions highlighted in the 21CC are indeed critical for the 21st century and need to undergird everything that students learn in school. Respect, integrity, care and concern for others and the environment, resilience and harmony are all vital for successful living in a VUCA world.

The idea of respect for the rights of individuals and gender equality are also important values that need to be taught in the school. As highlighted by Mr K. Shanmugam, Minister for Law & Home Affairs, the idea of gender equality, that everyone has to be treated equally and with respect, has to be taught from a very young age to all boys and girls (Shanmugam, K. 2020).

Thus, an age-appropriate sexuality education programme should be implemented throughout the different school levels so that young people will have a clearer understanding of the human anatomy, human reproduction, gender identity and orientation, and learn to develop healthy relationships. Sexuality education is important as it enables students to develop clarity in values, attitudes and dispositions, roles and relationships. This is necessary to bring about a whole paradigm shift in how society views gender issues such as gender bias, misogyny, violence against women, sexual harassment in the workplace, voyeurism, homophobia, and so on. Mindsets need to change, and it can happen only when these ideas of equal rights and respect are inculcated at a young age.

In order for students to be self-aware, they need to develop a positive personal identity and have a good understanding of themselves, their likes, dislikes, strengths and weaknesses. Resilience is important and they should develop a growth mindset, feel empowered to explore and ask questions, and be curious and eager to learn. Teachers should help students to see errors and failures as opportunities for growth and encourage children to have the discipline and willpower to persevere even in the face of repeated failures. Discipline means that they are not averse to repeatedly work at seemingly mundane tasks in order to master the necessary skills.

Students will need to learn social skills in order to get along well with others, communicate effectively and embrace cooperation and collaborative work. Empathy, compassion and care for others, particularly those with special needs, should also be emphasised in the curriculum. Bullying is rather pervasive in schools. This may take the form of verbal, physical or even cyber bullying. This is abhorrent and students in my ideal school will be taught not to be tolerant of bullying in any form and to speak up for the weak. As cyber bullying has become more prevalent with technological advances and increased use of social media, students will be taught social netiquette, how to be respectful, thoughtful and considerate in what they share and say online. They will also learn how to protect themselves against cyber bullies and how to help friends who are being bullied.

Critical and creative thinking

Besides values and dispositions, what else is critical in the curriculum? For a long time, the emphasis in Singapore schools has been on STEM subjects. When I was a student, the practice was to channel students into Science, Arts or Commerce courses according to their academic results. If you were channelled into classes studying the three sciences (Physics, Chemistry and Biology), it meant you were the cream of the crop. That was when Singapore was a young, industrialising nation and graduates in science and technology were required for the economy. With the change in our economic focus to a knowledge-based one, the focus on teaching subject-based content in isolation from each other is no longer sufficient to prepare our children for the future. The solutions to current-day real world problems require more critical and creative thinking and the application of cross-disciplinary approaches.

Across the levels, from elementary to post-secondary school, the curriculum should therefore not be overly focused on content and on memory work. Instead, the focus needs to be on developing critical and creative thinking, problem solving, and application of learning in real world problems and issues. However, it does not mean that the teaching of content will be completely discarded. Core content will need to be taught for thinking cannot take place without knowledge of key concepts and principles, but emphasis should be placed on applying the theories, principles and core concepts in meaningful contexts. Students do need to have a strong foundation of essential knowledge, the substantive and syntactic concepts of the disciplines to be able to carry out inquiry, think critically and creatively, problem solve or make sound decisions.

Students of all levels should also actively engage with the community to learn about and experience the social issues and challenges faced by people in the community. They can do community service or take social action if they identify an issue in their community that needs to be resolved. In these ways they can learn about active citizenship. This is necessary so that we will grow a generation of citizens who will have the knowledge, skills and desire to improve society and not have a complaining attitude or an entitled mindset.

Wider cross-cultural exposure

Cross-cultural experiences are important for acquiring intercultural knowledge and skills. Students will not be limited to our present-day racial categorisation of Chinese, Malay, Indian, and Others. This categorisation is artificial and no longer sufficient nor relevant as it does not consider the increasing diversity resulting from rising numbers of foreign students and products of interracial marriages.

I envisage that there will be many cultural celebrations in the school and students will have opportunities to learn about and develop greater understanding of the cultures of their peers. This knowledge will go beyond the '3 Fs' (food, fashion and festival) and students will be encouraged to share with their peers about their family lives, traditions, practices, religious beliefs and values that are significant in their own cultures.

Learning about the past, including the development of societies and civilizations, the interactions between societies as well as human-environment interactions are important for a deeper understanding of where we are and how we got here. While learning about the past, it is important to include a study of the lives and achievements of women. This is because the prescribed content of history that is taught in schools is gender biased towards men's activities and their achievements while women's contributions are under-represented and often excluded (Kho, 2013). As a result, women do not appear to have contributed significantly to human development. This needs to change if we are to change society's mindset about the role and position of women in society and the importance of gender equality.

It is also essential to have more representations of women in traditionally male-dominated professions in school texts. In Singapore, there are five sectors that continue to be male-dominated — politics, aviation, engineering, maritime industry and information technology (Bay, 2016). Although female enrolment in science and technology courses has increased, there is still a significant gender imbalance in these sectors. Having more female role models highlighted in school texts will go some way in helping girls aspire towards these professions and correcting the gender imbalance.

Nurturing the aesthetic and physical development of children is also an important aspect in their holistic development and so music, art and physical education should be integrated into the curricula in the school. Students will be exposed to and encouraged to participate in a variety of sports and visual and performing arts. There is also emphasis on the development of student competencies in digital and critical literacies, harnessing Information and Communication Technologies, as well as developing students' collaborative and communication skills. Many opportunities will be provided for students to showcase their talent and skills through concerts, exhibitions and student demonstrations. Such showcases aim at developing student confidence and communication skills.

The organisation of these events will mostly be carried out by students with some help from teachers. The school is run on democratic principles and students have a very big part in the running of the school. Students will learn about responsibility and democratic principles through participation in committees to organise and manage school processes. These can range from simple activities such as ensuring the successful conduct of lessons to maintaining the school garden, ensuring provision of healthy food in the cafeteria, running weekly school assembly or organising a whole school celebration.

Student evaluation and examinations

With regards to student evaluation, it is important to use diverse measures of success as children are so unique in so many different ways and have such diverse intelligences. They are unique in their different ways of thinking, learning and expressing their understanding of what they have learned and there is no one standard way of measuring such diversities. Thus, many different modes of authentic assessment will be used. Instead of assessing only via standardised testing and examinations, students will be involved in performance tasks and qualitative feedback on their performance will be given. Most of the competencies and values within the MOE's 21st CC are soft skills and need a different assessment mode from the usual pen and paper exercise.

Social-emotional competencies such as self and social awareness, and responsible decision making and competencies for a globalised world such as cross-cultural skills, collaboration and information skills cannot be accurately evaluated through pen and paper tests and examinations. Performance tasks such as inquiry projects, laboratory investigations, oral presentations, talent showcase, show and tell for lower levels and creative problem solving will enable students to better demonstrate such competencies.

Many of such performance tasks require collaborative work and communication skills. Hence, they also provide opportunities for students to acquire the desired 21st century competencies conceived by MOE. Students will accumulate a portfolio of their work with the qualitative feedback over the span of years that they spent in school. These portfolios are demonstrations of their knowledge, skills and dispositions and at the same time, track the progress of their learning in school. These will provide useful information to potential employers or for admission to institutions of higher learning.

While no examinations will be required for students to advance through the grade levels in school, students may opt to take certification examinations if they so desire. This is for students who wish to advance to institutions of higher learning that require such proxy qualifications. They can opt to take the International Baccalaureate examinations or the GCE 'A' Level examinations since these are internationally recognised as rigorous and are proxy qualifications for entrance into universities. Classes will be organised to prepare all students who wish to take these examinations.

School facilities

The school design is disabled-friendly with ramps, elevators and toilet facilities that can comfortably accommodate wheelchairs: Directional tactiles are also constructed to ensure easy and safe passage for the visually impaired. The classrooms are spacious, well equipped and designed to support instruction and cater to different permutations of collaborative or individual seat work. All teachers and students will have their own mobile devices for teaching and learning. These will be secure, protected against online threats and powerful in delivering engaging learning experiences. Students are taught and required to use these devices responsibly and safely. Besides Form rooms, there are also special interest rooms which are designed and equipped with the relevant learning apparatuses and instructional media. Students also have easy access to the library and computer labs throughout school hours.

Other school facilities include reading and work areas for project discussions or individual work. Eateries and canteens catering to different dietary requirements are situated at convenient places in the school. Sports facilities include a sports stadium for track and field events, a swimming pool, a playing field for soccer, softball or any other outdoor play and multiple indoor courts for games such as badminton, basketball, netball, floorball, volleyball, tchoukball, sepak takraw, etc. There are also music and dance rooms and a performing arts theatre for students interested in these performing arts. There is also a visual art workroom with a gallery to display students' art pieces. All these facilities are necessary to broaden and enrich students' overall learning experiences in school.

Achieving the dream

Singapore's education system has progressed significantly and the realisation of such a dream school is not inconceivable. What is needed for this vision to be realised? Key to the change in education is visionary leadership. Leaders themselves must have the open-mindedness to examine their own preconceived biases and stereotypes about ethnicity, gender, social class, and so on, and to have a mindset shift so that inclusiveness can be effectively realised in the school. Leaders will also need to have the courage to take the step of doing away with examinations in the school.

There needs to be trust in the rigour, validity and reliability of school-based assessments. Furthermore, there needs to be a determined move towards reviewing and reducing the mandatory curriculum to free up space for more learner interest-driven curriculum. In that respect, the MOE should engage officers who are qualified curriculum developers. The current situation of having teachers seconded to MOE for a period of time to develop and design curriculum is not ideal.

For the dream school to be realised, the school must have efficient administrative and technical staff to handle the administrative and logistical affairs of the school so that teachers will only have to focus on instruction and attending to student needs. Teachers in the school need to understand the importance of respecting the individuality of students. They are not prejudiced by their own constructed ideas of appropriate gender roles and behaviours or have racial or other biases which may affect their interaction with students.

Besides having the right mental frame, teachers need to have depth of knowledge of their discipline to be able to develop curriculum based on student interest. They should have a wide repertoire of teaching approaches and be versatile enough to change and adapt their teaching to meet the diverse needs of their students. Instead of being instructors, they need to be facilitators, mentors or coaches to their students. They are tech-savvy and able to appropriately harness technology to enhance student learning. They also have easy access to instructional resources and attend professional development courses regularly to keep abreast of developments in their field of study or instructional innovations.

Teaching assistants who will help teachers design and develop instructional materials and teaching aids are required. Additionally and perhaps, most importantly, a key teacher disposition must be that of being able to embrace change and being comfortable about delving into material that they are not familiar with and having to learn along with their students. This is necessary because sometimes curriculum arises from student interest and teachers may not always be knowledgeable about areas that students are interested in.

On the right track

Recent developments in education augur well for Singapore. In 2022, the MOE announced that mid-year examinations at all levels will be removed. Instead, ongoing assessments to identify student learning and areas for improvement will be used. The Minister for Education, Mr Chan Chun Sing, added that curriculum and assessment demands will be reviewed as "[a]ny one standard curriculum will necessarily not be able to meet the diverse learning needs of our student". (https://www.channelnewsasia.com/singapore/mid-year-exams-all-primary-and-secondary-school-levels-will-be-removed-2023-moe-2544051) This recognition of the need to cater to the diverse learning needs and use different assessment modes to evaluate learning is indeed a step forward.

In March 2023, the MOE also announced that full subject banding will be rolled out to all schools from 2024 and students will be in mixed Form classes, allowing for a more heterogeneous multicultural mix of students in the school. (https://www.channelnewsasia.com/singapore/full-subject-based-banding-secondary-school-posting-groups-express-normal-streams-3315171). This is definitely a step towards the vision of inclusiveness in the school.

The Director General of Education (DGE), Liew Wei Li, in a recent opinion piece highlighted how technological advances have brought about the need to transform teaching and learning. Liew (2023) asserts the importance of balancing the teaching of content and skills but more importantly, underscores the necessity of developing the 21CC dispositions and competencies required to help students function effectively in a VUCA world. Furthermore, she reiterates that the removal of mid-year examinations and the revision of curriculum to include more interdisciplinary learning and collaborative work are aimed at providing more opportunities for developing these competencies.

In another article in *Principia*, a journal published by the Academy of Principals, DGE Liew also pointed to the need for students to learn to manage their emotions, consider different perspectives and "develop cross cultural skills to navigate highly contested and polarised environments." (Liew, *Principia* 15(1):4). She also drew attention to the need for teachers to adopt new mindsets and be comfortable with not always being in control as home-based and self-directed learning become more common. Teachers have to take on the role of facilitator and guide rather than dispensers of knowledge. With such a myriad of new and interesting fields of knowledge, teachers also need to be prepared for students desiring to learn things that they are not familiar with. This implies that teachers themselves will need to continually keep on learning new things.

The leadership in education are taking steps in the right direction, but it will take a while yet for these moves to bear fruit and spur the leaders to make bolder moves to overhaul some accepted and established traditions such as duration of school, the focus of school rules, and examinations. It will also take some time to produce a generation of teachers who have the required knowledge, skills and disposition. And it will also take time for society at large to accept and be comfortable with these changes. It may be another twenty to thirty years before such a school can become a reality.

Conclusion

This is my dream school, and it is limited by my own experience, imagination, and sense of reality. There are aspects of school that I have missed, and others may have different ideas of what an ideal school looks like. But I think most would agree that education of our young is essential for the continued existence of our society. It is also an important way by which families can break out of the poverty trap. To ensure that children become educated, they need to enjoy going to school, a school where they can be themselves and learn and grow in a safe, warm and stress-free environment. Children naturally love learning and schools need to continue to nurture that love.

My hope for future generations of children is that they will be able to attend such an ideal school where they can joyfully learn and grow holistically together in a multicultural environment, where everyone is included and respected, where differences are celebrated and not merely tolerated, and where there is equitable access to all they need to achieve their potential.

KHO EE MOI was a senior lecturer at the National Institute of Education (NIE) where she was involved in pre-service education and professional development of teachers. She was actively involved in promoting History and Social Studies education through her work in NIE as well as the History Association of Singapore where she was President from 2005–2017. She is a firm believer in values education and continues to provide support in this area through various consultancy work with schools and publishers.

References

Ang, Q. 21 May 2022. "About 1 in 3 youths in Singapore has mental health symptoms: Study". *The Straits Times*. https://www.straitstimes.com/singapore/about-1-in-3-youths-in-singapore-has-mental-health-symptoms-study.

Bay, D. 2016. "5 male-dominated sectors in Singapore that need to think about gender equality". *Asiaone*. https://www.asiaone.com/5-maledominated-sectors-singapore-need-think-about-gender-equality.

Hirschmann, R. 2022. "Education in Singapore — statistics & facts". https://www.statCambriaPressista.com/topics/5766/education-in-singapore/.

Kho, E. M. 2013. *The Construction of Femininity in a Postcolonial State. Girls' Education in Singapore*. NY: Cambria Press.

Liew Wei Li. 2023. "Education in a technology-transformed world: What and how we learn must evolve". *The Straits Times*,T 8 April.

Ministry of Education. 14 Dec 2022. "21st Century Competencies". https://www.moe.gov.sg/education-in-sg/21st-century-competencies.

OECD. 2019. "Programme for International Student Assessment. Results from PISA 2018. Country Note". https://www.oecd.org/pisa/publications/PISA2018_CN_SGP.pdf

OECD. 5 Dec 2023. "Programme for International Student Assessment. PISA 2022 Results: Factsheets". Singapore. https://www.oecd.org/publication/pisa-2022-results/country-notes/singapore-2f72624e#chapter-d1e11

Robinson, K. & K. Robinson. 2022. "What is Education For?" https://www.edutopia.org/article/what-education.

Shanmugam, K. 20 Sep 2020. "Conversations on Women Development". Speech by Mr K. Shanmugam, Minister for Home Affairs and Minister for Law. https://www.mha.gov.sg/mediaroom/speeches/conversations-on-women-development-speech-by-mr-k-shanmugam-minister-for-home-affairs-and-minister-for-law/

Yeung, WJ.J. & X.J. Chen. 2023. "Achievement gaps before school in Singapore: Family SES, parental values and young children's self-regulation". *Early Childhood Research Quarterly* 65: 352–362. https://doi.org/10.1016/j.ecresq.2023.07.012

"Whether you ultimately achieve your goal, or not, is inconsequential. It is The Process that counts… So be a little more Zen as you venture along your way — keep your antennae up, you may very well find that digressions from your chosen path may turn out to be the most meaningful after all."

~ Toy piano virtuoso Margaret Leng Tan, State University of New York at Cortland 2011 Commencement address

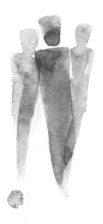

CHAPTER 12

Uncharted Paths

Danelle Tan

Path 1 at 6 — Unopposed beginnings

*My first obstacle to playing football was a drain, a 'longkang'
as it is known in Singapore. A treacherous gap 6-year-old me
had to jump across to get to training. Flanked on both sides by
muddy patches of grass, every step pulled me further into the
ground. Boots caked in mud, brown spots flaking my pristine
red socks, I attended my first football training session.*

An unorthodox sport for a girl, but not in my parents' eyes.
My two brothers (one older and one younger) were already
attending football classes at a club, JSSL FC, near our house.
When I expressed interest in following them, my parents did not see
any issues. I have always thought myself blessed that I did not have
to fight against many gender stereotypes growing up. This was one
of the first deterrents to playing that I might have faced simply
because I was a girl. I remain grateful that I never had to worry that

I was playing a 'boy's sport' and could instead focus on improving my footballing skills.

Path 2 at 13 — Football in a boys' world

The coach called for a water break. I stood in one corner gulping down water, while the boys clustered together, chatting and drinking in another. We were all in one team, but no one could have guessed looking from the outside.

Although I played in an all-girls' team growing up, I had always competed against boys so playing around boys was not unusual. In 2017, I started playing on boys' teams. Suddenly, I was the only girl on the team.

During my first training session, I was met with many strange stares. I cannot confess to being able to read people's minds, but that day, it was pretty clear what most of the boys were thinking, 'What is this *girl* doing on *our* team??' And in those early training sessions, there were many times I asked myself that same question. But it is when you are outside of your comfort zones that you grow the most. When I joined the team, I had two options: One, to continue feeling awkward and out of place, or two, to train hard and show the boys why I was on their team, not as a girl but as a teammate. You can guess which I chose.

Path 3 at 14 — Age should be timeless

The goal suddenly looked tiny, the goalkeeper massive. The fatigue from the 90 minutes of football I had just played seemed to hit my legs all at once. Legs shivering, breath quivering, I took five steps back from the penalty spot and prepared to shoot. All the tension built up released when the ball hit the back of the net.

I made my debut for the senior national team at 14. Fourteen years, 294 days to be exact. Those numbers are now inscribed on the walls of Jalan Besar Stadium, which some consider to be the birthplace of Singapore football,[1] next to the words Danelle Tan and Youngest Goal Scorers. It is nice to score on your debut for your club or country because it is a statement. You can imagine how much better it felt not just to score on my debut, but to stamp my name down in the history books of Singapore football as Singapore's youngest goal scorer. Both male and female.

I have always been a huge believer that if you are good enough, you are old enough. Thankfully, the coach of the senior team at the time, Melisa Ye, also recognised that and had the faith to start me in my first game against Timor Leste. The goal was historic, but it was the whole process it took to get me there that made it extra sweet. I still remember when I was 12, playing for the under-16 youth national team in my first international game. I was struggling physically and wasn't able to impact the game much. Fast forward two years and as the youngest player on the senior team, I was controlling the midfield and orchestrating the attack. Writing it now, it feels like a flick of the switch that made that change happen — one moment weak, and the other dominant — and I wish it were that easy. Yet, it was hours and hours dedicated to improving myself as a footballer that made that change possible. It was all the sacrifice that made the goal special.

Path 4 at 17 — 11,000km out of my comfort zone

My hands were stuck in the fleece-lined pockets of my puffer jacket. A scarf wrapped tightly around my neck. The winter months of the UK were not only bitingly cold, but sunlight was

---

[1] https://www.roots.gov.sg/en/places/places-landing/Places/historic-sites/jalan-besar-stadium

also sparse and definitely not the bright, hot Singapore I was
used to. In those early days, walking back from school alone,
I dearly missed the comfort of friends and family.

I had not always dreamed of becoming a professional footballer. In kindergarten, my teachers made us draw how we saw ourselves in the future. My 'dreams' of what I hoped to be fluctuated constantly with many of them lasting all of a day but becoming a professional footballer had not occurred to me. I did not know that female professional footballers existed, much less dream of becoming one.

With women's football now one of the fastest growing sports in the world, that is changing rapidly. Many girls now grow up watching the women's World Cup, the women's Euros, and look up to these female players. Although the women's game is still a far cry from the men's in terms of wages, with male footballers earning roughly 100 times more than their female counterparts, it is really nice to see girls growing up aspiring to become professional footballers.

When I had my sights set on becoming a professional footballer, I knew I had to move overseas. Staying in Singapore, my progress would only stagnate, so I took the next big step out of my comfort zone. I enrolled in Mill Hill School, in London, and lived in a boarding house with 50 other students.

Living my whole life in Singapore, moving to London on my own was a huge shock. The grim weather, the bland food, the uneven pavements. But also, the laundry, the cleaning I now had to do myself, the sudden independence. None of my family or friends were awake back home when my school day finished because of the time difference. Nights would often grow long, with only my books to accompany me.

The price to pay for progress is often comfort. I knew that although many days were challenging, the discomfort would only benefit me in the future.

Path 5 at 18 — Studies are overrated

With our luggage bouncing around in the boot of an Uber, and my dad and I squashed in the back seats, we headed to Princeton, New Jersey, on what I like to think of as our 'US tour'. I passed the 3-hour ride by being creative with finding the best sleeping positions. But with the occasional bumps that would shake you awake, and the driver's seat pushed all the way back, leaving you no space, sleep was at a premium.

I was granted a partial athletic scholarship by the College of William and Mary (W&M), ranked in the top 50 US colleges,[2] and became the first Singaporean footballer to be accepted into a National Collegiate Athletic Association (NCAA) Division 1 (D1) soccer programme. It was a huge privilege to accept the offer, knowing that only the top 0.5% of high school soccer players get accepted into D1 soccer programmes and receive scholarship aid. It felt like a step in the right direction. Sometimes, when you embark on unfamiliar paths, you are unsure if you are even going the correct way. The offer felt like confirmation I was doing the right things.

Then I chose to give up my spot on the W&M roster to join one of Europe's biggest clubs, Borussia Dortmund. It might seem crazy to give up such an appealing opportunity and my studies to pursue a career in football, but a professional footballer only has a short life span. I didn't want to let the opportunity pass and then look back and think 'what if?'. As my dad always says, "You can study at any age, at any time; but you only have till you're 40 max to play football." With that in mind, I chose to take the unconventional route and give my aspirations a chance.

---

[2] Ranked 41st in Forbes 2022 America's Top Colleges https://www.wm.edu/about/rankings/index.php

It was not a flippant, rash decision of a young child hoping to rise to fame and earn money. I understood the severity of the decision and the implications it would have — that if football did not work out, I would be left with nothing but an A-Level certificate. But in the end, it boiled down to a little girl wishing to chase her seemingly outrageous dreams and her parents who supported her all the way, no matter what that meant.

Future paths — Unopposed beginnings for all

When I joined JSSL FC at six, there were around 20 girls and 400 boys going to training. That is 20 times the number of boys playing football at one club in Singapore. At the time, I was in the only club in Singapore that had a girls team.

Football and sport have changed my life in so many ways. Not many people, much less 18-year-olds, can say that they've travelled to 15 countries to play their favourite sport. Football has widened my perspectives and stretched my world view. It has shown me how important sport is to society; it unifies people.

I strongly believe that more girls should be given the opportunity to experience the power of sport. Equal opportunity has to start right at the beginning. You can bring two people to the same pond and give them both fishing rods; but if you have not taught one of them how to fish, you're not giving them an equal chance to catch fish.

I hope change starts at all levels. I hope at the age of six, more girls will dream big, and with full support from their parents, chart their own paths. That they will believe wholeheartedly that they can shape a better, more equal society for the future they will live in. I hope at 13 years, girls competing with boys will not be unusual or awkward but will be met with more receptivity.

I hope at 14 years, the potential of these girls will not be limited because they are too young. I hope at 17 years, more girls will be willing to step outside their comfort zone to push for their goals. I hope at 18 years, more girls will not be scared to take an unconventional path if that is what they desire.

But change cannot only happen with individuals, it has to start with parents, who should be open-minded with their definition of success for their kids. Parents who, like mine, should not limit what their kids can or cannot do, and allow them to simply dream. It will also have to start with a society that supports the ambitions of these youths, giving them the platform and opportunity to enact changes. It has to start with everyone. This is my hope for the future.

DANELLE TAN is a 19-year-old Singaporean footballer. She is best known as Singapore's youngest goal scorer who scored on her debut at 14 years young. She has trail-blazed a path being the first Singaporean to be offered a scholarship at a US NCAA Division 1 college, the first Singaporean to play in a European League, and the first Asian woman to play for the famed Borussia Dortmund.

The Science of Inquiry

"You set some goal and then you try to achieve it. Once you have achieved it, there's a great sense of satisfaction. I like to push the limits of what I can do."

~ Trailblazing pilot Anastasia Gan, in the documentary
'Beyond Limits: 8 Singapore Women', MediaCorp, 2014

CHAPTER 13

We Need More Women in Scientific Research

Ding Jeak Ling

The STEM (science, technology, engineering, and mathematics) sector has historically been dominated by men, but there have been some remarkable discoveries by women. For a long time, the contributions of women to scientific research were not always fully acknowledged. The key role played by Rosalind Franklin, for example, in the discovery of the molecular structure of DNA was initially unrecognised by academia. I am glad that acknowledgement is now shifting, with articles, books, and even films being produced about women in science.

Exactly a century after Franklin's birth, the female duo of Jennifer Doudna and Emmanuelle Charpentier were awarded the Nobel Prize for Chemistry for their groundbreaking discovery of CRISPR. The publication of their findings some years earlier led to a revolution that has shaken the very foundations of science and enabled humanity to rewrite its own genetic code.

We need young girls to learn about the exciting scientific discoveries women scientists have made in order to inspire them to embark on promising careers in scientific research and unleash their full potential. As a woman scientist and researcher, I have always encouraged more women to enter the field. Women are well suited to science research, and I speak from personal experience. They have the tenacity and ability to be both meticulous and creative. We have the passion, perseverance, and dedication to follow our scientific curiosity and search for the solutions that our world so sorely needs.

But science research can mean very long hours of detailed work in the laboratory followed by more work after office hours, often at home. Academics teach, carry out research (which involves grant applications, publications, and lab management), and handle administrative tasks. The workload is considerable, especially with the additional duty of managing or co-managing the family.

This can be a big hurdle for women scientists — how to balance research, which has no fixed 9–5 schedule, with the burden of childcare and family life. I was fortunate to have strong family support which enabled me to devote time and energy to research and other academic and administrative duties. But even so, when my two children were young there were many occasions when I was at work and felt very guilty about not being with them at home.

So if we are to hope for more women to undertake science research, it would be good for universities to create a supportive environment for young researchers, both male and female, who have families. Ideally, universities can create opportunities for young parents in the same situation to come together and share their coping strategies for balancing the demands on their time at work and at home.

Universities might want to engage mentors to help organise 'women parent-scientist club' meetings to provide advice and support and share their experiences. Male counterparts could be invited to join special working-group meetings to raise awareness and for them to gain better understanding of women scientists' needs. It would help if men played a more active role in raising their families and share the workload of caring for the home and the children. The message is slowly getting through, but a lot more can be done to change the gender stereotypes that have prevailed for so long.

Mentoring is important

Many good initiatives now exist to attract more women into STEM and to help them develop their careers, such as Singapore Women in Science which is forging supportive networking, collaboration, and mentorship opportunities for women in all aspects of science. I have personally mentored young scientists and provide as nurturing an environment for them as possible. I remind them it is possible to do high quality research while also raising a family and encourage them to persevere in the pursuit of their scientific goals. This will in turn lead them to set examples that foster observation, inquisitiveness, and logical thinking in their own growing children, which provides an added bonus all around.

The National University of Singapore (NUS) is keen to nurture scientific research talent. However, we are challenged by the lure of greener pastures abroad, both academically and in terms of the general environment which may appeal to some of our most talented scientific minds. This would be a loss of precious human capital from our small population.

Meanwhile, NUS aims to attract young talents — PhD and post-doctoral fellows — from around the region and further afield. Those who have studied and/or worked abroad for some years to gain experience and exposure and who have excelled in their fields are incentivised to apply to work in Singapore as assistant professors on three-year contracts. Their trajectory is tracked closely, they are nurtured and guided over a couple of contracts, and offered tenure for their sustained productivity and significant results.

Stimulating the spirit of inquiry

In order to truly develop scientific research in Singapore we must recognise and value local PhDs as highly as we rate foreign PhDs. Our tertiary institutions have achieved high ranking globally and we need to overcome the idea that foreign talent is somehow better. We need more trust and respect for locally trained scientists, and we also need more sharing, interaction, and collaboration within the scientific community. Our *kiasu* or scared-to-lose culture can mean that we work in silos, guarding our territory instead of reaching out to share and learn from each other. I am pleased that we are now beginning to see a positive shift in scientific collegiality and culture in Singapore.

I am hopeful both for the overall research environment in Singapore and efforts to attract more women into STEM and scientific research. I once taught a freshman module using world-renowned women scientists as role models. This class was very well received by the students, not only the girls but also the boys. We should be doing more of this — recognising what women have achieved and holding them up as role models. There is now a lot more recognition in Singapore of the need for attention to gender equality, and for men to share the childcare and homemaking burden, so I am optimistic.

Meanwhile, we should do all we can to stimulate the spirit of inquiry in our young. We should encourage intellectual rigour, responsibility, respect, and trust; no less for women. Get them to take an interest in learning how things work and encourage them to experiment. One does not need expensive 'educational' toys for this. I grew up in a humble home where we used our creativity and imagination to make our own toys and games from everyday items like eggshells, twigs, and matchboxes. When I was six years old, I found that holding a spectacle lens that had fallen out of its frame to focus the rays of the sun onto a corner of a straw mat could create fire! This was an exhilarating experience for me, and it might have been one of the sparks that triggered my scientific career. Research has been my lifelong interest and I hope the years ahead will see many more women flourish in scientific research.

DING JEAK LING is an Emeritus Professor at the Department of Biological Sciences, National University of Singapore (NUS). Her research focuses on understanding the basic biology of "Host-pathogen Interaction, Innate immunity and Cancer Immunomodulation". Her research discoveries have been published in some 300 journal articles, book chapters and monographs including Nature Immunology, Sciences Advances, EMBO J, Proc Natl Acad Sci (USA), PLoS Pathogens, Cell Death & Differentiation, Science Signaling, J Immunology, *and* Advanced Therapeutics. *She has translated some of her discoveries into commercial products. She holds some 20 patents.*

"Whether it's sport, a job or even a hobby, you have to work hard at it. You must set a goal for yourself and go for it. There's no short cut to success."

~ Sprint queen Glory Barnabas, in an interview
with The Straits Times, May 2014

CHAPTER 14

Why I Want to be a Biomedical Researcher Rather than a Doctor

Shakti Vijayakumar

The path to becoming a doctor is undeniably noble and impactful, but my heart is set on a career as a biomedical researcher. I have a deep-rooted passion for unravelling the mysteries of the human body and making significant contributions to the field of medicine.

My desire to pursue a career as a biomedical researcher stems from a combination of my wanting to have an impact on society and a profound appreciation for the potential of scientific discovery.

As a biomedical researcher I would be able to contribute to the advancing of medical knowledge. I would dedicate my efforts to understanding the intricate mechanisms of diseases, exploring new treatment modalities, and uncovering breakthroughs that can improve healthcare outcomes. By involving myself in research, I would potentially be able to help save or improve the lives of thousands of people.

When focusing on research, I can actively contribute to the collective knowledge of humanity and drive progress in healthcare that benefits not only individual patients but also society as a whole.

As a young woman who is passionate about scientific research, I would like to see many more women in science. Gender diversity in the scientific community would bring immense benefits to both society and the field of science itself.

Historically, women have been underrepresented in the science, technology, engineering, and mathematics (STEM) fields, including biomedical research. And where there have been women in science, all too often their discoveries have been attributed to their male colleagues.

This phenomenon, known as the Matilda Effect, has resulted in a systemic bias that downplays the contributions of women scientists. Their work is often underrepresented in academic curricula, scientific publications, and award ceremonies. Many accomplished women in STEM remain unsung heroes, their stories consigned to the footnotes of scientific history.

The Matilda Effect is named after Matilda Joslyn Gage, a prominent 19th-century suffragist, women's rights advocate, and writer. The term was coined by Margaret W. Rossiter, a historian of science, to draw attention to the historical and ongoing marginalisation of women's contributions in academia and science.

Examples of the effect being prominent throughout the science world starts with Rosalind Franklin. Her work on X-ray crystallography was crucial in uncovering the structure of DNA. Despite her significant contribution, Franklin's name was largely omitted from the Nobel Prize awarded to James Watson, Francis Crick, and Maurice Wilkins for the discovery of DNA's structure.

Another remarkable woman in science is Ada Lovelace, often regarded as the world's first computer programmer. In the 19th century, Lovelace wrote an algorithm for Charles Babbage's Analytical Engine, a precursor to modern computers. Her visionary insights into the potential of machines to go beyond simple calculations laid the foundation for the field of computer science. Lovelace's work demonstrates that women have been at the forefront of technological innovation since its early stages.

These examples illustrate how women's contributions in STEM have been consistently marginalised. The Matilda Effect underscores the need for greater recognition of women's achievements in science and academia, highlighting the importance of addressing these biases and promoting gender equality in STEM fields.

We need to highlight the stories of the women in STEM and their accomplishments. Their stories are a powerful source of inspiration and empowerment for future generations. When young girls see women successfully pursuing careers in traditionally male-dominated fields, it challenges stereotypes, broadens their horizons, and encourages them to dream big.

Representation matters, and by showcasing accomplished women scientists, engineers, and mathematicians as role models, we inspire young girls to believe in their own capabilities and pursue their passions, regardless of gender. This ripple effect creates a virtuous cycle, leading to increased participation of women in STEM, and ultimately, a more diverse and inclusive scientific community.

In choosing to become a biomedical researcher, I am motivated by my desire to contribute to the advancement of medical knowledge and make a lasting impact on healthcare, as well as to create a difference in the under-representation of women in this field. The world of research offers the opportunity to delve deeply into the intricacies of diseases and develop innovative treatments.

I strongly believe that increasing gender diversity in science is not only a matter of fairness and equality but also a catalyst for scientific progress and societal transformation. By embracing the contributions of women in science, we unlock new perspectives and foster creativity, ultimately driving breakthrough discoveries and paving the way for a more inclusive and prosperous society.

SHAKTI VIJAYAKUMAR is a 12th grade student at United World College SEA East Campus. She plans to pursue her scientific education at universities and research labs in the UK or US and earn her PhD before returning to Singapore to further her career. Apart from her passion for science, she is also active in the theatre community, where she has completed trinity examinations including earning her ATCL diploma in speech and drama as well as planning a production that involved a series of monologues written by girls 13+ about feminism where all the proceeds were donated to AWARE. She also participated in the Vagina monologues in 2022. She has a strong interest in dance specifically Indian classical dance known as Bharathnatyam which she has been pursuing since she was 5 years old.

"This is not a career but a life-time journey that allows me to learn and do many different things. There's a tremendous amount of growth, that's the fun part. Even when things are not going smoothly, I persist because I love science and want to make a difference."

~ Award-winning nanobiotechnology researcher Jackie Yi-Ru Ying, in an interview with rahyafteha.ir, July 2016

Chapter 15

From Being Inspired to Inspiring Girls in Science

Isabel Ho Si En

Questions, questions, and more questions.

Throughout my early life, my family always encouraged me to ask questions, to inquire and to probe. This sparked my interest in science from an early age.

In my early childhood, I loved conducting science experiments at home and this fuelled my curiosity for science. My favourite question is "*Why?*" From the age of eight, I knew that I wanted my life to centre around science.

Attending a medical panel discussion aged nine opened my eyes to the world of science and seeded the thought that science could be my career. Professor Jackie Ying was one of my first mentors in science, and she was kind enough to chat with me when I was twelve. This came about because I sought her views on my choice of secondary school.

Interning when I was aged 13 in a science laboratory at the National University of Singapore with Professor Stella Tan, after I had emailed her, was an amazing experience and also taught me what makes a good mentor.

At 14, in the midst of the Covid-19 pandemic, I organised a trip to various U.S. universities to discuss science with professors and be inspired by them. Many kindly allowed me to visit their laboratories. It was wonderful to have been able to visit the Berkeley laboratoryof Professor Jennifer Doudna has always been an inspiration to me as she revolutionised the field of genetics with CRISPR.

Professor Florian Engert from Harvard, a neuroscientist working on zebrafish to build a biological neural network, shared with me that "We study not only to learn how to solve problems, but more importantly to learn how to *think*." I love hearing different perspectives and incorporating them into my world view to pay it forward.

> "*The first step to inspiring others is to make sure you are inspired yourself.*"

> — Carmine Gallo.

Inspiring girls in science

Inspired by incredible female role models, I knew that I wanted to serve and inspire others as well. And that is what I did.

Starting with small steps, I volunteered to help run workshops for various programmes in NUS High School of Mathematics and Science, including an MCurie Programme , which focuses on empowering girls. Next, I mentored research projects in similar programmes.

Often, I was the youngest volunteer in the room (I am the youngest contributor to this book as well). Never let age or gender hold us back from achieving our dreams, because we already have what it takes to serve. One step always leads to the next, even if we cannot see the rest of the staircase.

While sharing at a recent MCurie session, I was heartened to hear the stories and perspectives on science shared by other female mentors. They sounded so much like my own, yet their content differed, bringing to mind the saying "Different strokes for different folks" as we all inspire in our own unique ways.

Wanting to give back, I reached out to various primary schools when I was 14, asking whether I could share my experience through talks, titled "Learning through Science". Several schools, including Tao Nan Primary School, St. Hilda's Primary School and Raffles Girls' Primary School invited me to share with upper primary students.

Later, I was invited to contribute to this book by two of my role models, Margaret Thomas and Dr Kanwaljit Soin, who are both pioneers in empowering women. This came about because I contacted Ms Thomas to learn more about her journey in advocating for gender equality and empowering women.

Every step led me on a path that I could not have foreseen, following actress Michelle Yeoh's advice at Harvard Law School's commencement speech to "stay loose", which means to stay adaptable and take opportunities whenever they arise.

Next, what would I like to see for Singapore in the future and its interplay with science.

In the future

The future Singapore is one where there is gender equality, especially in science.

The future Singapore will have more female exemplars in science, empowering girls to believe that they too can achieve their dreams in science. This visualisation is powerful because it empowers us by affording us a glimpse of a future that we are capable of creating.

Gender equality starts from childhood. In the future Singapore, instead of giving girls dolls and boys Lego sets and toy cars, we should provide children with a choice for their toys. Perhaps boys should play dress-up and cooking while girls receive science and robotics kits.

The term gender equality is widely used in society today. But what does equality really mean to us?

When there is an equal number of women and men in science or perhaps when most scientists are females? We may find that radical, but remember, just 100 years ago, almost all scientists were males, and we found no fault there.

The unconscious and inherent bias against women in STEM (science, technology, engineering, mathematics) is a learned social construct, and one that is possible to unlearn, which is my hope for the future Singapore. Together, let us do our utmost to break down barriers for women in science. We can do this just by changing a single individual's mindset, because we change the world one person at a time.

In this journey of moving towards gender equality, support networks are crucial. In NASA (National Aeronautics and Space Administration) in the 1950s and 1960s, a group of female engineers and 'human computers' did most of the calculations that enabled the launch of humans into space and onto the moon.

The close-knit, all-female group supported each other, deviating from the norm of the no-talking rule in NASA as they built stronger connections by sharing their personal lives with each other They encouraged each. They encouraged each other to enrol in night school, studying engineering and computer science, to upgrade their skills, because at that time many universities would not admit women for STEM courses. Childbirth was no barrier, with Helen Ling, who supervised the female engineers and 'human computers', implementing an early form of maternity leave, by hiring female NASA employees again after they left to give birth.

Let us encourage girls to shoot for the stars in science. Let us look at how we can as a community provide support for every single female who wants to embark on her journey in science.

I am immensely grateful to all those women, and men — including my papa — who paved the path for equal representation and opportunities in science. We need to not only continue their legacy but also continually redefine what equality in science means to us and adapt to our changing society.

The Internet provides so much information on the future of women in science. I believe that our society already knows the course of action that needs to be taken. Now, we just need to act and to take the initiative to change the lives of women in Singapore and around the world. Let us not be defined by our gender but as people.

I am not just a female in science, I am an aspiring young scientist.

We *have* the power to create the future that we want to live in. What is the future that *you* want to create?

* * *

ISABEL HO SI EN is 15 and a student at the NUS High School of Mathematics and Science. Science is her passion as it transforms the lives of others. She partners with programmes promoting science amongst primary school students, including the MCurie programme for girls. To inspire primary school students, she shares her experience through talks titled "Learning through Science". She has a YouTube Channel — InspiHERing Science that shares the stories of STEM professionals to inspire younger students through Science. She is eager to find out what else the future holds.

Body, Mind, and Globe:
The Female Factor

"In this society, everything is men, men, men. So I come along and say, 'Pay more attention to women. I'm a woman.' I would like to have more done for women. It's as simple as that."

~ Pioneering gynaecologist Oon Chiew Seng, on why she made a large donation in 2011 towards research on women's health and ageing issues.

CHAPTER 16

Women Hold the Key to the Success of Healthier SG

Jeremy Lim Fung Yen & Nurul Amanina binte Hussain

By 2030, 1 in 4 Singaporeans would be over the age of 65 years. This rapidity of aging is unprecedented in the world. As Health Minister Ong Ye Kung stated in Parliament in April 2023, "The United Nations defines a country as 'ageing' if the share of its population aged 65 and above crosses 7 per cent. It is considered 'aged' if the share exceeds 14 per cent. Once the share reaches 21 per cent, it is 'super aged'. France took 115 years to transit from 'ageing' to 'aged' in 1980; Sweden took 85 years and became 'aged' in 1975; US took 69 years to become 'aged' in 2013. Singapore took only 19 years and became 'aged' in 2017. The gap between 'aged' and 'super aged' is estimated at only 9 years, which means we will attain 'super aged' status in 2026. Today, we are one of the fastest ageing countries in the world."[1]

---

[1] Speech by Mr Ong Ye Kung, Minister for Health, "Super-aged Country, Superb Singapore". 20 April 2023.

Singaporeans are living longer but advancements in longevity are not commensurate with improvements in quality of life. Furthermore, the healthcare budget has ballooned with a tripling of spending in the last two decades. Singapore has responded to these challenges with the introduction of Healthier SG, a bold effort to reframe healthcare as health promoting and disease preventing in equal measures to curative interventions.

Healthier SG heralds the biggest reforms to the Singapore health and healthcare system since its Independence in 1965. If successful, the reforms would enable Singaporeans to age actively and independently within the community, which would translate to a better quality of life. Singaporeans would increasingly take ownership of their own health and collectively improve population health, consequently, resources for health could also be distributed more efficiently.

A system that has been built on driving efficiency in healthcare is now re-focusing on nudging behaviours for health; a system that was built around the hospital is now doing its utmost to shift care into the community and the home. As of the time of writing, Healthier SG has three main public-facing thrusts, and one that is more behind-the-scenes but no less transformational: capitation of Singapore's public healthcare clusters.

The first public-facing paradigm shift is a government-encouraged partnership between a Singapore resident and his/ her chosen primary care clinic to attend to both healthcare and health-promoting needs. The underlying rationale is that preserving and enhancing health needs professional support and that the general practitioner (GP) in the community is best placed to guide the individual and marshal the needed resources on behalf of the Singapore resident.

Secondly, tangible incentives are offered for preventive health measures such as free vaccinations and disease screenings. This is no small policy shift as Singapore has traditionally utilised user fees or co-payments to force citizens to have 'skin in the game' and minimise wastage and misuse. There is now recognition that imposing financial requirements further dis-incentivises behaviours that not enough Singapore residents embrace in the first instance and that removing 'friction', whether in the form of fees or inconvenience, will be necessary.

Thirdly, there is a strong social component, recognising that community connections improve health, and the reverse also holds true. As American Surgeon General Dr Vivek Murthy wrote for the *New York Times* in April 2023, "Loneliness is more than just a bad feeling. When people are socially disconnected, their risk of anxiety and depression increases. So does their risk of heart disease (29 percent), dementia (50 per cent), and stroke (32 per cent). The increased risk of premature death associated with social disconnection is comparable to smoking daily".[2] Singapore Health Minister Ong Ye Kung has repeatedly spoken about 'social prescribing' and the importance of lifestyle factors such as sleep and stress. Local community organisations, often with some support from government agencies like the Health Promotion Board, will step up to host community events to bring residents together, foster bonds of friendship and address the very real risk of loneliness in Singaporeans' busy lives.

Capitation has been the least discussed in the media but will further shape hospitals and clinics operational behaviours. In capitation, the healthcare providers, in this case the three clusters- Singapore Health Services, National Healthcare Group and National University Health System — will be provided a lump sum budget based on the number of residents in their catchment area with an

---

[2] *The New York Times* "Surgeon General: We Have Become a Lonely Nation. It's Time to Fix That" 30 April 2023.

adjustment for age. The clusters then need to manage all healthcare utilisation of the residents within the budget.

Capitated models are not new. Kaiser Permanente in the United States of America is probably the best known globally. How is capitation different from our current fee-for-service model? Put simply, in a fee-for-service model, every surgery performed, every test ordered is revenue for the provider. In capitation, these are all costs. The ideal patient in a capitated model is one who eats healthily, exercises regularly, religiously attends all health screenings and receives all appropriate vaccinations, thus in the main not falling seriously ill and requiring little resources for healthcare. In the event of hospitalisation, this ideal patient would stay in the hospital the minimum number of days and convalesce in the home setting dutifully monitored remotely through hospital provided tele-medical devices.

While these measures may effectively reduce barriers for individuals to practice personal responsibility in health, reform should happen beyond the structural shifts to ensure success in Healthier SG. It is also pertinent to address other social determinants of health, which Minister Ong correctly highlighted as contributing to 60 percent of health outcomes, particularly factors that influence the public's perception of health and their health-seeking behaviours. In these, a gender perspective is important as men and women think and act differently.[3]

Women as decision makers

In most societies, women are expected to provide care and maintain the general well-being of each family member. Aflac, the supplemental

---

[3] Speech by Mr Ong Ye Kung, Minister for Health at the Global Launch of the Healthy Ageing and Prevention Index, Geneva, 23 May 2023.

insurance provider, colourfully describes this as "Every home has a chief medical officer… This is the person who researches, analyses, and decides on the best course of health care for everyone in the home. This is the one who tacks postcards from the dentist about six-month cleanings to the fridge. The one who files the insurance claims. The one who Googles medical terms after a confusing doctor's appointment, the one who saves receipts for health savings accounts, the one who keeps track of who needs to see which specialist and when", and the chief medical officer at home is most likely to be a woman.[4] In the United States, women make approximately 80 per cent of the healthcare decisions for their families. Elsewhere, it is similar and multiple studies show that women are much more active than men in healthcare decision-making, adopting positive health behaviours, and seeing the doctor when required. Shilpa (2023) demonstrated this in a local survey conducted with women, whereby 75 per cent of the respondents reported having the ability to independently participate in health screenings and having a sense of empowerment to seek care if necessary.[5]

Women start with a sounder base of knowledge and multiple studies have shown women fare better than men in knowledge about health matters. For example, women outperformed in the health and long-term care section of the quiz in a large American survey on retirement literacy. However, women correctly answered 46 per centof questions on average, which is hardly reassuring for a decision maker.[6]

---

[4] Aflac Inc., "Meet the people making your employees' health decision: Women", 2023.

[5] S. Surendran *et al.* (2023), "Understanding Barriers and Facilitators of Breast and Cervical Cancer Screening among Singapore Women: A Qualitative Approach". *Asian Pac J Cancer Prev* 24(3): 889–895.

[6] The American College (2021), "Women's Retirement Literacy Report". [Internet].

In Asia, a survey revealed that 84 per cent of their female respondents are more active in seeking health information online.[7] Being the main decision maker and steward of well-being in the family could result in neglect of their own health needs. A regional survey done by Philips (2023) revealed that 95 per cent of the female respondents recognised the importance of preventive health, yet only 29 per cent of them were able to go for regular health check-ups and screenings. A high proportion (48 per cent) of the respondents from Philip's survey identified the 'lack of time due to work, family, and personal commitments' as the main barrier to health-seeking ability.

This could partly explain why women have a longer life expectancy but are more susceptible to chronic diseases and disabilities than men. Consequently, women may not have the privilege to enjoy a high quality of life in their later years, should this trend persist.

Women as caregivers

With the increasing shift of care from inpatient facilities such as hospitals to the home setting, women will inevitably take more of the 'outside hospital' responsibilities. Women have traditionally assumed the caregiving role, especially single women and this is unlikely to change in the short term.

One American study from two decades ago highlighted that "husbands were less likely than wives to help their sick spouses with household tasks", and "husbands who helped were more likely to have other helpers".[8] Whereas wives tended to be sole caregivers, providing approximately twice the hours of care that husbands provided. At home, a 2012 Singapore Government-commissioned

---

[7] Philips, "Philips underlines commitment to gender equity in healthcare on International Women's Day". [Internet, 8 March 2023].

[8] S.M. Allen (1994)," Gender differences in spousal caregiving and unmet need for care". *Journal of gerontology* 49 (4): S187–95.

study found that 60 per cent of caregivers were women and that most were middle-aged, aged between 45 and 59 years.[9]

This trend was also reflected by other recent local studies such as those by Sambasivam (2019), Yuan (2020), and Riches (2023), and for care recipients with different health needs, including dementia, chronic illness, terminal illness, and intellectual disability.[10–12] In 2023, a study led by Dover Park Hospice focused on caregivers of terminally ill patients showed that not much had changed — women still disproportionately contribute to caregiving, the majority of women in caregiving roles were married (65 per cent), and there was a substantial group of single (never married) caregivers (26 per cent). Worryingly, the survey also found that four in ten caregivers were at risk of depression.[13]

The physical, emotional, and social strain and burden experienced by many caregivers could contribute to their eventual decision to quit work or take up infrequent employment. Caregiving is not a short-term endeavour, with a study surmising that caregiving duration varied from 6 months to more than 20 years.[14] Progressively, caregivers may have poorer quality of life and health, compounded by prolonged stress, which could not be easily and solely addressed under Healthier SG reform as it requires broader social and cultural interventions. Despite having more community resources that are

[9] Touch Community Services (2022), "Caring for Female Caregivers".[Internet]

[10] R. Sambasivam, *et al.* (2019), "The hidden patient: chronic physical morbidity, psychological distress, and quality of life in caregivers of older adults". Psychogeriatrics 19(1): 65–72.

[11] Q. Yuan *et al.* (2020), "Coping Patterns Among Primary Informal Dementia Caregivers in Singapore and Its Impact on Caregivers — Implications of a Latent Class Analysis. *The Gerontologist* 61(5): 680–692.

[12] V.C. Riches *et al.* (2023),"A study of caregiver support services: Perspectives of family caregivers of persons with intellectual disabilities in Singapore". *Journal of Policy and Practice in Intellectual Disabilities* 20(1): 117–131.

[13] *The Straits Times* (6 April 2023), "Over 40% of caregivers at risk of depression amid challenging environment: Survey".

[14] V. Y. W., Lee *et al.* (2016), "Managing multiple chronic conditions in Singapore — Exploring the perspectives and experiences of family caregivers of patients with diabetes and end stage renal disease on haemodialysis". *Psychology & Health* 31(10).

increasingly available and accessible for caregivers, existing cultural and familism norms may deter vulnerable groups of people from seeking appropriate support and recognising the need to prioritise their own health.

Improving gender stereotypes

More women are participating economically, societally and are holding executive or leadership roles now than ever before. The shift in traditionally gendered roles and diversification of care roles are attributable to rising costs and increasing care needs. Since 2020, there has been about 20 percent improvement in attitudes towards gender roles in Singapore. However, one out of five Singaporeans still agrees that "men should have more right to a job if scarce" and that "women earning more than men may cause problems in the household".[15] Despite commendable improvement in women's rights and female representation over the years, the traditional gender-based division of labour especially in family and household issues remains. As summarised earlier, these gendered roles may have a disproportionately negative impact on women's health and quality of life. Therefore, it is imperative to address gender inequality upstream to prevent perpetuating these norms and jeopardising the benefits of Healthier SG for women.

Conclusion

With Healthier SG, all Singapore residents will have smaller, more frequent encounters with the health system through the Healthier

---

[15] Mathew Mathews *et al.*, "Our Singaporean Values: Key Findings from the World Values Survey". Singapore: Lee Kuan Yew School of Public Policy, 2021.

SG doctors and their teams. It would be naïve to believe that everyone, male and female will take ownership of their health and partner with their doctors. In all likelihood, many seniors and even middle-aged men will abdicate this role to daughters, daughters-in-law, and wives, and women will need more and better support to navigate the health system. Healthier SG doctors will need to be mindful that women tend to 'neglect' their own health needs and coverage. Therefore, in caring for women and their families, healthcare practitioners must especially pay attention to the health plans for the women themselves.

The hospital-to-community and -home paradigm is the right one for Singapore and a needed one for a health system already under tremendous strain. But as a country, Singapore has to recognise this will impose even more onerous burdens on women and proactively take steps to mitigate this.

Expanding respite care options, expanded day services, and caregiver support, both financially and psycho-socially, would be invaluable in ensuring that in Healthier SG, we do not simply transfer the stresses faced by the health system to women caring for their families. Following social prescribing implementations in the United Kingdom, Singapore could also explore recruiting care coordinators whose role would be to link patients of Healthier SG clinics to the relevant community partners and periodic monitoring of health goals.

Care coordinators could act as an extension of community nurses or care managers and general practitioners, overseeing the individual's ability to follow through with their health plans. This would greatly ameliorate the burden of responsibilities women often hold in promoting well-being within the family. Caregiving allowances borne by the state to identified familial caregivers should also be much more generously enhanced to recognise the societal contributions of individual caregiving, the need for caregivers to have the means for self-care and to enable women who will be predominantly the caregivers opportunities to build up some degree of financial independence.

Mao Zedong famously said "Women hold up half the sky," to emphasise that women were a resource for the economy and not just the home. In Healthier SG, women, whether as decision-makers or as caregivers, will hold up more than half the sky. Society should recognise this reality and organise to enable women to play these roles well.

Acknowledgement

We would like to thank Ms Marianne Lim, from Singapore University of Technology and Design, for her help with the background research for this chapter.

JEREMY LIM is an Associate Professor at the National University of Singapore (NUS) Saw Swee Hock School of Public Health. His practice and academic work focus on health systems strengthening including financing reforms and the use of digital technologies in healthcare.

NURUL AMANINA BINTE HUSSAIN is a researcher in the NUS Saw Swee Hock School of Public Health. Her academic interests include social determinants of health and health systems strengthening.

"I want women to have confidence in themselves, and to make choices in their lives for themselves and not for others."

~ Adventurer and explorer Sophia Pang, for The Lives of Women exhibition at the National Museum, Jan–Mar 2022

CHAPTER 17

The Gender Gap in Mental Health

Kamini Rajaratnam

The gender gap in mental health disorders has always worried me, both as a psychiatrist and as the mother of two little girls. Women, across their life span, are at higher risk for anxiety and depression. This has been found in studies conducted both locally and globally.

The Singapore mental health study in 2017 found the lifetime likelihood of major depressive disorders to be higher in women, at 7.2 per cent, than in men, at 4.3 per cent. Similarly, in the U.S., a report in the American Psychiatric Association's *Journal of Abnormal Psychology* in 2011 put the lifetime prevalence of depression in women at 22.9 per cent compared to 13.1 per ent in men, and the prevalence of anxiety in women as 5.8 per cent compared with 3.1 per cent in men.

To add insult to injury, women are often belittled, their concerns dismissed, and their experiences invalidated when they seek help for their struggles. I have lost count of the number of times I have seen a patient who has been labelled 'weak', 'hormonal', or 'too sensitive', when in reality she has been struggling with an untreated mental illness.

This is what led me to pursue a career in women's mental health. Why is there this gender gap in mental health? One view is that women are better at recognising they need help and seeking it. But even so, this does not take away from the fact that women have to contend with situations and challenges in life that put them at higher risk of developing a mental illness. These are some of the challenges women face.

Young girls

It's not as stark as it used to be, but gender stereotyping at home, in school, and in society generally is still prevalent. Girls raised in environments where traditional gender roles are enforced and gender stereotypes are perpetuated can experience anxiety and depression, as well as feelings of inadequacy, low self-esteem, and social isolation. If girls are constantly told they should be passive, emotional, and nurturing, they will feel pressured to conform to such expectations even if these do not align with their personalities, abilities, and interests.

At school, teachers and peers may unintentionally reinforce gender roles through differential treatment, such as praising boys for their academic achievements more than they praise girls or encouraging girls to pursue traditional female-dominated career paths, such as nursing or teaching.

School uniforms can reinforce gender stereotypes, giving girls and boys no room for choice. Similarly for extra-curricular activities that vary for boys and girls. All of this sends a poorly veiled message to girls from a young age that they are not the same as boys.

Teenagers

Meta analytic studies[4,5] which have systematically examined data since the 1990s have proven that men tend to have higher self-esteem than women, and that this gap emerges in adolescence. Even when adjusting for cultural differences, the gender differences seem driven by universal factors and biological processes that transcend culture and context.

Teenage girls have their appearance and behaviour put under the microscope, both in daily life and on social media platforms. Most of the teenaged girls I see talk about the pressure they feel to look and behave a certain way in order to fit in. This constant anxiety about the way they look, and a heavy reliance on external validation from their peers and social media, takes a toll on their self-esteem. Hormonal fluctuations during puberty also wreak havoc with

[1] Nicholas R. Eaton *et al.* (2011), "An Invariant Dimensional Liability Model of Gender Differences in Mental Disorder Prevalence: Evidence from a National Sample". J. *Abnorm. Psychology* 121(1):282–288.

[2] F. Van Droogenbroeck, B. Spruyt, & G. Keppens (2018), "Gender differences in mental health problems among adolescents and the role of social support: Results from the Belgian health interview surveys 2008 and 2013". *BMC Psychiatry* 18(6). https://doi.org/10.1186/s12888-018-1591-4

[3] L. Picco, M. Subramaniam, E. Abdin, J.A. Vaingankar, & S.A. Chong (2017), "Gender differences in major depressive disorder: Findings from the Singapore Mental Health Study". *Singapore Med J.* 58(11):649–655. doi: 10.11622/smedj.2016144.

[4] Wiebke Bleidorn *et al.* (2016), "Age and gender differences in self-esteem — A cross-cultural window". *Journal of Personality and Social Psychology* 111(3): 396–410. https://doi.org/10.1037/pspp0000078

[5] Kristen C. Kling *et al.* (1999), "Gender differences in self-esteem: A meta-analysis". *Psychological Bulletin* 125(4): 470–500. https://doi.org/10.1037/0033-2909.125.4.470

teenagers' emotions. All of this puts teenage girls at higher risk of developing anxiety and depression.

An emerging problem I see in this age group is the increased rates of sexual harassment, assault and trauma experienced by girls compared to their male peers.

A longitudinal study in the UK in 2022 found that at age 17, one in five girls had experienced sexual violence in the previous 12 months, while about 5 per cent experienced assault and 20 per cent experienced unwelcome sexual approach. Compare this with 5·4 per cent of boys experiencing sexual violence, 1·0 per cent experiencing sexual assault and 5·2 per cent unwelcome sexual approach.

The problem is that when someone tries to report or just talk about the sexual assault and sexual harassment they have experienced, often it is dismissed by the person or people they are reaching out to, be it a family member, a friend, a colleague, or a teacher.

When I see patients with longstanding refractory anxiety or depression, it is almost always a red herring for underlying trauma. With this comes the guilt, anger and shame that a lot of girls feel and are dealing with alone because of the huge barrier they face in getting the help they need. They question their role in the assault, often blaming themselves and questioning their morality or feeling ashamed for something that was not their fault at all.

Schools may take a conciliatory path or minimise the actions of the perpetrator and mediate between the victim and perpetrator. This is far more damaging for the traumatised victim and makes it seem as if the blame should be equally borne by the two parties.

I have seen a school subject a victim to a lengthy investigation spanning years, further traumatising her and causing her to be discriminated against by classmates and teachers. As the investigation dragged on, the victim battled bouts of depression and anxiety and eventually had to leave school.

Reporting a sexual offence to the police is even more daunting for young girls. They would have to sit through a detailed interrogation, recounting all the details and risking being re-traumatised. The thought of testifying and facing the perpetrator in court can be a big barrier to reporting the crime. Often the victim decides not to report it and just tries to move on.

This leads to very deep-rooted feelings of shame and guilt which form the bedrock of their anxiety and depression, and it may only manifest years later. When I see a teenager or adult with refractory anxiety or depression, I always do a trauma screen and the sad fact is that more times than not it comes back positive.

Young adults

In young women who are starting out in the work-force, workplace discrimination is not uncommon. Discriminatory hiring practices, being passed over for promotions, lower salaries compared to their male peers, being invested in less and getting less support from their supervisors — these are the realities many face. Although there are laws against such discriminatory practices, it continues.

For young women who encounter these obstacles it is usually easier to just leave and find another job in what will, hopefully, be a fairer workplace. But these experiences create a fertile breeding ground for the imposter syndrome that many young women report, and this can lead to them falling prey to depression and anxiety.

Young women, more so than young men, have to deal with societal expectations that they will marry and start families by a certain age. The concept of the ticking 'biological clock' can create a lot of unnecessary anxiety.

Marriage and motherhood

Marriage brings a unique set of struggles for women in this day and age. Most women have jobs, but many have to juggle the demands of their paid work with their caregiving responsibilities. The burden of caregiving, whether it be of the children, ageing parents or other relatives with health or mobility issues, continues to be borne primarily by women. This can lead to a sense of being overwhelmed and unsupported, as well as feelings of guilt and inadequacy if they are unable to meet the expectations.

Women may have to reduce their work hours or leave the work force altogether to take on the caregiving responsibilities. This can have long-term financial consequences and impact their sense of self-worth, all of which puts them at higher risk of developing mental health issues.

Another issue I encounter is the fact that men are very resistant to seeking help for their mental health issues, and even just taking the first step of admitting that they are struggling. This can lead them to vent their frustration at home on their wives, putting tremendous strain on the marriage. We can't talk about women's mental health without addressing men's mental health as they are inextricably linked.

As a society, we are making some progress. The husbands and dads of today are far more involved and ready to share household care and parenting responsibilities with their wives. But even in the most progressive households, women still take on a heavier emotional and mental load when it comes to caregiving. It isn't just about sharing chores; it is the management and running of a home — deciding what needs to be done, who needs to do it, and then checking to make sure it has been done.

A typical mother is in charge of coordinating school pickups, after-school schedules, meals for the day, doctor's appointments, parties, who needs to bring what and what to pack for each day. It is never-ending, and it is a recipe for burnout. And I have seen this play out so many times in my clinic. Often women don't see the mental load they are shouldering, and they blame themselves for not being strong enough to handle it all. This leads to a lot of guilt and resentment which further worsens the burnout and puts them at a higher risk for anxiety and depression.

Peripartum depressive symptoms are seen in as many as one in five pregnant women, though not all amount to major depression. For a long time, women experiencing peripartum depression received little help as they struggled to cope with it.

The postpartum period can be a particularly trying for women. A study done in Singapore in 2011 found a 12 per cent prevalence of antepartum depression and about 7 per cent for postpartum depression.[7]

It is heartening to see that major obstetric departments are now paying attention to this aspect of motherhood, and there is more antenatal and postnatal screening and early intervention.

Stay-home mums are particularly vulnerable as they tend to be very isolated with few opportunities to socialise outside of the home. This can lead to feelings of loneliness and depression as well as a sense of being overwhelmed and unsupported. Feelings of inadequacy are common, but they hesitate to reach out for support and professional help because they feel that since they do not have the additional demands of paid work, they should be able to manage their caregiving responsibilities.

[6] F. Bentivegna & P. Patalay (2022), "The impact of sexual violence in mid-adolescence on mental health: A UK population-based longitudinal study". *Lancet Psychiatry* 9(11):874–883. doi: 10.1016/S2215-0366(22)00271-1.

[7] Helen Chen *et al.* (2011), "Identifying mothers with postpartum depression early: integrating perinatal mental health care into the obstetric setting". *ISRN Obstet Gyneco* 2011:309189.

[8] D.H. Phua, T.W. Ng, & E. Seow (2008), "Epidemiology of suspected elderly mistreatment in Singapore". *Singapore Medical Journal* 49(10):765.

Mum guilt is a huge problem among both new and seasoned mums. They struggle to cope in the face of the onslaught of information telling them how to parent their child, and there is also the constant judgement by society of the way mothers are bringing up their children. Almost every mother I see tells me this, and it's a battle getting them to switch perspectives and show themselves the compassion they are entitled to.

A major concern for new mums is returning to work after having a baby. Some worry that they will be made redundant, while others may face discrimination because it is assumed that they are now less committed and so they are passed over for important roles and promotions. Some may have their requests for flexible work arrangements refused.

Older women

Menopause typically occurs between the ages of 45 and 55 and is defined as the permanent cessation of menstruation. It is caused by a decline in the production of oestrogen and progesterone hormones by the ovaries. These hormonal fluctuations can have a number of effects on mental health.

For example, women going through menopause may experience symptoms such as irritability, mood swings, anxiety, and depression. These symptoms are thought to be related to changes in hormone levels, which can affect the balance of neurotransmitters in the brain. Menopause can also lead to sleep disturbances, which can further exacerbate mood problems. Hot flashes and night sweats are common during menopause, which can disrupt sleep and contribute to fatigue and irritability.

Elder abuse is a serious problem that affects both men and women, but women are disproportionately affected. In a study done in

Singapore over a period of 12 months in 2005–2006, 42 cases of suspected mistreatment were detected. Women made up about two-thirds of these cases.

Elder abuse refers to any form of mistreatment or harm inflicted on an older person, usually by a caregiver or family member. This can include physical, emotional, sexual, or financial abuse, neglect, or abandonment. Research has shown that elder abuse can have a significant impact on mental health, especially in women.

Women who experience elder abuse are at higher risk of depression, anxiety, and post-traumatic stress disorder (PTSD). They may also experience feelings of helplessness, shame, and guilt. Women are more vulnerable to elder abuse because they often have longer life expectancies than men and are more likely to live alone or in institutional settings. Women are also more likely to experience age-related health problems, which can make them more dependent on others for care.

Intergenerational trauma

Intergenerational trauma refers to the transmission of trauma and its effects across generations. The impact of intergenerational trauma on women can be particularly significant due to their roles as caregivers and transmitters of culture and values. Women who have experienced intergenerational trauma are at increased risk for mental health issues such as depression, anxiety, PTSD, and substance abuse.

These women may also experience feelings of shame, guilt, and hopelessness, and may struggle with relationships and trust. Women who have experienced intergenerational trauma may struggle with parenting, as they may have learned unhealthy parenting behaviours from their own parents.

These women may also have difficulty trusting others with their children and may struggle to form attachments with their children. Despite the challenges posed by intergenerational trauma, many women are able to develop resilience and overcome the effects of trauma. Through supportive relationships, therapy, and other forms of healing, women can learn to cope with the impacts of intergenerational trauma and move forward in their lives.

Closing the mental health gender gap

The world today is a better place for a woman than the world in which my mother grew up and her mother before her. What I want to see for my daughters is an even better world, one where they are not burdened by gender stereotypes that will limit their choices and potentially affect their mental health, where gender is just another facet of a person and not a factor that determines your role and opportunities in life.

How do we bring about such a world?

Schools need to do more to reduce gender stereotyping and introduce flexibility in the choice of attire and CCAs both in single and mixed gender schools. They need to eliminate messaging that directly or indirectly perpetuates gender stereotypes.

Schools also need to redirect their focus from standard sex education to a more comprehensive programme covering consent, mutual respect, and equality. School counsellors need to be trained to deal with allegations of sexual assault or harassment in a trauma-sensitive way and they should provide victims with immediate access to mental health care.

Workplaces need to be more inclusive and supportive. Instead of viewing working mothers as a liability, they should help them balance the needs of work and family life by letting them shape their workday as they want.

Company HR policies should be more progressive, with more generous paid childcare leave and flexibility to work from home. Health insurance coverage for employees should include mental health conditions. This is rarely included today, and it is one of the biggest barriers to women seeking professional help.

Public healthcare programmes need to be tweaked to factor in the gender discrepancy in certain mental health disorders, and there should be more targeted programmes dealing with primary prevention and early intervention.

The future I envision for my girls is one where they can feel safe to voice their opinions without being dismissed as being too sensitive or emotional, where they can be safe around their friends knowing that their wishes will be respected, and boundaries not breached without their consent.

If they choose to have a child, they should not have to worry that this will affect their progress at work. They should be able to enjoy the experience knowing that they are supported fully both at home and at the workplace. Gender equality simply means that there is a level playing field for women and men, and that is what I want for my daughters.

KAMINI RAJARATNAM (MBBS, MRCPsych, FAMS) is a patient-centred psychiatrist who is committed to providing compassionate and holistic care to her patients. She is especially passionate about working with women facing emotional issues during and after pregnancy. One in seven women suffer from postnatal depression and 80 per cent of women experience mood disturbances in the postpartum period. As a mother herself, the challenges of pregnancy and motherhood resonate only too well with her. She has made it her mission to guide mothers who are facing emotional difficulties, or are on the brink of burnout, to make the changes necessary to reach their optimal health and functioning. She is certified in the Mindful Motherhood programme and Bringing Baby Home programme, and she uses these powerful tools in combination with other interventions and medication when necessary. There is help available for anyone feeling increasingly overwhelmed, experiencing mood disturbances, anxiety, insomnia, irritability, and fatigue.

"By 2050, climate change, and other environmental challenges will transform not just how we work, live & play, but what we value. Women must have a pivotal leadership role if we hope to adapt and survive. As traditional child-bearers and caregivers, women have the resilience, patience, tenacity and humility to set humanity on the right path to a sustainable future. The society, nation or world that values and respects women and the environment will be the one that is successful and sustainable."

~ Environmental activist Geh Min, for The Lives of Women exhibition at the National Museum, Jan–Mar 2022

CHAPTER 18

What Fuels Gender Inequality is What Fuels Climate Change

Woo Qiyun

What does it mean to be a woman living in a climate-impacted society?

When I got the brief to talk about gender and environmentalism, I was kind of stumped. The fight for gender equality and the fight for climate action are two causes very close to my heart and yet I never saw them as interconnected fights until very recently.

A phrase that has grounded most of my advocacy is that no one is spared the impact of climate change. When a typhoon hits a city, everything and everyone in its path of destruction will be affected. And all the more so a woman who is already at a disadvantage from lacking access to education and physical security and facing financial precarity — key factors crucial to being able to adapt to the impact or to avoid it in the first place.

As I prepared the comic, I thought it was quite funny to use the phrase rising tide lifts all boats, considering that Singapore policymakers like to use it to talk about tackling inequality. The rising tide is an environmentalist's worst nightmare. I hope you readers will appreciate the irony.

But jokes aside, this piece has helped me see how intertwined both fights are. I hope that we can be better allies to each other in our joint pursuit of a fair and liveable future.

The thing is, climate change does not discriminate. No one is spared from its wrath.

However, the impact of climate change is highly unequal. Let's go back to the rising tide example.

If your boat is disadvantaged, you'll be struggling to keep water out of your boat.

(If you're preoccupied with other problems, who has time to fix the hole??)

If you couldn't afford a good boat, you will struggle to just stay afloat.

Not to mention, if you lack access to safety resources, you're in some serious trouble when things go south.

The thing about climate change is that it's an amplifier. It amplifies existing inequalities in our society.
There is evidence that violence on women increases during times of stress and displacement.
Source: World Health Organisation
The lack of sufficient sanitary and maternal care during floods means increased miscarriages and illnesses.
Source: The Guardian
When women lack access to education & decent employment, they are far less likely to be able to access information to deal with the impact of climate change
Source: UNFCCC
As human rights defender, Matcha Phorn-In, puts it "If you are invisible in everyday life, your needs will not be thought of, let alone addressed, in a crisis situation,"
Source: UN Women
How now?
THE WEIRD AND WILD

It's not so much about lifting more boats at this point, but making sure that more boats don't sink when the tide rises.

We need to address the inequalities that plague our society like...

equalize the load of care work

ensuring that women have access to safe conditions and resources

ending discrimination and provide women with equal opportunities

And addressing both these issues means ensuring that women have a seat at the table to make these decisions.

This is still a huge work in progress for us in Singapore...

Women have been persistently under represented on boards in Singapore. As at the end of 2020, the largest 100 primary-listed companies on SGX achieved a 17.6% participation rate of women on boards.
Source: AWARE Omnibus Report on Gender Equality

In 2020, full-time female employees aged 25 to 54 earned 14.4% lower than their male counterparts.
Source; MOM Update on Singapore's Adjusted Gender Pay Gap

Stay-at-home fathers in Singapore face stigma & family policies in Singapore continue to signal that childcare is a woman's responsibility which reinforces unequal care burdens.
Source; Institute of Policy Studies (IPS) study

The number of reported sexual violence cases has increased in recent years.
Source: AWARE Omnibus Report on Gender Equality

Gender inequality not only makes communities more vulnerable to the impacts of climate change, it continues to create problems if climate solutions aren't designed to care for already-marginalized communities.

THE WEIRD AND WILD

In Singapore, our fight for gender equality comes hand in hand with a more sustainable future.

We need to take climate action to prevent the worst of climate change. There's still time.

When we put our hearts and minds together for both causes, we can create a more equal, more habitable and sustainable world for all.

THE WEIRD AND WILD

WOO QIYUN is an environmentalist and self-taught illustrator with a goal of making climate issues less scary, more diverse and culturally relevant on her platform, The Weird and Wild. Qiyun has worked with brands such as Mercedes-Benz, Carousell, Decathlon, Temasek, The Earthshot Prize, National Geographic Society to develop environmental education material. Besides keeping the lights on, her work is also used to advocate for policy change, be it getting people to understand technical policy, write to their MPs, attend in-person rallies, or participate in public consultations. She continues to draw in the hope that her resources can facilitate people in their own journeys to advocate and appreciate all things weird and wild about our natural environment.

The Ties that Bind

"After marriage, women typically give up their careers to become carers and child bearers — and this happens to many of the women in the arts and cultural scene. In the year 2050, I would like to see greater support and encouragement in spurring these women to continue pursuing their dream in the Arts. I hope that these women are empowered to continue their passion for performing and singing and allow their talents to shine for our nation."

~ Singapore's first lady of song Rahimah Rahim, for The Lives of Women exhibition at the National Museum, Jan–Mar 2022

CHAPTER 19

The Future of Families in Singapore

Paulin Tay Straughan & Mindy Eiko Tadai

S ingapore is set to become a 'super-aged' society by 2030. The current decade represents a golden window of opportunity to advance new interventions aimed at addressing the barriers to fertility and family formation, be it financial or ideological. Our pro-family policies rival some of the most generous and comprehensive in the world, and yet we have not been able to arrest the downward trend of our total fertility rate (TFR) since the 1970s. Why is this the case and what more can be done? The answer is embedded in a mosaic of new meanings and entrenched contradictions concerning marriage, children, motherhood/fatherhood, and work (Jones, 2019; Straughan *et al.*, 2007). Any sustained breakthroughs will not be through financial incentives alone but through the normalisation of true gender equality at home and in workplaces.

Taking a back-casting approach, we envision a future for Singapore that endows its young couples with greater agency, social support, and work-life balance to grow their families earlier and larger. In this chapter, we aim to address the main factors affecting couples' decisions about marriage and parenthood, and what might help to improve Singapore's TFR over the next few decades. It is our intention to unpack some of the key layers of tension between fertility and human capital accumulation.

We start with an overview of the changing shape of families and expectations of marriage and parenthood, followed by a frank discussion on whether recent enhancements to Singapore's pro-family policies will shift the 'needle' towards higher fertility. Ultimately, we hope for young couples to achieve their ideal family size without having to suffer great marital strain or sacrifice their career aspirations.

The changing shape of families in Singapore

Over the past decades, our population has been rapidly ageing amidst a backdrop of changes to family structures. The shapes and sizes of households today reflect key demographic and societal shifts — including delayed marriage and parenthood, preferences for singlehood and childlessness, and longer life expectancies. Importantly, we are seeing a rapid "feminization" of our ageing society as women continue to outlive men and reside alone in larger numbers (Thang and Lim, 2012).

Singapore's TFR, which refers to the average number of babies per woman during her reproductive years, has been in steady decline from 1970 to 2022 (see Figure 1). In 2023, it fell to a historic low of 0.97, dropping below 1.0 for the first time ever (Tan, 2024). This demographic trend is in part a reflection of young Singaporeans' shifting priorities and aspirations. Singlehood has become a new norm. The proportion of singles rose across all age brackets for both men and women between 2011 and 2021, with the largest increases seen among women in their late 20s to early 30s (Singapore Department of Statistics, 2023).

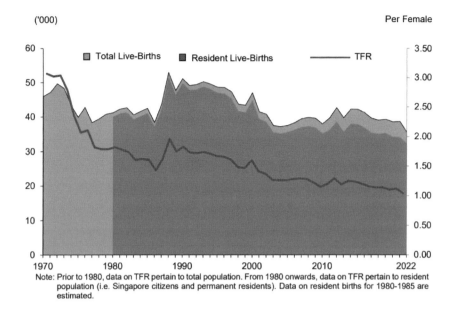

('000)   Per Female

Note: Prior to 1980, data on TFR pertain to total population. From 1980 onwards, data on TFR pertain to resident population (i.e. Singapore citizens and permanent residents). Data on resident births for 1980-1985 are estimated.

Figure 1.   Total Live-Births and Total Fertility Rate (TFR)

(*Source*: Singapore Department of Statistics, 2023)

We are also seeing more women marrying in their early 30s compared to their late 20s a decade ago (Singapore Department of Statistics, 2023). Among women, the median age at first marriage also rose across all educational groups between 2011 and 2021, and those with higher levels of education continue to marry later than their peers (Singapore Department of Statistics, 2023). In addition to rising trends of singlehood and delayed marriage, family sizes are shrinking. The average number of children born to married women fell across all age groups between 2011 and 2021 (Singapore Department of Statistics, 2023).

New expectations of marriage and parenthood

Declining marriage and fertility rates speak to changes in social norms over time concerning couplehood and parenthood. It used to be that we would marry to start families. However, as societies modernise and opportunities for women to train and work alongside their male counterparts improve, we have come to see a shift in gender role ideologies and a corresponding shift in expectations of marriage (Davis & Greenstein, 2009).

Now, we are seeing more couples marry to valorize couplehood. These couples tend to marry later and remain childless and are part of a growing category of 'DINKs' (double income no kids). This phenomenon of career-oriented, child-free couples has been brewing for some time. Data shows that, for all age groups, the proportion of married women without children has increased between 2010 and 2020 (Singapore Department of Statistics, 2020).

For those contemplating starting a family, prescribed ideals and expectations of parenthood can influence fertility decisions. In contemporary Singapore, what it means to be a 'good' parent echoes an ideology of intensive parenting that requires parents — and particularly mothers — to channel tremendous amounts of time and resources into paving a successful path for their children (Hays, 1997; Straughan *et al.*, 2007). As the demands of intensive parenting are both heavy and expensive, these may conflict with the lifestyle aspirations and career goals of young Singaporeans, and thus delay or deter parenthood. Importantly, prevailing social values and expectations of couplehood and parenthood have evolved into formidable barriers to fertility and family formation in Singapore.

Greater support for family formation — will it move the needle?

In February 2023, the Singapore government released a new budget introducing an enhanced suite of financial incentives and work-life initiatives for young married couples aspiring to start and expand their families. Singapore's pro-family policies cover multidimensional needs and is one of the most comprehensive schemes in the world. The basket of provisions, including increased Baby Bonus payouts, more government contributions to the Child Development Account, extended paternity leave, and additional unpaid infant care leave, is expected to cost the government $240 million for each cohort of children (Ng, 2023). Beyond Budget 2023, the recent overhaul of the Housing & Development Board (HDB) classification system accords young families (under the Family and Parenthood Priority Scheme) greater access to affordable housing, signaling new heights in support of family formation.

Will the recent pro-family policy enhancements move the needle in raising Singapore's fertility rates? Probably not palpably (Straughan *et al.*, 2007). They will be most welcomed by those who are already planning to start families or expand family size. However, they are unlikely to persuade the DINKs to change their aspirations, and most significantly, unlikely to move the singles to get married.

On the whole, the impact of pro-family policies in the Asian context has been limited because "countering the forces making for ultra-low fertility requires the adjustments of entrenched cultural, institutional and familial arrangements that are not easy to achieve" (Jones, 2019). Studies show that financial incentives tend to have only modest and temporary effects on raising fertility rates (Thévenon & Gauthier, 2011). The revised policy package may partially alleviate some of the financial and time-related constraints associated with balancing family and work but covers only a small fraction of total lifetime costs. Recent scholarship, however, has raised an important question as to whether Singapore's TFR could have declined even further in the absence of its pro-family provisions (Tan, 2023).

Among young Singaporeans, issues of work-life balance and cost of living are currently the most highly cited reasons for remaining childless or keeping family sizes small (Goh, 2021). This suggests that work-life initiatives, including increased parental leave and a new set of Tripartite Guidelines on Flexible Work Arrangements (FWAs) that will be rolled out in 2024, are crucial to reducing barriers to fertility.

There are dual forces at play. On one end, the existing work-life initiatives do not adequately address entrenched gender role ideologies and the lack of social support that young couples face, resulting in lower take-up rates. We know, for instance, that only slightly more than half of all fathers fully utilized their paternity leave in 2019, based on the Ministry of Social and Family Development's latest figures. On the other end, the prevailing ideologies and practices within workplaces make it difficult for managers to adopt more holistic measures of work performance that would benefit working parents (Straughan & Tadai, 2018). For true work-life balance to exist, there needs to be a *re-thinking* how we appraise employee contributions and a *re-calibration* of work expectations at different stages of life and parenthood (Lin, 2021).

Hope for raising Singapore's ultra-low fertility rate

No matter what pro-family policies are on the table, we are unlikely to see overnight changes in the intrinsic motivations guiding young Singaporeans' decisions on fertility and family formation. At the very least, continued government investments in social policies aimed at increasing gender equality, enabling work-life balance, and widening the fertility window may serve to sustain Singapore's TFR and better support couples who are determined to have children. These couples represent a very important group that may be most amenable to pro-family policy enhancements. As such, we should continue to pave smoother pathways to enable these couples to grow their families earlier and larger.

A key thrust is how we can continue to normalise the implementation and up-take of work-life initiatives, particularly FWAs (in terms of time, space, and workload) to reduce the motherhood penalty. This will require an ideological shift towards understanding how we can redesign jobs and workplaces, and further digitise aspects of work, to better support dual-income families and harness their capabilities at different stages of life. Ultimately, we should aspire towards creating the conditions that enable and empower young couples, and especially women, to take on a fulfilling balance of social roles in work and non-work pursuits.

In conclusion, the future of families in Singapore depends on new approaches to integrating the traditionally separate realms of family and work, as well as evening out the asymmetrical loads that working mothers and fathers carry. There is hope in striving towards true gender equality, which can make inroads for the sustainability and well-being of our greater Singapore family and economy. Of significance will also be the inevitable normalisation of the single-member households as more women (and men) remain single either by choice or circumstance.

PAULIN TAY STRAUGHAN is Professor of Sociology (Practice) and Dean of Students at Singapore Management University, and Director of the Centre for Research on Successful Ageing (ROSA), a centre dedicated to expanding the healthspan of Singapore's ageing society. Paulin serves as consultant on numerous projects commissioned by various government agencies, including the Marriage and Parenthood Surveys commissioned by the National Population and Talent Division. She has published in both sociology and medical journals. Her books include Marriage

Dissolution in Singapore: Revisiting Family Values and Ideology in Marriage, *and* Ultra-Low Fertility in Pacific Asia: Trends, Causes and Policy Issues *(with Gavin Jones and Angelique Chan). She was a Nominated Member of Parliament from 2009 to 2011, during which time she argued for work-life balance and the nurture of a more pro-family social environment.*

MINDY EIKO TADAI is a research assistant at ROSA and contributes to the centre's translational research output. She obtained an Honours degree in International Relations and Political Science at Syracuse University (USA), and subsequently went on to complete a Master's degree in International Studies at the University of Washington (USA). Her research interests lie broadly in family sociology, work-life balance, and health and well-being over the life course. She has three children under the age of 9.

References

Davis, S. & T. Greenstein. 2009. "Gender Ideology: Components, Predictors, and Consequences". *Annual Review of Sociology* 35. https://doi.org/10.1146/annurev-soc-070308-115920

Goh, Y. H. 21 November 2021. "Work-life balance, cost of living among S'pore couples' key concerns in building a family". *The Straits Times.* https://www.straitstimes.com/singapore/politics/work-life-balance-cost-of-living-among-spore-couples-key-concerns-in-building-a

Hays, S. 1996. *The Cultural Contradictions of Motherhood.* Yale University Press.

Jones, G. W. 2019. "Ultra-low fertility in East Asia: Policy responses and challenges". *Asian Population Studies* 15(2): 131–149. https://doi.org/10.1080/17441730.2019.1594656

Lin, C. 2 July 2021. *"I don't think I will regret it': Why more married couples are remaining childless"*. Channel NewsAsia. https://www.channelnewsasia.com/singapore/census-more-married-couples-women-childless-no-kids-1998331

Ng, A. 14 February 2023. "Bigger baby bonus, more paternity leave: 7 takeaways for parents from Budget 2023". CNA. https://www.channelnewsasia.com/singapore/budget-2023-parents-families-baby-bonus-paternity-leave-cda-3276766

Singapore Department of Statistics. 2020. *Census of Population 2020 Statistical Release 1: Demographic Characteristics, Education, Language and Religion*. https://www.singstat.gov.sg/-/media/files/publications/cop2020/sr1/cop2020sr1.ashx

Singapore Department of Statistics. 2023. *Population Trends 2023*. https://www.singstat.gov.sg/publications/population/population-trends

Straughan, P. T., A. Chan & G.W. Jones. 2007. "Where is the stork? Sociological insights into barriers to fertility in Singapore". In *Sociology for Change* (pp. 143–162). Brill. https://doi.org/10.1163/ej.9789004157064.i-245.58

Straughan, P. T. & M. E. Tadai. 2018. "Addressing the implementation gap in flexiwork policies: The case of part-time work in Singapore". *Asia Pacific Journal of Human Resources* 56(2): 155–174. https://doi.org/10.1111/1744-7941.12126

Tan, J. 2023. "Perceptions towards Pronatalist Policies in Singapore". *Journal of Population Research* 40(3): 14. https://doi.org/10.1007/s12546-023-09309-8

Tan, T. 28 February 2024. "Singapore's total fertility rate hits record low in 2023, falls below 1 for first time". *The Straits Times*. https://www.straitstimes.com/singapore/politics/singapore-s-total-fertility-rate-hits-record-low-in-2023-falls-below-1-for-first-time

Thévenon, O. & A. H. Gauthier. 2011. "Family Policies in Developed Countries: A 'Fertility-Booster' with Side-Effects". *Community, Work & Family* 14(2): 197–216. https://doi.org/10.1080/13668803.2011.571400

Thang, L. L. & E. Lim. 2012. *Seniors Living Alone in Singapore*. Singapore: Fei Yue Community Services.

"My wish is for women to be recognised for the multitude of roles they play. A woman must be respected as a 'Mother' who provides peace and eradicates all hatred from society. This status of mother should not only be bestowed upon aged women or individuals who physically have children, but on any and every female, regardless of age, religion or race."

~ Pioneering dancer and choreographer Santha Bhaskar, for The Lives of Women exhibition at the National Museum, Jan–Mar 2022

CHAPTER 20

Love in a Stash of Peanuts

Defying the Odds: The Selfless Journey of a Single Mother before the #MeToo Era

Ken Jalleh Jr

———•〜◦〜•———

Gloria Tan Swee Neo was a sweet wisp of a woman, slight of stature, gentle by nature.

You do not know her, but you should. She belongs to the small print of Singapore's pioneering women who, in Mao's gross under-estimation, hold up half the sky.

She was from an era before the #MeToo movement and the emancipation of women. Like many of her generation, she was plain in accomplishment, but no less precious, and entirely worthy of note and tribute.

I write with unabashed bias. Gloria Tan Swee Neo was my mother. This is her story.

Her once-upon-a-time was in 40s and 50s Singapore, well before the stridency and cacophony of social media opinion, before the first-world opulence of opportunity, progress and modernity.

After the birth of her fourth child when she was in her 30s, she was left to face the future alone, the victim of a philandering husband. And so she was thrust into the plight of a single mother, slighted by conservative society and stigmatised by the zealotry of her church.

She was given custody of her two youngest children, a boy and a girl. The court granted her alimony. It was neither paid nor enforced.

A two-room flat in Circuit Road was all that was left of her marriage.

And so, with two toddlers in tow, she faced a fork in her path. One led to despondency; the other to a personal, powerful discovery of inner resilience.

Before the tyranny of technology, there was the now-quaint prospect of work as a clerk. With little education, her job at a bank provided some relief from uncertainty. The kids were left in the care of grandma while Gloria went from single mother to working woman.

Even as we amplify accomplishment, pursue worthy ideals and explore progress for Singapore women in the chapters of this book, we should honour the everyday trailblazers, their trials and tribulation, their triumphs.

I believe to the very core of my soul in the power of women — their capacity for compassion, their intuitive, maternal calm, a balm against disruption, a ballast to uncertainty.

We often equate the physically stronger of the species with chauvinistic superlatives; Herculean? No, women have proven to be far more. They are mesmerising, vibrant, mysterious, but also enduring with wills of steel.

They are, aptly, Amazonian.

My life and those of my brothers and sister are testimony to my mother's selfless devotion. So, too, I'm sure, is yours.

Some time after she was given custody of my sister and I, my two elder brothers were driven out of their father's home by their step-mother.

They turned up at my mother's flat with a tiny bundle of clothes. Gloria, the young, struggling single mother, saw at her doorstep that her burden, already laden, had become daunting.

Yet, never once in the long struggle as a single mother did I notice regret or self-pity.

Certainly, there were fears. Certainly, there were moments of despondence and despair.

I did see her cry once. We were in church when the priest called for the congregation to step forward and receive Communion.

She stood rooted, alone in the emptying pew, in tears. She could not receive communion, she told me. She was a divorcee, and thus deemed unworthy.

In that moment of vulnerability, I saw how a woman of steely resolve could be overcome by perceived inferiority. Such is the insidious, loathsome prejudice of small-minded society.

I have since remained an atheist.

Four kids were schooled. Gloria was mum and dad, housekeeper, handyman and breadwinner. Thankfully, she had the support of a loving, highly-capable, rotan-wielding granny.

It was not easy managing three teenage boys growing up in the Woodstock era of rebellion, drugs, long hair. Money was always tight. Expenses — school uniforms, fees, bills, mortgages — had to be paid. The oft-espoused philosophy of the Government of the day: "No free lunches."

We lived on the precipice of penury.

Fast forward and one among the three boys graduated from university in London, another thrived with his own construction business and the youngest found his calling in journalism.

It is a legacy she can hold dear. It is unique in the way that it was never meant to be.

As Adrian Wooldrige, in his seminal 2021 book, "The Aristocracy of Talent" says, referring to the US: "Sixty per cent of births to women with only a high school certificate occur out of wedlock, compared with only 10 per cent to women with a university degree."

Why is this pertinent to the story of Gloria Tan Swee Neo? It matters, because, as Wooldridge notes, "the rate of single parenting is the most significant predictor of social immobility".

To sum up a life of sacrifice in the linear timeline of a blurry newsreel would be a gross injustice. Without anecdote and context, her life would merely be small and inconsequential.

Life was not all unpleasant for Gloria. She found love again, but never remarried. He gave her joy and some measure of material comfort.

In keeping with her independent streak, she learnt to drive and bought a car. He helped pay for a landed home.

But through it all, her children remained, instinctively, intuitively, at the core of her being.

True to the spirit of thrift of the time, telling in her maternal devotion, was *kacang*.

Always, after returning from wedding or restaurant dinners, she would wrap the free peanuts in Kleenex tissue and smuggle the contraband home for her children.

In those moments, in the late-night crunching of teeth on peanuts that we take for granted today, we tasted the tender gesture of a mother's love.

Like most Asian families, there were few moments of showy, lovey-dovey hugs and daily declarations of love. Love was sufficiently articulated by a stash of peanuts.

Gloria Tan Swee Neo died in 1999. She was 70.

And still I see her.

I see her in my Filipino helper. Joey is one of thousands of her fellow migrant domestic workers (MDWs) who venture abroad, thrust, alone, into the unknown, supporting families of strangers to support her own.

I see my mother in the aunties at restaurants, or bent over trays at food courts, serving others to survive, to raise their children or grandchildren as best they can.

I see her in the lady of the toilet, collecting coins amid the stench, cleaning up after the uncouth and the unsanitary.

And I especially see her in the mother of my son, in the way she instinctively puts the two men in her life first, in everything she does as wife and mother.

They are not women of means or scholarship, of opinion or ambition. In their DNA, an inexplicable devotion, an extravagant mission: To give their all for their children.

They are extraordinary in what society blithely defines as ordinary. They must, as Maya Angelou suggests, be "tender and tough".

She writes, in her 1993 book "Wouldn't Take Nothing for My Journey Now": "The woman who survives intact and happy… must have convinced herself, or be in the unending process of convincing herself, that she, her values and her choices are important.

"In a time and world where males hold sway and control, the pressure upon women to yield their rights of way is tremendous. And it is under those very circumstances that the woman's toughness must be in evidence."

Gloria Tan Swee Neo's life evokes awe and wonder in the manner that Maya Angelou encapsulates.

I remain grateful, but also perplexed. Some of the many questions continue to haunt me. What, I wonder, was it like to possess such steel of will to strive, to sacrifice so much, so selflessly?

What is the measure of a single woman raising four children successfully, playing both mum and dad, sans MDW?

What was on her mind many years later, seeing her children grow to have comfortable lives and families of their own? Was there gratification? Or regret that most of her life was ours to demand, as self-absorbed and entitled kids?

Was it all worth it? *Were we worthy?*

In the context of this tribute, allow me to tweak what the great Czech writer Milan Kundera once wrote: "The struggle of women against perception and prejudice is the struggle of memory against forgetting."

I live each day grateful for the life, love and legacy of Gloria Tan Swee Neo. I rail against reckless indifference. I fear forgetting.

Thank you for helping me remember.

KEN JALLEH JR was a journalist for more than 40 years. He conceptualised and was founding editor of two newspapers (The New Paper on Sunday, and Streats), and a socio-economic news magazine styled on the Economist (Lexean). He was in the pioneer team that launched The Singapore Monitor and The New Paper, where he held various senior editing positions before becoming CEO of Think Inc, a visual content arm of SPH Media. He began his career in The Straits Times as a sportswriter and moved into writing/reporting on a range of beats, including crime, politics and socio-economic issues. His experience includes stints at LA Times, Detroit News, and The New York Daily News.

"I hope that by 2050, there is more equality and social integration in Singapore, and that there will be no discrimination, bias, or unfair treatment. This applies to not only sex, but also age, race, gender reassignment, disability, religion or belief, sexual orientation, marriage or civil partnership status, pregnancy or maternity. For example, there should be no need to complete forms or answer questions regarding these biases."

~ Equestrian and Paralympian Laurentia Tan, for The Lives of Women exhibition at the National Museum, Jan–Mar 2022

CHAPTER 21

Who is Free to Love? Queer(ing) Life in Singapore after The Repeal

Shobha Avadhani

How do I love thee?[1]
Let me count the ways
I love thee [for]…

…The right to shelter
The right to work
The right to citizenship
The right to raise children
The right to share resources
The right to be represented in mainstream media spaces
The right to support from family, community, and society
The right to a second chance
The right to grow old with dignity

---

[1] A reference to Elizabeth Barrett Browning's "Sonnet 43", the first three lines of which I have taken the liberty of using as a springboard for new ideas.

In the Flower Dome at Gardens by the Bay in Singapore, there is a sculpture by Bruno Catalano entitled "La Famille De Voyageurs". The blurb on the website tells us that this translates to "A travelling family", and that this work of art

> "…depicts a family visiting Gardens by the Bay before heading home. As they depart Singapore, they take with them beautiful memories and leave a part of themselves behind. Inspired by the universal theme of travel, French sculptor Bruno Catalano's eye-catching works, with their dashed bodies and the deliberate lack of volume, invite the viewer to mentally reconstruct the possibility of the human potential."[2]

A closer look at the sculpture suggests a different way of reading its meaning — a liberty that one hopes any artist allows their audience the moment they release their art to the public. The expressions on this wonderfully detailed sculpture are not happy

---

[2] The quote has been taken from the website of Gardens by the Bay: https://www.gardensbythebay. com.sg/en/things-to-do/attractions/art-sculptures.html

ones. They look anxious. Exhausted. Father, mother, and child (we are meant to assume that this is how they are related to one another) all have furrowed brows, grimly set lips and tightly clenched jaws. Their erased body parts do not seem to have been enthusiastically surrendered in a welcoming city. Instead, they appear to have been ripped away against their will. A bodily tax — more than a pound of flesh. Leaving gaping wounds that, far from inviting us to imagine human potential, provoke us to think about what the disciplining of our bodies by the politics of citizenship takes away from us. This heteronormative family seems to have done everything right. One man. One woman. The product of their fertility. Yet their efforts to perform the ideal family (either through the conspicuous consumption of tourism, or the forced fleeing of a country — it is hard to tell) have taken their toll.

La Famille De Voyageurs shows us that there is little joy in this performance. But we do not need to accept this claim on the basis of one sculpture. We know that performing family is difficult, because the ideal state-sanctioned family is held together by a raft of policies, and because for many who aspire to this ideal, one deviation from the ideal means that they are swimming against the tide. Who, indeed, is free to feel the warmth of love, from their family, community, and nation?

On the 3 January, 2023, Section 377A of Singapore's Constitution, which criminalised sex between consenting gay men, was repealed. This was hailed by LGBT activist groups as the positive outcome of years of petitions, constitutional challenges, community outreach projects, and the yearly organisation of Pink Dot — a gathering of citizens in support of LGBT rights. At the same time that the repeal was announced, however, the Singapore Government also indicated that it would take a protective stance towards the reservation of marriage as being between "a man and a woman". While this caveat casts some gloom on the long-awaited and hard-won repeal, it remains to be seen how exactly the state plans to ringfence what conservative lobby groups refer to as the traditional marriage model. Has the LGBT community finally gained the "freedom to love", its rallying cry since the first Pink Dot event in 2009? What does the future for love in Singapore look like? Who is free to love in this nation? Whose freedom to love do we still have to fight for?

In a 2014 paper entitled "Queer time in global city Singapore: Neoliberal futures and the 'freedom to love'", geographer Natalie Oswin[3] explains how queerness in the context of the freedom to love is not just about sexuality, but about how certain groups of people are constructed as the "other". LGBT love is far from being assimilated into the norm of family structures and socially approved arrangements of care, of course, but Oswin's point is that the path to normalisation should also take into account others who are deemed by the state to be undeserving of love and care — the single parent, the migrant worker, the immigrant spouse, and the poor, among others. So many are unfree to love, and if we are to consider what the future of love in Singapore might look like, we should, according to Oswin, think about how all these queered subjects are connected in their construction as being deviant from the proper family model. How, after all, can a nation survive if love is reserved for only a select few? Such a nation is in its death throes. A rapidly emptying signifier. For a more radical visualisation of a loving future, Oswin argues, we need to rigorously interrogate how the "proper family" model was derived in the first place, and what is the work that it does to shore up the state's developmental project. This will allow us to work towards a future where everyone has the freedom to love and be loved.

Apart from the repeal of 377A, another entry point for visualising the future of the freedom to love is the announcement in Parliament

---

[3] N. Oswin (2014), "Queer time in global city Singapore: Neoliberal futures and the 'freedom to love'". *Sexualities* 17(4): 412–433.

on the 24 February 2023 that Singapore's resident total fertility rate had hit an all-time low of 1.05 in 2022. It is difficult to ignore the gruesome syncopation, as this bemoaned slow death knell is brought into contact with the urgently dispatched displacements of migration, labour, social welfare, and drug policies. Who is free to love, to form families, to nurture those families, to keep those families intact, to be supported in giving their family members second chances, to access the services that allow their family members to be who they are? In a post-repeal Singapore, where the stated intention is to even more tightly guard the access to legitimate care arrangements, to ascertain the significance of the falling birth rate is a complex task, with uncertain objectives. If so many are not free to love, and if that freedom to love is a prerequisite for the arrangements of care that sustain the desire and ability to bring children into the world and keep them alive, this seems to suggest that we do not in fact have a vision for the future. We have no future, if we are not prepared to unpack what Oswin has identified as Singapore's developmental project.

La Famille de Voyageurs is not the only sculpture that catches the eye at Gardens by the Bay. In a 2020 article entitled "Reversing demographic decline: Singapore's experience in trying to raise its fertility rate offers lessons for other countries", Poh Lin Tan[4] offers explanations for Singapore's failure to address the falling birth rate. For example, she notes that the pronatalist policies are built on the knowledge that younger women are not keen on giving birth, and so provide access to medical support for older mothers as a way of countering this. Yet she points out that this is unsuccessful because fertility treatments have negative side effects, and so only very few take them up. Tan also explains that the lack of cultural change

---

[4] P.L. Tan (2020), "Reversing Demographic Decline". *Finance and Development* 57.

means that childcare falls on women, despite the access to low cost domestic labour and state-supported childcare services. Finally, Tan tells us that the focus on developing human capital means that ambition and economic success are valorised, situating child-raising as burdensome and traumatic. What this suggests is that the very principles that purportedly created Singapore's success as a nation state are also responsible for its lack of sustainability. Tan notes that immigration is positioned as a solution, but she dismisses it as a "policy patch".

Tan's article paints a bleak picture of Singapore's future, and is accompanied by an image of another sculpture from Gardens by the Bay. Entitled "Planet", this massive bronze piece by artist Marc Quinn:

> "...portrays an oversized reproduction of the artist's own son, Lucas, as a baby. The sculpture's weight is masterfully balanced on the infant's right hand, creating the illusion that the sculpture is floating in the air."[5]

---

[5] The quote has been taken from the website of Gardens by the Bay: https://www.gardensbythebay.com.sg/en/things-to-do/attractions/art-sculptures.html

The giant white baby, floating immobile in the air, framed on the one side by towering skyscrapers, and on the other side by an assemblage of horticultural structures, built on land constructed with sand taken from surrounding countries under controversial circumstances,[6] is a perfect metaphor for the inevitable culmination of the state's developmental project. Without the roots of old trees, the harmonious co-existence with other lands, the space for organically emerging alternate ways of loving, living, building, relating, and creating, this is the baby we are left with. As our birth rate continues to plummet, and so many who yearn for children and family are disallowed from having them, the logical extreme of the tightening boundaries around the freedom to love is more and more queered subjects — migrant workers, transnational families, poor people, single parents, LGBT individuals, drug mules on death row — who are rendered the "other".

In her 2007 book *Terrorist Assemblages: Homonationalism in Queer Times*, Jasbir Puar[7] argues that countries such as the U.S. have used their progressive stance on gay rights as a basis for claiming an advanced level of modernity over other countries that do not recognise gay rights. In coining the term "homonationalism", Puar was not dismissing the need for gay rights. The focus of her research was the way in which the establishment of gay rights was used as a political tool. For example, it has been used to construct Muslim people as always homophobic and heteronormative, and therefore undeserving of the full rights of citizenship. With the repeal of 377A in Singapore, the planned tightening of boundaries around family-formation policies, and the ongoing othering of excluded subjects

---

[6] See for example, V. Lamb, M. Marschke, & J. Rigg (2019), "Trading sand, undermining lives: Omitted livelihoods in the global trade in sand". *Annals of the American Association of Geographers* 109(5): 1511–1528. In this paper, the authors argue that sand mining affects, among other things, fisheries in Cambodia, riverbank agriculture in Myanmar, and migrant labour in Singapore,

[7] J. K. Puar, *Terrorist assemblages: Homonationalism in Queer Times*. Duke University Press, 2007.

from the freedom to love with all its implications, it is time to think about what post-repeal queer politics could look like in Singapore. Whom does a queer politics need to embrace? Whose hand do we take as we gently walk together into the future? What could that future look like if, instead of yearning to be included in homonationalist projects, we allowed ourselves to imagine a completely different future?

The COVID-19 pandemic highlighted the porous boundaries of family. Lockdowns, restrictions, registrations, and virtual contingencies for work and school were built on formalised notions of households. Various news reports and social media posts showed us that many people were not coping well with these policy-defined boundaries. Elderly people and adolescents who needed their friends and usually spent as little time at home as possible, children who were used to interacting with multiple family members across different houses and having some parent-free social interaction in school, migrant domestic workers who were isolated from their weekend communities, migrant construction workers who were locked in their crowded dormitories, queer couples who couldn't be together, transnational families who were split up, and so many other people whose everyday lives, safety and happiness depended upon fluidity, mobility, and access to their chosen family. Would we have been able to manage this better if we had accounted for their desires?

The writer Arundathi Roy ends her 2020 essay[8] "The pandemic is a portal", with the following provocation:

"Historically, pandemics have forced humans to break with the past and imagine their world anew. This one is no different. It is a portal, a gateway between one world and

---

[8] The essay was published on the website of the *Financial Times*, and can be accessed here: https://www.ft.com/content/10d8f5e8-74eb-11ea-95fe-fcd274e920ca

the next. We can choose to walk through it, dragging the carcasses of our prejudice and hatred, our avarice, our data banks and dead ideas, our dead rivers and smoky skies behind us. Or we can walk through lightly, with little luggage, ready to imagine another world. And ready to fight for it."

In considering whom we want to bring with us into a post-repeal Singapore, we will also need to give careful thought to what we want to leave behind.

SHOBHA AVADHANI lectures at a Singapore university where she specialises in the dynamics of race and gender in digital media culture. She has published academic work on media literacy and technological citizenship, as well as non-academic work on her lived experience as a Singaporean Indian woman. An award-winning feminist educator and lifelong learner, she actively works on community-building around teaching for social justice. She also teaches public speaking, which she sees as a way to empower students to fully participate in their desired domains — whether personal, professional, or political.

"In the year 2050, I would like to see Singapore women, nearly all well-educated, enjoying good health and holding good jobs if they choose to work, with greater equality among them. This is not to be taken for granted as globally in affluent countries, even as they get richer and older, the gaps between different groups of people and women increasingly get wider. I hope in Singapore we avoid that. This levelling up will enable all women to have the ability to shape their own lives. I am not asking for the moon, but it is harder to achieve this than you think. I would like to see Singapore become a more tolerant and generous society, able to accept diversity in all its manifestations, and be open to foreigners who are allowed to come into Singapore to live and work and add to our development."

~ **Academic and diplomat Chan Heng Chee, for The Lives of Women exhibition at the National Museum, Jan–Mar 2022**

CHAPTER 22

Outsiders Within: Female Migrants in Singapore

Shailey Hingorani

In 2016, I migrated to Singapore from New York, where I was working with Open Society Foundations. I was a trailing spouse. My partner, whom I had just married in New York's City Hall, was set to start his first post-PhD teaching job at an academic institution that had established itself as the first liberal arts education-provider in Singapore.

The move took place exactly two years after we had first visited Singapore for his job talk. On that first visit, employees of my partner's academic institution — they were trying to court highly skilled migrants like my partner and, by extension, their families — would frequently stress Singapore's 'Asian values' as a reason to migrate. "Imagine a Western city with its attendant cleanliness and robust infrastructure in a multicultural setting where individuals are not atomised, families are put first, and all manner of communities flourish," said one of them, with the confidence of someone who had struck gold.

I would later learn the role migrant women (and men) played in helping Singapore secure this reputation. As construction workers, domestic workers, and indeed as spouses, migrants contributed to the extraordinary success of Singapore. And yet they remained "outsiders within": They lived in Singapore, worked there, performed social reproduction roles, and had families there, but they were neither fully incorporated into their marital families, nor into the Singaporean nation-state.

As I became more familiar with Singapore, I noticed how firmly my identity as a 'migrant woman' was entrenched. Singapore wasn't my first time living abroad — having grown up in Delhi, I had left for Boston to study (and subsequently work) when I was 28. And yet somehow, emotional and bodily experiences in the U.S. didn't make me feel as much of a migrant as they did in Singapore.

In Singapore, I was continuously marked 'foreign', whether by taxi drivers who asked me invasive questions (where I was from, why I looked different from the local Indians, how much I was paid, how many bedrooms my flat had), or by bank tellers who told me that as a 'dependent' (the type of visa I was on, as a trailing spouse) I could not open an independent bank account and had to share my husband's.

These everyday experiences were situated against a policy backdrop which used ethnic composition as the guiding principle of organising public housing, drafting immigration policies, dictating language policies in school, and so on. The social engineering implicit in these policies reinforced my status not just as a migrant, but as an *Indian* migrant.

This growing (forced) realisation of my positionality as a migrant woman made me pay close attention to the state narratives and media discourses around migration, especially the cultural script we follow in assigning 'worth' to female migrants and discussing whether or not they deserve immigration, citizenship, and other rights. There are three types of female migrants in Singapore:

1) Migrant wives, i.e. women married to Singaporean men;
2) Trailing spouses, i.e. women like me married to men who migrate to Singapore for jobs, and;
3) Migrant domestic workers, colloquially known as "helpers".

In the interest of space, I'll focus on migrant wives in this essay.

The aforementioned script is based on two questions: The first question asks, why did you migrate? And the second question asks, how will you contribute to the collective resources of the state?

The script is embedded in the wider hierarchies operating along gender, age, ethnicity, and class. It is crucial to dissect because it tells us how migrants, their experiences and aspirations, are categorised and contained in popular and policy discussions. Regardless of actual experiences of migrant wives, we — state, media, and civil society — prescribe one dominant frame to understand their experiences. The script does not only deny the heterogeneity of the experiences of migrant spouses, but also does something far more insidious: It serves to justify their disempowerment and exclusion from our social contract.

Let me explain.

'Why did you migrate?'

In response to this first question, the cultural script situates migrant spouses at two ends of the spectrum: those who enter into 'marriages of convenience' as a way of circumventing immigration laws to gain a foothold in Singapore; and those who 'married for love'.

The 'marriage of convenience' narrative is more common. In fact, even when migrant spouses say they married for love, they tend to be asked: 'But did you really?'

Yet the spectrum of experiences in between these extremes shows a great deal of diversity in actual motives, consequences, and experiences. Migrant spouses may have married to improve their economic status, improve their social status, or achieve greater autonomy. They may enter into marriage to escape the oppressive gender systems in their countries of origin. I remember a migrant spouse telling me that she preferred a Singaporean man, because — at least in her imagination — they were not like men from her home country, who according to her drank too much, couldn't hold down a job, and had too many girlfriends.

In my experience as a researcher, migrant spouses' perceived motivations behind migration are used to deny them full incorporation into the family and the nation-state. We have heard some social workers use this template — 'migrant spouses enter into marriages for convenience' — to deny them their full support. (As if, if a person had actually married for 'convenience', e.g. to escape economic deprivation, they would not be worthy of being part of a local family.)

Somehow, we never ask Singaporean men why they marry migrant women. Because it's presumed that men, and by extension their families, have social reproduction needs that can only be met by the unpaid labour of women — a type of labour that local women are seen as unwilling to perform.

Even if migrant spouses are not fully aware of their husband's motivations in marrying them, they are quickly and frequently reminded of their domestic responsibilities: both through state-sanctioned pre-and post-marriage courses that teach them how to deal with conflicts and in-law relationships in a cross-cultural context, and by their marital families, most frequently by their in-laws.

Lurking behind the main question ('why did you migrate?') is a more fundamental question: 'Who are you?'. If the answer is that you are of a Southeast Asian nationality that's economically poor relative to Singapore, then you are more often than not pushed to the lowest rung of the family hierarchy, asked to provide domestic labour to your husband, his parents, his siblings, and sometimes extended family, too.

You are incorporated into the family unequally, in a way that's deeply gendered, and fraught with tensions.

'How will you contribute to the collective resources of the state?'

The second question guiding the cultural script is somewhat rhetorical. The answer is already prescribed by the nation-state when they first admit the female migrant into the country.

For example, although both domestic workers and migrant wives are expected to perform domestic labour, the labour itself is defined slightly differently. Migrant domestic workers are expected to contribute to the collective resources of the state by enabling middle-class Singaporean women to participate in the labour force (i.e. by tending to their domestic spheres).

Migrant wives, on the other hand, are expected to reproduce the next generation of Singaporeans. Once female migrants are slotted into one of these two categories — enabling productive labour for Singaporean women, or reproductive labour for Singaporean men — it's difficult to switch between categories or take on additional roles such as being political actors, cultural mediators, and economic contributors.

The reproductive abilities of domestic workers are regulated through the Marriage Restriction Policy and mandatory six-monthly screenings for pregnancy. The productive abilities of migrant spouses are regulated by the type of pass they are on (in many cases requiring a letter of consent from an employer) and their legal ineligibility to work as self-employed persons.

In our work at AWARE, we tend to conceptualise citizen and immigrant rights as 'contributory rights', i.e. they are based on the principle of contributions to collective resources in exchange for long-term benefits. Individuals can typically make contributions to society through war service, or social reproduction, or paid work. In the case of migrant spouses, social reproductive labour in service of the Singaporean family is intimately linked to their legal and substantive citizenship. Their access to citizen and immigrant benefits is mediated through a sponsor — a Singaporean family member, most likely the husband.

Although the citizenship and immigration regimes remain opaque, and there's little transparency on the criteria for each type of pass or the length of individual passes, one relevant factor I have gleaned from doing case advocacy on behalf of migrant spouses may include the presence of a citizen child.

Once they have citizen children, many migrant spouses are able to access social assistance — but chiefly for their children, in the form of childcare and student care subsidies. With citizen children, a migrant spouse's case to stay in Singapore is made stronger, especially if they can prove that they are the child's primary caregiver. The access to both these benefits reinforces the idea that migrant spouses are primarily valued for their reproductive labour.

Still, we have seen cases where even when migrant spouses perform the expected reproductive labour — raise children, care for the ageing, do housework, and so on — certain rights, such as the right to work and to access public housing, social assistance, and health subsidies, are not granted to them. Indeed there are many migrant spouses who are separated from their children or are forced to bring up their children in their countries of origin without their husbands.

The status of migrant spouses as "outsiders within" was reinforced when the government did not extend its COVID care and support package to migrant spouses, even those with citizen children. At AWARE, we interviewed 36 low-income migrant spouses and found that they were struggling to pay rent, and were having to cut back on expenses on basic needs, such as food.

Migrant spouses sustain the lives and relationships of families in Singapore, and yet they struggle to belong.

SHAILEY HINGORANI is a human rights professional who has spent over 13 years advocating for the rights of the most marginalised women and children in South Asia, United States, and Southeast Asia. She has worked with the Association of Women for Action and Research (AWARE), Open Society Foundations, and Save the Children.

"I wish for mothers to be deeply valued for their role in the home. They sow seeds of love and nurturing into their children, seeds whose fruits will not be seen for many years — but these should not go unacknowledged. Whilst their work cannot be accurately measured in monetary remuneration, there should be a tangible affirmation for mothers, especially those who choose to stay home and forgo income, to plough deep in the soil of their families. This will be a nod to how our country doesn't just price economic progress but values every child who grows up here."

~ Adventurer and explorer Esther Tan, for The Lives of Women exhibition at the National Museum, Jan–Mar 2022

CHAPTER 23

A Grandmother's Wish

―◦◦◦◦―

Aline Wong

When my granddaughter, at the age of 16, was leaving for her A-level studies in a boarding school in the United Kingdom, I gave her a red packet containing money, as is customary among the Chinese to wish the young ones good luck. I had intended to include a note that I had written to her but decided to withdraw it at the last minute.

In that note, I had wished her not only God's blessings, but also for her to enjoy her experience abroad, and grow up to be an independent, confident, caring, and generous lady. What made me hesitate to give the note to her at that point was the fear that she might take my message negatively, to mean she was anything but that kind of person at that time.

Thinking back, perhaps I did not need to tip-toe around her as if she was a member of the so-called fragile, 'strawberry' generation. But I did, because she was in truth a very sensitive, still maturing adolescent who was living in her own world of social media and struggling to find her own identity.

How does a person in her eighties, who was born during World War II, communicate with a young girl of 16? Beyond giving them love, preparing their favourite dishes, ferrying them to school and tuition classes, occasionally taking them on outings and such like, how do grandparents bond with grandchildren these days?

I am writing this essay in an effort to understand the current young generation, their world, and the future of their world, as well as to understand myself, and the way my generation figures in social history. This essay is in part a personal reflection. In part, it is to start a deep conversation with my grandchildren. It is also partly a sociological essay that hopes to fill a gap in perspectives purveyed in the earlier volume *Our Lives to Live: Putting a Woman's Face to Change in Singapore.*

Generations: Concept and lived experience

Analytically, the term 'generation' refers to two separate concepts. One is the biological concept of lineage (as in great grandparents, grandparents, parents, and their children). The other is a sociological concept that describes a group or a cohort of individuals born and living contemporaneously, who share a certain 'collective consciousness' (*gestalt*), because they lived through a common location in historical time, with significant socio-economic and political changes that shaped their thoughts, attitudes, values and behaviour.[1] Popular depictions of generations in the 20th century

---

[1] The sociological concept of 'generation' was defined by Karl Mannheim in his 1928 essay on "The Problem of Generations" in Paul Kecskemeti (ed.), *Karl Mannheim, Essays on the Sociology of Knowledge.* London: Routledge and Kegan Paul, 1952. According to Mannheim's theory, the perspective of youth (social consciousness) is very much influenced by their shared experience of major socio-historical events that occur during their maturation period, and in which they were actively involved. This consciousness would influence their lives and in turn shape the events that influence the future generations.

and up to now, the first decades of the 21st, include the well-known cohorts of 'traditionals, baby boomers, X, Y and Z generations'.[2]

The popular depictions of social cohorts are, of course, generalisations which are nonetheless useful tools to describe certain differences between generations as they live through different eras. In real life, the biological generations also live through some common times across cohorts, as people live longer and over-lapping lives. And in real life, individuals lead their own unique lives within the same generation (same cohort) as well.

In this essay on grandparenting and inter-generational relationships, I will use both the above concepts to describe, first, the changes in the social roles of grandparents (biological generations) and, later, the so-called generation gap between different social cohorts (sociological generations). To establish a dialogue between generations, it is necessary to understand how the older generations lived and what the younger generations aspire to for their lives.

What did grandparents do?

Even though the biological generation is based on reproduction and lineage, it has enormous sociological significance. Throughout the past, the grandparents had important roles to play in the production of the household economy and reproduction of everyday life within the family. They were the culture bearers responsible for the preservation and transmission of collective memories, values, and traditions. Grandmothers, especially, were often at the centre of hearth and harmony for the extended family. Thus, in those days, the older generations were much revered for their experience,

---

[2] The loose application of Mannheim's conceptualisation gave rise to the popularised versions in Western social science and the mass media of the Traditional, Baby-Boomer and X, Y and Z generations. They were, respectively, influenced by their shared experience of the Great Depression, the two World Wars, post-War economic recovery and prosperity, the anti-Vietnam war and civil rights movements, and the rise of the Internet and globalisation.

wisdom, and anchoring roles in the kinship group. This was so in both the West and the East.

As society changed rapidly through industrialisation and urbanisation, family structures and relationships changed. Families became much smaller, women became educated, more of them went out to work, and the nuclear family became the norm for married living. Accordingly, the role of grandparents became diminished.

Diminished, but not vanquished. There has long been research evidence from the developed world to show that the nuclear family still maintains regular ties with the grandparents who may live a long distance away (through visits, telephone calls, and now Skype and Facetime.) For marginalised groups, such as minority Black families, or single mothers, or families with incarcerated members, the grandmother has been recognised in research studies as the main provider of childcare and other forms of support for their adult children.

More recently, there is increasing research on the inter-generational flow of resources and support in both Western and Asian societies. In both types of societies, the actual and expected economic support given from adult children to parents has declined (but is still quite common in Asia). Other kinds of inter-generational support such as emotional support and practical help, are existent to a significant extent.[3] More interestingly, there is emergent research on a reverse

---

[3] A well-known research project on inter-generational transfers is the Global Ageing Survey (GLAS), a large-single survey of older population with 44,000 respondents from 24 countries in 2005–2008. It was undertaken by the Oxford Institute of Ageing, (with George Leeson and Sarah Harper as principal researchers), as part of the HSBC funded Future of Retirement Project. This study has given rise to numerous research publications on many aspects of ageing, including some interesting papers on contemporary grandparenthood.

In Singapore, the National Surveys on Senior Citizens conducted periodically since 1983 by the former Ministry of Community, Youth and Sports, have detailed information on the kinds of support provided by adult children to their elderly parents. The latest survey was carried out in 2011. See, S.H. Kang, E.S. Tan, and M.T. Yap, *National Survey of Senior Citizens 2011*. Institute of Policy Studies Report, National University of Singapore, 2013. The analysis covers grandparenting activity patterns. See also, Ministry of Social and Family Development, Insight Series Paper 01/2022. *Ageing Families in Singapore 2010–2020*. https://www.msf.gov.sg/research-and-data/Research-and-Data-Series/Documents/Ageing_Families_in_Singapore_2010-2020.pdf

kind of inter-generational transfer of resources (from grandparents to adult children), including financial assistance, as the current grandparental generation is better educated, and has more financial assets to share than the generation prior to them. Following the mass migration of labour from rural areas to cities (such as in China), recent studies have focused on the changes in family structure and relationships with the grandparents becoming the main caregivers of young children left behind in the village.

It is often assumed that Westernisation and declining cultural values such as filial obligation of children towards their parents is a main cause for the older generation's dependency on the state.[4] However, there is emergent evidence in the opposite direction: that the level of inter-generational transfers within the family is related to/varies with the extent of the welfare state.[5] The fact that one can expect/is entitled to a certain level of state support in old age would decrease one's expectations of support from children, and also decrease children's sense of obligation to support their parents.

However, these studies are just emergent, as the academic interest in grand-parenting is only a recent occurrence. I think this has to do with the fact that, in Family Sociology, the nuclear family has long been taken to be the universal, modern norm of family living and the rightful unit of analysis. This has rendered grandparents almost invisible in the academic literature. Yet in real life, even in today's urban setting of individualised living, grandparents are there waiting to be re-discovered.

[4] For a brief discussion of the 'modernisation and ageing' hypothesis, as applied to various countries in Asia, see Thang Leng Leng, "Social-Cultural Aspects: Family and Filial Support", in K.H. Phua, L.G. Goh, and M.T. Yap, (eds.), *Ageing in Asia: Contemporary Trends and Policy Issues*, pp 177–202 Singapore: World Scientific, 2019. Thang's chapter focuses on the old age support policies of some Asian societies, including Japan, Taiwan, South Korea, India and Singapore.

[5] G. Leeson and H. Khan "Levels of Welfarism and Inter-generational Transfers within the Family: Evidence from the Global Ageing Survey" in S.A. McDaniel and Z. Zimmer (eds.), *Global Ageing in the Twenty-first Century — Challenges, Opportunities and Implications*, Chapter 16. Burlington, USA: Ashgate, 2013.

What can grandparents do?

As populations age, and as people live longer, the presence of grandparents will once more become more visible. Their roles (or lack of roles) in society will become more recognisable either as an asset or as a problematic in future, because they are an integral part of the ageing population.

With population ageing having become a global phenomenon (and which is happening at a faster rate in Asia now), there was once a fear among economists and politicians of a so-called 'inter-generational conflict'. In this conflict, the older generation is depicted in the form of a rising old-age dependency-ratio, meaning, as a financial burden for the younger generation. As opposed to this perspective, there is now a more positive view on ageing. The elderly population is seen as a resource that can be tapped in helping sustain GDP growth, and this resource could be enhanced through a supportive environment that encourages healthy, active, and productive ageing. These concepts are currently widely promoted by the WHO and many national health agencies.[6]

In the intermediate future (10 to 15 years), we will see an increasing proportion of the aged population who are better-educated; they will remain productive and will work longer. They will enjoy more years of healthy living into old age. Many would have become grandparents in their early 60s, given the trend of young adults marrying around age 28–30. They would have 25 or more years of time for being grandparents and some may become

---

[6] WHO. *Active Ageing: A Policy Framework,* 2002. And, WHO. *World Report on Ageing and Health,* 2015. For a succinct account of the evolution of policy perspectives on population ageing (active ageing, healthy ageing and productive ageing), and the policy actions to attain these goals in various Asian countries, see T. Kay and M. Nodzenski, "Active and Productive Ageing", in K.H. Phua, L.G. Goh, and M.T., Yap (eds.), *Ageing in Asia: Contemporary Trends and Policy Issues,* pp 151–176. Singapore: World Scientific, 2019.

great-grandparents.[7] They could possibly play an important role in both the family and society once again. The question is whether they wish to, and whether they would be 'allowed to' by the middle generation.

In my generation (I was born in the 1940s), young adults married somewhat earlier. I became a grandparent the first time in my mid-fifties. As I was still very much involved in my professional career then, I did what little I could to help take care of my grandchildren; which was not much. Interestingly, many of my peers (who had had higher education, were also working or had enjoyed an independent lifestyle) actually let it be known that they did not want to be the 'traditional grandmother' whose life revolved almost totally around taking care of the third generation. A generational shift among grandparents was happening, with regard to the value they put on their grandparenting roles versus their personal freedom to pursue their own interests.

I think this also came in parallel with a generational shift in parenting style that posed some constraints on what a contemporary grandparent could do. Parents of the Y generation (children born between 1980–1995 who are also known as Millennials) adopt a very hands-on approach to child-rearing. These are the 'helicopter' parents who closely watch over their children's activities and growth.

In a highly competitive society like Singapore, they have high expectations of their children's academic achievement and devote a lot of time and resources to ensure that their children will excel. This often creates enormous pressure and tension between parents and their schooling child. Parents then over-compensate by indulging

---

[7]   The median age at first marriage for Singapore citizens was 30.3 years for grooms and 28.7 years for brides in 2021. The median age of mothers at first birth among citizens was 31.0 years. (National Population and Talent Division, Prime Minister's Office, *Population in Brief 2022*.) *https://www. population.gov.sg/files/medicentre/publications/population-in-brief-2022.pdfe*. Life expectancy at birth was 81.1 years for males and 85.9 years for females in 2021. (Department of Statistics, *Singapore Population Graphics*). *https://www.singstat.gov.sg/modules/infographics/population*

the child in various ways. To avoid conflict with their daughters or daughters-in-law over different views and practices, the grandparents would not have much chance to influence the way grandchildren are brought up, and their roles vis-à-vis the young children become mostly one of 'helping out on demand', i.e. when needed. This picture is based on rather common anecdotes, as there is little or no study on grandparenting per se locally.

When the young married adults first become parents, most of them depend to a great extent on the help of grandparents with the new-born infants. This trend has persisted. Even where the help of domestic workers is available, young working couples would still like their parents to help ensure their children are in safe hands. Many would move house to be near to their parents in order to receive help with childcare from them. At this early stage then, the grandparents would feel valued, and appreciated. Some may feel taken for granted — but then, most grandparents feel happy to be of help. As the grandchildren grow beyond the infant and preschooler stage, many grandparents gradually feel side-lined.

As old age is a time of loss and often of social isolation, loneliness among the elderly (particularly those living alone on their own) has caught the attention of researchers and social agencies. However, some studies on the elderly do not show loneliness as much of an issue — grandparents, even though side-lined in their roles, feel positive satisfaction with their life, as they have families which still care about them and vice versa. Social ties and engagement in community activities are found to correlate with good mental well-being among the elderly.[8]

---

[8] Centre for Ageing Research and Education, Duke-NUS Medical School. *Research Brief Series: 4, Home Alone: Older Adults in Singapore*, 2018. This research report shows an unexpected finding that it is loneliness and not living arrangements per se that is associated with mortality. In fact, a higher percentage of older Singaporeans who are living with children only (i.e., not with spouses or others) expressed feelings of loneliness compared to those living alone, p.10. The report points to the importance of social ties and engagement in social activities outside the home for the mental well-being of the elderly.

How can grandparents relate to the young Gen Y, not to speak of Gen Z? Is the 'generation gap' unbridgeable, given the very different generations that grandparents and grandchildren were born into?

What do young people want?

I come now to the sociological concept of generations. In an earlier paper, I had attempted to modify the popular, oft-mentioned generations (in the West) to the local historical and social context of Singapore. The following is a short summary of my (equally imprecise) descriptions, based on some published sources.[9]

Here in Singapore, the traditional generation lived through the colonial era, and suffered through the hardships of World War II and the Japanese Occupation. They worked hard and believed in traditional virtues such as thriftiness, filial piety, respect for elders, and obedience to authority. The Baby Boomers also grew up in turbulent times during Singapore's early independence: law and order problems, unemployment, Communist and communalist strife, Merger and Separation, and the recession of the 1970s. However, they later became the beneficiaries of Singapore's development in the 1980s and the prosperity of the 1990s.

My children's generation (Gen X) straddled this period, growing up during Singapore's rapid economic development. They benefited from the rising educational and economic opportunities, prospered, and became the solid middle-class society that we are today. To them, material success is a validation of their talents and hard work in a meritocratic society.

---

[9] Aline Wong "From Generation to Generation: Growing Up in Singapore", in *Speaking of Children*, The Singapore Children's Society Collected Lectures., pp 65–95. Singapore: World Scientific, 2016. I adopted the conventional age-demarcation of the different generations: Baby Boomers are those born between 1946–1964. Their parents are called the Traditionals. Generation X were born between 1965–1980. Generation Y were born between 1981–1995. Generation Z are the post-Millennials. To provide context for profiling these generations, I used the socio-historical events that occurred in the local and regional contexts, which were more relevant for their shared experiences.

Gen Y (my three older grandsons' generation) were born with the computer and the Internet. They grew up when globalisation was in full swing, and Singapore joined the ranks of the knowledge economy. According to some studies of Gen Y, they are confident, tech-savvy, unconventional, and restless. They consider it a norm to take career sabbaticals and make frequent job switches. Travel, life-style pursuits, finding work-life balance, and finding self are important; and environmental concerns are also a 'big thing' for them.

Although this young generation received a very good education as well as great opportunities offered by the globalised world, their world is also full of great uncertainties, what with SARS, bird flu, mad cow disease, financial crises, natural disasters, and terrorist threats. And now the Covid-19 pandemic, the geo-political tensions between the world's major powers, and the destructiveness of climate change. As we shall see later, these uncertainties do affect their outlook on life, their future, and their priorities.

My youngest grandchild is my 16-year-old granddaughter. As a member of Gen Z, what will she be like when she grows up? What will her world be like?

Since 2002, the National Youth Council (NYC) has conducted regular national surveys as a time series study on young people (adolescents to young adults) between age 15–34. These surveys focus on young persons' major concerns: schooling, work, life goals, values, attitudes, use of social media, family and social networks, civic participation, and sense of well-being and resilience. The sixth survey (2019) provides some interesting data, on both commonalities and differences between the current Gen Y (age 25–34) and Gen Z (age 15–24) populations.[10]

The NYC surveys show that, on the whole, Singapore youths are quite pragmatic in their outlook. Over the last decade, their important

---

[10] National Youth Council, *The State of Youth in Singapore 2021: Youth and Their Diverse Priorities.*

life goals have remained largely unchanged. They continue to give priority to strong family relationships, home-ownership, acquiring new skills and knowledge, having a successful career, and travelling the world. Their five major concerns include the high cost of living in Singapore, work-life balance, global warming and environmental issues, mental health, and job competition.

Across all age groups, 8 in 10 say that they would care for their parents in old age regardless of the circumstances. Across all age groups also, the perceived necessity of marriage has declined as there is an increasing acceptance of singlehood and co-habitation. Those in a relationship find marriage to be stressful, as they feel this requires certain prerequisites such as financial stability and home ownership. Youths are increasingly civically conscious and active. Social media are used extensively for sharing information and championing causes.

There are some variations between the two age bands (Gen Y and Gen Z) in terms of use of the social media, with the former using it more for obtaining information on current affairs as well as communication with friends and family, while the latter group uses it more for connection, entertainment, and self-validation. Interest in social issues also varies somewhat with the age band, with the older age groups more interested in bread-and-butter issues and work-life balance, whereas the younger age bands are more interested in issues such as bullying and racism. The younger age groups are more liberal in social values such as sex before marriage, but across all age groups, there is an increasing tolerance of diversity and a wider range of social behaviour.

What do young people fear?

As I interpret the results (somewhat contrary to the positive tone of the report itself), I think one of the most concerning findings from the 2021 survey is on the Sense of Well-being among the youths.[11] Global events such as the Covid-19 pandemic, economic downturn and political instability make it difficult for the young people to visualise their future. Among a range of stressors faced by the youths (e.g. studies, finances, emerging adult responsibility), they feel most stressed by future uncertainty. On their perception of physical and mental health, the scores were moderately positive across the age groups (3.5 average on a range of 1–5), with perceived mental health being slightly lower among the younger age band (Gen Z), as compared to the older band (Gen Y). The older youths appear to hold a more positive evaluation of their lives (happiness, life satisfaction, and confidence in the future) as compared to the younger age groups.

Mental health issues among youths had come to the fore of public attention even before the Covid-19 pandemic. Various factors have been contributing to the rising level of anxiety, depression and more severe forms of mental problems (including self-harm and suicides) among young people. These include: pressures of the highly competitive educational system, expectations of parents, self-esteem and peer pressure, identity and social media usage, and cyber-bullying. Covid-19 exacerbated these trends.

The Covid-19 pandemic posed unprecedented challenges everywhere in the world. During the height of the Covid-19 pandemic from 2020 to 2022, its impact on youths was felt in many areas of their life: study, work, family and social life, physical and mental health. Mental stress was heightened for both the younger groups e-schooling at home, and for the young parents working from home. A Special Edition on Covid-19 was added to the 2021 NYC report,

---

[11] National Youth Council, *The State of Youth in Singapore 2021: Youth and Their Strides Towards Flourishing.*

documenting the ways in which young people felt impacted by these challenges, faced them and adapted to them.[12]

As expected, the pressing concerns for the present time, coupled with worries over the future, have affected the overall levels of subjective well-being of the youths when compared to pre-pandemic levels. They worried about their own academic progress, job prospects, loss of social ties, fun activities, and overseas exposure. However, there was a bright side to their experience. Being tech-savvy, many of them were also learning new skills and entering new frontiers online. At the same time, they showed concern for the vulnerable members of society, migrant workers, and the frontline workers such as the healthcare personnel and essential service workers. Many organised charitable projects and volunteered. It is said that the pandemic brought out the grit, resilience, and heart of our young people.[13]

Where have all the girls gone?

The NYC State of Youth reports are invaluable sources of information on our youths today. But one thing that jumps out to me is that only responses by different age groups and trends over time are reported, with no distribution by gender.

Can one assume that gender does not make any or much difference to how youths think, feel, act or wish for? Or that, only significant differences are reported; and since no significant differences are found between the two sexes, these are not published in the reports?

---

[12] National Youth Council, *The State of Youth in Singapore 2021: Covid-19 Special Edition*. Another interesting report on the impact of Covid-19 on youth mental health is in the Institute of Policy Studies summary of its *Closed Door Discussion on Tackling the Challenges of Youth Mental Health in Singapore*. IPS Update — October 2021. *https://lkyspp.nus.edu.sg/docs/default-source/ips/youth-mental-health-closed-door-discussion-report.pdf*

[13] Chew Han Ei and Vincent Chua, "Singapore Youth: InDefence of 'Strawberries'", INSIGHT, *Straits Times*, 19 September 2022.

I would doubt so, even in Singapore's context where today boys and girls receive roughly the same levels of education, have almost equal opportunities to work, and many more women have reached great heights in many occupations. The fact that the Singapore version of the #MeToo movement caused such public interest and outcry in 2017, was a clear enough sign that young (and not so young) women are troubled by sexual harassment and gender role issues. I am sure that if the NYC studies were more gender-sensitive in their approach and analysis, some significant differences in youth aspirations and concerns along gender lines would emerge.

However, what is the intensity of concern about gender inequality *as such* among our young people? Does the current generation of young women feel personally the barriers of sexual discrimination at work, in the family, in civic and political participation? They apparently don't. Many of the successful young women who participate in public discussions on gender equality state that they have not encountered much of a gender barrier to their rise in their professions, except that they have to work harder than men to prove themselves.

The young women of Gen Y and Gen Z have taken for granted the rights and opportunities that we, grandmothers, never had in our lifetime. Young women today do not know much nor care about the struggles that earlier women put up for the legal, political, and social recognition of women's status and contributions. In *Our Lives to Live*, I gave a brief account of the tremendous progress women gained over the past five decades, which was in no small measure due to the advocacy efforts of women pioneers, including the efforts of the earlier women politicians. I also noted that feminism is hardly a concern among young women nowadays. But I am reconciled to the fact that this is a case of young people of every generation wanting to 'move forward', not 'look backward'. Each generation has its own causes to fight for.

In future, perhaps gender will not matter much anymore. It is not that perfect equality or true gender equality will be finally attained during my granddaughter's lifetime. The UN Convention on Elimination of All Forms of Discrimination Against Women (CEDAW) is an aspirational document. Even for Singapore, which has climbed up quite remarkably on the global Gender Equality Index, the 2022 White Paper on Women and Development will serve mainly as a guideline for action for the future in various aspects of gender equality.[14] Meanwhile, other urgent issues have emerged to grab the next generation's attention.

Back to my world, our shared world

Barring a World War III on account of the intensifying geo-political rivalries between the great world powers, the ongoing Russian-Ukraine war and the Hamas-Israel conflict, the first and clearest signpost of Gen Z's times is the promise and the peril of digitalisation. The second is the enduring impact of the Covid-19 pandemic on the nature and organisation of work, reshuffling of life goals and priorities, and mental health issues. The third is Climate Change, the fire and fury of which has come upon us during their time. These concerns will engulf both my granddaughter and my grandsons. Perhaps they would also worry about the ageing population that they will have to live with and support when they are in their mid-career or mid-life years.

Claire Chiang, writing in her essay "Silent Revolution" in a book looking into Singapore's future, described the changes in the way four generations of women had "wished to work", as our society

---

[14] *White Paper on Singapore Women's Development: Towards a Fairer and More Inclusive Society,* 2022.

progressed over fifty years of independence, and women's choices became much wider. I quote:

> "My grandmother's fight was for survival, my mother's was progress, mine was for equality, and my daughter's is for personal control and self-actualisation."[15]

Personally, my own fight has been for progress and gender equality. My granddaughter already enjoys the privilege of personal control and self-actualisation. But I think her generation will be fighting for survival again.

Having arrived at where we are today on the scale of gender equality, I see the issues facing us all, men and women, older or younger generations, to be much bigger and much more critical in future than gender issues. Climate change, extremist ideologies and terrorism, modern forms of enslavement, nuclear war threats, cyber insecurities and so on. These are the most pressing, global fights for survival.

It is not enough for me to simply not pose a care burden on my children. I wish to be included in this very important dialogue with my grandchildren: on how the different generations can come together and tackle the Next Big Things that challenge our shared lives, shared world and shared earth.

For this to happen, I believe we, the older generation, must try to equip ourselves to be able to carry on a meaningful dialogue with the younger generation on these issues, a dialogue that should lead to purposeful actions however big or small for us to play a part in tackling these critical challenges. No doubt, one can remain healthy and can live longer if one is active and engaged. One can enjoy healthy,

---

[15] Claire Chiang, "Silent Revolution", in Euston Quah, (ed.), *Singapore 2065: Leading Insights in Economy and Environment from 50 Singapore Icons and Beyond*, p 59. Singapore: World Scientific, 2016.

active and productive ageing. Perhaps the issue here is that of Purposeful Ageing.

On the other hand, I think the young people need to appreciate and learn from the lessons of history. After all, the older generations have also desired the same things as the younger generations — safety, security, social justice, and a happy and meaningful life. The older generations have also faced the uncertain futures of their times, and have proved to be resilient. Would the young people include us as partners in their quest for a safe, secure, equitable and peaceful future for all ages?

ALINE WONG obtained her PhD from UC Berkeley and was Professor of Sociology at the National University of Singapore. She entered politics in 1984 and served as Minister of State for Health and for Education (1990–2001). She then became Chairman of the Housing and Development Board (2003–2007) and Academic Advisor at SIM University (2003–2015). She is currently Hon. Advisor of the SR Nathan School of Human Development at the Singapore University of Social Sciences, and a member of several advisory boards in social research and services.

Where To #MeToo

"I wish and pray for an end to all forms of violence against women and girls. Is this possible? I say, why not? This has been a work in progress over many years and there are now more willing hearts and hands of men and women. We must succeed in this effort if we want the world to be a better place."

~ Lawyer and women's rights activist Anamah Tan, for The Lives of Women exhibition at the National Museum, Jan–Mar 2022

CHAPTER 24

Gender Violence Will Not End if We Do Not Redefine Masculinity

⁌ↂↂↂ⁌

Corinna Lim and Kelly Leow

Open the crime section of a Singapore paper on any given day, and you'll probably be struck by a thought like this: *The news is pretty bad for women.* The sheer breadth of ways in which people — mostly men and boys — hurt other people — mostly women and girls — can be staggering.

The past few years have given us their fair share of headlines about men in Singapore enacting various forms of violence against women. Many of these cases involve physical violence, sometimes taken to tragic extremes: Take Teo Ghim Heng, who strangled his pregnant wife, Choong Pei Shan, and four-year-old daughter, Zi Ning, to death in 2017, after Choong called Teo a "useless" husband and father. Or Ahmed Salim, who strangled ex-girlfriend Nurhidayati Wartono Surata to death in 2018, after she compared him unfavourably to her new partner. Or Pak Kian Huat, who hacked longtime partner Lim Soi Moy to death with a chopper in 2019, after she declined his request to sleep in their home's bigger bedroom.

Many other cases involve sexual violence, which again can take various forms, including rape. Singapore was recently shocked by the gang of seven men who conspired to drug, assault, and non-consensually film each others' wives over the course of eight years, from 2010 to 2018. This 'wife-sharing rape case', as it was dubbed by the press, first came to light in 2020, though details only emerged in 2022 and 2023 as the men were charged in court.

Other prominent incidents of sexual violence — specifically, of technology-facilitated sexual violence — may not involve physical contact at all. Singapore's best-known such case is referred to colloquially as 'SG Nasi Lemak', after the most notorious Telegram group of its ilk, which came to public attention in 2019. These Telegram groups, which range in size from a couple thousand members to SG Nasi Lemak's peak of 44,000, function as clearinghouses for the digital distribution of sexual, nude, and intimate images, mostly of women and girls. It is safe to assume that the vast majority of the images have been distributed without their subjects' consent — if not also obtained without consent, e.g., through voyeurism, hacking, DeepFake technology, and so on.

As members of AWARE, Singapore's leading gender equality organisation, we watched the above stories unfold in the news with sinking hearts — not only because such cases occur with depressing frequency, but because the general public appears so poorly equipped to make sense of them. Discourse about violence against women often seems to circle the crux of the matter without landing at its heart. Online conversations about Teo, Ahmed, and Pak, for example, connected their deadly actions to crises of mental health and stress, or to failures of emotional regulation — framing them as outbursts, 'crimes of passion', temporary rages that possess an otherwise unremarkable person. Social media commenters posited links between violence and various addictions, e.g., to gambling or substances. In Ahmed's case, some commenters even, deplorably, framed violence as the domain of 'foreigners'.

By proclaiming these violent acts foreign in some way — illegible, pathological, beyond the comprehension of reasonable persons — we distance ourselves from the men who commit them. Doing so, we surreptitiously reassure each other of our own innocence... and rush into a kind of willful ignorance. We don't stop long enough to examine the grim family resemblance between seemingly disparate examples of male violence. We don't tug on the thread that runs through not only the actions of these perpetrators, but through our entire society, our systems and our ideologies.

So, we once again let ourselves off the hook.

Misogyny has a way of hiding in plain sight by cultivating blindness in its subjects. We fixate on red herrings (mental illness! cultural differences! anger management issues!)[1] so as to not admit the painful truth: that violence against women, even when severe, is not an aberration or a deviation but a logical, functional part of life under a patriarchy. The control and subjugation of women — and others marginalised by gender, including transgender and non-binary people — is baked into our society, culture, and institutions so deeply that we seem to have conditioned ourselves not to name it. We brush off its more banal forms as annoyances, we plead confusion over its most extreme manifestations, and we are utterly incapable of imagining alternative — non-violent, non-patriarchal — modes of relating to each other.

---

[1] Most people with mental illness or substance addictions do not commit acts of violence; most of the perpetrators identified in this essay are Singaporean-born Chinese; and none of them struggled, at least reportedly, with 'managing anger' around friends, colleagues, or other people in their lives. It does a disservice to not only violence against women but to mental illness, addiction, and racialised migrant experiences to conflate them.

Apply a gender lens to the aforementioned incidents, though, and their basis in the rigid, regressive ideas commonly known as 'toxic masculinity' shines through. Toxic masculinity revolves around the set of norms traditionally associated with 'manhood', such as strength, aggression, emotional stoicism, risk-taking, sexual conquest, heteronormativity, and the ability to provide for and protect others. Although many of these traits are not in and of themselves 'healthy' or 'unhealthy', societal pressure to conform to them (and thus demonstrate affiliation with maleness) can lead to extreme behaviour, ranging from physical assaults to male body dysmorphia, homophobic bullying, or risky driving.[2]

How does this happen? What we perceive as masculinity is enacted and absorbed in myriad ways. From a young age, boys are subjected to gender-policing messages. For example, parents may tell them to 'man up' by not expressing emotions, or siblings and playmates may ridicule them for displaying vulnerability, perpetuating the idea that sensitivity is a kind of non-masculine 'tell'. Social scripts around romance tie masculinity to paying for dates, buying gifts or making extravagant gestures to pursue the objects of their affection. The media normalises images of financially successful men who drip with lavish material possessions and attractive partners, or hardworking blue-collar fathers who tirelessly provide for their families above all else. Meanwhile, pornography typically depicts men as dominant and primarily focused on their own pleasure, while women are objectified and portrayed in subservient roles. In cases of violence against women in particular, toxic masculinity manifests as an urge to exert power and control over vulnerable others, and as an assumption of a position of ownership.

---

[2] Note that 'masculinity' does not literally mean 'men', although the perpetrators of violence against women are almost always men. 'Masculinity' refers not to actual persons but to a set of ideologically inflected norms, which anyone — not just cisgender men — can imbibe and enforce.

A number of feminist writers provide key insights into how toxic masculinity, and men's drive to iterate and reiterate it, relates to violence against women. Take, for instance, American anthropologist Gayle Rubin's landmark 1975 essay "The Traffic in Women: Notes on the Political Economy of Sex", which positions male-to-male relations, *not* male-to-female ones, as primarily important in societies based around heterosexual marriage. Drawing upon Claude Lévi-Strauss's writing on kinship — fundamental patterns of social relationships within human society — Rubin identified marriage as the oppressive mechanism by which men (givers) exchange women (gifts) with each other, thereby establishing male affinity and power. "If it is women who are being transacted," she wrote, "then it is the men who give and take them who are linked, the woman being a conduit of a relationship rather than a partner to it... As long as the relations specify that men exchange women, it is men who are the beneficiaries of the product of such exchanges — social organization."[3] Similarly, "the exchanges upon which patriarchal societies are based take place exclusively among men," observed French philosopher Luce Irigaray, pointing out the male homoerotic implications of this. "Woman exists only as an occasion for mediation, transaction, transition, transference, between man and his fellow man, indeed between man and himself."[4] Finally, Argentine-Brazilian anthropologist Rita Segato conceived of a "mandate of masculinity", under which violence against women serves as something like a ritual sacrifice into a male brotherhood or guild. "I discovered," she wrote in a 2019 essay summarising her work, "that aggression against women's bodies was a declaration of masculinity to the world; an expressive, not an instrumental, form of violence; that such a

---

[3] Rubin, Gayle. "The Traffic in Women: Notes on the Political Economy of Sex", *Towards an Anthropology of Women*, edited by Rayna R. Reiter, Monthly Review Press, 1975, pg. 174.

[4] Irigaray, Luce. *This Sex Which is Not One*, Cornell University Press, 1985, pg. 192.

statement was simply obedience to a mandate that the group issued to each of its members: the mandate of masculinity."[5]

With all the above in mind, let's revisit recent incidents of violence against women in Singapore, elucidating the specifically masculine combination of entitlement, ownership, and "expressive" misogyny at their heart. By describing these systemic forces, we do not excuse individual perpetrators' actions or take the blame off their shoulders; rather, we give their behaviour its full and necessary context, with an eye to interrupting its recurrence.

We should mention here that our knowledge of the circumstances surrounding these criminal cases is imperfect. The narratives we have to work with are mediated not only by perpetrators and their legal teams, but by reporters and editors; in many cases the victims did not or could not publicise their own side of the story. Even so, these narratives contain such evident tropes of toxic masculinity that we believe them sufficient as texts.

Fatal intimate partner violence

International research has identified a number of 'triggers' for violence against women. These include such quotidian actions on the parts of women as: arguing, not obeying orders, not preparing food on time, not caring 'adequately' for the children or the home, going out without permission, and refusing sex. Similarly, many fatal cases of violence against women reported in the Singapore news over the past five years share common triggers: in particular, the undermining of male authority over finances and living spaces, and male sexual jealousy (e.g., rejection, infidelity, or sexual comparison). Unsurprisingly, these triggers touch on arenas of life

---

[5] Segato, Rita. "The Writing of Women's Bodies," *Miriam Cahn: I As Human*, edited by Marta Dziewańska, Museum of Modern Art in Warsaw, 2019, pg. 130.

over which — gender stereotypes dictate — men are supposed to have mastery. Under the masculine mandate, even relatively minor challenges to male mastery become insupportable threats, and require a response in the way of misogynistic violence.

A number of triggers collided in the case of Teo Ghim Heng, who strangled his wife and daughter to death in 2017. Teo had reportedly struggled with gambling, losing large sums of money while his family racked up debts. According to news reports, he attempted to conceal this fact from his wife, Choong Pei Shan, for some time, but — as of one week before her murder — Choong had become aware that her husband owed between $100,000 and $150,000 in debt.[6]

The conventional 'masculine' figure is the ideal breadwinner: strong, productive, successful, and perfectly capable of fulfilling the economic needs of his charges. The collapse of that fantasy for Teo was arguably the key factor precipitating his turn to deadly violence. Both parties in the marriage seemed conscious of the gendered implications of their situation: Choong apparently aimed her criticism directly at Teo's status as breadwinner, thereby giving voice to toxic-masculine stereotypes. In his testimony, Teo recalled that Choong had bemoaned his inability to pay their daughter's pre-school fees. "Other families can take care of three kids," she reportedly told him, "you can't even provide for a family with one child, you're so useless."[7,8]

On top of these financial anxieties, Teo had sexual anxieties. He told psychiatrists that Choong had been having an extramarital affair,

---

[6] Lum, Selina. "Woodlands double-murder trial: Victim knew of husband's debts and wanted to help clear them", *The Straits Times*, 29 January 2020, straitstimes.com/singapore/courts-crime/woodlands-double-murder-trial-victim-knew-of-husbands-debts-and-wanted-to

[7] As we can see, toxic masculinity is not the sole domain of men; women too are complicit in upholding it. (However — and hopefully this goes without saying — women do not deserve to be killed for expressing such views.)

[8] Lam, Lydia. "Woodlands double murder: Accused says wife scolded him, called him a 'useless father'", *Channel NewsAsia*, 3 July 2019, channelnewsasia.com/singapore/woodlands-double-murder-teo-ghim-heng-wife-called-useless-father-868776

and that he suspected that the girl he killed was not his biological daughter.[9] Indeed, it is not uncommon for perpetrators of violence against women to express preoccupations with their partners' fidelity and their children's paternity — with, in short, the prospect of being a cuckold. Pak Kian Huat, for example, voiced similar suspicions to police officers: that not all the children of ex-partner Madam Lim Soi Moy, whom he killed in 2019, were fathered by him.[10] Whether or not these suspicions have any basis in reality is immaterial (even if they did, that would never justify violence). Yet, the fact that they are often raised in defence of violence speaks to a strain of entitlement to women's sexual and reproductive lives.

That these murders, or attempted murders, sometimes have an explicitly demonstrative or 'expressive' element is also key to our understanding of the masculinity mandate. In 2019, Murugan Nondoh doused his wife, Krishnaveny Subramaniam, with petrol in an attempt to burn and kill her after a suspected affair. Murugan sent voice messages to a friend beforehand, saying amongst other things that the matter "'should come out on newspapers' so that... everyone would think Murugan is 'a real man'".[11] One would be hard-pressed to find a clearer iteration of Rita Segato's observation that "it is from his peers that the mandate of masculinity issues, as well as the title of 'man' that is assigned to anyone who carries out that mandate."[12]

---

[9] Lam, Lydia. "Woodlands double murder: Accused `adamant' daughter not his, suspected wife of affair", *Channel NewsAsia*, 5 July 2019, channelnewsasia.com/singapore/woodlands-double-murder-accused-adamant-daughter-not-his-suspected-wife-affair-869321

[10] Goh, Charlene. "'Vicious, horrifying': 15 years' jail for 86-year-old man who hacked partner to death with chopper", *TODAY*, 22 May 2023, todayonline.com/singapore/vicious-brutal-man-86-jail-15-years-chopper-death-partner-2176391

[11] "Jail for man who abducted, doused wife in petrol on suspicion of affair: Report", *Channel NewsAsia*, 29 September 2021, channelnewsasia.com/singapore/jail-man-abduct-wife-pour-petrol-suspect-affair-2210191

[12] Segato, pg. 131–132.

Telegram groups

This entitlement over women's bodies — viewed as commodities for men to, as Gayle Rubin would say, exchange — comes even more clearly into focus when we look at the next example of violence against women: the non-consensual obtainment and distribution of sexual, nude, and intimate images via Telegram groups such as SG Nasi Lemak. These forums, with their explicitly sexual (i.e., masturbatory) purposes, facilitate the objectification of women and girls at an unprecedented rate and scale, due to the acceleration of technologies such as encrypted messaging apps and camera phones. Such objectification divorces the bodies of women and girls from their humanity and commodifies them into products for male sexual pleasure — enabling a patriarchal society to habitually dismiss and devalue female personhood, and thereby continue to subjugate and disenfranchise women.

While the painful repercussions of technology-facilitated sexual violence (TFSV) on women and girls are fairly well-known by now, it's also worth looking closely at the masculine dynamics at play within the communities that perpetuate TFSV in Singapore.

SG Nasi Lemak gained popularity in 2018 alongside other Telegram groups of its nature. Screengrabs at the time show that SG Nasi Lemak had upwards of 44,600 members in 2019 (and while it was later shut down, it's reasonable to assume most members just regrouped elsewhere). The popularity and frequent activity of these groups might be due in part to certain structural features designed to encourage user engagement — reminiscent perhaps of tactics employed by social media or entertainment platforms, or even by multi-level marketing companies. For one, members are purportedly required to keep uploading new material in order to remain in the groups, an effective way of ensuring a continued stream of eyeballs as well as a sense of in-it-together camaraderie.[13]

Furthermore, interviews with former members describe a pecking order of sorts that developed within the community (presumably based on factors such as frequency of posts), which in turn facilitated the rise of "VVIP" groups into which "high-ranking" users were "recruited".[14] In the messages sent by group members — made public via screengrabs leaked to the press and on social media — users display a fraternity-esque rapport, at times fawning over each other: In response to a newly posted image, a member of one group thanked the poster with "u r my savior" [sic].[15] When he was invited into more exclusive group SharingIsCaring, SG Nasi Lemak administrator Leonard Teo was hailed by others as a "hero".[16] "I feel like I've been knighted," he quipped in reply.

Think of Segato's description of masculinity as a "corporation", having "two essential characteristics" in common with other structures of power and prestige: "Loyalty to the corporate group is the supreme value… and its internal order is strictly hierarchical and authoritarian."[17] Certainly, the gamification and chummy mutual valorisation in these Telegram groups form the bland mask with which toxic masculinity sells itself, downplaying the costs of the members' callous actions (e.g., to women's consent and bodily autonomy and men's empathy). Accordingly, members perpetuate various narratives to defend their actions, "disavow[ing] responsibility

---

[13] "SG Nasi Lemak Telegram chat group administrator sentenced to mandatory treatment", *TODAY*, 3 June 2021, todayonline.com/singapore/sg-nasi-lemak-telegram-chat-group-administrator-sentenced-mandatory-treatment

[14] Sholihyn, Ilyas. "SharingIsCaring: Secret Telegram group circulating pictures of schoolgirls on MRT", *AsiaOne*, 18 October 2019, asiaone.com/digital/sharingiscaring-telegram-group-circulating-pictures-and-videos-schoolgirls-mrt

[15] Cheung, Rainier and Ilyas Sholihyn, "At least 2 more Telegram groups circulating pictures of local women surface; police investigating", *AsiaOne*, 24 July 2020, asiaone.com/digital/least-2-more-telegram-groups-circulating-pictures-local-women-surface-netizens-take-action

[16] Sholihyn, Ilyas. "Hailed as a 'hero', SG Nasi Lemak's Leonard Teo was also involved in SharingIsCaring", *AsiaOne*, 23 October 2019, asiaone.com/digital/hailed-hero-sg-nasi-lemak-leonard-teo-was-involved-sharingiscaring.

[17] Segato, pg. 131.

for any content uploaded"[18] and placing accountability entirely on their victims. "You [women] are the one to blame… You are the stupidest ever person to let your BF/GF take SEXUAL VIDEOS to be leaked out," wrote an SG Nasi Lemak administrator in a message.[19] (Even if that argument was valid, it ignores the fact that many of the images shared are obtained without the subjects' knowledge, e.g., by hidden camera; in many cases too the subjects are minors, who could never consent to appearing in sexual videos.)

In the long run, exposure to these communities may even radicalise men into more violence: "Kinis", a "regular contributor" of voyeuristic videos, told Channel NewsAsia's *Undercover Asia* in 2020 that "after watching so many upskirt videos, it's worth it to get your own."[20] And Don Weng Kai Jun, who in 2023 pled guilty to transmitting obscene material on Telegram and making an insulting communication likely to cause harassment, claimed to have done so because "he had a 'fear of missing out' for not contributing to the Telegram channel."[21] Toxic masculinity ultimately privileges male pleasure and social status above the rights of women and children.

Inter-marital rape

The same masculine dynamics animating communities such as SG Nasi Lemak are evident in the case of the seven men who drugged, raped, and posted non-consensual sexual videos of each others' wives between 2010 and 2018. Reading news coverage about the case, what

---

[18] Lay, Belmont, "4 men aged 17 to 37 arrested over 'SG Nasi Lemak' Telegram chat group", *Mothership*, 15 October 2019, mothership.sg/2019/10/sg-nasi-lemak-arrested

[19] Sholihyn, Ilyas, "What is SG Nasi Lemak? Inside the Telegram chat group circulating local NSFW content", *AsiaOne*, 2 October 2019, asiaone.com/digital/what-sg-nasi-lemak-inside-telegram-chat-group-circulating-local-nsfw-content

[20] Ng, Desmond and Yuxin Peh, "The rise of non-consensual porn in Singapore, and the battle to stem its spread", *Channel NewsAsia*, 26 April 2020, channelnewsasia.com/cnainsider/the-rise-of-non-consensual-porn-singapore-battle-stem-its-spread-767066

[21] Koh, Wan Ting, "Man tried to link woman to porn video by posting her pictures; victim later propositioned for sex on Telegram", *Channel NewsAsia*, 12 September 2023, channelnewsasia.com/singapore/man-tried-link-woman-porn-video-posting-her-pictures-victim-later-propositioned-sex-telegram-3764216

stands out is not just the perpetrators' urge to subjugate their wives, but the sense of fraternity that developed between them over the course of their actions — which after all revolved as much around the pleasure of other men as around the violation of women.

The men met on the online forum Sammyboy (notorious local cesspit of misogynistic discourse), where they hatched plans to sedate their wives with sleeping pills and have each other rape them, sometimes photographing, filming, and/or live-streaming the assaults. Afterward, some men would, as described by Channel NewsAsia, "prolong the 'experience' by chatting feverishly afterwards via texts about their encounters."[22]

These texts are revealing in their establishment of two parallel themes. The first is the misogynistic putting down of women, emphasising their ignorance and thus their inferiority to men: "Woman like [my wife] and [your wife], no matter how smart they think themselves are, eventually also kanna outsmart by her man [sic]," wrote the perpetrator dubbed "J" by the courts in 2015. "Bet both of them still thinking they are their husband's chaste and loyal wife." The second theme is the puffing-up of men via male-to-male ingratiation: Another perpetrator, known as "K", told J that K's wife was "always yours". K also told J that he liked the idea of J impregnating K's wife (in a kind of inverted reprise of Teo and Pak's preoccupation with intimate partner infidelity and the 'legitimacy' of their children).

Yet again, there is a public 'expressive' aspect to the actions of these perpetrators, akin to that of SG Nasi Lemak's members (whose fawning tone is echoed in "always yours"). J and K seem driven not just to demean women, but for the demeaning to be witnessed by other men; they continually reiterate male dominance, in their celebration of male collective intelligence, of male access to women's

---

[22] Lam, Lydia, "7 men, 1 depraved sex network: Unravelling the full story behind the wife-sharing drug rapes", *Channel NewsAsia*, 15 May 2023, channelnewsasia.com/singapore/wife-sharing-rape-cases-drugs-sex-network-victims-3471896

bodies as a sort of communal chattel, and of the male-reserved ability to propagate freely. Once more we think of the male homosocial benefits that drive the commodification of women (and indeed this case is a sort of overdrive version of Rubin's 'exchange of women' paradigm, with men seeking *additional*, extramarital exchange of women who had already been 'exchanged' via marriage). Segato also describes this "endless staging": "it is to his peers — whether physically present or merely a presence in the aggressor's mental realm — that he dedicates the exhibition, the great 'spectacle' of the forcible possession of and exertion of control over his victim's body."[23]

Put another way, if toxic masculinity is about dangerous and extreme attempts to prove one's affiliation with maleness, then by necessity it requires an audience — specifically, an audience of fellow adherents, equally literate in masculinity's iconography and invested in its upkeep. Thus individual and collective concerns elide, one's personal masculine dominance taking a backseat to one's fidelity to the principle of *collective* masculine dominance. By this token, the oppression of women at the heart of this case redeems, perhaps, the perpetrators' ingratiating exchanges and plays at being 'cuckolded' by other men — typically counter to the masculine tenets of sexual conquest and jealousy. Perhaps J and K, on some subconscious level, gave up their private sexual access to their spouses, i.e., their supposed 'rightful domain', in the name of dominance for men *as a class*, and subjugation of women *as a class*. This is arguably the ultimate goal of toxic masculinity, which survives through the reinforcement of that universal hierarchy.

The above cases of violence against women should not be read as unusual, incomprehensible, or deviant but as manifestations of deep-seated masculine norms that have persisted for generations

---

[23] Segato, pg. 131.

and in which we are all complicit. These patriarchal masculine norms — power and control, entitlement and dominance — form the root of gender violence.

But if the sham at the heart of toxic masculinity — its very unnatural-ness as a value system — is laid bare by how hard men work to enact it, and the violent lengths to which they go to inch up its specious hierarchies, perhaps there too lies hope. Perhaps that instability holds the key to toxic masculinity's ultimate undoing.

Most of the initiatives undertaken by Singapore organisations, including AWARE, to address gender violence have focussed on strengthening legal protections, increasing awareness of family and sexual violence, and empowering bystanders and family members to be more supportive. These are essential, but do not fully address the root cause of gender violence. Because the crux of the matter lies in how we conceive of masculinity, it's a mistake to frame gender violence as a problem for women to solve — we must shift our gaze towards men, the expectations placed upon them, and the expectations they place on others in turn.

So, what can we do to reshape masculinity for good? An important avenue for change, one that AWARE has strongly pushed for, is comprehensive sexuality education. We have for years conducted sex ed workshops with youths in Singapore, closely following the recommendations of the UN's international technical guidance on sexuality education,[24] but we know that's not enough — so we launched a programme called Birds & Bees to better equip parents and other adults who can play a vital role in shaping children's values and attitudes. By nurturing an environment that explicitly addresses stereotypes about masculinity, and encourages empathy and fairness, these adults can help kids challenge rigid ideas about gender from an early age.

---

[24] "International technical guidance on sexuality education: An evidence-informed approach" (Revised edition), United Nations Educational, Scientific and Cultural Organization, 2018, unfpa.org/sites/default/files/pub-pdf/ITGSE.pdf

Another avenue we've explored centres on corporate training and male allyship programmes. Workplaces have been the traditional sites for patriarchal, relentlessly capitalistic, toxic modes of human interaction. But we've encountered companies and organisations in Singapore that are genuinely interested in advancing gender equality, as well as providing support for victims of violence and implementing policies that address discrimination and harassment. We work on getting these organisations to prioritise education, awareness, non-violence, and accountability: enabling their male employees to understand that current conceptions of masculinity are failing them too, though these failures might not be immediately apparent. As such, men wish to be part of the solution. They acknowledge themselves as bearers of power, authority, and the privilege to lead real change. We've also seen them have vulnerable conversations about the pressures, dilemmas, and fears they experience as men in the workplace — thereby providing each other positive role-modelling and much-needed emotional support.

Further, even more spaces should be created for men to engage in open discussions about the challenges and aspirations they experience around masculinity. The Government should consider establishing more support services that are couched in an understanding of prevailing norms and gendered expectations. Conducting a comprehensive survey on the state of masculinity in Singapore could yield valuable insights to guide interventions and policies effectively. By providing resources that address the specific needs of men and boys in a non-judgmental and supportive manner, we can hopefully create avenues for individual growth, emotional well-being, and healthy relationships.

We would be remiss not to say that — although the cases we've examined in this essay are all examples of individual male violence — the solution does not lie only in remoulding behaviour on an individual level, but in identifying and uprooting the patriarchal thinking embedded into the very structures of society, from laws and policies to language. That calls for nothing short of a full-blown reimagining of gender relations in society. We hope that this generation, and those that come after it, will be up to the task.

CORINNA LIM is the Executive Director of AWARE, the Association of Women for Action and Research. As a dedicated women's rights activist, she has been an advocate for issues such as the promotion of gender-equal workplaces, the addressing of gender-based violence, and the provision of greater support for single parents and lower-income women. In addition to her advocacy work, she spearheaded the establishment of the Sexual Assault Care Centre at AWARE in 2011. Corinna has a Master's in Public Administration from Columbia University and is a Fulbright Scholar. She graduated with an LLB from the National University of Singapore and was called to the Singapore Bar in 1988.

KELLY LEOW is an Erasmus Mundus scholar currently completing a joint Master's degree in Women's and Gender Studies at the University of Bologna and University of York. Born and raised in Singapore, Kelly received a B.A. in English from the University of California, Los Angeles, then served as deputy editor at MovieMaker, a quarterly magazine about filmmaking. Returning to Singapore, she was senior communications manager at gender equality organisation AWARE from 2019 to 2023, during which time she co-created the award-winning podcast Saga, Singapore's first narrative long-form podcast. Kelly's fiction writing includes the short story "Breakwater", winner of the Epigram-Storytel Horror Prize in 2022.

"I think women of my generation, we dare to be different. We like challenges, and that's why I chose a career as a fighter pilot in the RSAF."

~ Lee Mei Yi, Singapore's first female commander of a fighter squadron, in an interview with Her World Singapore, June 2015

CHAPTER 25

Gender, Sexuality, Masculinity: What Two Young Men Have to Say

Ho Ren Chun and Liu Ray Chun

The #MeToo movement is rewriting the rules of engagement between women and men. More and more women are speaking up about the sexual harassment and sexual abuse they have endured, and there is growing understanding of why there is so much sexual violence and how gender equality is crucial if we are to curb the violence.

Much of the #MeToo discussion and debate has been by women. What do men have to say about it? We put some questions to two Singaporean men in their late twenties and asked them to have a conversation. As one of them was then based in London, we set up a Zoom session. They talked for nearly two hours. This is the edited transcript of their conversation.

Q: Where would you place yourself on the spectrum of views about gender, that is, feminist on one side, misogynist on the other.

Ren Chun

Well, I am more on the feminist side. I am not sure who would happily identify as a misogynist. I support equal opportunities for women whether socio-economically, like in the workforce, or politically, like with substantive legal rights. I think these are important things to address since the situation may still vary from country to country.

Ray

Yes, I agree. Definitely more towards the feminist side. But I think we should not be taking any side of the spectrum to extremes. At the end of the day, I think the focus should still be for equality in general and challenging some of those archaic gender roles which are oppressive to women. Or men even.

Ren Chun

Yeah, we want to avoid a kind of militancy on either side of the spectrum. But then there's always the challenge of the static, moderate middle. If we want to redefine social norms or build more inclusive norms, it probably requires positive action.

Ray

That's a very good point. People like myself! The challenge is to not being too extreme on either side, but also being strong enough in terms of having a voice and having a call to action. I suppose that's the goal that society should strive towards.

Ren Chun

How could that feed into social practices in Singapore? Do you think it would be helpful if we had, for example, in a school context, a workshop or something about gender roles? You know, talking about the importance of not having rigid gender constructions or norms and talk about the roles that both men and women play in terms of balancing the landscape. When we were in high school — would that have been interesting, at least just to expose people to the considerations?

Ray
I think the biggest steps we can take towards equality would be in education, through the media, or at home. Just to sort of get people thinking, and challenge different perspectives. Get some constructive conversations going.

Q. How easy or difficult do you usually find it to talk about masculinity, gender, or sexuality with other men.

Ray
I think that depends on who you're talking to, but in general it wouldn't be difficult to have a casual chat or discussion about such themes. So long as everyone involved is respectful with the intent of constructive dialogue, even if the views are different. If someone's views are extreme and if they don't seem very receptive to other perspectives, I may keep the conversation at arm's length. I'm unlikely to get into an argument with someone over this.

Ren Chun
Do you feel there is any demographic difference? In the UK, for example, it seems to be a bit more in the public consciousness, things like gender fluidity, LGBTQ issues and issues of gender and sexuality. Maybe it relates back to what you said about media. There is probably more discourse in the UK media about such issues, so people are more inclined to talk about them. In Singapore, if we have more media commentary, then maybe it will spark more natural discussions among men.

Ray

I was in Canada for an exchange programme and people are a lot more open about such topics. The way many of my classmates carried themselves openly conveyed that they stood up for women's rights. In comparison, these are generally less discussed topics in Singapore.

I suppose it would be difficult when you're in a setting where you feel your views are very conflicting with everybody else's. Maybe you're with a bunch of guys and they're all like 'Oh, men should do the breadwinning as opposed to women etc.' If one doesn't agree, it could be difficult to say so.

Ren Chun

In Asia there is this expectation that the man will be more of the breadwinner, contributing more financially to the household and so on. It's more prominent in Asian society than Western society where there is more of an active effort to support the idea of men being house husbands or doing more of the work at home.

Q: Are there certain ideas about gender or sexuality you find yourself wrestling with or coming back to over and over in your mind?

Ren Chun

One thing that I do think about is how can we articulate a constructive vision of masculinity in the 21st century. Is it possible to give it a definition?

Ray

I think it is kind of hard to define and that there isn't a one-size-fits-all answer.

Ren Chun

Let's say we start from the supposed traditional basis that women are supposed to take care of the family and the household, and men go out to work and have gainful employment, rights, and so on. This is archaic, obviously, with women in the workforce, often very successfully so, that distinction no longer applies anymore.

I notice then that with some right-wing male activists, part of their discourse is about trying to resuscitate an old vision of manhood. You know, being aggressive, going into the wilderness and surviving in the outdoors. But in mainstream society perhaps the role and the place for those traditional male attributes is not as relevant as it used to be.

So the thought is whether it is helpful to even try to define masculinity or should there be no definition because it should be on a person-by-person basis.

Ray

The other way we could look at it is in terms of what to avoid instead. So it would be a matter of identifying the attributes or traits which constitute toxic masculinity that are clearly bad for society.

For everything else, it's up to you as an individual to think and see how you want to work it out between two people. In the context of a couple, they would work out how they want to divide the work of running a household and how it fits best.

I don't think that there is a hard and fast rule where it should be this or that. If you are in a relationship with someone and you have this great system going but it's not what is traditionally viewed as masculine, the guy should not have to feel bad about it.

I think it's very much open to personal preferences. At the end of the day, I think it's okay as long as it's comfortable and it works for both parties.

Ren Chun

Yeah, I agree. If we try to have a definition of masculinity, we would be imposing norms on people. Different couples, different pairings will have their consensus on how they want to do things, how the two partners contribute in different ways and take on different roles in their relationship as they deem fit.

Q: What was the last thing relating to gender and sexuality that you changed your mind on?

Ray
Lately, I feel it's actually quite natural to have some different gender roles. I mean, men and women are fundamentally different in certain ways, right? There's no need to force them to be the same.

So certain occupations may be just better suited for men or women, and there's really nothing wrong with that as long as it's not in an oppressive sort of manner.

Ren Chun
It's the nature versus nurture thing, isn't it? To what extent are there predispositions in the genders?

There's this stereotype that women are better at caring roles — nursing or elder care or social work. The occupations that require some element of interpersonal care — the stereotype is that women are better at it because they're more emotionally available or better at nurturing tasks because of their child-bearing experience and responsibilities.

But some feminists would say, hey, that's a patriarchal way of looking at it. Just because through history women have performed these roles and occupations, are you saying this is where we belong? And if a man is performing caring work at home or being a nurse, it's less manly?

This is something worth thinking about. I hear your point. I totally agree that we can't ignore potential biological differences. But then we shouldn't stigmatise people's choices, right? We should remove the expectation that this should be for this gender, and that should be for that gender.

Ray

Yeah agreed. Increasingly, the right way to go is to focus on what people really want and enjoy regardless of their gender.

Ren Chun

It's about individual agency, isn't it? And I think it relates also to sexuality and dating. In the earlier days of LGBTQ discourse, the argument seemed to be that you were born that way. You were born a gay man, or you were born a straight man.

But I think now the understanding is more that sexuality can be fluid. So for example, when you were young, you might have thought you were just a straight man. Then in later life you felt a soulful connection with another man and maybe you identify as bisexual. I think the movement past static categories with a concept of fluidity is something that I've come to understand a bit more.

Q: Post #MeToo, have you noticed any shifts in how people around you think or speak about gender and sexuality?

Ray

The people I interact with don't really talk about it that much. I do think that for the all people who were affected and harassed, it's good they realise that they aren't alone and can speak out. So that was quite remarkable. I'm glad that they have an avenue to share what they were facing and hopefully get some help.

Ren Chun

Yeah. In Anglo-American discourse at least it seemed like a watershed moment where society became more receptive to women stepping forward and sharing their story. Before that, imagine what it was like if you were a victim, and you were very afraid to voice what happened to you.

For me, and for perhaps men generally, I think it also emphasises the importance of thinking harder about consent. Knowing where people's boundaries are, knowing what people are comfortable with versus not comfortable with. Not assuming anything because then things can be misconstrued or misunderstood. And being mindful of your own actions.

Would you say that this is something that's now more in the public consciousness?

Ray
Yes, I agree, this helps build that sense of community that helps people open up about what happened to them instead of keeping silent due to fear of shame. I'd say it would be some much-needed catharsis for many.

Ren Chun
That's interesting, the idea about shame. I remember reading about how shame kind of fosters silence. So if you feel ashamed about something, you are very unlikely to say anything about it.

So when you have some issue in your life, and you can share that with a group of people who are supportive, who do not judge and do not criticise, that dispels the shame.

I think this applies to other topics we have talked about. Like if you're a young boy and you feel you can talk about how you perceive masculinity or about your sexuality or whatever, whether it is with your parents or your teachers or your peers — that probably would be helpful.

Ray
Yes, it's having an open and safe platform for communication, whether at home, in school, online, or anywhere. I think that is

going to be a more effective tool than just straight up education about gender roles or masculinity. If there are communication channels where people have a safe space to talk about their feelings, this can help foster validation and affirmation, reducing feelings of isolation.

Sometimes there may be certain feelings that baffle you. Putting it out in the open not only provides relief, but often grants you new perspectives that help you understand yourself a little bit better.

If one supresses their feelings, they may take social cues because they don't know how else to behave in front of other people. That's when one starts looking for social norms online or around them and behave based on that rather than how they truly feel.

Ren Chun

I absolutely agree that channels of communication are more important than education. Education tends to be top down, and it runs the risk of creating labelling. So imagine you are at a seminar, and you're told that there are these labels or types of people. You might be wondering, oh, which category to identify with? What am I?

What if I feel in flux? You might be afraid to share your own experience and you might not be sure exactly where you land. And what if the stuff that is being taught has the preconceived bias of whoever's making the materials.

Whereas if it's more about encouraging parents — 'hey, please reach out to your children, have an honest discussion about their sexuality and gender experiences'. Or for teachers to be more receptive and foster a conducive atmosphere for different kinds of people and to have honest conversations and communication. I think that makes more room for the individual to come into their own. It's an exploratory process. You need to have that atmosphere so that boys feel like they can discover themselves or come into their own.

Ray

Exactly. Everybody is different and it's a highly individualised process to truly discover what's best for themselves. We should cultivate an environment that naturally encourages self-discovery, allowing individuals to explore and understand who they are intrinsically.

Ren Chun

One thing that is a bit tricky in Singapore is that we have National Service for boys, and this encourages a certain kind of normalisation, doesn't it? The nature of National Service is that it's about regimentation.

That may be a good thing for Singapore, but what is the implication for the whole gender discussion? NS is like, 'Okay boys, this is what you should do. This is how you should be and that's how you should train, and you got to fall into line' and all that.

Ray

Well, to have an effective military, uniformity tends to be necessary. As such, that would come at the cost of individuality and typically encourages everyone to embody a certain behaviour.

Ren Chun

I wonder whether we can extricate all of the stuff about strict regimentation and so on from masculinity. I know that in the U.S., for example, there are prominent soldiers and generals who are openly gay. So clearly, the military experience doesn't have to be super macho in a conventionally heterosexual manner, right?

But I think in Singapore the older generation is more likely to police concepts of manliness. If you are not heterosexual and you are doing your NS, you run the risk of being made fun of — your sergeant might tease you or make comments about you.

Ray

Yeah, it tends to be an uphill battle. A lot of the things you see in the army, you could almost say it's breeding grounds for misogyny with all the talk about being a 'man' and behaving a certain way.

Ren Chun

Yeah, like your sergeant might say 'don't be a woman'.

Ray

Or don't be so sensitive. It's potentially an environment for some that can lead to development of toxic masculinity traits. I think the leaders in the military can make some tweaks to prevent this sort of thing by adjusting their choice of words. Instead of saying things like 'be like a man', they can say 'be strong' instead.

Ren Chun

Yes, being strong or being weak should not be a gendered issue. So if you're doing a mission the superior shouldn't be saying things like, 'hey guys, don't be little girls'. Instead, say something like 'don't give up easily here, guys'. Strength and weakness — you should not be using gender language to refer to it. That's probably the toxic part.

Q: Recent years have introduced us to concepts like incels, alpha versus beta males. What is your relationship to these terms and does it differ from that of other people in your life.

Ren Chun

I once looked into this. From what I understand there was this biologist who observed the behaviour of wolves and wolf packs, and he found that there's usually one wolf that is in charge of the pack, the alpha wolf. People extrapolated from that and said human relationships, male hierarchies especially, operate in a similar way. And it kind of stuck in the public consciousness.

But subsequent researchers found more fluidity of leadership, even in wolf packs, with a lot of groupings based on parents and pups. So even the notion of the alpha male in wolf packs is debatable.

But taking that further, other researchers have suggested that a much closer proxy for human behaviour are the great apes. This makes so much sense to me. When you look at the behaviour of our closest monkey relatives, say chimpanzees, there is competition between males, but also close bonds and alliances. In fact, some studies suggest that the males who are the most social, with many ties of association, are the most likely to survive. Not to mention bonobos, which we are as closely related to as chimpanzees, which are actually matriarchal and have a lot of solidarity between females.

In any case, all great apes are collaborative. They have complex tasks to handle — find which areas have food, organise the squad, break up the fruit, etcetera. There are tasks to coordinate. There's teaching of the younger ones.

So this notion of the alpha male — it's actually very unhelpful because it encourages the notion of a guy who bulldozes through people and just does whatever he wants.

Actually, in the real world, I think leaders are the people, both men and women, who are very good at encouraging teamwork. Collaborating with other people, sharing ideas, helping to spur on action and being very welcoming, inclusive, helping the group develop.

So I think the notion of an alpha male is actually outmoded and inapplicable. We need a more constructive way of looking at it.

Ray
Yes, agreed. I don't really buy into the association that 'alpha' behaviour makes a person superior to others and that there is

naturally occurring evidence to prove it. To your point, I'd say a person at the top of a collaborative hierarchy could be more justifiably considered to be superior.

However, I wonder why is it that alpha males, despite the negative connotations, are also often very positively attributed with decisiveness and leadership.

Ren Chun

So do you think decisiveness is typically a male trait?

Ray

Oh no. I wouldn't say it's a male trait. However, in societal norms nowadays, it's rather common to observe that women are more attracted to males who have these traits whereas males are less frequently attracted to women who exhibit these traits.

Ren Chun

That's absolutely true from my experience as well.

Ray

Maybe the focus should be on someone's decisiveness or natural leadership skills rather than the association of whether a person is 'alpha' or 'beta'. That's probably a more constructive way of looking at things.

Ren Chun

Yeah. So we have this interesting over-arching theme of freeing positive attributes from the confines of gender language. Being strong or being weak is not an issue of being a man or a woman. Sure, women might prefer a man who is able to step up to the situation and be decisive. But at the same time, it can be very attractive to a man when a woman is sure of herself and decisive.

Let's move on to the topic of incels. How much do you know about incels?

Ray

Not too familiar, I know that the term generally refers to males who are unable to attract women and are resigned to their fate of being single.

Ren Chun

Well, let me explain what I understand regarding the incel world view. I once read about it after there was a violent incident. I was morbidly curious.

Incel is an abbreviation. It stands for involuntary celibate. Some men identify as involuntary celibates because they say they will be unable to ever have intercourse with the opposite sex. So they are saying that the situation is forced upon them.

An incel world view is that in traditional society, say in traditional agrarian society or in the pre-globalised world, men and women lived in smaller communities like villages. In that small-scale setting, there was a lot less mobility. Very often your parents would arrange a marriage for you, or you would fall in love with someone in a nearby village. In other words, men were more or less guaranteed a wife because of that small-scale village setting. Also, the incels argue that female norms were that they were meant to be submissive to men.

Then they say that in the modern globalised world, you have freedom of choice. People can move around different countries. Their argument is that there is basically like a pareto principle, the 80–20 principle where 80 per cent of women go for the top 20 per cent of guys. Or even worse, 99 per cent of women go for the top 1 per cent of guys. These ultimate guys or "chads" are the guys who are super amazing who are dating all the 99 per cent of the women.

And therefore, if you're an average guy and not a chad, you'll never be able to have romantic success. It's a condition that's forced upon you. You have no agency. You have become an involuntary celibate.

Ray (laughing heartily)
They're literally drowning in self-pity!

Ren Chun
Yeah, it can be funny when one tries to articulate it this way. These incels, they make a lot of Internet memes, and they make a lot of these funny images and it seems like fun and games.

But it started becoming very dangerous because on the incel forums, lot of these guys were egging each other on with hateful ideas. What binds them is a shared self-pity, and they project their hate on to women and on those they deem to be successful men.

They really hate the chads, all those supposed successful guys. They say these guys are so selfish and they're the reason for their situation. And they also hate women. They have all these derogatory terms for women, like fembots as though women are robots.

Ray
Ah yes, and the term 'feminazis', I've heard that one before.

Ren Chun
Yes, feminazis. I think their argument is that women are so shallow and don't give ordinary guys like them a chance. This links to one of the toxic masculinity attributes of sexual entitlement — as though women are supposed to endow them with sex as a default. Why?

I think probably the dangerous thing is they use this kind of language and then they say we should take revenge. Guys, we should stand up for ourselves, kind of thing. We should take revenge on them. We should show them what we're made of. And that's when the violent action starts — shooting people, killing people.

Ray

Thanks for sharing that. Very, very interesting and rather scary to think about...

Sounds like a very sad and unfortunate group of people. They should know that they are basically just victimising themselves and drowning in self-pity. And those are actually the attributes which are making you unattractive.

Honestly, you could be a handsome man or a beautiful woman, but if your attitude is self-victimising and fatalistic, people are unlikely to want to be in a relationship with you.

Ren Chun

Their world view creates a deprivation of agency, and it creates something like a blame game. It's a victimisation blame game where it's like I'm not at fault — I'm the one who has had this forced upon me — and then you cast hate on other people.

And their world view is unhelpful because it links to a lot of these gender norms as though they're very fixed things. It's interesting because there have been guys who come forward in response to incel hate crimes and they talk about it constructively and they say that they used to identify as incels but now they want to publicly break away from that and also they disapprove of the extremist, violent actions.

They say they realise it's really a matter of not blaming people and dropping into self-pity but really working on their fitness, their education, their own motivation and life. That it is not that women should owe you something, which could be one of the dangers of toxic masculinity.

Ray

This incel movement is a great example of a destructive community, as opposed to the kind of constructive communities that we were talking about earlier that we want to move towards.

We need forums, education and media that encourages them to talk about it in a constructive manner with their friends and family. I can empathise that these people must feel frustrated and there's nothing they can do. Thus, when they meet others like themselves in an online forum, that probably gives them a safe place to confide in one another, a much-needed respite for their feeling of helplessness.

However, if the culture of this group is destructive in nature, then it is rather worrisome. I believe we need to funnel more of these people into constructive groups. Where they can address their needs, their feeling of helplessness and there is actionable assistance for them to improve their situation.

Ren Chun
Yeah, I agree. This links to the second point I was going to make — about how communication can be a double-edged sword. How do we ensure that it is positive rather than negative. It's very difficult. And this links into the bigger topic of media, censorship, media discourse.

On one hand we don't want to encourage hate speech. So there should be safeguards in place, whether it is online or in print media. But then does that go against freedom of speech?

Something like Internet forums, it's so hard to control. You can't control what kind of a forum a young boy goes on. Maybe it's more about trying to just bring in the positive values through the other mainstream communication channels — parents and teachers, and the mainstream media — so that at least some positive values are instilled.

If there are channels where you could speak honestly and safely to your counsellors or schoolteachers or friends or whoever about your anxieties and other issues, you wouldn't have a lot of pent-up rage to go into anonymous forums and talk and say whatever.

Ray

Exactly. I think that that's a key point you've just made — create some manner of curated channels where people can have their issues addressed before they turn to these rogue forums.

Let's consider the scenario of a kid at school who is unpopular because he is considered conventionally unattractive. When he tries to talk to a teacher or his parents because he feels frustrated, they may be dismissive or address his concerns in a way that does not alleviate his feelings of helplessness. He may not feel they understand what he is going through.

So eventually he's going to be looking for a channel to release that pent-up frustration and he might end up on an incel forum that welcomes him to the community with open arms. They can share relatable experiences and then it would be no surprise that he may choose to identify with this group of people rather than suffering alone in silence.

On the other hand, if his parents managed to sort out the issue, or perhaps there was an online forum moderated to be more constructive, he could avoid developing toxic traits. I'm sure that the majority of these people aren't hateful people to begin with, they're just people who need a little bit of help.

Ren Chun

That makes me think. Obviously, we have a lot of work still to do on gender equality and female rights, but I feel that it's going to be quite important to have more male support groups as well.

There's a bit of stigma around males being vulnerable and opening up about their issues. If you're a guy and you know that there are these constructive, inclusive places, whether online or offline, where you can go to talk about your issues and other men can counsel you or share their thoughts — that will probably be quite encouraging for young men with problems. So it's about creating a safe space for men and supporting men in their journey.

Ray

Yes. If we had these channels, we could filter people towards a path of recovery rather than leaving them on their own to deal with loneliness, stigmatisation or not being able to feel vulnerable. This could help mitigate toxic masculine traits developing over time.

Ren Chun

The rejection breeds the hate they feel. First of all, they feel rejected and then it gets combined with a toxic mindset of sexually objectifying women. They're kind of bottling it up. Then it ferments and breeds a lot of hate. The very famous shooter case in California, it was discovered after the fact that he had these extensive diaries where he was writing all of his morbid thoughts.

We should try to help people before it gets to that stage where they feel like nobody understands them and the only way is to lash out with very extreme action.

Q: Who needs to do what to bring about gender equality?

Ren Chun

I think we can think of it in terms of various angles — the workplace, the household, the school, and between kids or between individuals.

For the workplace, we talked about having more inclusive notions of leadership and decisiveness. Do away with the unhelpful notion of being an alpha male and getting your way. It's really about inclusive leadership, from the male point of view and also from the female point of view. Obviously from the male point of view, the onus falls upon a lot of men because statistically a lot of business leaders are still men.

There is the ongoing issue of improving female representation at the C Suite level, at the managerial level, on boards, at the heads of organisations. But beyond that there is the issue of leadership styles. We said that if there is a choice between a workplace with a domineering top-down culture and a place with a more inclusive open culture, obviously we would choose the latter.

Then about the household, we should encourage parents to be open minded, to have frank discussions with their children, especially when they reach puberty and adolescence. Create a safe space where parents listen to their kids, ask them how you feel about gender, how do you feel about sexuality.

This links to the school. We talked about how maybe top-down education will not be that helpful because it might reinforce labels and categories. So maybe future educators should be taught about the value of mindfulness, of the skill of active listening.

Tell teachers 'Make sure you don't police norms; make sure you don't use language that creates distinctions; make sure you don't tolerate bullying. Make sure you don't tolerate toxic behaviours.' And if you see that something is going on with one of your students, reach out to them and say, 'I'm here to listen, what's on your mind?'

So we can help to train teachers about what to look out for and then encourage them to be mindful and active listeners to try to create those open channels of communication with students. This feeds into the whole parent-teacher relationship.

Of course then there is civil society. It's always been important for activists to bring more attention to issues. One of our points was the importance of raising public consciousness. So the work of the activists and the journalists is important. And this conversation we are having, for this book — this is also part of the effort to raise public consciousness and to get people into the conversation.

Get them listening and thinking about the issues, and to pass it on to their peers.

This links to our point about male peers and National Service — making sure that language is not inadvertently used to emphasise or reinforce toxic masculine identities. The leadership could perhaps be more mindful about this.

And finally, back to the individual level. First of all, it is really about trying to free our notions of attributes from the confines of gender. Stop thinking of certain attributes as being of this gender or that gender. Just link attributes to the individual.

And secondly, having that receptivity to the fluidity and the choice of the individual. Every individual is on their own path, we're all on our journeys. People will have explorations. They might feel one way at a certain point in time, they might feel a different way at another point in time.

And ultimately, it's going to be very difficult to try to say what masculinity is. We can instead say what it's not. It is not about being the alpha male. It is not about bullying and pushing your way through. That is not what we should have in masculinity. Then leave space for men to define it for themselves within their lives, and with their loved ones.

Ray

Well said! For me, the emphasis is on raising that awareness and empathy. Just having this conversation gets me thinking about how we can put in place better systems and create communication channels where we can be more inclusive of everyone's opinions and beliefs.

As you've mentioned, this should be through a multitude of channels, from the workplace to NS and at home. This can provide people different insights and perspectives, on gender roles, highlighting how one's beliefs may need to be changed or adjusted for a more harmonious society.

Hopefully this can promote empathy and people with contrasting beliefs ultimately collaborate with one another rather than be firmly divided. I believe that change that comes intrinsically from empathising with others is more effective than hard regulations where people only adhere to them because of extrinsic factors. Although the hard regulations are there to protect social order, more emphasis needs to be put into the long-term solution which is education.

That is the over-arching theme for me — more mindfulness and awareness, more open communication so that we can build a society that feels more inclusive and harmonious. That way, we can bring out the best in people, rather have them fall astray and end up developing toxic behaviour.

Thanks for this opportunity! It was an incredibly insightful conversation.

* * *

HO REN CHUN is a lawyer and writer, now working in corporate strategy, based in Singapore. He is a graduate of the University of Cambridge, where he was the recipient of the Winifred Georgina Holgate Pollard Memorial Prize for the most outstanding results. He was also the founder of the Cambridge University Poetry and Prose Society, the first university-wide literary society. Ren Chun has published in journals such as the Quarterly Literary Review Singapore *and in anthologies like* Poetry Moves, *and has received the Friend of the Arts award for his philanthropic work supporting the arts in Singapore.*

LIU RAY CHUN is a business strategy manager based in Singapore and a graduate from Singapore Management University. He has also undertaken study abroad programmes at Harvard University and Queen Mary University of London. Ray is a recipient of the Canadian-ASEAN Scholarships and Educational Exchanges for Sustainable Development (SEED) scholarship at the University of Alberta and now pursues making a difference through his work in ethical enterprises.

"Women's strengths will be rightly valued and not seen as weakness or stereotypical and frivolous. Her empathy, compassion, practical sense tempered with judicious judgement, and gentle approach will be allowed to shape society's values. Beginning now and always, boys and girls should be educated to see themselves as team-mates not competitors; throughout life contributing their inherent talents to build nation and society, together."

~ Poet Anne Lee Tzu Pheng, for The Lives of Women exhibition at the National Museum, Jan–Mar 2022

CHAPTER 26

Teaching Children about the Birds and the Bees

Tan Joo Hymn

When my children were younger, they liked roughhousing with one another: tickling and play-wrestling all over the mattress we had on the floor. If one of them said something like "no" "stop" or "ow", I would stop the game and explain that they had to respect their sibling's request. It was no longer fun for one of them, and the others should not have fun at his/her expense.

When the youngest was able to communicate verbally, I tried not to interfere in their play. There was once I heard some raised voices behind the closed door of their room, and then one loud shrill cry, followed by sobs. After a few minutes of busy rustling and hushed voices, I heard giggles and delighted shrieks, and I walked away. I figured that they understood my earlier lessons.

When they were in primary school, they would often tell me, "I do not give you my consent to brush my teeth" and "It's my body, and I do not want to have a shower". One of them just said to me, "I do not give you my consent to practise piano" when I told them I would like to include anecdotes from their preschool days in my essay. Ah, the joys of being a parent who has taught her children the importance of consent!

It is unusual for a parent, especially in Singapore, to forefront consent and sex education in interactions with children, and I have had my share of eyerolls and "Mum, please!" from my children. I do this not (just) to protect my children, which I recognise is impossible, but also so that other young people will be safe with my children. In the play "This is What Happens to Pretty Girls" written by Ken Kwek and staged by Pangdemomium, the mother character played by Serene Chen is the one that I found most memorable, and which haunted me for weeks after. What would I do if my child were a perpetrator of sexual assault?

A recent Reply to a Parliamentary Question[1] stated that a total of 11,868 people made police reports about being sexually assaulted in the five years from 2018 to 2022. By contrast, a survey done in 2015[2] found that 16 per cent of young persons in Singapore aged 17–25 said they had been sexually assaulted. Meanwhile, 11 per cent admitted having touched, kissed, or had sex with someone without making sure their partner consented. Applied to the approximate total population of 17–25-year-olds, this means that 70,000 young people have experienced, and 50,000 young people have committed, some form of sexual assault.

This is borne out by the experiences of the young people attending the sexuality education workshops we run at AWARE. One young woman stated at the start of a workshop that she was there to learn

---

[1] https://www.mha.gov.sg/mediaroom/parliamentary/written-reply-to-pq-on-sexual-assault-cases-involving-minors-under-16-years-old-in-the-past-five-years/

[2] https://www.aware.org.sg/2015/03/survey-1-in-3-young-people-have-faced-sexual-violence-few-seek-or-receive-help/

that "what happened to her was not her fault". I had to take a deep breath after hearing her say that. Another asked questions throughout about how best she could support her friend. It's not just from the young people that we hear of such accounts; parents who attend our workshops have shared similar experiences.

It is not unthinkable that one of our children could become a survivor or perpetrator of sexual assault. It is therefore absolutely vital that we have many conversations with them on the topics of consent, healthy relationships, and sex.

Don't the schools teach it already

Sexuality education, or SEd as the Ministry of Education (MOE) calls it, is taught in schools from primary five to junior college. The MOE website[3] does provide information (in fact, the entire SEd syllabi), but it would be a committed parent who can find all the relevant segments and then really understand it.

The first principle of the MOE programme is that "parents play the primary role in educating their children and for teaching and transmitting values on sex and sexuality". However, the MOE website does not offer parents any guidance on how to have conversations about these matters with their children, nor does it tell us what actually happens at the SEd lessons in classrooms.

Tellingly, the word "consent" does not appear in any of the syllabi posted on the website (nor in the curricula posted on the websites of secondary schools).

The most important aspect of sex education is not what students will learn, recognise or understand, but what they actually will do in real life with a romantic partner outside the classroom.

---

[3] https://www.moe.gov.sg/education-in-sg/our-programmes/sexuality-education

This gap between knowledge and real-life behaviour was pointed to by experts interviewed by media[4] about the rising sexually transitted infections (STI) rates amongst young people. The experts said young people know about condoms and safer sex but are not using them for a variety of reasons, including embarrassment and peer pressure. This can comprise both attitude ("It's dorky to stop the action to put on a condom") and skill ("I don't know how to tell my partner I want to use a condom"), the other two learning objectives the United Nations described as critical[5] in addition to knowledge.

One additional question that my co-trainers and I had from ploughing through the MOE website is this: whether the teachers know enough about the impact of trauma. Given the known statistics, it is highly likely that there will be students in the classroom who have experienced violence of some sort. The teacher, in promoting the importance of responsible decision making (in the syllabus for Sec Two), can inadvertently make a young person who has experienced sexual violence feel it is their fault for not having taken all the steps they should have done — even though they probably did not know about these steps when the violence took place. It is a common reaction amongst survivors who have sought help at AWARE's Sexual Assault Care Centre to think that it is somehow their fault.

There is a long running tendency to focus more on what a person can do to prevent being sexually assaulted, rather than on what can be done to not be a perpetrator. One of my co-trainers once asked a student, "If a perpetrator is sitting right here, and hears that you

---

[4] See for example https://www.straitstimes.com/singapore/health/more-young-people-get-sexual-infections; see also https://www.todayonline.com/singapore/hiv-positive-18-why-teenagers-risk-their-sexual-health-and-what-parents-can-do

[5] The United Nations, *International Technical Guidance on Sexuality Education*, 2018. https://unesdoc.unesco.org/ark:/48223/pf0000260770

have just told her that she should not have gone to a bar and drunk alcohol, what is the message he will get?" The student replied, "That it was not entirely his responsibility". The student, and others in the room, hopefully were prompted to re-look at their attitude.

What do we need to make sure our children know
Safe and unsafe touches

News reports of young children being molested or raped appear every few weeks. Many of these children would have internalised the message that they are to respect and obey adults like teachers, school staff and older relatives. When the molest or rape happens and they sense that it is wrong, they may not know what to do. Or they may not even realise that it is wrong. Furthermore, they may not talk about it to anyone for fear of getting into trouble or because the adult told them to keep it a secret.

There are horrific stories of children realising during their primary five sexuality education classes that what was done to them when they were as young as four or five was wrong.[6] [The media stories also raise questions about the Replies given to Parliamentary Questions stating that MOE Sexuality Education begins at Primary 1.[7]] These stories give a glimpse of the intense emotional turbulence experienced by survivors of sexual violence.

Healthy and unhealthy relationships

Parents are often fighting a losing battle with media portrayals of relationships. Harassment, pressuring, and stalking behaviour are

---

[6] For example: https://www.todayonline.com/singapore/man-admits-repeatedly-trying-rape-4-year-old-daughter-who-later-engaged-self-harm-2050411

[7] https://www.moe.gov.sg/news/parliamentary-replies/20210706-response-to-the-adjournment-motion-sexuality-education-in-schools-as-first-line-of-defence-against-sexual-violence

often portrayed positively as persistence and romance, with the object of the pursuit eventually falling in love with their harasser. The qualities that are actually vital in a healthy relationship — which include respect, boundaries, safety, communication, and mutuality — are often dismissed as wimpy and unexciting.

While "respect" is a word that is ubiquitous in the material on MOE's website, do young people know what it means? An important accompanying characteristic, mutuality, is often absent from discussions. Is it respect if, for example, a girl expects her boyfriend to attend all of her violin recitals but very politely declines to attend any of his basketball matches?

Consent

Young children can already understand the basic concept, so the mention of it often elicits groans and eyerolls in young people. However, do they know how to navigate it in real life? If two people are making eyes at each other as they slowly lean in, surely, they don't need to be captain obvious and ask if it is ok to kiss?

What if the girl is really into this and cannot wait for their lips to meet. Does she have any preconceived ideas about the boy and his gender? Does she think, all boys want to make out so he must want to even though he is moving so slowly.

Or perhaps the boy thinks that all girls act coy even if they want to, so it's only natural that she seems a bit hesitant, but she wants to for sure. Or is he already aroused and flooded with hormones so that he perceives any movement as being towards him even when she is actually trying to slowly move further away?

Consent is one of the areas where knowledge contributes only a small amount towards practice. A large part of it lies in attitude, including stereotypes, power dynamics, and hot states (i.e. being in an emotionally or sexually heightened state), just to name a few. The maxim "We don't see things as they are, we see things as we are" is especially important to keep in mind in intimate relationships.

Another factor that impacts consent is the ability to accept rejection. Recent research[8] shows that humans are hard wired to avoid rejection as it could have made the difference between life and death in prehistoric times.

How many of our children have practised accepting a "no" graciously, without sulking or throwing a tantrum?

Parents can have conversations about aspects of consent at home, and all of these help the young people refine their understanding. However, workshops of peers have a clear advantage over parental conversations at home because young people can experience for themselves the very many different points of views that people have, including, potentially, their romantic partner. Or as one participant put it, some people do not seem to have the same level of common sense.

Pornography

Pornography is a topic that many parents find very hard to broach. However, many of our children have come into contact with some form of it. A survey done in 2015[9] found that 91 per cent of boys had been exposed to porn by age 15. For girls, the number was a much lower 35 per cent.

Some time ago, I was invited to be 'the expert' in a Mediacorp programme[10] on YouTube about sex education. The teen was very open in talking about how her peers watch and talk about porn.

---

[8] For example, https://www.ncbi.nlm.nih.gov/pmc/articles/PMC4734881/

[9] https://www.straitstimes.com/singapore/nine-in-10-teen-boys-exposed-to-porn-survey

[10] https://www.youtube.com/watch?v=QMXPjKfmMLg

I found it absolutely refreshing that it was possible for a teen to have such a conversation with a young adult, and for both of them to exchange ideas and learn from each other. I very much hope that the sex education programmes in schools allow for this type of open discussion, though the description of it on MOE/school websites makes it sound unlikely, especially as boys and girls are separated.

While it may be tricky for parents to have these conversations, it is useful to refer to the New Zealand Government's holistic education package.[11] The focus is on providing young people with the information, knowledge, and skills they require to make responsible choices. It acknowledges young people's natural curiosity about sex without shaming them and allows for authentic dialogue amongst the young people.

Bystander support

Do our children know what to do if their friends are being harassed? Or being the harasser? The 2015 survey[12] which found that 16 per cent of young persons had been sexually assaulted also found that four in 10 respondents knew someone who had perpetrated unwanted sexual contact, and every other young person knew someone who had been harassed. The average young person is thus more likely to be a bystander than a survivor or a perpetrator. This makes them an important point of intervention. If more of our children knew what to do, our country would be safer for everyone.

Pleasure

Sexual pleasure is a topic that is taboo in Singapore. MOE promotes abstinence before marriage, with attendant warnings of the physical

---

[11] For more parent-friendly material, see: https://www.keepitrealonline.govt.nz; for research, see: https://www.classificationoffice.govt.nz/resources/research/

[12] See note 2 above.

and emotional repercussions of pre-marital sex. Such an approach allows little scope for talking to young people frankly about their sexual needs, and about sexual pleasure and how it can be simply a physical reaction.

As a result, young people may be confused when they experience sexual pleasure as a physiological reaction when doing everyday things, and this can lead to feelings of guilt and shame. Survivors of coercive sex who experience pleasure during the assault may wonder whether they were indeed assaulted.

If sex and sexual pleasure are depicted to children and youths as being 'dirty' and taboo, little wonder if as adults they are hesitant to talk about consent and contraceptives, let alone their sexual preferences. Could shame about sexual pleasure be a contributing factor to Singapore's extremely low total fertility rate, along with the concerns about living costs and other factors?

Sexual orientation and gender identity

This is another taboo topic. Percentages of people who identify as non-heterosexual can vary a lot according to how the surveys are conducted. Estimates vary from around 5 per cent to as high as 19 per cent.[13] It is very possible that our children or one of their close friends identifies as LGBTQ.

A 2013 survey (unpublished) of the LGBTQ community found that almost 60 per cent had as students experienced bullying or discrimination and 5 per cent had been physically assaulted. As a comparison, verbal bullying of students with disabilities is about 20 per cent. These numbers should give us pause. Why in a society that prides itself on being cosmopolitan and multi-racial is bullying of peers perceived as different so high?

---

[13] https://www.statista.com/statistics/1318449/singapore-distribution-of-people-by-gender-identity

The attitudinal changes required for this situation to improve are huge but not insurmountable with enough will and courage. As a first step, scientifically incorrect materials should be strictly prohibited. There is plenty of research that it is not a 'lifestyle choice', and historical records from Asian countries will show that it is not a 'Western import' either.

If we believe that Singapore's resource is its people, we cannot stand by while some students are denied the opportunity to achieve their full potential. Factually accurate information about sexual orientation and gender identity must be part of the syllabus and discrimination against LGBTQ+ persons must be dealt with as firmly as discrimination against racial or religious minorities.

The sex ed we deserve

Try as we might as parents — and I speak from personal experience — there are things that conversations at home are unable to achieve in the way that workshops amongst peers can. From the response to the workshops that AWARE has conducted, there are clear signs that all young people in Singapore would benefit from and also enjoy comprehensive sexuality education programmes (CSE). One participant wrote "The facilitators covered all of my concerns and provided necessary information regarding the topics shared." Another said, "Reach out to more! More girls and boys needs this knowledge." When asked, many said they would recommend the workshop to their friends and peers.

Many people have asked how they can "educate" young people to know or do certain things. And our response generally is that we cannot make them do anything that they have not seen the value of and internalised. It is far more valuable to create spaces for young people to explore their beliefs and perspectives, and to formulate for themselves what they truly find important and what they would like to do.

Obstacles in our path

Attempts to provide more holistic sexuality education have been met with covert or overt opposition, the strongest example being the takeover in 2009 of AWARE by a group of religious women who took exception to aspects of the organisation's CSE workshops. (The takeover group was ousted some weeks later at an Extraordinary General Meeting but the ruckus they raised about the CSE programme led to AWARE being banned from running it in MOE schools.)

Traditionally, it has been thought that parents are worried that talking about sex would encourage their children to try it. However, in a survey done in 2020 by AWARE in collaboration with Blackbox, only 26 per cent[14] of parents expressed this concern. Meanwhile, 86 per cent felt it was important to teach consent and sexual self-protection. Almost a quarter of parents did not know what was being taught in schools.

Education in Singapore has always been about academic performance; therefore parents and teachers usually have little capacity to pay much attention to sexuality education. It is unlikely to be an area MOE would like to take the lead on, given the potential backlash from the more vocal communities. While there are many matrices measuring academic learning, it would be interesting to gauge if any of the MOE learning objectives for sexuality education have actually been achieved.

Another huge obstacle is teacher selection and training. Provision of sexuality education is largely done by teachers in schools. We

---

[14] Survey done in collaboration with Blackbox: https://www.aware.org.sg/2020/07/parents-comfortable-sex-ed-consent-abstinence-aware-blackbox-survey/

have heard anecdotes of teachers being so awkward they could barely name the genitals. In addition, most teachers are already burdened with curricular and co-curricular responsibilities, and unlikely to be able to devote the time and resources that this topic requires.

Whither the way forward?

The United Nations and the WHO[15] have issued strong statements about the need for education about sexual health. Studies done in other countries and quoted by the United Nations[16] show that comprehensive sexuality education in schools, and confident loving parent-child communication about relationships and sex, both have positive outcomes. These include delaying first sexual intercourse, fewer sex partners and reduced frequency of sex, and more consistent use of contraceptives including condoms. In the USA, increased emphasis on abstinence education was positively correlated with increased teen pregnancy and birth rates.[17]

It would be helpful for MOE to provide a dual track sexuality education syllabus, i.e. the existing programme as well as a more comprehensive one for which parents can opt in. Subsequently, comparison longitudinal studies can be done. Several other Asian countries, such as Taiwan and the Philippines, have adopted or are in the process of adopting CSE.

Young people deserve to have healthy and respectful relationships where consent is appreciated by both parties; where they do not have to worry about date rapes; where being rejected says nothing about

---

[15] The World Health Organisation (WHO) website (https://www.who.int/health-topics/sexual-health#tab=tab_1) states: "Sexual health is fundamental to the ***overall health*** and well-being of ***individuals, couples and families***, and to the social and ***economic development*** of communities and ***countries***. Sexual health, when viewed affirmatively, requires a positive and respectful approach to sexuality and sexual relationships, as well as the possibility of having pleasurable and safe sexual experiences, free of coercion, discrimination and violence." (***emphasis*** mine)

[16] https://www.unesco.org/en/health-education/cse

[17] Research done in 2005: https://www.ncbi.nlm.nih.gov/pmc/articles/PMC3194801/

their masculinities; and where they are free to achieve their fullest potential without worrying about stereotypes.

The AWARE workshops demonstrate that young people are receptive to and appreciate such workshops. It is a long, long road ahead to convince the authorities to make CSE available to all youths. But it is a road we must take if we want to permanently reduce incidences of sexual assault, STIs and unwanted pregnancies, and if we want our young people to have healthy and satisfying romantic relationships.

For now, as parents and people who care about children, you have a decision to make. There are many loud voices opposing CSE, and it is unlikely to be implemented in schools any time soon. So, what is important to you? What do you want children and young people to know, and do? And what are you prepared to do now to make it happen?

TAN JOO HYMN is a facilitator, storyteller, trained early childhood educator, and lawyer. She has been a volunteer with AWARE for over 20 years, and a past president of the organisation. She is currently AWARE's programme director for Birds & Bees workshops on consent, sex, and relationship for young people and parents. She is also a proud mother to three amazing beings, who inspire her to wear the label activist with pride. Joo Hymn would like to thank her Birds & Bees co-trainers and colleagues Mathangi Kumar and Chie van Slobbe for their inputs and suggestions for this essay.

[Note: All websites referred to in this essay were accessed on 6 December 2023.]

The Language of Change

"..there are still multiple areas that require change to achieve greater gender equality. There is no silver bullet in this journey. Clearly, policy and legislative changes will have significant impact. At the same time, government efforts must be coupled by contributions by other social and economic actors. Urban design professionals like architects, and developers have a role to play in delivering cities and buildings that are friendly to women's needs. Businesses have a role to play in taking seriously training on biases so that diversity and inclusion is not a luxury but a necessary activity."

~ **Educator and geographer Lily Kong, at a dialogue about women's development, March 2022**

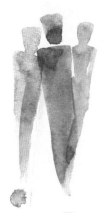

CHAPTER 27

Brands, Language, and Gender in the Age of Technology

Linda Locke

In the 1980s and early 1990s, women were generally shown in the media as homemakers, mothers, or objects of men's sexual desire. Consider the well-known Tiger Beer coffee shop posters with their suggestively dressed ladies; or a TVC for the now defunct Marco Polo Hotel in which a lady in a hip-high, sexily slashed evening dress is led up the steps on the arm of a smartly dressed man. Even the iconic Singapore Girl of Singapore Airlines portrayed a meek and docile woman only too willing to serve; thankfully, she is now shown travelling the world, a strong, independent woman graciously caring for you.

Being a woman in the advertising industry at that time was surprisingly not that unusual especially in media, finance, account servicing, and even the creative department. This was because advertising was a career path frowned upon by parents of male children, who expected them to be lawyers, doctors, teachers, scientists, or bankers. While this should have allowed for less stereotyping of women in advertising, many of the clients were men with quite fixed ideas about how they wished their brands projected, and society itself was far less evolved than it is today.

China Silk House, Linda Locke, and Leo Burnett Advertising

Having said that, there were opportunities with intelligent clients like China Silk House, who agreed to a campaign to amplify the way silk makes women feel — shockingly, for their own pleasure.

Or UOB's Lady's Card launched in 1989, designed to appeal to financially independent women, and tied to insurance products designed to support women's health issues, providing protection just for them. The product and the communications empowered women to take care of themselves, rather than depend on men.

Women turn up the volume

Women continued to change and evolve significantly. More and more women were travelled, educated, and finding their path in non-traditional positions and contexts. And not just the young, but older women too were continuing in careers after becoming mothers, and even grandmothers. And their careers were in areas once the domain of men: bankers, scientists, lawyers, doctors, surgeons, politics, and in all types of businesses; with many running their own successful companies.

Some women entrepreneurs, however, were guilty of depicting women in a less than a positive light to push them into buying their products and services.

> *"Mothers were shamed for their postpartum bodies and were encouraged to fix them (with Marie Bodyline, no less). And young women were encouraged to experience their skin going lighter by the week, only with Garnier Skincare or your money back."*
>
> — *Pat Law, Founder, Goodstuph*

It is easy to play the blame game and point the finger at the agency and the media, but in many cases, it starts with a brand and its products or services and is heavily influenced by prevailing attitudes, both male and female, towards gender roles and appearance within the norms of local culture. A client who deliberately makes a skin lightening product does so because research has told them that dark skin is considered unattractive, and an agency will therefore exploit this insight to sell the product.

Client attitudes are changing rapidly, however, due in part to the Internet, social media, education, and also because of their agencies and research.

> *"With the recent 'It's not crazy, it's the Navy'[1] campaign, the use of the young daughter to open and close the spot is a step forward for diversity. This is a strong ad, and it may sound clichéd but needs to be heard. Kudos to the agency and client for going there."*
>
> — *Koh Hwee Peng, Creative Partner, Blak Labs*

Kudos indeed to the Navy and the Singapore Armed Forces as a whole for recruiting women in various positions since the late 1980s. One could argue that it has been societal attitudes, more than an unwillingness on the part of the government and the Armed Forces, that have impeded more rapid progress.

> *"Ever since UOB's iconic "The Men Don't Get It" campaign for the Lady's Card, more ads have made women aware that they can be empowered while also embracing their feminine side in Singapore society. Who you write for is as much about who you exclude. And there's a growing sense that men appreciate the strong role that women play in society."*
>
> — *Koh Hwee Peng, Creative Partner, Blak Labs*

Brands like Perk by Kate, founded by entrepreneur Kate Low, are doing their part to change perceptions not just of how others see women, but of how women see and feel about themselves. The brand acts as a cheer leader for women to enjoy and revel in their sexuality. The knock-on effect of these portrayals, when seen by men, has the

---

[1] https://www.youtube.com/watch?v=8clfbPEGCuk

potential to make them re-evaluate their personal view of the women in their lives.

> *"Being a lingerie brand fronted by a woman, it was important for the brand to showcase lingerie as experienced from a woman's point of view, and not from a man's point of view. Lingerie is more than just something you wear for a special occasion. Putting on a piece of beautiful lingerie can boost your self-confidence, as narrated to me by women going through self-esteem issues or those going through a difficult period in their lives — particularly post-partum or post-surgery. It has now become a form of social responsibility for me to depict women being most beautiful in their own skin. Lingerie brings out that glow that's inside everyone."*
>
> *— Kate Low, Founder, Perk by Kate*

Brands and their owners have come a long way from shaming women into purchasing their products and services, demeaning them rather than lifting them up; or featuring them in stereotypical roles that are no longer true or are too narrowly defined. They are doing a better job of reflecting a more authentic view of women in society today. Some, however, are responsible for going too far and 'faking it'.

The noise created by social media, the Internet and media in general, as well as the growing voices of advocacy groups across the spectrum of gender issues from female empowerment to the LGBTQ+ community cannot be ignored. We see more and more brands attempting to show they are in touch with these groups and their causes. Too many, however, do it at face value for the purpose of driving revenues and profit.

All kinds of washing

We have all heard of green washing and now we are looking at fem-washing and rainbow-washing. These are brands that bang the drum about female empowerment or supporting the LGBTQ community, but who do so without actually supporting them in any meaningful way.

Attaching a token pink ribbon for breast cancer or a rainbow one to packaging is not real support. Tie-ups with brands in the LBGTQ+ community, for example, that do not use any of the earnings to help the community is not real support. It is deceitful and risks making a mockery of hard-fought battles for recognition by all these groups and the emotional price many have paid just to be respected, seen and allowed to live their lives.

Treating these causes as if they are short-term novelties and trends is highly damaging to all concerned, including the brands that deceive themselves into thinking they will not be found out. And 'brands' includes media platforms. Google is a good example of a brand and media platform that actively provides financial and communication support to the LBGTQ+ community.

Agencies need to play their part by keeping themselves and their clients honest. They have a powerful opportunity to open minds to all women who fight hard to be accepted and welcomed.

Global brands have an even bigger voice and can literally change world attitudes, for the right reasons and in the right way — starting with their boards, their staff and company culture, propagating inclusivity; and then manifesting this change through their products and services; and the marketing and communication of them.

Globally, companies influence the culture and society of the markets in which they do business. They do their company and brands — and ultimately their bottom line — a great disservice by not reflecting enough of the constituents who make up our world. One female board member therefore is not enough. One gender specific member is not enough.

This process however needs to be genuine and intelligent. No one should be excluded because of their gender, but by the same token, no one should be hired simply to fulfil a quota and tick boxes, but rather on merit.

Locally, there are brands trying to lead change in perceptions and promote inclusiveness, but it is important to understand that it is a sensitive area requiring care, thought, and the right approach. What we say is as important as how we say it and show it. We are not helping to break stereotypes if, for example, an insurance company tries to sell its products to women by telling them they should take care of themselves — so that they can take care of others.

It helps, of course, if the brand is run by a woman or women. Good examples are Love Bonito that actively supports women in general and the LBcommunity+, and Perk by Kate that tries to be inclusive to all women.

> *"I was recently told this — my product is not just a product that sells sex. I have the ability to change the way women feel about themselves. Why not use this privilege I have to make an impact? Diversity in body shapes, for example, is a big topic — and I would say it is a work in progress. We as a brand have to balance aspiration with reality.*
>
> *We choose to use a mix of models and real women — no woman should be discriminated against. Models are professionals, and they should be accorded respect for what*

they do. That said, the rise of social media has created a new generation of content — the user-generated content — which showcases products worn by real women. That element is crucial to a brand's success."

— *Kate Low, Founder Perk by Kate*

AI and the danger of perpetuating stereotypes

The speed at which Artificial Intelligence (AI) is developing is extraordinary, out-pacing the technological transformations that five years ago we thought were moving the world in new directions at warp speed. The advertising industry is rapidly embracing and adopting AI. In many ways it is beneficial as it reduces inefficiencies and tedious aspects of the work, increases performance measurements and speedily and cost-efficiently allows targeted campaigns to be created with specific messaging that can be delivered where, when, and to whom it needs to be directed.

But alarm bells start ringing when we factor in gender stereotyping, because the old adage 'garbage in garbage out' is still very much the case and it can get a lot worse considering the speed at which AI is allowing us to function. AI is not static, rather it is dynamic and 'learns' at speed, but it still utterly reliant on what it is fed and this places an enormous pressure on brands and agencies to ensure that what it is fed is not biased, limiting, and ultimately incorrect.

"AI employs precision, enabling ads to reach an audience with the highest probability of expressing interest in the promoted product. However, when shaped by past data, this notion of 'high probability' regrettably encompasses ingrained stereotypes that have persisted through time. Take, for instance, the scenario where AI recommends typically 'masculine' products

like soccer balls to men while suggesting 'feminine' products such as air fryers exclusively to women.

This perpetuates the damaging notion that certain products are intended solely for specific genders. Furthermore, AI may be informed by the data it is trained upon to discriminate against certain groups, effectively excluding individuals based on their race, gender, or other factors.

If this data happens to be tainted by sexism or biased perspectives, the AI system will inevitably reflect these flaws in the ads it generates. The result? A landscape populated by stereotypical and hyper-realistic advertisements, reinforcing gender stereotypes to such extremes that they are pushed even further along the spectrum."

— Eugenia Tan, Managing Director,
Managing Partner, Goodstuph

In other words, its very ability to be relevant and timely can be subverted by the core data it is fed and trained on. This issue if not corrected will potentially flow into the advertising it creates. The impetus is therefore on the client and agency to self-regulate.

Sound bites and hyper segmentation of media

The media landscape has exploded in the last 20 years due to the impact of technology, the Internet, and social media channels. Mass communications is out, and smaller, tailored and personalised channels are in, and in many cases controlled by the users themselves — by passion and interests such as gaming, cooking, fashion, travel, movies and more. This has negated broader-based advertising and more naturally requires a clearly defined, targeted approach.

"Yet, even as we revel in the delights of this hyper-segmented media landscape, we must confront the spectre of echo chambers and the potential reinforcement of existing biases like gender stereotypes."

— Eugenia Tan, Managing Director,
Managing Partner, Goodstuph

In other words, we are exposed to fewer alternatives and our world has shrunk and will continue to shrink in many ways — requiring more Word of Mouth (WOM) to spread knowledge and information beyond our normal media diet. This is despite so many new and varied ways to receive and channel ideas, knowledge, and cross cultural and gender experiences. There is a danger that we become more likely to interface narrowly, with only the like-minded. The cost will be the loss of discussion, debate, and other perspectives to create balance, including around the increasingly complex issues of gender definition and equality, and the language around it.

In our fast-paced life, media has not been spared. We have short and disappearing video stories on Facebook, Tik Tok, and Instagram; Twitter and main media channels deliver appetiser portions of news and information, serving the god of speed we all crave, but limiting the full story and its potentially different points of view which might lead the consumer to draw very different conclusions.

"One of the significant challenges of short-form media lies in its susceptibility to reinforcing stereotypes. By their very nature, these formats often rely on simplified, easily digestible, and comprehendible narratives. Unfortunately, this convenience can inadvertently perpetuate harmful beliefs, spread misinformation, and reinforce gender stereotypes. Oversimplified portrayals of gender roles and expectations can hinder progress

toward achieving gender equality, limiting the nuanced understanding of the complex issues at hand."

— *Eugenia Tan, Managing Director and Managing Partner, Goodstuph*

Moving women forward

Thankfully, we are seeing a positive shift as more women break the mould and advertising and client alike embrace it. For example, Vaseline's Knife Sharpener commercial which features a woman taking over a family business, learning the trade, and gaining acceptance. Media companies are doing their part to galvanise the change in traditional perceptions, such as Netflix's Street Food series showing a *putu piring* lady also taking over a family business.

Local media is increasingly giving shout outs to pioneering women that break glass ceilings and stereotypes about women, building brands, such as the all-women dental clinic The Orthodontic Clinic; legal tech company Founders Doc; Spark Architects; and funeral parlour The Life Celebrant.

We are lucky to live in Singapore where a woman can be President and almost 30 per cent of parliamentarians are women. We have made a lot of progress, but more effort is needed. Brands and agencies are listening harder and paying attention but the still low number of women on company boards suggests there is still work to be done to see positive change across all aspects of gender equality.

Companies and brands need to pay careful attention as social media has provided the audience — and customers — with a very loud and persuasive voice that speaks truth to power. In turn these voices can and do affect sales and reputation. The audience owns the brand as much as a company legally does.

"I want to be clear that I'm not a fan of the Cancel Culture, but when managed correctly, the audience does serve as a conscience for brands. Audience engagement can be leveraged to challenge stereotypes, and social media platforms serve to drive those conversations around gender roles to get people to rethink their biases."

— Pat Law, Founder, Goodstuph

In the case of Ai algorithms, clients, and media alike, all need to take responsibility and ensure that the quality of data and its sources are constantly checked and reviewed for prejudice, intolerance, depth, and quality. Data needs to be fact checked, algorithms made transparent, and diversity and balance of viewpoints sought.

"Collaboration between AI technology developers, advertisers, and advocacy groups dedicated to advancing gender equality is necessary. By joining forces, these stakeholders can synchronise their efforts and work towards a common goal: designing AI systems explicitly aimed at dismantling gender stereotypes and fostering inclusivity. Media platforms must take deliberate steps to foster a more diverse and balanced narrative."

— *Eugenia Tan, Managing Director &*
Managing Partner, Goodstuph

Advertisers and advertising agencies both have the potential to change the narrative. By creating ground-breaking, insightful and compelling ideas and content that harness the power of short-form media, by embracing rather than excluding the marginalised, and by empowering them and sharing their stories they can open minds and hearts and move society beyond the stereotypical perceptions of all genders and help us see them as they are, which is equal human beings. Ultimately and inherently, it is in the interest of both brands and agencies to ensure this is the case.

* * *

LINDA LOCKE was CEO and creative director of Saatchi & Saatchi Advertising Singapore, and chairperson and regional creative director of Leo Burnett Advertising, with over 300 creative awards to her name. She later started her own consultancy, Godmother Pte Ltd, and held several key positions at Club21, a luxury fashion distributor. Now an author, she has published eight children's books, including Agnes and Her Amazing Orchid, *a picture book about the creator of Singapore's national flower, the Vanda Miss Joaquim. Linda now serves on the board of Culina.*

"To me, the greatest purpose of literature is to surmount barriers of time and distance to influence thousands of readers, transforming their mental outlooks and impacting their emotional worlds. This is also why even till today, I have never stopped writing."

~ Award-winning writer Tham Yew Chin, in an interview
with Esplanade Offstage, October 2016

CHAPTER 28

Censorship of the Letter

Matilda Gabrielpillai

When I was teaching women's writings at an academic institution at the start of the new millennium, I would go around with a mug that said 'Women who seek to be equal to men LACK AMBITION'. That was often misconstrued according to the stereotypical distrust of feminists, that we want to steal men's power and privilege, that we want more than our fair share. But it wasn't my meaning. For me, feminism is about women challenging patriarchal culture. The 'equality' demand for me is about women seeking to be the same as men, to work the same as men, to demand a chance to play the same game. I am not impressed by women in boardrooms or political parties who are bosom buddies with the male elite, seeking to disempower ordinary citizens. In Parliament, such women rarely argue for policies that would make life easier for mothers and wives; in court rooms, they celebrate their own cleverness at sending under-privileged, hapless men to their death. I've learned to distinguish 'patriarchal women' from feminists. A true feminist in my books seeks women's DIFFERENCE from the prevailing patriarchal order.

You could say I returned from graduate studies in Vancouver a new woman from the one that had left Singapore in 1991. I had been introduced to the writings of Hélène Cixous, who theorised that culture was intricately bound up with sexuality and gender roles, that whether you experienced single orgasms or multiple orgasms determined the way you think. Rather extreme, but you get the idea. She spoke of "phallocentricity", where the masculine perspective was privileged in understanding meaning or social relations. Cixous also linked men's affinity for hierarchy, control and rigid either-or thinking with their sexuality. Men even told stories differently from women, she said — they liked the classical, single perspective form with terminal climaxes whereas women were comfortable with writing that had multiple climaxes and narrators in it. Cixous and some psychoanalytical feminists fired my imagination with the notion that I could overthrow the identity imposed on me by society and tradition as long as I was critically aware of it and instead construct and perform identity for myself. Later, I would run into the feminist "politics of difference" where South Asian, African American and Chicana 'women of colour' rejected the feminism of 'white women', stating that their oppression was multi-layered, given their subjection to both ethnic patriarchal and European colonial cultures.

Where previously I had identified as a modern, Westernised, educated woman, unable to embrace the cookie-cutter Indian woman image on offer to me, I came back with a stronger sense not only of my female identity but also of the intricate binding of European, South Asian and Southeast Asian histories in that gendered identity. Naturally I assumed that I would find a niche in the local women's movement and contribute to it. As a woman of an ethnic minority who had experienced racism at school and at work and even in dating culture, I was especially interested in linking up with South Asian women and sharing histories of discrimination and denigration of our sexuality on television, in the newspapers, at school, and at work. I took it for granted that the local women's movement would be interested in tackling the discriminatory treatment of women from ethnic minority groups, and that they would oppose the government's race-oriented policies.

But I met with a kind of silence, literally and figuratively. There were no Women's Studies departments in the local universities, unlike those proliferating in North America and the UK, and I had a difficult time merely trying to teach my 'women's writing' course for more than a few years despite it being popular with students. I was lucky to meet some of the women in the local women's movement, and admired their organisational abilities, their ability to juggle full-time careers with voluntary work for women, and their resilience in working with a conservative government for the betterment of women's lives. But they were not much interested in exploring problems at the intersections of race, class, gender and sexuality. They were instead extremely active in fighting for equal opportunities at work and in pay, for equal representation in positions of authority and for laws to protect violence against women and children. If the feminists abroad were fiery and confrontational, these women were working with those in power, negotiating with government, collaborating with them, and often letting the men take the credit for their work.

This was perplexing to anyone familiar with the dramatic start of the Singapore women's movement early in the formation of the nation. From the early 1950s, the Singapore Council of Women, led by Shirin Fozdar, had lobbied the British Governor and other officials, the Labour Front government, and opposition parties like the People's Action Party (PAP) as well as Chinese associations to end polygamy and to pass laws to guarantee women's rights to property. These were big demands as it meant taking a giant axe to the heart of Chinese patriarchal culture where female sexual oppression and material fortunes became intertwined with male privilege. Women were politically active, winning seats in the Legislative Assembly and even starting a women's wing in the PAP. They had gotten the vote in 1955 and calculated that any political party that wanted to win had to contend with them as they made up half the electorate. The PAP as a leftist opposition party with feminist firebrands like Chan Choy Siong in its midst was much more ready for women's rights than other parties. Sure enough, women's rights became a central plank of the PAP in its 1959 election manifesto as it courted this important section of the population. The rest, as they say, is history and Singapore's Women's Charter came to be passed even before the nation gained its Independence.

That spectacular start would fizzle out for a while from the 1970s to 1983, which Corinna Lim, Executive Director of AWARE, has aptly named "the Men's Years" (IPS Lecture 1: Herstory). The PAP's feminist MPs had largely defected to Barisan Socialis in 1961 and there were no women in Parliament from 1970 to 1984 because the PAP did not field any female candidates. Women from the opposition parties did not win seats. Educated and with a role to play in Singapore's industrialisation programme, local women focused on turning 'modern' and entered the workforce in huge numbers. There was less time for politics. It took time for our women to realise that modernity had its own patriarchal perils, that their bodies could be oppressed in new ways: that they would have to do double duty as daytime office workers and sunset homemakers and their sexual reproduction would have to be curtailed to fit national prerogatives. They wisened up in 1983 with the culmination of state interference in women's reproductive rights, when the government switched from the 'Stop at Two' policy of 1972 to a discriminatory policy of encouraging university-educated women to have three or more children while less-educated women were to 'Stop at Two'. AWARE, today's leading feminist organsation, was formed in 1985 out of anger that women were being blamed for falling fertility rates and with a mission of improving the social and legal status of Singapore women.

However until the new millennium came around, despite the breakneck speed at which new theories and schools of feminism were developing in other advanced countries, Singapore women would be tied to a liberal style, second wave, mainstream feminism that wouldn't go much beyond fighting for equal rights. The Singapore style of authoritarian governance no doubt would explain some of this lack of pace. But we can, I think, narrow this down further to also involving censorship, a politics of language.

Feminists have long recognised the importance of language to gender as a construct. Works such as Robin Lakoff's *Language and Woman's Place* (1975) and Dale Spender's *Man Made Language* (1980) began by exploring how sexist attitudes in society can be traced to the connotations and denotations of seemingly innocuous words that put women down and elevated men's qualities. Language is intrinsic to the way society denies women authority and legitimacy as human beings. It is also the means by which women can dream themselves anew, inventing new words and self-myths when they have to.

Given the way language can determine reality, feminists have since the 1980s made it a project to 'disappear' sexist words and to coin gender-empowering new words. Today, many teens grow up not hearing the word "spinster", which has for ages represented unmarried women as 'defective,' and this has corresponded with a decreasing stigmatisation of women's choice to be single. On the other hand, the promotion of the word "herstory" as female-gendered history has raised awareness that mainstream "history" is largely a male perspective of the past and tells of men's lives. The feminist neologism has also created a ballooning of scholarship about women's roles in the past and spurred feminist critical perspectives of dominant historical narratives. Words also have conceptual significance, determining the parameters by which objects and events can be understood or analysed. Given all this, is it possible to consider that the women's movement in Singapore was hamstrung in the last two decades of the 20th century by a 'censorship of the letter', by explicit or implicit taboos placed on certain words significant for the women's struggle, words such as "politics", and "patriarchal culture" and "feminism" itself?

There is in Singapore a containment of dissent that is effectuated by a censorship of language, a sense that certain words have to be unspoken. As ethnic minorities will concur, the fight for minority rights has to take place without the uttering of the "racism" word, which is considered to be in bad taste and immediately renders your discrimination claim to be illegitimate. Similarly women activists had to practise linguistic caution if they wanted to be heard. As Leonore Lyons notes ("Believing in Equality", 1999) all associations in Singapore have to include language in their Constitution that commits them to "not indulge in any political activity". The word "political" is very elastic — although it may directly forbid associations from aligning themselves with the activities of any political party, it can also mean that associations should not challenge government policies or perspectives, even verbally, as doing so would make it "political". As Chua Beng Huat observes, such a position would mean that women's organisations can only demand changes that are "reformist in character," i.e. simply tweaking or improving existing government policies and practices (*Communitarian Ideology and Democracy in Singapore*, 1995, p. 208).

But perhaps more crippling for the women's movements would be strictures placed on the word "patriarchy" or its related phrase, "patriarchal culture". On the one hand, the terms "patriarchy" or "patriarchal culture" may be simply understood as anthropological descriptors of families or clans that are controlled by the father, eldest male or male group in society, where men are the only ones who inherit and possess property. In traditional societies, men also commanded sexual power in the family with multiple wives and concubines. Given that polygamy is outlawed in Singapore civil law, that women can inherit and own property and share control of the dual-income home with men, it would seem that the days of "patriarchal culture" are over.

But for feminist writers from the 1970s and 1980s, the terms "patriarchy" and "patriarchal culture" are analytical concepts that point to the institutionalisation of sexism in laws and culture. For Kate Millett writing *Sexual Politics* in 1970, the power of men over women resides in social norms and cultural ideas that we often take as 'natural', for example, romantic love as a "patriarchal" idea where male courtship of women manipulates women and seduces them into accepting domination by men. Millett spoke of patriarchal culture as performing an "interior colonisation" of women where women internalise their own roles as the weaker sex. For some feminist theorists social structures such as the family, laws, the political system and religion organise society and permit men to subjugate and exploit women and girls while for others gender roles and duties are patriarchal ideologies that justify gender domination as being due to nature or divine command. Simone de Beauvoir underlined the significance of socialisation to 'constructing' gendered identity when she said that "one is not born, but rather becomes, a woman".

Feminist history linked the emergence of patriarchal culture in the second millennium BC to sexual control of women, when women, who had been important to the maintenance of human communities, could now only gain status and privilege by limiting their child-bearing capacity to one man. "Patriarchal culture" became an even more important analytical concept when socialist theorists linked male power motives to the emergence and development of capitalism, when men directed the household production of goods in a gender-biased manner, made themselves the head of households and rendered property inheritable by gender. Feminists saw in modern capitalistic culture's social stratification, hierarchical polities, institutionalised violence, and ego-driven individualism forces that structured the oppression of women in society. Not only families but states were viewed as 'heteropatriarchal', leaning on each other to maintain male power. Now cultural change was seen to be even more germane to female equality and emancipation: Sara Ruddick, for example, queried who would be a 'good mother', the one who raised sons to be competitive, individualistic and comfortable with hierarchies or the one who socialised sons to be cooperative and communalistic.

It is clear from the above that by forbidding the use of the 'patriarchy' word, Singapore men could keep women from ripping the veil of gender domination, from questioning why gender roles had to be just so, why women had to conduct themselves in 'modesty' and demonstrate sexual 'virtue' while men did not. The word made visible that there was a man-made system of beliefs in place that existed to keep men in power and control. If you don't speak that word, male domination could be made to appear to be a phenomenon entirely dictated by nature.

The Singapore Government did not as such issue a diktat that the word "patriarchy" was not to be used in public discourse. But the cultural climate of the 1980s and the 1990s in the nation — when Confucianism and our traditional Asian ethnic cultures and identity were being promoted and celebrated by the state against Western modernisation — was definitely the wrong time for local feminists to champion the critical examination of our inherited and different Asian patriarchal cultures. They would have been accused of a cultural betrayal, of using a Western discourse (of feminism) to hack at the patriarchal roots of their own ancestral culture. The national microphone was also exclusively in the hands of a powerful male elite, who spoke a language that made the masculinity of the state invisible even while it highlighted the female gender of working mothers.

In 1975, then Prime Minister Lee Kuan Yew said, "Our primary concern is to ensure that, whilst all our women become equal to men in education, getting employment and promotions, the family framework in bringing up the next generation does not suffer as a result of high divorce rates, or, equally damaging, neglect of the children, with both parents working." He would repeat that message in 1983, saying, "...Equal employment opportunities, yes, but we shouldn't get our women into jobs where they cannot, at the same time, be mothers. You just can't be doing a full-time heavy job like that of doctor or engineer and run a home and bring up children."

The subtexts here? Female gender equality is a choice that the state makes or a gift it hands out, not an inalienable right for women. The "we" and "our" pronouns in these sentences refer to the supposedly ungendered state, to be distinguished from the "men" and "women" that Lee spoke about. Other subtexts: 'broken' families are caused by overly ambitious women who neglect their family responsibilities to focus on career success; only mothers/women can raise children and manage domestic work. Not that other advanced countries then did not have domineering male political leaders who spoke similar sexist rhetoric, but they didn't have a state machinery that could silence other perspectives for decades.

There were women who did use the two "p" words, "patriarchy" and "politics" at that time: in academic journals that were kept separate from mainstream discourse sites such as newspapers and the broadcast media. There were also women who critiqued our inherited Asian patriarchal cultures but in disguised metaphoric language and tropes in poetry and fiction.

The theoretical connections between the two 'p' words and feminist theory also meant the 'f' word, "feminism" had to be erased. The archives of *The Straits Times* show that the word was largely mentioned in relation to developments in the West in the 1980s. An article "Not Weak and Gentle" by Evelyn Wong on 28 Jan 1985 confirms the word's lack of popular appeal in Singapore. Wong notes that "despite their concerns for women's rights, many women don't like the word 'feminism'". In addition to fearing a Western discourse that would challenge their Asian cultural values, Singapore women thought the word 'feminism' "precluded femininity": stereotypical images of bra-burning American women who refused to wear make-up substituted for any real understanding of the intellectual content of the women's movement.

In her paper "Believing in Equality: The Meanings Attached to Feminism in Singapore" (1999), Leonore Lyons noted that AWARE activists often used the term "feminism" in its internal documents but refrained from using the word in open public discourse as they feared being "dismissed, not on the quality of their argument but on the negative perceptions of the public". AWARE instead chose to use "the language of 'women's rights' and 'gender equality'" (Lyons). In 1995, there would even be an attempt within AWARE to declare itself to be a "feminist" organisation but those promoting the move lost the vote in an Extraordinary General Meeting.

AWARE accomplished a great deal for women's rights on the strength of fighting for "gender equality" and no one would challenge its feminist identity. Nevertheless, its chosen use of language limited the way it could intellectually reach out to women. Lyons, for instance, observes that in a survey of AWARE members' views that she carried out between 1994 and 1997, there was a strong correlation between AWARE members who did not identify as feminist and those who believed that childcare could never be a substitute for family care, that a woman's primary duty was to care for her family. These women also rejected the idea that a quota system — rather than one based on 'merit' — should be used to usher women into Parliament. If they had been exposed to feminist thought, they would have likely questioned any essentialising equation of women with domestic roles and would have been sceptical that any idea of 'merit' upheld by a male-dominated political party in choosing parliamentary candidates could be free of gender bias and patriarchal motives.

The decision to rely on the language of "gender equality" perhaps also made it easier for men in power to perpetually paint women as the weaker 'unequal' sex, as victims who need help to be equal. For instance, there was never any adequate explanation for why the ruling party readily accepted some of Dr Kanwaljit Soin's 1996 suggestions in Parliament for police to investigate and prosecute family violence but refused to accept any need for a "family" act. Instead they imported these amendments into the Women's Charter, linguistically presenting "family violence" as something that happened to women even if, in reality, men and children were often also targets of domestic abuse.

Similarly, in 2020, the government presented a project to improve 'gender equality' in Singapore as one that would focus on "Women's Development", where the state would seek to "empower, protect and uplift our women", language that represents gender equality as something that involves surmounting female weaknesses or 'backwardness', where women would be the object, not the agents, of action. If it did not appear ironic that the mover of the quest for female equality was a male Law Minister, that was because 'gender equality' is understood by the Singapore male political elite to be the struggle of women seeking to fit themselves into a patriarchal order, not that of challenging it.

In an opinion piece in *Today*, "Now to Be a Woman Again" on 13 March 2006, Dr Soin recognised that 'feminism' meant something more than the quest for female equality. She said the struggle for women's equality, which she periodised as belonging to "the second phase of feminism", was "achieved at the expense of women's personal identity", that many women had felt that in seeking equality at the workplace they had to deny their "gender difference". The nostalgia-laden title of her article suggests that this quest for gender equality involved an amputation for women of their sexuality, which they had to set aside in order to fight for workplace rights. By noting that improved infant mortality rates and the availability of abortion had changed women's sense of themselves and their possibilities in life, Dr Soin signals that female subjectivity is a historical phenomenon that can alter and radically transform over time, that it would be doing women an injustice to view their identities even in modern terms in a Post-Modern era.

Is it a mere coincidence that the moment that has been lauded as a turning point in the Singapore women's movement is also the first time that the word "feminism" was uttered repeatedly in a mass public gathering? Or that the event featured an eruption of women's voices talking about everything from gay rights to the importance of maintaining the secular in national spaces and reflecting on the difference between corporate culture and civil society ethos?

One afternoon in March 2009, a group of women, trailing supporters, had come into AWARE headquarters during its AGM and elected themselves into top positions on the NGO's executive committee. It turned out later that the group were corporate women who also belonged to the same Christian church, and that they had hijacked AWARE to dismantle its gay-friendly programmes and transform its liberal culture from within. The conflict between the deposed leadership, who wanted to claim back their NGO, and the usurpers was played out in the media and led to an EGM in May. On the day in question, their voices and minds unbridled by the government's decision to stay out of the fray, Singapore women finally spoke up. In their recollections of the event in a recently produced series of award-winning podcasts, it becomes evident that Singapore women 'experienced' feminism for the first time that day in an integrated, holistic manner, encountering it as a space of female solidarity and connecting their identity as women to their wider values about social justice and the unjust exercise of power.

The AWARE Saga, as the event has been dubbed, released new feminist energies. Although previously AWARE had stayed away from raising race and class issues as these were not seen as directly related to their interest in "gender equality", today AWARE boldly describes itself on its website as an organisation that advocates for gender equality and women's rights as "an integral part of human rights" and that it also works with other civil society organisations on "push[ing] for" (not simply "promot[ing]") democratic governance and institutions, freedom of speech, expression and assembly, and the elimination of all forms of discrimination (https://www.aware. org.sg/about/policy-and-position-statements).

A few months following the EGM, in his 2009 National Day Rally speech, the Prime Minister would finally talk about the event. He was not surprised that the bid by a religiously-motivated group to impose its agenda on an NGO provoked a push-back that "happened vociferously and stridently as a fierce battle", engaging metaphors belonging to patriarchal discourse about feminists (https://www.

pmo.gov.sg/Newsroom/prime-minister-lee-hsien-loongs-national-day-rally-2009-speech-english). But what bothered him was that the media's "amplifier was turned up a bit high", suggesting that it is okay for women to talk loudly but that the media ought not to let them be heard by the public.

It would be a grave mistake for women activists to underestimate the determinative effects that language has on the oppression and liberation of communities. Just as implicit taboos on certain words inhibited the force of the women's movement in Singapore for a few decades, the licence on language offered by our access to global media is providing daily opportunities now for local women to revision themselves and represent their needs to the nation in powerful new words.

In 2011, in an event marked as starting a new era of grassroots activism in our women's movement (Corinna Lim, IPS Lecture 1: "Herstory"), two women adapted a transnational movement against rape culture to fit into the confines of Hong Lim Park, the only place where protest is allowed in Singapore. Slutwalk Singapore did not involve long protest marches as in other cities but it hurled patriarchal language that objectified and denigrated women back at their users. Then there is Diana Rahim, editor of the blog 'beyondhijab.sg', who also links language to women's liberation as she speaks of her purpose in providing a platform for Muslim women to share their stories. By telling their stories, the nightmarish reality of women's lives gets a chance to escape from the tightly woven illusion of patriarchal perfection spun by the state. Stories, she said, also make you wonder about the connections between male gender power and traditional ethnic customs such as "tutup aib" (the Malay equivalent of 'not airing one's dirty linen in public'), the way these function to enable women's oppression. "Stories are never just stories. They are the bed upon which the prevailing ideology, the status quo, rests....Stories are powerful things because within each story lies a kind of meaning," Rahim says (https://beyondhijab.sg/2020/03/20/interrogating-the-uncomfortable/).

Increasingly in Singapore today, feminism is regarded as not only being about the struggle of women for equality but also about the transformation of culture, of life as we know it, by women's experience and their sense of the ethical. Language plays a crucial role in this. In recently published books, for instance, we can see how the new linguistic freedoms offered by the Internet enable women to de-sacralise patriarchal ideas of race, of class, of capitalistic success and redefine notions of family, of home, of being Singaporean or Asian. In the AWARE anthology *What We Inherit — Growing Up Indian*, we discover that being 'Indian' is a multi-layered, intersectional fiction that often signifies women's oppression, giving the lie to the state's narrative of coherent racialised identities. In the Ethos publication *Making Kin — Ecofeminist Essays from Singapore*, one woman revisions motherlove in terms of releasing her autistic son to live his perfect life apart from her in a haven of nature in another country while another recalls family life as a childhood horror unleashed on her by a religious concept of 'salvation'. Many others float above their female identities to contemplate their inter-species kinship with the non-human denizens of this green earth, imagining new forms of being in this world.

Thankfully too, the censorship of the "patriarchal" word is behind us now. On 24 May 2022, as part of the government's effort to address gender inequality in the nation, Corinna Lim, executive director of AWARE, stood up at the lectern and lectured men about "toxic masculinity", and pointed to aspects of National Service culture as contributing to this masculinity and thereby to sexual violence against women. In her third IPS-Nathan lecture, "Reset: Men, Women, Violence", Lim crashed through the conflictual simplistic maxim that "men are from Mars, women are from Venus" to suggest that social pressures on men to be strong, stoic, brave and aggressive did not just hurt women but they also hurt the men themselves in the undue pressure this imposed on them. In addition to National Service, Lim also found an unwitting institutionalisation of gender inequality in the sex education delivered in our schools that did not go beyond preaching abstinence. Her research found that the inadequacy of this led to boys turning to porn as their "default sex educator", inculcating sexist mental attitudes that led to the ill-treatment of women, including violence.

As seen above, the sites of women's oppression are not always self-evident, especially when gender intersects with race, ethnicity, class and age. Sometimes it's hard to trace cultural customs or institutional or social practices where inequality is being seeded. We may also want to think about gender equality within larger contexts of women's rights and freedoms. All these require self-reflection and deep diving into one's national and ethnic cultures.

The government's White Paper on Singapore Women's Development indicates that our thinking about gender equality has stretched to include more facets. We're going beyond the workplace in addressing equality in the home and in the family with regard to sharing parenting and housework responsibilities. In a long overdue recognition that women play more significant roles in caregiving of children and the elderly, the government is now considering facilities to provide both emotional and financial support to caregivers. With these new provisions, women will find it easier to combine mothering with building a career as they get more access to childcare services, flexible work arrangements. Plans are afoot to make it easier for women to re-enter the workforce after taking a hiatus to raise children.

Government agencies have also been tasked with promoting and enforcing greater representation of women in corporate leadership roles as board members and directors. Billed as a whole-society effort, the Conversations on Singapore Women's Development that preceded the presentation of the White Paper apparently held 160 conversations with nearly 6,000 Singaporeans. However looking through the list of organisations and groups as well as community and corporate partners that contributed to discussions, I noticed that no artists and writers' groups or media organisations were listed. Even though the government sees the need for a "deep mindset change" in undoing gender stereotypes, an action plan to bring about those cultural and social changes in perspectives of gender were not included in its White Paper.

That omission however could be fortunate for local women: we don't need a patriarchal state controlling our tongue. Far better for us to take advantage of our access to unregulated online mass communication channels and reach for greater freedom of thought and expression of women's voices. The onus should be on women, not on the government, to let their voices be heard. We need to lift ourselves out of our apathy, even if our tongues had been tied by previous restrictions and taboos placed on our thoughts.

The mindset change that has been called for should not only be about persuading men to think of women as their equals but should also encourage women to escape from patriarchal ideas about female identity and their place in society. Singapore women need to think about what keeps them from attaining equal self-fulfilment in life as men; they should probe the difference between their desires and needs and those imposed on them by patriarchal culture. We should certainly think about what kind of 'mothers', 'wives', 'sisters', and 'daughters' we want to be if we could decide these for ourselves.

How can we re-imagine the meanings of these gender-related words or labels? How do women from various ethnic and socioeconomic groups differentiate their female identity and gender problems from those of women in other social groups? How do we want our female leaders to behave — what values would we like to see them uphold? What changes would we like to see in government, in institutions of learning, in healthcare, or in urban development that would better meet our needs as women? Do we like the way we are portrayed in the media and how would we like society to see us?

Only by thinking about such questions can we even begin to map the ways in which we are unequal to men in our society. But don't just think: speak, write. Flood the airwaves with your words. Write in your diary, write to your MP, write to the press, write the stories of your life and those of your mothers.

The fastest way to mainstream women's voices and their perspectives would be to assert our presence in the mass media. Newspapers, online or off, remain the leading means by which a city, or a country imagines a coherent identity for itself, setting out the ideas and attitudes it finds acceptable. Unfortunately newspapers are also the site where the ruling and business elites establish the dominance of ideas and values that serve their interests, excluding those of less empowered social groups. Like women. The newspaper is a major vehicle that reproduces norms of masculinity and upholds male power. You only have to read *The Straits Times* to understand how women are ciphers in Singapore, little known and understood, that they lack a voice and are continuously being erased and scripted by men. The few women journalists who do write for the newspaper are allowed to speak as long as they use a man's voice and language, performing a kind of verbal drag act. This is the glaring gender inequality that is never addressed in Singapore — the under-representation of women's voices and perspectives in public spaces.

Flip through *The Straits Times* on any given day and you will find that men's faces and their voices dominate the pages despite the presence of many female by-lines. Profiles of women and their views only appear in the arts and entertainment section of the newspaper, Life! It would seem that for *The Straits Times*, the business, politics, education, health and court events are 'male' arenas of life whereas arts and entertainment, and even romances of stars, are the 'female' arenas. This is shocking, almost primitive in one of the advanced countries of the world. The male-centred nature of the newspaper is obvious even in the sports pages. On a day in April 2023, I see that only one out of 17 sports stories features a woman. A story about a national female sprinter who has stunned the country with a series of new records is dominated by the voice of her male coach: the voice of the athlete herself merely appears at the tail end. The headline focusses on the coach's emotional response, "It's Unbelievable: Cunha" (3 April 2023).

On the same day, however, in an article about the poor performance of a local male soccer team, both coaches and players are interviewed ("Young Lions will be one of the weakest teams at SEA games: Ex-Lion Sasikumar", https://www.straitstimes.com/sport/football/young-lions-will-be-one-of-the-weakest-teams-at-sea-games-ex-lion-sasikumar). The expertise level of male coaches and male players are treated as equal. Sexist and ageist language is also used to headline a story about Petra Kvitova's 30th win of the WTA singles title: "Kvitova Still a Golden Oldie" (https://www.magzter.com/stories%252Fnewspaper%252FThe-Straits-Times%252FKVITOVA-STILL-A-GOLDEN-OLDIE%2F/).

Curious about what female leadership might mean to a newspaper, I conducted an impromptu experiment, comparing that day's *The Straits Times* content with that of *The Washington Post*, which is headed by Sally Buzzbee. *The Post* has stories about abortion rights and black female athletes, but *The Straits Times* offers no women-related stories in the main newspaper. It is the day after Jacinda Ardern's final speech in the New Zealand Parliament and both newspapers refer to her "empathetic" style of governance, a gender-coded adjective. However, only *The Post* relates it to liberal feminism and presents Ardern's thoughts on leadership and femininity as expressed in her speech. "Young people," Ardern says, should not be "deterred by outdated perceptions of what makes a good leader," adding, "I do hope that I've demonstrated something else entirely. That you can be anxious, sensitive, kind, and wear your heart on your sleeve" ("Jacinda Ardern quits politics, joins Prince William's environment charity, https://www.washingtonpost.com/world/2023/04/05/jacinda-ardern-final-speech-prince-william-earthshot/). *The Straits Times* report, "Jacinda Ardern delivers final speech in NZ Parliament" (5 April 2023, https://www.straitstimes.com/asia/australianz/jacinda-ardern-delivers-final-speech-to-nz-parliament) is not up to lauding female leadership styles but does remind us that Ardern had been a victim of online abuse and "social media posts filled with violent and sexist language" (code: woman stereotyped as victim). The article ends by suggesting that Ardern had resigned as Prime Minister in order to spend more time with her four-year-old daughter although Ardern herself had earlier said that she no longer had "enough in the tank".

It is crucial that we expand our notion of gender equality to include issues concerning the representation of women and the greater inclusion of their voice and perspectives in the cultural and intellectual space of the nation. Words and stories matter if women are to grow their identity and take their equal place in Singapore. We may be a common sight in our newsrooms but there is little parity in terms of stories that profile us or those that answer to women-specific needs and interests. Women journalists need to consciously push for changes in content and seek women's perspectives in various areas of expertise.

Women both inside and outside the media, including educators and civil society, need to advocate for a fairer representation of women in all their diversity and call out gender-stereotyping. We could do with stories on television that better reflect the more complex realities of women's lives in millennial Singapore and newspapers that give more space to women as newsmakers and interpreters of social and cultural developments in the country. Our universities too need to equip a new generation of journalists with gender-literacy skills. Words not only reflect reality, they also construct reality. The newspaper is a mirror to society. If society is stubborn about changing, switching up the mirror can bring new realities into being.

MATILDA GABRIELPILLAI was a journalist with the local media and later an academic in Singapore. She has researched and taught women's writings and post-colonial literatures, focusing often on Singapore culture and nationalism as well as race and gender issues. She also enjoys teaching and writing about the imagining of cosmopolitan identities. At present she is a freelance writer and tutor of Literature in English. She maintains a Literature Education website www.literaturehelpdesksg.com that provides study resources for students in local and international Literature programmes.

"I am always glad that whenever I felt I had to do something, I just did it there and then, rather than wait. There are things in life that you will never do once the moment is past."

~ Global refugee crises problem-solver Janet Lim Yuen Kheng,
talking to The Straits Times, March 2014

Chapter 29

The Machine is Us

Nurul Jihadah Hussain & Nurul Amillin Hussain

"The machine is not an 'it' to be animated, worshipped, and dominated. The machine is us, our processes, an aspect of our embodiment. We can be responsible for machines; they do not dominate or threaten us. We are responsible for boundaries; we are they." (Haraway 1991: 180)

This was an essay that was almost left unwritten. While I felt honoured to be asked to contribute, especially by two women I look up to, I was (am?) completely overwhelmed. Being a new mother has consisted of every challenge I'd been warned of, and all the new ones I discover in my every day. As I struggled with new responsibilities at home and at work, writing this was my last priority.

And then I thought…let me just ask for help. And we'll see where this goes. My brilliant, wonderful sister — herself figuring out new configurations of what, how and why, reached out to me to offer the generosity of her spirit and time. Whatever ends up being written will be what we end up writing, and that will be what we have for this book. So if you're reading this, then this essay was written.

In figuring out what to use to anchor our ideas, we chose the metaphor of a 'cyborg' that Donna Haraway discusses in her 1985 essay, "A Cyborg Manifesto". Things that talk about technology usually become obsolete really quickly — the early Internet, 'cyberworld', analogue technologies, livejournal and myspace, anything pre-Facebook, and sometimes about Facebook. This essay does not feel old. It feels timeless, like the interactions between women and technology have been repeated endlessly through the march of inventions.

Why the 'cyborg'? An anchoring metaphor in her essay, Haraway writes of the image of the cyborg as a kind of "cybernetic organism", a "hybrid machine", "a creature of lived social reality…[and] fiction". Haraway's four descriptions of the cyborg (cybernetic, hybrid, of the present, of the future) are not discrete, but rather, co-determinate. This means that there is no real space between, for example, a creature "of lived social reality", and one "in fiction", because one category is constantly defining and refining the other. This co-determination, Haraway argues, can be used to understand how feminists deploy the notion of "women's experience", using it both as "fiction and a fact of the most crucial, political kind".

The cyborg will change what counts as experience for us women.

Muslim women understand what this has meant for us, for decades. What we know: the media, especially in a post-9/11 world, has depicted a range of Muslim women, most of them problematic and spectacular. The spectacle has enabled the dehumanisation of many Muslim communities around the world. What we're beginning to realise is that the spectacle derives its power from that push and pull between lived reality and fiction. The stories we create, deconstruct, we rally behind, and condemn — these stories build the reality of our everyday lives, which in turn determines the stories that get told.

As we move from essentialising ideas around women, and particularly Muslim women, to something that can account for hybridity, complexity, and change, the material with which we create these cyborgs will be our stories. Who is a woman? Who is a Muslim woman?

These are not questions that are constituted by the same stories, and it is time that we start telling new ones — the vacuum left by a discomfort around being too specific, too loud, too obviously 'about Muslim issues' will leave a space we regret we didn't fill when we had the chance. There are women who are doing this who hold competing, complementing, expanding and expansive identities who are holding space for the them they have created. They are not only brave but also visionary for understanding that participating in culture is important in order to shape culture and we need to not just act but create.

We will need to question not only stories but also the mediums by which we receive them. It matters who builds the cyborg. The rise of artificial intelligence asks the question of how intelligence comes into being — how it is created, trained, and manipulated, and how this will impact those who do not have any say in any part of the making of the cyborg. The platforms we use to tell our stories should be responsible to all of us — because they determine who we are. We should not be de-platformed, de-legitimised, and minimised simply because the systems that are building the cyborg continue to be the systems which have always considered us as "other".

Cyborgs are hybrid and provisional, and for this reason, Haraway argues that they don't stick to a single political category that requires a stable, essentialist identity. Rather than using identity as a political category, Haraway advocates feminists to consider building coalitions based on the more cyborg-friendly notion of "affinity".

What does this strategy of affinity consist of? How we understand affinity politics is to compare it to identity politics, and see what it does differently. Identity politics is based on stable identity categories — for example, women support women because they are women. It draws on essentialised ideas of what being female means. Affinity politics, on the other hand, is developed through a recognition of one's biography, of otherness, difference and specificity, rather than identity. Identity becomes an impoverished indicator of one's politics. Affinity explores our shared needs and goals, our desires and challenges, in ways that move beyond traditional identity politics.

We need affinity politics, not identity politics.

Allyship does not mean agreement, but to stand together against the darkness of othering — the enforced loneliness that comes with deciding that only you should exist. For those of us who are othered — it is not just our success that is impossible to imagine, but our existence. We do not exist in the common collaborative imagination of who is. We will ourselves into existence and create our spaces in the emptiness of the lack of imagination that we find ourselves in.

The Codette Project could not have existed without imagination — because we were not imaginable. Our belief that women like us existed almost seemed to will women like us into being as we were finally able to coalesce into a coalition to build a space that did not measure us against anyone else but took us, ourselves, as being enough. We imagined what would be possible with an intersectional network of women and allies that centred on the experience of minority/Muslim women and that reimagined what regenerative work would look like for communities if we sought to divert resources back into our community without using traditional capitalist structures. We imagined connections as an infrastructure for thriving in not just empty but unfamiliar environments.

The future will require more imagination. There is a hopelessness that comes from imagining the future with all the challenges of now including the threats of AI, climate change, and war. Hope requires imagination for a way forward. The cyborg does not have to be a threat. Monsters might have always "defined the limits of community in Western imaginations" — but the cyborg does not have to be the monster. Who is the other in community is just who gets to belong. We need to reimagine a future in which we understand technology as a way for us to live collaboratively with the past — centring more indigenous, marginalised experiences as ways to help us move forward into the future where we can be more expansive in our ideas of who gets to belong.

There remain so many questions that need to be answered in this bridge between the now and the future.

– How can we translate all this into practical emancipatory politics?
– What are the values that should guide this politics? How have Codette's values changed?
– How do we know what is true in a world where reality is not experienced but consumed?

We leave you with these questions without answers, because we have none. One might ask: why did we spend time we didn't have, to write an essay on cyborgs? Why is this essay even useful in helping us think about what women are, and can be?

The short answer is: the metaphor of the cyborg has made us understand how the machine IS us. Not in the way that we are mothers, aunts, partners, sisters and daughters to the men that are building this new world — but that we are this new world. Through a politics of affinity, the possibilities and limits that used to define the worlds we could inhabit are being challenged in meaningful ways.

As we realise our collective obligations to each other, and the intersections of oppression that exist in our lives, we start to tell different stories. That, perhaps, will be the greatest enemy of our 'monster'; that the possibilities technology promises broadens our horizon into a utopia that we now have the tools to build a road towards. We are those that will write new fictions, negotiate new realities, and build not just equitable, but better, worlds.

As we write this, me (the mother) furiously trying to stay awake after putting my 1-year old son to sleep — editing the words my sister has written in her own home as she works with her music on and her cat awake, I/We hope you see what we do: that it is not just our husbands, or sons, or fathers, who will be the architects of the world we live in. We, too, will be theirs. And we do so by first being honest about who we are to each other, and ourselves. We are they.

NURUL JIHADAH HUSSAIN is a globally recognised community leader and founder of non-profit The Codette Project that aims to get more minority/Muslim women into technology. The Codette Project is working towards long-term change through developing tech skills, building a collaborative community as well as reclaiming narratives of success to include underrepresented women's stories. She has one son, Aaron, who is her why.

NURUL AMILLIN HUSSAIN is an Assistant Professor in the Division of Sociology at Nanyang Technological University (NTU). Amillin's research looks at sustainable and smart infrastructures in high-rise housing estates, focusing on Singapore. She is also a published author of a collection of poetry, BEEF. She received her BA in Sociology from NTU, an MPhil in Social Anthropology from the University of Cambridge and will receive her PhD in Geography from the University of Oxford.

References

Haraway, Donna. 1991. "A Cyborg Manifesto: Science, Technology, and Socialist-Feminism in the Late Twentieth Century". In *Simians, Cyborgs and Women: The Reinvention of Nature*, edited by Donna Haraway. New York: Routledge. 149–181.

https://www.mediasupport.org/navigating-a-changing-world/we-are-all-cyborgs-how-machines-can-be-a-feminist-tool/

https://rossdawson.com/futurist/best-futurists-ever/donna-haraway-cyborg-manifesto/

Senft, Theresa. 2020. "Reading Notes for Donna Haraway's Cyborg Manifesto". 10.13140/RG.2.2.28370.99521.

"The whole practice of making art is about an individual struggling with her inner thoughts and trying to make sense of this conflict. It is about finding that real and true you, and this process is still ongoing for me. That is why being an artist is a lifelong job, and there is no such thing as retiring."

~ Trailblazing artist Amanda Heng, in an interview with the Singapore Council of Women's Organisations, January 2023

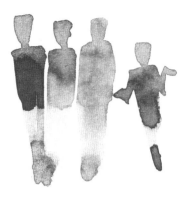

CHAPTER 30

Woman. Artist. Citizen: Running with Her Dreams

⁓◦⊙◦⁓

Dana Lam

It is 1994. A woman looks up from the pages of a book. Her gaze meets the face of a clock on the opposite wall; its hands at 11 o'clock. It is mid-week. Most people she knows are at jobs somewhere else in the city. The peculiar luxury of her station strikes her. She smiles to herself, relishing the moment.

I am the woman; recently enrolled as a Foundation Year student at the LASALLE College of the Arts.

* * *

I was 41. And the mother of two primary school-going children.

The year 1994 had begun with a crushing episode for the Singapore artist. An act by a young male performance artist in the wee hours of New Year's Day was picked up and sensationalised by the tabloid media. It brought the wrath of the State down on the organisers, an artist initiative, led by two women. Accusations, condemnations, police action, and a de facto ban followed. But it is not like this had never happened before.

A pall of apathy and ennui hung over the college campus.

The LASALLE College of the Arts was founded in 1984 by the late Brother Joseph McNally. An artist and educator, Brother McNally was the first to advocate the necessity of a Fine Arts curriculum in Singapore. With the authorities unconvinced, he went ahead to dedicate a small classroom in St Patrick's School for the teaching of drawing, painting, and sculpture. It provided students with the opportunity for an alternative pathway of learning. The centre was later renamed LASALLE College of the Arts and now boasts Diploma, Graduate and Post graduate programmes across various disciplines in the Arts.

For many of my fellow students in foundation studies back in 1994, art school was where you went when you had nowhere to go. They looked, the majority of them, listless and unhappy. To pass the time, they installed themselves as fixtures in rows upon rows of canteen benches; their young bodies weary and hunched over, heads bowed in headsets and, nicotine clouds. It was before smoke-free campus became a thing. Somebody once asked, "Why do art students look like zombies dragging their dead bodies around?" I laughed. Late to the scene, I was by contrast annoyingly ebullient, I am sure.

Away from campus, the period of the late 1980s to early 1990s was both triumphal and tumultuous. It would later be recalled by some as a time when the Singapore artist dreamed big and then watched their dream turn into nightmare. The few women who ran with their dreams left significant legacies whose reverberations, though muffled, are still felt today. But the names most closely associated with this chapter of Singapore art history have tended to remain male.

I am woman: Hear me roar

Like it or not, Eighties Singapore reverberated with the voices of women rudely awoken to the realities of an openly patriarchal government, thanks to a phalanx of pro-natal policies directed at them. Women organised.[1] The forum, Women's Choices, Women's Lives (1984) hosted by the National University of Singapore Society[2] included an exhibition of women's contributions at work-places and a chronology of milestone achievements and setbacks. A year later, in 1985, AWARE (Association of Women for Action and Research)[3] was registered. Its mandate — to end all discrimination and violence against women and to improve women's lives by promoting their full participation in all areas.

From the earliest, AWARE's strategies were rooted in women's creative energy, providing women with a platform for intellectual engagement, artistic expression, and advocacy. AWARENESS, its monthly newsletter published art and poetry, first-person narratives, policy research and analyses by women for women. A first AWARE Occasional Paper on current issues asked questions of policy makers few Singaporeans thought to ask. How is the 5.5 million 'optimal' population number arrived at? And how does the government plan to manage the stress such an increase would bring to bear on the social fabric; issues such as overcrowding, housing, transportation, and healthcare, for instance?

A poster campaign against domestic violence featured unflinching close-ups of women's faces and bold fonts in the style of American

---

[1] Women first organised in Singapore in 1951 when the Singapore Council of Women was founded by Shirin Fozdar to advocate for women's rights, especially in the domain of marriage.

[2] NUSS member Zaibun Siraj and academic Vivienne Wee put the forum and exhibition together. See Mandakini Arora, ed., *Small Steps, Giant Leaps: A History of AWARE and the Women's Movement in Singapore.* AWARE, 2007.

[3] The founding Committee comprised Lena Lim, Kanwaljit Soin, Chua Siew Keng, Sylvia Jackson, Lim Li Kok, Margaret Thomas, Hedwig Anuar, Lai Ah Eng, Jennifer Ang, Zaibun Siraj, Vivienne Wee and Evelyn Wong.

conceptual artist Barbara Kruger, famous for her iconic text-based work on women. Somewhere in the AWARE archives is a tee shirt emblazoned in bold black text on a blood-red ground by the internationally established Suzann Victor, then a young artist from LASALLE.

AWARE's strategies included regular public forums, mostly at the Queenstown library, and letters to the press. For the first time in a long time, women's issues were brought to the fore and the structural causes of their private grief exposed. Something like a feminist ethos was being birthed, even though the F word was still discomforting to many for all the usual reasons. The point is: the condition of women in Singapore, the systematic prejudices against women, were now exposed. It was up to the individual woman to look this in the face, take cognizance of it, and of her own agency. Many did.

Concurrently in the Arts, similar forces were at work.

A golden age of English Language theatre

The Eighties have been characterised as a 'golden age' of English Language theatre by National University of Singapore academic Robin Loon.

TheatreWorks Singapore (now T:>Works) was founded the same year as AWARE. Friends Lim Kay Tong, Lim Siauw Chong, Justin Hill, Sylvia Leow, Lena Bandara, Jenina Bass, Kim Ramakrishnan, Kalyani Kausikan, Jessieca Leo, and Goh Eck Kheng pooled their money to start the private limited company.

Justin Hill remembers the women's role in the founding of TheatreWorks as pivotal. The company debuted in April 1985 with Be My Sushi Tonight, an adaptation of a black comedy by the English writer-director Mike Leigh. Original Singaporean scripts were hard to come by then. The ambition to professionalise was so that theatre makers could get paid for their work and, in time, consider a viable career within the industry. There was also the drive to hold to a higher standard of production. In 1990, TheatreWorks converted from a Private Limited Company to a not-for-profit company limited by guarantee. This qualified the company for government arts subsidies and tax exemptions for donor supporters.

As an independent professional theatre company, TheatreWorks was preceded by Act Three Ltd, a professional company for children's theatre founded by Ruby Lim-Yang, Jasmin S. and R. Chandran in 1984. Both companies have continued to thrive.

The push for a Singapore/Singaporean theatre was propelled by a fomenting civil society and not confined to the professional companies.

A year earlier, in 1983, Wong Souk Yee, then a newspaper reporter, founded The Third Stage with nine friends who shared a similar ambition to create theatre that spoke to the lived experience of Singaporeans. Their ambition, by no means unheard of, would set the stage for the first of two traumas of the time.

Between 1983 and 1986, Wong and friends staged a total of eight original plays. Their attempts at creating relatable characters in recognisable situations included the use of Singlish on stage at a time when Singlish was not as cool as it may be today.

Their brutal fall from grace was predicated on Esperanza, a social realist drama co-written by Wong and another founding member, Tay Hong Seng. Originally performed at the Drama Centre as part of the 1986 International Arts Festival fringe, the play received favourable reviews for its portrayal of power dynamics between a foreign domestic worker and her employer. It even received a small government grant for re-staging.

But the tables turned abruptly. In May 1987, police suddenly arrested 22 people allegedly involved in an international Marxist conspiracy to topple the Singapore Government. Among them were

Wong, Chng Suan Tze, William Yap, and Tay Hong Seng from the Third Stage and three AWARE members. The authorities took as evident the association of social realism with Marxism. The rest of us later watched in disbelief Wong and the other detainees' forced confessions on TV, and subsequent incarceration without trial.

All 22 detainees refuted the allegations and historian Mary Turnbull and others have questioned and debunked the so-called Marxist Conspiracy. Some form of restitution is overdue.

Ironically, the same year that Wong and company were incarcerated, The Necessary Stage (TNS), another similarly motivated socially conscious theatre group, came into being. It has managed to thrive despite the long shadow of the 1987 Marxist conspiracy. TNS founders Alvin Tan and Haresh Sharma were briefly detained in 1994 for their involvement with forum theatre.[4]

For me, the episode concerning The Third Stage was especially scarring and contributes in part to a continuing deep resentment and scepticism of the government and its mechanisms. Wong Souk Yee was both a colleague in journalism and in the pursuit of the arts. As was Chng Suan Tze. I admire their motivations and aspirations as writers, then and now.

The engagement with social issues in arenas like the theatre and AWARE was paralleled in the Visual Arts. And contributed in part to the emergence of a contemporary art scene distinguished by its temperament and movement away from conventional forms. Artists, responding to the push and pull of national policies and their infringements on personal space looked to and embraced new forms of expression; new ways of making, seeing, displaying.

This resulted in a mélange of offerings that was occasionally cacophonous. Collaborations, installations, happenings took place

---

[4] Forum Theatre is now an accepted form.

outside of the 'white cube' of regular exhibition spaces. The polished formalism of Modern Art gave way to an unrecognisable aesthetic prompting questions of 'Is this art?' Performance Art, unscripted and edgy, where the artist's body is the medium (and sometimes the message), tended to be the more suspect in the eyes of an anxiety-prone state authority. This soon became the site for another enduring trauma of the time.

A home for the arts

"The Substation cannot begin to survive unless we start creating a new space within our inner selves — a space which is responsive to creative, pluralistic, artistic ventures...by nature "untried, raw, personal, unglamourous, slow in developing and often 'not successful', 'not excellent'.[5]

The Substation, Singapore's first independent, multidisciplinary arts space, opened its doors on 16 September 1990. The vision for an arts centre open to all art forms from the traditional to the highly experimental was proposed by the late Kuo Pao Kun in 1985. From the first — an open invitation to participate in painting its garden walls, to my first anti-war vigil — The Substation was a nurturing, transformative space.

It was at The Substation's signature conferences — Art vs Art: Conflict and Convergence (1993), Space, Spaces, Spacing (1995), for example — that I first was acquainted with the issues of art and its relationship with life. In 2021, under pressure from state authorities over funding challenges, The Substation moved out of its home of 30 years. It feels like the profoundest betrayal and abandonment.

---

[5] https://biblioasia.nlb.gov.sg/vol-17/issue-4/jan-to-mar-2022/early-years-substation/

Two ground-up artists' initiatives stand out for their alternative vision between the late 1980s and early 1990s. Like The Substation, the Artists Village (1988) and 5th Passage (1991) were place makers for art and artists and the first of their kind. The Artists Village which began as an informal commune was converted to a formal entity in 1992. The 5th Passage (1991) was a private limited company at the outset and converted to a not-for-profit artist cooperative, a company limited by guarantee, following in the trajectory set by TheatreWorks. Sadly, the 5th Passage is no longer operational.

Although completely divergent in principles and vision,[6] both the Artists Village and the 5th Passage have left indelible marks on contemporary art in Singapore and those of us who practise it.

An artist commune in Singapore? Really?

The Artists Village (TAV) was founded in 1988 by Tang Da Wu on his return from the UK. Amanda Heng, then a mid-career fresh graduate from LASALLE, was one of only two women in the original group. The other, Hazel McIntosh, was married to Tang. Heng is today widely regarded as the first to introduce a feminist tract to Singapore contemporary art.

The number of women associated with the Artists Village would increase over the years. Many like Jennifer Teo, Agnes Yit, Eve Tan, and Yeo Shih Yun have established enduring and significant practices. But the character and reputation of TAV have mostly remained cast around Tang, its father-figure.

For two years, TAV occupied a disused chicken farm in Lorong Gambas, Sembawang, where members lived and worked and showed

---

[6] Susie Lingham, "A Quota on Expression: Visions, Vexations & Vanishings (Contemporary Art in Singapore from the Late 1980s to the Present)", in *Negotiating Home, History and Nation: Two Decades of Contemporary Art in Southeast Asia 1991–2011*. Singapore Art Museum, 2011, pp 55–70.

together. They held two Open Studios in the first year, reportedly attracting nearly 500 visitors, including a group of kindergarteners. A Drawing Show in the same year showed 400 drawings from 48 artists.[7]

It was fodder for the mainstream media but not without a measure of caution and anxiety. An indiscriminate group of artists sequestered together away from view could not have been the most comforting thought in control-obsessed Singapore. Soon enough, TAV lost its idyll to 'land redevelopment', itself a contentious issue.

While it lasted, the rural commune offered a solution to a persistent hurdle, and handicap, for the Singapore artist — the need of studio space. The farm was practically rent free.

After Sembawang, TAV briefly occupied the vacant Hong Bee warehouse, doing all the work of making it habitable themselves. In 1992, it registered as a formal entity with the Registrar of Societies in a bid to secure funding for the space from the newly minted National Arts Council (NAC).[8] That did not work out and a period of hiatus followed.

5th Passage. A corporate sponsored artists run space. And a woman-founded ollective

"The 5th Passage is room for all artists in all fields
actors, musicians, painters, poets, sculptors
a lodge for Giants in the Making and those who dare to dream."
(Invitation card to the official reception of the 5th Passage: Access to the Arts, Parkway Parade, Singapore, 19 April 1991. M Antoinette, 2020)

---

[7] Seng Yu Jin, "Re-visiting the Emergence of The Artists Village". http://www.tav.org.sg/files/TAV 20YearsOn.pdf
[8] The Space Fringe Festival, 1992.

In the words of the late Kuo Pao Kun, a worthy failure is more valuable than a mediocre success. To my mind, the 5th Passage did not fail, nor was its success during its tenure mediocre.

Its vision is unsurpassed in ambition and execution, and this is attributable in no small part to its erudite artist co-founders, Suzann Victor[9] and Susie Lingham.[10] The acuity of the co-founders was such that the 5th Passage was well received among its artist constituents, including officialdom. Two years after its formation, the NAC invited 5th Passage to apply for its then nascent Arts Housing scheme. As the first corporate-sponsored artist-run space, the 5th Passage looked set to become a replicable model for the arts and community to co-exist and thrive. Until the fateful event of 1994 pulled the brakes on it.

While the Artists Village was sequestered in a disused chicken farm with a few remaining clucking birds, the 5th Passage elected to occupy the urban centre by putting the art practice right in the heart of Singapore's newest capitalist symbol at the time — the now ubiquitous shopping mall. Suzann Victor had the brainwave and temerity to approach the management of the popular and populous Parkway Parade with a proposal to turn the passageway between the building's carpark and its office block into an artists' space. The unusual proposal found support in the then Centre Manager, Elizabeth Soh, and a deal was struck. 5th Passage got to use the space for two years rent-free.

Named after the fifth-floor space, the initiative set precedents as the first corporate-sponsored artist-run space and a women-founded collective at a time when male artists clearly dominated. Among its

---

[9] https://suzannvictor.com/biography/

[10] An interdisciplinary thinker, writer, educator, curator and artist, Dr Susie Lingham was the first female Director of the Singapore Art Museum from 2013-2016.

array of multi-disciplinary programmes were ground-breaking shows on women by women: The Selves (1991), Personae I (1994)[11] and Personae II (1996). From the start, the 5th Passage was motivated by an open, non-hierarchical model of management and a critical approach to programming. Between 1991 and 1994, it produced 40 exhibitions and events on issues ranging from the environment to gender and sexuality, to race, to children's interests. Nor were its activities confined to its corridor space. Right off the bat, the 5th Passage initiated collaborations with diverse communities in Singapore. These include H.E.A.L. (Human Ethics for Animal Liberation) which took the form of an exhibition and rock concert; Our Expressions, where the artists worked with the then-named AESN (Association for the Educationally Subnormal) showing the children's arts and crafts, and Legs- Seats of Thought, with product design students from LASALLE and the popular Sharity events with the National Council of Social Services. Personae II in 1996 was an exhibition of site-specific works created by women artists at the Kandang Kerbau Maternity Hospital (KK Hospital). The project owes in no small part to the imagination of another woman, then-CEO of the hospital, Dr Jennifer Lee, who dared to commission it.

In 2000, nearly a decade after 5th Passage's founding and six years after its demise, eight women artists involved in Personae II got together as W.A.P. to mount HOPE, on the grounds of CHIJMES. The artists' works comprised site-specific installations of wood and fabric sculptures in response to the venue's previous life as a convent and baby-drop.[12]

---

[11] Suzann Victor, Eve Tan, Chu Chu Yuan, Susie Wong, Chng Seok Tin showed at the newly opened Pacific Plaza.

[12] The artists were obliged to take down the installations under pressure from the venue's tenants who feared the sculptures would keep customers away.

Writer–researcher M. Antoinette notes the 5th Passage remained motivated by a comparatively non-hierarchical and egalitarian management scheme with Victor attending to it full time without pay and Lingham, who had a full-time job, contributing what she could to its running from her salary.[13]

The 5th Passage's cross-cultural, multi-disciplinary programming which included 12-hour events featuring local indie bands, visual arts and literary readings paralleled The Substation's in scope and vision. And 5th Passage, from its beginning, was working with the various artistic sectors without any government funding.

The 5th Passage's contribution to Singapore contemporary art, its generous and visionary scope, was abruptly halted, wiped out even, by what is lodged in the popular imagination as a piece of obscenity — the "Joseph Ng pubic hair" incident.

Ng made front page news in January 1994 for snipping off his pubic hair in performance, complete with a blown-up photograph of him "in the act" with his back turned to the viewer. The act, a symbolic gesture in the last few seconds of a 20-minute piece, titled Brother Cane, Ng's response to the government's entrapment and prosecution of 12 gay men, was part of the Artist General Assembly (AGA), a 12-hour mini arts festival co-organised by 5th Passage and TAV. As it turned out, 5th Passage took the full force of the authorities' displeasure (anxiety?) which included a ten-year de facto ban on performance art across the board. 5th Passage artists found themselves ostracised from official support.

WITAS and AWARE

Two events in 1999 were to be of significance to me personally. One was the founding of WITAS (Women in the Arts in Singapore). The

---

[13] A third member, Han Ling also contributed. Michelle Antoinette (2020), "Vanishing acts: remembering 5th Passage in Singapore's Contemporary art history (a story about making art public)". *World Art* 102-3). https://doi.org/10.1080/21500894.2020.1810753

other was my election as President of AWARE (Association of Women for Action and Research).

WITAS was the first artist-run women arts collective of its kind here. Like the 5th Passage, it adopted a non-hierarchical model of participation but existed purely as a space for women to share and support each other in their work. It was an initiative by Amanda Heng who had helped found the Artists Village (TAV) ten years earlier, in 1988. Heng's feminism disapproved of the personality-driven leanings of TAV and fought against any similar currents in WITAS.

Widely regarded as the first to introduce a feminist tract to Singapore art, Heng opposed the option to formalise WITAS when it came up. It would have meant coming under the control of the Registrar of Societies — the very thing Heng wanted to avoid. Two decades later, artist-academic Margaret Tan, remembers: "WITAS created a space for women to come and share and support each other in the challenges we were facing."

WITAS was fuelled by the women's curiosity and appetite for knowledge-building, and community. True to a feminist-activist tradition, a regular programme of artist talks and forums formed the core activities.

Gothenburg-based, Malaysian performance artist Chuyia Chia, then a young artist in Singapore, remembers: "WITAS was a wonderful experience, especially for a young artist like me then. I remember there were talks by visiting artists from overseas — Faith Wilding from the Chicago Institute of Art, Jane Kaisa from Denmark. There was a talk by a copyright lawyer on protecting ourselves from being taken advantage of. The Housework project was an important collaboration with Transient Workers Count Too (TWC2). But we had already been discussing the issues — like what is the value of housework to women and women artists. What happens to women after graduating from art school?

While WITAS was a women's group, it did not confine its activities, nor its concerns, to women. When another group of artist-curators, Jennifer Teo among them, gathered at 10 Perumal Road (P10) in 2004, members immediately saw the opportunity to collaborate. A suite of four artist talks on interdisciplinary collaboration followed. Shirley Soh spoke on art, science and technology. Ulrich Lau spoke on the multi-disciplinary work of theatre-maker and performance artist, Noor Effendy Ibrahim.

Another contribution from WITAS was its archive. Heng, who was allotted a space in the Teluk Kurau Studios in 1997, under the government's first Arts Housing scheme, remembers asking administrators why she was the only woman in the group. They replied there were no other women. This became the impulse for the archive. As many as 40 women including expatriate women deposited their portfolios in Heng's Teluk Kurau studio in two hefty ring files. I have an indelible mental image of the bulging files on Heng's flimsy shelves.

The purpose of the WITAS archive was to make names available to anyone interested. Eventually, the idea of a WITAS website with a page for every woman took shape. Ginette Chittick took on the design and layout of the web pages. Jing Chiang handled the domain name and server platform. The drivers for the project included Margaret Tan, Shirley Soh, and Amanda Heng. The group later expanded to include Kelly Reedy, Chuyia Chia, Sabrina Ng (a student of Tan's from NUS School of Computing), and myself. We took turns administering the site, relearning operating steps every time it was our turn. Chiang had prepared step-by-step instructions. Still, it proved a challenge every time.

How I became AWARE

Sometime before 1999, Amanda Heng talked with Philip Cheah, Artistic Director of the Singapore International Film Festival (SIFF).

Woman About Woman, a collaboration with the Singapore Art Museum and the 11th edition of SIFF in 1998, was the result of their conversations.

An invitation to participate in the show turned out to be fortuitous for me. I had never been exhibited and the invite caught me by surprise. I was pleased to be included but hesitated to accept. I was worried about being typecast! But, as soon as I put the phone down and heard it click in its cradle (we had those kinds of phones then) I thought, Why not? That was how I came to debut with Who Says Who We Are in the show. As a video work, it was rudimentary, to say the least, but making it enlarged my world. I reached out to women ranging in age from 18 to 80. To cut a long story short, it led me to AWARE.

Among the many AWARE leaders I met, Constance Singam was pivotal. Under her mentorship, I embarked on my first-ever public project — a look at our education system. There were murmurs as to whether AWARE was stepping outside of its purview. Claiming our rights as mothers, sisters, teachers and supported by focus groups from in and outside of AWARE, we called on policy makers to "give our children back their childhood".

What was more, we found our schools in near crisis mode. Despite announcements of changes that included a much-trumpeted 30 per cent reduction in syllabus, students and teachers continued to be overloaded with worksheets and the like. Teachers were feeling drained of time and energy that could be better spent in the classroom. We took our findings to the Ministry of Education. Among our recommendations were smaller schools and smaller class sizes, less homework, review streaming and school banding, re-evaluate examination and tests as progress indicators. And a revamp of the primary school curriculum to give every child equal opportunity to experience the arts.

As a mother of young children at the time, I had occasionally wondered why nobody had ever asked me how I wanted my children educated. The AWARE report, Quality Education for All (2001), elicited a meeting with MOE officers and not much else at the time. But the issues and recommendations continued to stay relevant and appear in both public and official debates.

The experience leading the education review for AWARE taught me that I did not have to wait to be asked. And that I was not alone in thinking what I was thinking. The experience opened my mind to a wider civic consciousness and responsibility that extended beyond the immediate family.

My awakening was compounded by the book, *The Unconscious Civilization*, by John Ralston Saul that, among other things, introduced the concept of active citizenry. My appetite whetted; I took the next opportunity that presented itself. In 2000, I stood for election as President of AWARE. It meant putting off an earlier plan to embark that year on a Fine Arts degree.

Back in 1999, the BA (Fine Arts) department was abuzz with the arrival of Irina Aristarkhova and a new feminist programme she was offering. Adeline Kueh, Margaret Tan, Shirley Soh from WITAS were among a small posse of students. I had the privilege of sitting in on their discussions — a weekly infusion of feminist thought and art-based knowledge.

It was an exhilarating time. I found resonance in the formal feminist texts, the artists' expressions, and the day-to-day encounters with other women at AWARE. I was discovering connections that I wanted very much to share.

One of the first things I did as AWARE President was to throw open the AWARE Centre at Dover Rise to artists' interventions. For one afternoon in July, we filled every room, every nook and cranny (it's not a very big centre!) with artwork and performances. Margaret

Tan and Shirley Soh created a history wall from a collage of photocopy transfers of newspaper headlines documenting AWARE's voice and impact over the decade. Tan's *Restless* comprising a performer (Samantha Hutton) painted in a wallflower pattern against a similarly painted wall by Tan was the main act.[14]

The painted wall and images from the performance were retained by AWARE, courtesy of the artist. They adorned the main function room at the centre for some years. Other artists who donated their time to the AWARE Open House included Tay Bee Aye whose surrealist white glue sculptures were installed in a counselling room. And a performance by the late Juliana Yasin, then a young artist exploring issues around her identity as a Muslim woman. The Open Mic event attracted speeches and poetry which, incidentally, included a reading by award-winning poet Cyril Wong, then starting out as a poet!

AWARE suffered what some people called an image problem in those days. Most people either had not heard of the organisation — in spite of our headlines-making work — or did not think we were relevant to their lives. I, therefore, took it as my job to bring people to AWARE, and the Open House was one way.

Women@Work (AWARE, 2001). To celebrate International Women's Day, a photographic competition was arranged in collaboration with the Singapore Photographic Society. It included a forum. At the opening, Margaret Tan and Faith Wilding (widely regarded feminist multidisciplinary artist introduced to us by Irina Aristarkhova) performed Maintenance Performance which they created especially for the occasion. The multi-media presentation made an impactful statement on the invisible, often repetitive, and necessary work performed by women in the global economy.

---

[14] Then Member of Parliament Dr Lily Neo who was the guest of honour arrived late. It created a problem for Samantha Hutton who was in body paint from head to toe and feeling the pressure of a full bladder!

The houseWORK project (WITAS, 2003). An exhibition to encourage re-thinking on housework and who does it. It included a survey of 150 households. Several artists offered their services for household chores in exchange for tokens that audiences earned from their participation in the show. Natacha Blondeau, Cassandra Schultz, Shirley Soh and Margaret Tan provided ironing services on Ironing Day. Amanda Heng, Twardzik Ching Chor Leng and Vincent Twardzik offered mobile cleaning services. Karee Dahl and Juliana Yasin performed Wash n Ware with a washing machine.

The horrendous death in 2001 of a 19-year-old Indonesian domestic helper, Muawanatul Chasanah, at the hands of her employer, led to the founding of The Working Committee 2 (TWC2, later Transient Workers Count Too). The idea for an advocacy group for the rights of domestic workers, separate from AWARE, was mooted by Constance Singam at a meeting with Sara Dean, Braema Mathi, then Nominated Member of Parliament, and myself. At its launch, TWC2 attracted nearly 100 people including researcher Stephii Chok, Russell Heng and John Gee, who have continued to contribute to the leadership of TWC2.

Meanwhile, WITAS was making progress in its democratic, inclusive, and collaborative way. But my responsibility as AWARE President was intense, and I could not be wholly present for the WITAS experience and its momentum. Till today, I count that very much as a loss.

But I was getting another, not unsubstantial kind of learning experience. In those days, the president was the face and voice of AWARE and had to be well-informed, ready and able to comment on social issues, and respond to policy announcements on a regular basis. We regularly aired our views on the forum pages of newspapers. My predecessors were prolific, their letters well substantiated. I had a lot of catching up to do, and Constance Singam was a pillar of support.

I did go back to school eventually, completing my MA (Fine Arts) studies in 2007. In 2009, I was called again to serve when AWARE was briefly taken over by a group whose fundamentalist agenda threatened to override AWARE's then 24 years of accomplished work, and inclusive feminist culture. My second turn as AWARE President was challenging as the organisation was in transition and reeling from trauma. It meant putting off the personal ambition of a studio practice for another two years.

Where have all the women gone?

"The fault lies not in our stars, our hormones, our menstrual cycles, or our empty internal spaces, but in our institutions and our own education." Linda Nochlin, *Why Have There Been No Great Women Artists?* 1971.

In 1979, Singapore introduced the Cultural Medallion, the highest award for artistic excellence. Of the six recipients that first year, there was only one woman, dancer Madhavi Krishnan. To date, 29 of a total of 135 Cultural Medallion honourees are women. That is less than 20 per cent. Amanda Heng was awarded in 2010, five years after male contemporary Lee Wen got his.

In 2022, Shubigi Rao represented Singapore at the 59th International Venice Biennale (VB), becoming only the second woman artist selected in the 21 years that Singapore has had a national pavilion at the event. Rao's selection came after her high-profile turn as curator of the fifth edition of the Kochi-Muziris Biennale (KMB) in 2020 which, incidentally, landed her on the Art Reviews' Power 100 list.[15] Suzann Victor was the first and only woman of the six artists selected when the Singapore Pavilion opened in 2001.

---

[15] The Power 100 is an annual ranking by 30 anonymous international jurors, compiled by the 74-year-old Art Review magazine.

And yet, five of ten curators responsible for the selection of artists for the Singapore Pavilion over the years were women. They were Joanna Lee, Lindy Poh, June Yap, Michelle Ho, and Ute Meta Bauer.

The shift in the art scene, with more women in curatorial and administrative positions in institutions, prompted *Straits Times* Arts writer Clara Chow to say in 2014: "Whether this power is going to trickle down to more influence and esteem for women art makers remains to be seen."

Meanwhile, while female students continue to far outnumber male in our art colleges, there are far more male artists than women artists. Where have all the women gone?

A biennale called Natasha

The act of naming brings into being something. Was naming the 7th Singapore Biennale (16 October 2022 to March 2023) 'Natasha' a significant moment that curiously passed unremarked? The optics on the website — particularly artist Berny Tan's luscious knot of wool — certainly appear emblematic.

The point, according to the Singapore Art Museum (SAM)'s June Yap who is Co-Artistic Director in the all-woman team with Nida Ghouse (India), Ala Younis (Kuwait) and Binna Choi (South Korea), is this: "Naming can produce a sense of familiarity or intimacy (and) personal connection.[16] Foregrounding women in the naming of Natasha was conscious in the sense that when we decided we would name the Biennale, the name we preferred was a female one...to us, the gendered experience is a very real one and one we ourselves are familiar with, so it was natural and necessary that we reflect this in our work."

---

[16] https://ocula.com/magazine/art-news/why-was-singapore-biennale-2022-named-natasha/

And that is where it ends, apparently. The team stopped short of framing the Biennale on the female condition. Or on feminist terms.

The announcement of a feminist gathering by the Biennale thus came as a surprise. The Slideshow Party: A feminist sharing of art and other provocations[17] as a rallying call seemed a bit fraught, I thought. The organisers did their best. There was wine and cheese, familiar faces, and conspicuous absences. But it felt good. And reminiscent of the WITAS meetings in the 1990s.

There were 50 or 60 of us. Alecia Neo, Nurul Kaiyisah (Kai), Susie Wong and I gave presentations. Wong spoke of negotiating memory gaps when trying to recall the Dinner Party, her project after Judy Chicago, around 2000. And the HOPE project at CHIJMES where an installation referencing the venue's past as a depository for unwanted baby girls had to bow to commercial interests and be removed. Neo spoke stirringly of the influence of artist-researcher Chu Chu Yuan, a pioneer in community-based work and an early member of the Artists Village. Kai shared her curiosity and research on the friendship between two pioneer women artists — Rohani Ismail, a founding member of the Angkatan Pelukis Aneka Daya[18] and Nanyang artist, Georgette Chen. I shared my regrets and learning from what I consider a failed project, my re-creation of Amanda Heng's iconic, Let's Chat, at The Substation in 2005.

Being in the roomful of women practitioners was in itself uplifting.

London-based artist Erika Tan acknowledged the dissonance inherent in the room but insisted on the importance of connecting and the value of personal experiences and references heard over one another. Together with curator Adele Tan, she created a padlet, an

---

[17] The organisers, curator Adele Tan and London-based artist Erika Tan, had drawn inspiration from a ground- breaking event in 1978, An Informal Slide Evening, at London's Hayward Gallery. Among the all women artists-committee was the Singapore sculptor and print-maker Kim Lim.

[18] Association of Artists of Various Resources, APAD, Singapore's longest running art society for Malay artists.

online repository of women artists, artworks, exhibitions and events over the years. It is a stunning platform, breathtaking in variety, colour and texture. And an invaluable open resource for women about women and anyone interested.

Yet still the question posed half a century earlier by Linda Nochlin persists: why have there been no great women artists.

Erika Tan points to the fact that women making up half of the ten Singapore Biennale curators has not made a difference to the selection choices in over 20 years. And discussions about museum acquisitions inevitably produce names of male artists, while a predominantly male canon appears to be at play with the reopening of the Singapore Art Museum.

To quote Erika Tan: "We love to think of ourselves as a nation where merit predominates, but are less able to acknowledge our bias, blind spots and innate chauvinism."

Singapore, on the whole, demonstrates a schizophrenic attitude to the arts and artists. On the one hand, there is an increasing appetite for art (enrichment) from both State programming authorities and the public. Motherhood statements exhort citizens to participate in nation-building, exercise creativity, think out of the box as a matter of national survival. On the other hand, authorities are quick to react to opinions deemed at variance with the dominant official line. And, of course, there is that infamous 2020 survey by The Sunday Times citing artists at the top of the list of non-essential workers.

State-organised back-to-back, overlapping mega art shows where the return of investment is measured by visitor footfalls and sale revenues further centres art and art-making in a purely materialistic, capitalist value system. Creativity as understood by this system is no more than a means of goods production. The critical role of art and art-making in the cultivation of individuals and humanity is unrecognised, and most certainly, unrewarded.

When asked what women artists wanted, Shirley Soh, previously a broadcast journalist and active WITAS member, said: "Don't we know what we want by now? We want affordable studio spaces, we want independent art spaces, we want dialogue and discourse free from censorship. Yes, we don't want censorship, we don't want to apply in advance for an entertainment permit to perform in public, and yes, dare I say it, we want freedom to think and act. I know we can't have it. Period."

Women artists with traditional familial, child-rearing, and caregiving duties drop out of the race. Those who stay the course have to contend with institutional prejudice or blindness. In "Women Artists: Becoming Professional in Singapore, Malaya and Indonesia",[19] Yvonne Yanmei Low asserts "women although deemed missing have always been part of the enlarging process of the socio-cultural sphere". They have just not been given the recognition and the accolades their male counterparts have. And subsequent history writing simply reproduced women's absence.

At the time of writing, a group of eight women from the relatively newfound Fertile Art Refinery (FAR) are showing at the newly opened Punggol Regional Library. The exhibition, Strange Tools, comprises works made in collaboration with the National Library Board initiative, MakeIT at Libraries that offer workshops in Robotics and coding, 3-D printing, digital cutting, sewing and upcycling free of charge.

In the hands of artists Xiu Xiaochang, Smiha Kapoor, Agatha (Agy) Lee, Veronyka Lau, Jennifer Teo, Cynthia Delaney Suwito, Teo Huey Ling, TecheFractals, and curator Kamiliah Bahdar, these skill-sets become tools with which visitors are invited to look anew at the

---

[19] Yvonne Low (2015), "Women Re-Modelling Artworlds: Exhibitions and Projects on Southeast Asian Women Artists (1990–2015)". *The Journal of the Asian Arts Society of Australia* 24 (4).

ordinary and the mundane. The invitation is to experience beauty rather than to see it.

Among the neat (read cool) array of aesthetic works is an invitation to blow gently into a short tube to see how your action may have a direct consequence on Agatha Lee's delicate handsewn corals. Or travel the network of electrical cables up, under and around the library in Cynthia Delaney Suwito's computer game. Or follow the constellations of stars mapped onto the library's carpeted flooring (Jennifer Teo).

This is the third group showing by members of FAR since its inception in 2020. The collective is, by its own description, "a celebration of women-centric organisation in the Singapore art scene".

It came directly from the experience of organising Steeped Strong, an all-women show at the Far East Plaza in 2019. Nineteen women were involved in Steeped Strong. They were the Artists Village (TAV) stalwarts Eve Tan and Jennifer Teo and relatively "young artists" Veronyka Lau, Nicole Phua, Nicolette Teo, Isabelle Desjeux, Deborah Ong, Chen Ziwei, Agatha Lee, Sharmean/Sifar, Dorathy Lye, Fiona Seow, Maisarah Kamal, Teo Huey Ling, Xiaochang Xin, Amelia Desmond, Eunice Lacaste, and Illa Haziqin.

The women showed a refreshing range in form and material from painting to embroidery, soil to PVC pipes, multi-media installations to found objects to live-art (performance). And ranged in themes from environmental concerns, from coral habitats and tree life to human connections with place, from the personal to the political. The live-art programme included Lash Spa Lessons (Veronyka Lau), an hour-long part lecture, part movement performance of "joyous indulgence" staged inside one of 45 nail salons in the mall.

Following on the experience of Steeped Strong, the FAR vows to keep to a mode of cooperation that does away with traditional hierarchies, such as an elected committee. It continues to support and welcome collaborative work by any practitioner who identifies as woman.

FAR's motivation is "to maintain safe conversations critical to women art practitioners and to extend women's voices in Singapore art and outside".

A number of FAR members, Eve Tan, Veronyka Lau, Jennifer Teo, Bridget Tay are part of a current effort to revive TAV. Electing to continue is a way of honouring what has come before even as new modes of working are being evolved. The group wants to explore new implications of care and collectivism and new modes of collaboration and presentation both in the virtual and in the real.

Meanwhile, the PostMuseum,[20] which grew out of the P10 group in 2007, continues to make space for ideas and creative exchanges in the only way they know how. The PostMuseum began life in the hands of the indefatigable duo, Jennifer Teo and Woon Tien Wei, in a shophouse in Rowell Road, Little India. It began as an artist-run café with artists serving as guest chefs and also providing a space for artists to hang out. It later became known for its soup kitchen two days a week for migrant workers with produce from the small stall holders from the nearby market. The duo underwrote the rent. The PostMuseum currently operates nomadically. The soup kitchen still carries on every week. And a Really Really Free Market has been added for the exchange of ideas and goods.

The Future We Want

"The beautiful thing about the arts is that when we are participating in it, we are actually articulating what we wish

---

[20] Carolina Sanchez, Interview with the Founders of POST-MUSEUM: Jennifer Teo and Woon Tien Wei in On-curating, Issue 41, June 2019. https://www.on-curating.org/issue-41.html

for — to see differently, to change perspective, minuscule or seismic."

– Shirley Soh

Speaking for myself, "to see differently" calls for deep listening. And the will to question one's very own belief system which is often an internalised version of the dominant culture. This makes for a long, hard struggle requiring commitment, persistence, and stamina.

Away from the gallery circuit, artist Lin Shi Yun has been running something called the Tak Takut Kids Club (TTKC) in Boon Lay Drive on her own initiative and, until recently, out of pocket. Children in the neighbourhood gravitate to the two rooms at the bottom of the Housing Development block, drawn by curiosity and Lin's Open-Door policy. Something of a roll call of artists are among regular volunteers. The children are free to participate or not in the programme of workshops on any given day. A communal garden was planted with seedlings from private plots in the neighbourhood. Permaculture advocate Nora Nelson runs a Better Eat Better programme with the children.

The TTK club, The Post Museum's Renew Earth Project and Really Really Free Market are some current iterations of artist initiatives that are mostly women-led. These projects respond to what the artists involved identify as a need or gap in society. They do more than simply articulate a future they wish to see; they pave the way for change by acting on it.

Veronyka Lau whose journey began with TAV and who is currently leading its revival puts it this way: For change to happen, ideas must travel, people must have meeting places for conversations to happen freely.

The examples of current initiatives from women artists centre care, community building and sustainability; and the free exchange of ideas as both the creative process and output. Another thing they do is chisel away at institutionalised visual art language and create new public sites for change to happen. Making and holding space for imagining a different future is what they have in common with the line of artist initiatives before them.

History reminds us, it takes very little to set things back. In the case of 5th Passage, a few seconds of an act is enough to erase several years of good. The area around Armenian Street that used to house The Substation, that democratic, eclectic space where a young, untested person of any of the arts is as welcome as any master of the craft, where a generation of artists, Cultural Medallion recipients among them have come, is now just another sterile street in the gentrified museum district.

However, artists must do what artists do. And the work goes on.

Conclusion

I have tried to chart my personal journey alongside the collective actions I have had the privilege of association with as a fellow traveller and invested observer. My greatest fault is my inattention. By the same token, my saving grace may be that I do come around in time.

In keeping with the feminist tradition of making visible and audible I have made a point to name as many individuals as I reasonably can in the scope of this narrative. I do this in the spirit of solidarity with the artists and activists mentioned herein. Even so, there will be names that have fallen through the gaps of memory or inattention. I sincerely apologise for their omission.

I am grateful to Margaret Thomas and Dr Kanwaljit Soin for their inspiration in initiating the series of books for women by women, of which this is the second. And for the opportunity to think deeply on those events around my life. I needed to write this, for myself and for posterity.

I owe a special debt to academic Michelle Antoinette for her insightful essay on the 5ᵗʰ Passage; Seng Yu Jin for writing on the Artists Village; Veronyka Lau for her meticulous notes on Steeped Strong. And to Jennifer Teo, Isabelle Desjeux, Adele Tan, Erika Tan, June Yap, Shirley Soh, Margaret Tan, Hazel Lim, Amanda Heng, and Chia Chu Yia for generously giving of their time to answer my questions.

DANA LAM is a visual artist and writer and an associate artist with Checkpoint Theatre. Her visual journal, The Art of Being a Grandmother: An Incomplete Diary of Becoming, *is out in stores.*

Ageing to Perfection

"One shouldn't think of oneself as a senior citizen. As long as you can still go on doing things that you like, you should keep active."

~ Philanthropist and pioneering conservationist Yuen Peng McNeice, talking to The Straits Times, September 1991

CHAPTER 31

Ageing in Place with Dignity: That is the Challenge before Us

Constance Singam

I keep a journal and maintain a blog. Both record my ageing journey and the changes I underwent as I transitioned from being a restless, bored, and depressed old woman to someone who is settling down to an easier way of life. The change did not happen overnight. I struggled with fear and depression but with the help of wide-ranging conversations with friends and family I slowly changed my attitude and accepted that I am old and will get older.

So instead of capitulating to social expectations and the public image of the aged, I became an active agent of my own life and the paths I took. I defied the self-fulling prophecy of decline. Meanwhile I discovered what it is be old by living it. I am as alive to the world as I have always been — alive to everything I see and hear and feel.

Ageing points to a different way of living. I discovered that I enjoy solitude. I am reading more. I have returned to my early love of art, of pencil drawing. I have continued writing. I am lucky I have the advantage of a good education and a community of friends and family that provide the intellectual stimulation, the emotional support, and social life. No longer do I feel the loss of status associated with economic productivity.

I maintain a small garden which gives me great pleasure and sadly I need help to keep it going. I open my front door and delight in the glow of the brilliant sunlight. Some mornings the awe-inspiring beauty of the yellow hibiscus bloom in all its dappled glory in the sun greets me and I smile in delight of the fact that even the most ordinary flowers of our youthful days have the capacity to bring such joy. I watch the yellow sun bird, the bulbuls, and the mynahs come chirping into my little garden. Old age brings its own rewards.

I am astonished by my own acceptance of a simple life. It was just a year ago when I was restless, struggling to fill the empty spaces of my day and depressed beyond reason for want of something to do. Now, just sweeping the floor or watering the plants makes me feel fulfilled. Doing small practical things, even trivial things, gives a sense of achievement.

The change led me to focus on the present, which as philosophers and religious leaders have advocated is the way to joy and peace of mind. In this state of mind, projecting to the future of my ageing, as I am required to do in this essay, is problematic, grim, and depressing. It obliges me to project myself to a time I have not sufficiently thought about or that I have avoided thinking about.

* * *

We, the old, are many. By 2030, a quarter of Singapore's population will be over 65 years of age. By 2050 about half the population will be at least 65 years old. The old will no longer be invisible. They will be the mainstream.

But how many of us are, as individuals, prepared for this dawning reality? And for all that has been said by the policy makers about our ageing population, is what is being done sufficient?

I am witness in my own neighbourhood to the difficulties of ageing. What I observe gives me very little comfort or assurance. The following stories taken together offer a worrying glimpse of the future if we are not able to envision and organise a better world for the super-aged society that we will soon be.

My early memory of moving into an HDB estate, my first experience of HDB living, is how visible people's everyday lives were. There was this old man — partially blind, very unstable on his feet, wandering round the neighbourhood and sleeping wherever he could. One day my friend helped him from falling and on probing found that his family didn't want him in the flat during the day and only allowed him home at night to sleep. He is no longer around.

Another old man used to wheel his wife, who had dementia, around the neighbourhood. He stopped every now and then to tenderly wipe the sweat off her face. They were around together for a while. Then she died and a year later he was being wheeled around by a foreign helper. He too is now gone.

Then there was this old woman whom I used to notice at the window of her second floor flat. She was always looking out of the window. What could she have been thinking, I wondered. What was her life like? Did she have a family? Is she thinking of what could have been. Or is she just waiting to die. She is gone too.

Two doors away from me lived another old lady with her three sons and her husband, a bent old man. She became difficult to live with, perhaps because of dementia, and her husband and sons left. She was alone. Then she had a fall, and she needed a walking stick to get around. After some time, we hardly ever saw her.

One of the neighbours decided to look in on her. She found the flat in shambles, cooking utensils and plates piled up in a sink that had not seen any detergent for months and the bathrooms black with grime. My very kind-hearted neighbour armed herself with gloves and the strongest of household cleaning products and cleared away the dirt, the grime, and the stink. This generous neighbour, who was in her 70s then, later said to me: "Who is going to help me when I am older?"

I recall another man I met in the lift who from the smell emanating from him I guessed had not been in a shower for a while. Speaking in dialect and sounding desperate, he was asking another passenger in the lift for help to find someone who could help him clean his flat.

How could all of those old people have been helped to live a more dignified old age? What were their needs? How could their needs have been met? There might have been schemes and services that could have been of help to them, but they might not have known about these.

The Lien Foundation in its report *Care Where You Are*, published in 2018, found that "... even seasoned care providers sometimes find administrative frameworks to access services and grants difficult to navigate. The procedures and paperwork can prove mind-boggling. These many hurdles to access services reveal a lack of understanding about the lives of the majority of people...."

The report recommends empowerment of care recipients and caregivers by simplifying the complexity of the procedures to access services. This calls for a new readiness among policy makers and administrators to trust people, to put compassion before or at least alongside the need to control and prevent any abuse of the system.

The Singapore way has been to look to the family and community to provide what is needed for people to 'age in place'. Ageing in place has great attraction and relevance for someone like me for whom home is central to my sense of identity. But for my neighbours, ageing in place meant failing health, loss of long-time elderly neighbours, departures of children, death of spouses, social isolation and neglect. They would have required substantial support, both financial and material, to age in place with greater dignity and joy.

* * *

When did I start feeling old? Not when I was in my sixties. That was when I went back to university and obtained an MA in literature, and I also published a book on Singapore women. I didn't begin to feel old in my 70s nor when I turned 80. In my 70s I wrote two memoirs and continued to be active in civil society, and in my early 80s I wrote and illustrated four children's books.

But then at 83, I had to deal with sciatica. The pain and immobility brought on a sense of helplessness and powerlessness, and also the fear of dependency and loneliness. For the more existential anxieties there are no easy solutions. I fear losing interest; I fear becoming irrelevant; I fear the loss of best friends; I fear the loss of autonomy; I fear the loss of a way of life; I fear the manner of my death.

In the Wild Rice play 'Supervision', the character of Teck, 71 years old and wheelchair-bound, is memorable for its poignancy and depiction of reality. The playwright Thomas Lim brilliantly captured the dynamics between the various players in a situation of caring for a loved one.

The trio — the old father, his domestic helper, and the daughter who is herself a mother, wife, and worker — are all trapped in a situation of powerlessness. The daughter is forced by her circumstances to entrust the care of her father to a foreign domestic worker. The father resists losing power and control over his own life. It was heart wrenching to watch their struggles, each caught up in their own predicament and each having to deal with difficult problems on their own.

How different it would have been for Teck and indeed for his daughter if there were a community of care to turn to — people and agencies providing support for their emotional and physical needs. His daughter who, like many women, had to shoulder the burdens of two households, her own and that of her aged parent, while earning a living. The policy of leaving the care of the aged to families can weigh very heavily on women.

* * *

I had a neighbour, Betty, who upon retirement bought a flat. She was just about to move with her mother, who was in her 90s, into the flat when the older woman had a fall and was hospitalised. Betty made her daily visit to her mother, starting at 8.00 in the morning and returning at night after her mother was asleep. After about a year her mother died and Betty, for the first time in her life, was alone, and living alone.

It only took Betty a couple of months of living alone to decide it was not for her and she moved herself into a home. She was happy, she said, because there were other people around her, her meals were prepared, and entertainment organised. She is still there. I don't think she is 70 yet.

Meanwhile, there is the remarkable story of 99-year-old Toyo Shibata in Japan who, at the age of 92, picked up her pen and started writing poems about love, dreams, and hanging on to hope.

Her first collection of 42 poems, titled 'Don't be Too Frustrated', was in 2010 the most popular book on the closely watched Oricon charts for two weeks and was one of the top 10 sellers that year. "Although 98, I still fall in love. I do have dreams; one like riding on a cloud," Shibata confessed in one poem. She went on to write a second anthology. In January 2013 she died at the age of 101.

Shibata and Betty were both able to enjoy worry-free older life. Betty because she had the financial resources to do so. She sold her flat and used the money to live well the way she wanted. For Shibata, the Japanese culture of treating the old with respect offered her a dignified life into old age and death.

The story of Shibata's life reminds me of a passage in Singapore sociologist Teo You Yenn's excellent book *This is What Inequality Looks Like*. Writing about the Japanese culture of respect for older people, she says: "The respect accorded to older persons, the feeling one got of their continued belonging in society as they aged, the expressions and body language of security in one's self-worth among older people — these were images that felt alien to me. I thought to myself: This is what dignity really looks like."

The key to ageing well is 'dignity'. What do we understand by 'dignity'? Once again, I refer to Teo You Yenn in her study on poverty and equality. She acknowledges that the concept of dignity is difficult to grasp. Towards the end of her book, in commenting about our society, she concluded that 'the 'inherent right to respect as a human being and member of society' is not a right that is conceded nor a value that is understood in Singapore.

"When I reflect on the issue of dignity, ... as long as our well-being and worth as persons are deeply linked to economic productivity, income, a specific way of doing family, then everybody's dignity is essentially at risk. In this ethos, no one has inherent worth as persons."

Elsewhere in her book she describes dignity as: "It is a sense of being valued, a feeling of being respected, a sensation of esteem, of self-worth. How and from where does one get it? In everyday life."

For my elderly neighbours, dignity would have meant a clean home, a bed available day and night, hot meals, financial support, activities and services within reach, access to medical facilities, a sense of belonging to a community. These are the barest essentials for a dignified life.

Dignity, however, is not one of our core values. The culture we have shaped in Singapore equates success with material progress, with wealth. In such a culture, the poor and the old become invisible, and compassion is relegated to the ranks of the bleeding hearts. It is not a culture that makes ageing in place easy.

Can we change this culture? Are we prepared to have a rigorous societal conversation about what we value as a nation, about meritocracy, about poverty, about what it is to be human?

The UN Decade of Healthy Ageing (2021–2030) document outlines some guidelines for governments to reduce health inequities and improve the lives of older people, their families and communities. Collective action, says the UN, is needed in four areas: changing how we think, feel and act towards age and ageism; developing communities in ways that foster the abilities of older people; delivering person-centred integrated care and primary health services responsive to older people; and providing older people who need it with access to quality long-term care.

These are good targets. We should pursue them with new vigour.

* * *

As I progress through my 87th year I am discovering that my energy to organise my own community is diminishing. But this community is essential for my mental health and well-being. Studies have found that it is important to have a sense that you are part of a community.

Being part of a community means not only living with like-minded people but also communal activities, doing things together, learning from each other, and having reciprocal support, all of which create a sense of togetherness, belonging, and trust. Also important are the ability to continue to plan for the future, having a role in life, relationships with the family, and a feeling of control over your life.

These are factors that have enabled me to live my life with considerable satisfaction. So far, at least. By the time I am 100 the circumstances of my community would have changed, as would my own life because of health or financial issues. The Lien Foundation report estimates that by 2030, some 69,000 people in Singapore will be severely disabled. Will I be in that group?

Women, according to government released data, outnumber men in old age. Other studies tell us that women tend to suffer from mobility issues as they age. By 2030, the women who are currently taking care of their aged relatives will be aged themselves. The chances are that their earlier caregiving responsibilities would have limited their capacity to nurture a community and look after their own social and health needs.

What of my own future? For how much longer will I be able to live on my own and organise my own life? When the time comes for me to get some help with daily life, will I have the support of the state for my social, medical and financial needs without surrendering my agency and my privacy?

I envision an HDB building which has a mixed occupancy. One level is dedicated to older folks like me, living in single units with a central space as a common area for social activities and a veranda across the length of the floor for us to enjoy the sun and nature. In other words the kind of life I now enjoy, but with someone such as a nurse who checks in on me regularly, and a helper who pops in daily to take care of the cleaning and perhaps also some cooking.

Importantly, there should be opportunities to continue learning, and perhaps also to continue contributing in some way to the community around me. The danger of dependency and the perception of old age as deterioration can lead to a situation of denying agency to older people. This is my greatest fear about ageing — that I will lose the agency to make decisions about how to live my life.

Our ageing society has profound implications for our personal choices and for public policy. It calls for major shifts in our approach, for personal and social change. And change we must if we are to age in place with dignity and with a sense of self-determination. I worry about my old age. So it is very personal.

CONSTANCE SINGAM is a writer and civil society activist who can now speak with some authority about the experience of ageing.

"I hope for a stress-free nation with a calmer lifestyle. Our ageing parents should be able to spend their old age in a comfortable home with their loved ones or live independently in a comfortable home in conducive surroundings. Our children and youth as well as senior citizens should have common spaces for interactive activities that will promote bonding."

~ Pioneering Malay dance choreographer Som Said, for The Lives of Women exhibition at the National Museum, Jan–Mar 2022

CHAPTER 32

An Older Woman's Story

Mary Ann Tsao

As the sun begins to rise on a sunny morning in 2050, 85-year-old Florence Tan wakes up with a smile on her face. She stretches her arms and legs, feeling a sense of contentment in the life she has lived thus far. It is a life that has seen its share of trials and tribulations, but somehow, in her later life, she feels safe, secure, and assured of her future, as it has been enriched by countless advances and societal changes that have made her senior years better than she could have ever imagined.

Florence has led a fulfilling life even with all her life's challenges. With the support of family, friends, and community — together with senior-friendly advances — she feels she has had a new lease of life even in widowhood and older age.

Florence was married to her childhood sweetheart and had two wonderful children with him. She was a homemaker and devoted caregiver to her parents and her stroke-disabled husband until they passed away. While she enjoys close, loving relationships with her children, they have built lives overseas. Though she misses them, she accepts that they cannot stay by her side, and she does not want to burden them in any way. In any event, she is satisfied with their annual trips home and frequent videocalls.

Having proactively forged friendships in her community, particularly with younger people who help her remain engaged with and curious about social trends, she has a network of relationships that sustains her. She was engaged with friends and community in activities that she found purposeful and enjoyable, and even with her recent need for more care, she is able to live at home and get around independently with improvements in public transportation. Despite being widowed and with family far away, Florence has never felt unsupported or isolated.

Florence was born in a world that was quite different from the one she lives in today. In 2025, when she was 60, policies, services, and products were not developed with a gender perspective, and as a result, they were insufficient to address the needs of older women. Then, older women typically lived five years longer than men and had more years of disability, especially if they had been homemakers or not worked. They needed health care, but insurance premiums were more expensive for older women at a time when they were less able to pay.

According to Singapore's 2020 census, half the women 65 and over were single, be they never married, divorced, or widowed. Older women were particularly vulnerable financially especially in widowhood, as Florence was. They were more likely to have left financial management to their husbands and were less literate and inexperienced in money matters. When they became widowed, they were not adequately prepared to manage their own financial affairs. They were also frequently left asset rich because of home ownership but cash poor, especially if their spouse had a long illness that drained their nest egg.

Employment opportunities for mature women who had been out of the workforce were far and few in between especially when they could only work part-time due to family responsibilities, so it was difficult for them to earn and have savings of their own. Many had reluctantly to rely on their children for financial support in their old age, rendering them feeling disempowered and indebted. Maintaining social relationships was also challenging as they grew older, as their disabilities increasingly made it difficult for them to catch public transportation, especially when it involved negotiating stairs, such as overhead bridges. It was also a struggle to find appropriate housing options with support services and affordable transportation when they became frail or had disabilities. As a result, many older women became increasingly isolated, resulting in higher incidence of anxiety, depression, poor health, and low quality of life.

Florence faced a major challenge when she was widowed in 2037 at age 72. Her husband had a good job, and they were a solidly middle-class family, but by the time her husband passed away after years of disability, she was not left with much. Like many women, Florence worked before she was married, but became a full-time home maker in her late 20s after she started her family. She had some money in her CPF account, but it was far below the minimal sum, and certainly insufficient for what she would need to last until the end of her life. She considered selling her home, but the smaller flats designed for older people were far from her community and in unfamiliar neighbourhoods, and at 32sqm, they were too small for her taste.

Most importantly, she did not want to leave her marital home and neighbourhood — a place filled with memories and connections to the community. Not only was home and community easy and comfortable for her to navigate in her daily living, it was also an integral part of her identity. Leaving her home felt like leaving part of her being behind, and she could not bear it.

Fortunately, a recently established non-profit centre that provided senior employment services also offered financial planning for older women. Together, they devised a solution: she rented out her extra rooms and was able to earn additional income by providing breakfast and some meals. The centre also helped her find tenants — two overseas nurses who worked in a nearby hospital and another single older woman, resulting in the additional benefit of companionship and less housework with shared housekeeping responsibilities. Florence was thus able to have sufficient income to age in her own home and community, and she also liked the idea that when she eventually passes on, the sale of the flat would allow her to leave a substantial inheritance to her family as well.

Florence's financial security was also bolstered by advances in financial technology as well as new opportunities for older people to earn an income and establish their own businesses. From online banking and higher performing investment platforms to IT tools that connected seniors with work opportunities, Florence took advantage of these developments and sought to further strengthen her financial security while acquiring new skills and meaningful work. Though her financial situation stabilised through her rental income and limited savings, money was still tight for the quality of life she wanted, and Florence was determined to build stronger financial security for herself.

At age 73, the Silver Work Centre was able to find her a part-time job at a local bakery through job share with another older woman. She liked baking and found that she was good at it. With the encouragement of the staff at the Silver Work Centre, she was able to tap government funds for a professional baking course, studied how to start and manage a home-based enterprise, access investment capital from the community foundation in her area, and established a home baking business.

Starting from her home and selling limited batches every month, she eventually moved the baking to a communal central kitchen that supported local F&B businesses and grew it into business run by a cooperative of women who brought their relevant skills in finance, marketing, and other competencies required to grow the business. Florence found new energy and purpose in her life, as the business not only offered her substantial income, but also offered opportunities for women to earn an income doing something they enjoy and in a supportive environment. Never in a million years did Florence ever imagine that — at 73 and having been a homemaker most of her life — she would initiate a successful and meaningful business.

Florence reflects on the journey to this moment, and the many advances that have made her life so much easier. She remembers the day she entered her newly renovated apartment, with its wider doorways, no-step entries, accessible bathroom fixtures and all the latest technology to make her life easier as part of a flexi package scheme for seniors' home adaptation. Technology innovations such as a 24-hour safety monitoring system that automatically calls for help if she falls or needs help, medication alarms to remind her to take her medicine, online exercise classes with her friends when the rain made it hard to go out — these have all helped her to live independently and securely.

She also remembers the day she gave up driving and embraced public transportation. New services such as 'dial-a-ride' for seniors at affordable rates with mobility assistance are immensely helpful, as are hop-on/hop off neighbourhood shuttles (serving everyone but with reduced rates for seniors) that provide transportation to bus and MRT stations as well as neighbourhood shopping areas. With affordable and accessible options available to seniors, she has been able to get around town with ease, without having to rely on family members or friends.

Advances in healthcare such as telemedicine options allow her to consult with her doctors remotely, and AI-enabled personalised medicine helps her maintain her health as she ages. Reformed health insurance schemes that pool risk across men and women as well as long-term care insurance that pools risk across generations provide affordable assurance that she will be able to pay for her health and long-term care if the need arises. Enrolment in a health maintenance primary care practice allows Florence to have a consistent relationship with her primary healthcare team that provides not only chronic disease management but also acute care when she is not well. The team is her partner in her health journey, supporting her to live well by encouraging a healthy lifestyle, enabling her for self-care and providing timely preventive care through their integrated health and social care model. A doctor, nurse social worker, rehab therapist and counsellor are always there to help Florence manage her total well-being, negotiate the health system confidently and stay well. Florence has benefited from the many innovations and improvements in primary care.

Lately, Florence has noticed that her memory has been deteriorating and she is not physically as strong as before. So today she will be visiting the social worker of her primary healthcare team to find out more about creating a supportive environment for herself as her health starts to deteriorate and functional needs increase. She heard that there is a government-supported scheme for groups of people in the same neighbourhood to create their own NORCs (naturally occurring retirement community). The NORC is where they can share the cost of hiring a nurse care manager and social concierge to help them manage their health and personal care, home maintenance and housekeeping as well as social activities. This way, Florence will be able to continue living in her home even as she develops more long-term care needs.

As she sits in her home, sipping her morning tea, she feels grateful for the many blessings in her life. She has been able to enjoy living in her own home with a social network that has sustained her throughout her life. Whether it was friends, family, volunteer work or the support of her community, she has always been surrounded by people she cares about and who care about her and who want to help her succeed. What she cherishes deeply is the opportunity to continue learning and growing. With a plethora of courses available, she has been able to pursue her interests and passions, and with hybrid online courses, she can learn without leaving her home when her arthritic knees are acting up. Most importantly, she is able to pursue her own aspirations and personal growth and remain in charge of her own destiny.

In the quiet of her living room, Florence thinks about the future. She knows that she still has many years ahead of her, and she is excited about the possibilities. She has started writing a memoir and is considering taking on a new intergenerational 'menterning' role — being a mentor to the younger generations while also learning from them with the curious mind of an intern. Florence's life has been a testament to her determination and resilience, but it is also a testament to the power of innovation and progress. By taking advantage of the many advances in policies, products, and services, Florence has been able to make her senior years more fulfilling than she could have ever imagined.

As she manoeuvres her chair closer to the window, content in the knowledge that her life had been well-lived, Florence smiles at the thought of all the other people who would benefit from the many advances since her widowhood and those that are still to come. For Florence, the future is bright, exciting, and full of possibilities.

* * *

MARY ANN TSAO is the Chairwoman of the Tsao Foundation, a regional non-profit operational foundation dedicated to addressing population ageing issues, longevity, and the well-being of older people at policy and practice levels by catalysing constructive change. Mary Ann also chairs the Tsao Family Office and is a Board Director for Family Business Network (FBN) International as well as its Asia Chapter. Among other accolades, Mary Ann was named by WHO in 2022 as one of the first 50 healthy ageing pioneers — global leaders recognised for transforming the world to be a better place to grow older.

"Life is precious, help it last
Use it for some other's good
Then you'll not regret your past
For you have done the best you could."

~ **Pioneering women's rights activist Shirin Fozdar,
from a poem she wrote for her headstone**

CHAPTER 33

I am Caring for My Mother, But Who will Care for Me?

⁜

Patricia Ng

My caregiver journey started in 2011 when my mother had a hip replacement surgery following a fall. She was 81 at the time. We were extremely fortunate then because Mum was determined not to be bedridden, so spearheaded her own recovery. She had fallen on the eve of the eve of Chinese New Year. Before everything went into shutdown mode for the holidays, a physiotherapist came by the day after Mum's procedure. He gave her a walker and asked her to stand. Once she got up and felt little pain, she was, in a sense, off and running.

The original plan was for me to take a year off work, train the domestic worker, and then go back to a full-time job. Life had other ideas. The helper decided to steal money from us and that meant an immediate send-back to the agency and home. Mum vehemently refused to have any other stranger in the house. So that meant a change of plans since my brother and I didn't want Mum to be on her own, especially if she was out of the house. Thankfully, my line of work as an editor made it comparatively easy to transition to freelance work.

Caring for Mum was a breeze because she could function normally. She had no problems with public transport and only needed a little help getting off the bus. We visited almost all the public parks and she was able to do long walks, albeit with breaks in between. She was also one of those who had no problems at all with the escalator. Even though she used an umbrella *tongkat* for support when we went out, she was stable enough to do without it when we were at home. What all this meant was that I could leave her alone at home for a few hours if I needed to run errands, had meetings, or just wanted some time with my friends. And Mum was happy at home, watching her Chinese shows on TV, doing Word Search, and playing Solitaire with her deck of cards.

Fast forward about ten years and Mum decided to have a repeat performance, breaking the bone in her other leg. And this was on the eve of New Year's eve (hey, Mum is sort of consistent, if nothing else). But ten years makes a world of difference. She wasn't as robust as she was before and neither was her mind as focused. I had already noticed that her synapses weren't firing properly a few years before but had attributed it to old age. After all, even we who are younger, were starting to forget things and be less sharp, why shouldn't she?

This happened in the midst of Covid-19. The hospital was keen to discharge her about a week after her operation but I refused as she could not walk at all and needed to rebuild her strength. I asked for her to be transferred to a community hospital, and a specific one because it would be easier for me and family members to visit her. It would be two weeks before that materialised.

I was naïve to think that Mum could recover in the same way she did before. This time, she wasn't keen on walking and would complain of a pain in her knee. She would take a few steps then ask to sit down. The therapists tried but they could only do so much. After about a month and seeing no more improvement to her condition, I unilaterally decided to take her home and look after her on my own. Mind you, I really had no idea what I was getting myself into.

The realities of caregiving

Before her homecoming, much had to be arranged. We purchased a walker with wheels, geriatric chair, and wheelchair from the hospital and I went online to search for a guard rail for her bed and a shower chair. And lots of adult diapers and adult wipes.

Thankfully, our toilet already had grab bars as I had had them installed a few years before when the Housing and Development Board (HDB) offered to do these for free. Our home is one of those old flats where the bathroom and toilet are in separate compartments. This was actually a blessing in disguise because Mum is still strong and can hold on to these bars that were anchored onto the toilet wall as I clean her. The drawback is that she can't be wheeled into either compartment as there isn't enough room. So it's a good thing that Mum is rather petite and I am a big lump, which makes it easier for me to "manhandle" her and carry her short distances between the wheelchair and wherever she needs to be. Point to note, though, petite doesn't mean light. She can be deadweight if she decides not to hold herself up and then you feel like you're hauling a sack of potatoes.

Before her discharge, the hospital made sure to equip me with skills on how to move her to and from the wheelchair, as well as how to bathe her. These were fine, in theory, but once you get home and the situation is different, you have to figure out how best to adapt to the environment.

Taking her home was the easy part. Trying to care for her in her "new" condition was another matter. I didn't mind rearranging my life to suit a schedule that included looking after her. But as with most things, there were teething problems. The biggest one was when she kept fighting me about exercise. I tried to get to her to walk. She would move a little and then complain that it was painful and wanted to sit down. I tried to explain that it was the lack of exercise that contributed to the pain. We would usually end up quarrelling with each other. And Mum can be a drama-mama. She would pound her chest and ask God to take her home. I swear if Darwin were here, he would have pointed to her as the proof that humans, monkeys, and apes had a common ancestor.

In the end, I was the one who gave up. Honestly, the only person who was getting exasperated (to put it mildly) was me. After all, it was more my own hope that she would get back to what she was, able to walk and do basic things on her own. But she was older and that iron will she had previously lay in one of her synapses that wasn't connected any more. Once I accepted that this would be the new normal, I became less stressed.

To be fair, Mum's relatively easy to look after. She may need help with toileting and bathing but she is still able to feed herself once you cut up the food into smaller bites and she doesn't need a lot of attention. She's happy playing games on her tablet and if we're at home, spends most of her time in her geriatric chair, just playing her games. I take her with me when I meet my friends, who have been extremely accepting of the situation.

But there is a downside to all this. I still have to juggle work and caregiving duties and when you're chasing deadlines over a space of a few weeks, poor Mum sometimes has to be cooped up in the house, just like I am. Like it is with everyone, I notice that taking her out, even for a few hours, is beneficial for her and she's a bit more alert. So trying to find the right balance isn't so easy especially when work is just as important as you need the income to pay the bills.

And I will myself not to fall sick. No matter how poorly I'm feeling (and this happens when I don't get enough sleep), I still have to get up and tend to Mum. For a time, I gave up on doing courses because that meant someone would have to look after Mum in my absence. Thankfully, more institutions are offering fully-online courses so there is hope for the future. The next thing is I'm telling myself not to do is burn out. I can feel it starting to happen and I know I need a holiday, but the cost of respite care does not come cheap. Neither are staycations, as I discovered when I had to have cataract surgery done and the family had to look after Mum during that time.

Sure, you can call for help. The family is always willing to help but, personally, I don't think it's fair to them. I was the one who made the decision to look after my mother. So, while asking for help once in a while is fine, it isn't right to expect them to help every single time. A friend commented the other day that I seem to be coping well with the situation as she has a cousin who was in a similar situation and was extremely unhappy.

I didn't know what I was getting myself into and I still don't know what is to come, but I do know that with a willingness to try and learn new things, plus a heavy dose of humour and the support of family and friends, I will get by.

In my twilight years

Things seem rather uncertain as I edge towards my own twilight years. I have to admit that I am less than optimistic about having too many perks that currently exist (e.g. all the various grants, Pioneer Generation, Merdeka Generation) when I am old. Given that we've taken such a long time to get to where we are now, even though we've known for decades what the demographic was going to be like, I can only dream that of what I hope will be.

In the slew of initiatives targeted at the silver generation that cropped up after the pandemic, many seem to be aimed at the elderly who have children to look after them. One area that has been overlooked is that in the coming decades, many older folks will be singles who do not have children to look after or support them. It would be unfair to expect our siblings' children to do so as they have their own parents to look after. Keep in mind that many couples only have one child and that one child has to look after both parents. If you start adding on aunts and uncles, that's going to be too much for just one person to bear.

Ideally, of course, most of us single elderly would like to be independent. Assuming that I am able too, I would hope to still stay in my current home as I tend to be a creature of habit and am very comfortable where I am. However, I would like to see the flat being fitted with some of the amenities found in the assisted-living quarters such as the 24-hour emergency monitoring and response service as well as the housekeeping, laundry, caregiving and meal delivery services. The question is, of course, will we be able to afford this, especially if we are unable to work or earn anymore? When it comes to money, there are no easy answers. Government subsidies and grants would be beneficial but may not be feasible in the long run. One way might be to implement a scheme (something like an insurance-type endowment plan) where we put a certain amount toward paying for these amenities. After all, our finances will become more finite as we get older and not all of us may have passive income to tide us through. So something needs to be done while we are still able to get money in.

In the event that I need a nobility device to get around and doctors advise that I shouldn't be on my own, I hope that by then there would be something like a retirement village cum nursing home. Instead of living in a whole flat, it would be more like renting an en suite room in a community and as part of the rental you would get medical care, be allowed to move around in some sort of mobility device, have some community interaction and still be able to live fairly normally. My friends and I (single and widowed) once chatted about possibly having something like this. Jokingly, we even wondered if we could get a group discount if we all *choped* a place together at the same time.

My practical mind tells me that this type of retirement accommodation is not likely to materialise during my lifetime. So if I do need dedicated caregiving help, it would be good if there were specialised agencies that trained caregivers for this. It would be akin to a domestic helper but one who wanted to look after old people and understand what it entails. Ahbudden… how to pay for these "skilled" workers, especially, as mentioned, our finances are dwindling? Another scheme, perhaps, or a rider to the previous one for the flat?

If I am still mobile, I would still like to be able to travel a little. It would be good to have more insurance companies cover those over 80 (currently, I think only one does). I'm hoping to see more travel agencies or platforms offering special packages for the elderly. Something catered specially to those who can't walk fast or eat much but still want to experience a different slice of the world, even if it's just for a few days. And at an affordable cost. If they can also plan specialised trips for those who need mobility assistance, even better. This is sorely lacking now when you can't even plan a staycation in Singapore if someone is in a wheelchair, without making special arrangements and paying extra. It is just as bad if you want to go for a quick trip to a resort in a neighbouring country.

PATRICIA NG has two degrees, in English with Management and in Communication Studies and English Language. She was in book retail for six years and, safe for short forays into education, jewellery, and healthcare, has been in publishing for more than 25 years, working in established companies such as Marshall Cavendish and Scholastic Education. She authored All in the Name of Lust *and set up the publishing unit for SingHealth Academy. She has worked on many titles as a freelance editor, one of which is* Super Scaling *which won the Best Professional Title at the 2022 Book Awards in Singapore.*

"If you want to create change, you have to do it and not just say or think about it. We all have a role to play in whatever capacity we have."

~ **Pioneering Paralympic swimmer and advocate for disability sports Theresa Goh, speaking to The Straits Times, Sep 2019**

CHAPTER 34

Reimagining Care for the Elderly

Christopher Len

Caregiving for the elderly is a growing trend with our ageing Singapore population. In 2019, the local media reported that in an ageing Singapore there were over 210,000 caregivers and counting, with some 70 per cent of them aged 40 and above. As a guy in his mid-40s who left his job mid-career to look after his ailing mother, I became part of those statistics.

Generally speaking, a caregiver is someone who provides direct care to another person who is not fully independent, be it a child, an elderly person or someone who is ill. In my case, I took a further step by leaving my job to become a full-time caregiver. My decision caught my friends and colleagues by surprise. It caught me by surprise too.

A career break was something I had been thinking about for some time. Friends who know me have heard of my yearning to climb some mountains in Asia, go on extended meditation retreats, and to spend quality time with myself in self-reflection. While dithering on this idea, Covid-19 came along and the lock-down made such plans impossible. Ironically, my mother's sudden illness propelled me into such a decision as it was increasingly difficult juggling caregiving duties and my work responsibilities. Looking after her became the mountain I had to climb. I did not choose this mountain; it literally came to me!

Harsh reality

I experienced what a community aged-care physician referred to as the 'harsh reality' of caring for an aged parent. I was one of those who stumbled into caregiving with little preparation or warning as my mother became ill quite suddenly. In the initial months, I did not even recognise myself as a caregiver, even as the caregiving commitments crept up on me. I thought that my mother's illness was temporary, and she would soon recover to become her independent self again.

As weeks turned into months, I observed my mother's growing frailty and increasing need for dedicated attention and it was only then that that it dawned on me that I had become my mum's day-to-day caregiver. I have friends who are primary caregivers. I also recall my mother looking after my grandparents — my grandmother suffered from chronic illnesses while my grandfather had Alzheimer's — when I was young. Yet somehow, I was blind to my own circumstance until the creeping responsibilities started taking over my life.

In the course of reading up on caregiving, I came across an interesting quote by Rosalynn Carter, the Former First Lady of the United States. She noted that "[t]here are only four kinds of people in this world: those who have been caregivers, those who are currently caregivers, those who will be caregivers, and those who will need caregivers".

In this respect, caregiving is a universal issue that will affect everyone. A greying society does not just concern the elderly. There are wider serious knock-on effects for the family caregivers who are usually not compensated and bear the brunt of the responsibilities. Personal sacrifices have to be made, and while I did so without hesitation, there is always this lingering thought at the back of my head wondering if things could have been managed differently without me having to quit my job. Family caregiving is very much invisible work and I turned into a stay-at-home invisible worker, attempting to climb a mountain that many a times felt impossible to conquer.

Women are said to make up the majority of family caregivers and this adds another layer of concern for me. After showering my mother with a lot of love, care and attention — and thanks to the Singapore health system — my mother's condition has stabilised. As a man preparing to re-enter the workforce soon, I often think about how the potential employer would perceive me. I have read about the difficulties stay-at-home mothers face when they try to re-enter the workforce with employers questioning their qualifications and commitment. Are there return-to-work programmes ('returnships') to support stay-at-home-sons like me?

It was only through this direct experience when I personally realised the implications of our greying society on families and individuals. This demographic time bomb is a major challenge, and I could not help but wonder about my own future. As a man in my forties who is unmarried and without children, who is going to take care of me? Can I afford quality care and live a fulfilling and dignified life as I age? Is there any value in having a longer life expectancy if I do not have a healthy quality of life?

Changing family dynamics

I will reach retirement age in about 20 years and by then, the world will be a very different place. Just think about what the world was like 20 years ago. There are clear generational differences because of evolving societal norms, changing individual circumstances, and advancement in scientific knowledge and medical treatments. These developments will affect how successive generations are to be cared for. Whereas having three generations living under one roof was the prevailing norm in the past, post-baby boomers like myself increasingly prefer to live separate from our parents given the choice. The numbers of single person households and married couples without children are also on the rise.

These trends will inevitably have an impact on the availability of support, as well as the nature of care to be provided when people like me turn elderly. Even those with children will more likely end up living alone in empty nests as the younger generation are more individualistic and tend to want better privacy and autonomy.

Also, more and more Singaporeans are working and living abroad and thus unable to care for their parents. Unlike the older generation who traditionally expect and rely on their children for caregiving as an expression of filial piety, the younger generation expect the government to do more through public policy and state institutions to support their retirement and caregiving needs, shifting the burden of welfare support away from their children. The post-baby boomers are also more open to end-of-life planning such as creating a will, having a Lasting Power of Attorney in place, as well as determining treatment preferences through the Advance Medical Directive.

Looking into the future

The Singapore Government to its credit has been making comprehensive plans for an ageing population for decades with greater resources allocated towards various healthcare, housing, and financial initiatives. However, I feel that there is room for bolder policies. What would I like to see take shape? I have listed three suggestions below.

Improved caregiver support

First, I think the philosophy of care in caregiving needs to proactively include both the individual under care and the caregiver. Very often, the family caregiver, who plays the most critical role looking after the loved one, stumbles into the role without much knowledge and experience. A new caregiver is usually so overwhelmed by the tasks and responsibilities towards the sick person that one often neglects one's own needs.

Caregiver support should be part of an integral approach and not a secondary focus. A key consideration for my decision to become a full-time caregiver was that I wanted to enjoy quality time with my mother while she is still conscious and able to appreciate our time together. It is important to improve the caregiver experience so that caregiving does not become an overwhelmingly negative experience. Preventive care is important for the caregiver. I want to prolong my mother's life without shortening mine!

There are various initiatives in place such as the Agency for Integrated Care's Caregiver Support Action Plan, and the Care Corner's Caregiver Support programme. But to be honest, I only learned about caregiver support after struggling to cope on my own.

While I appreciate the attention given to my mother during her health checks and support from various community care groups who call me to check on her needs, it occurred to me belatedly that no one checked on my well-being as the primary caregiver. If my memory serves me right, it was at a later period, when she was assigned to the Centre for Geriatric Medicine at Tan Tock Seng Hospital, that a staff member asked if I needed any support myself.

We need to increase public awareness of caregiving issues and caregiver support as part of Singapore's healthy ageing campaign. Various organisations such as the Tsao Foundation, Lien Foundation, Association of Women for Action and Research (AWARE), the Next Age Institute at the National University of Singapore, Fei Yue Community Services, and TOUCH Community Services have done a lot of research identifying gaps and providing feedback.

Several recommendations that would have been helpful in my case are in the areas of early engagement and orientation of the family caregiver to help them navigate the resources available to them, extended paid caregiver leave for those having to look after their elderly parents, more affordable home healthcare services, as well as improved financial support for full-time caregivers whose careers, income and retirement plans have been disrupted. Caregiver stress is real; proactive engagement at an early stage will help to pre-empt elder neglect and abuse, as well as caregiver burnout.

National Service through community work

Second, another dimension in the philosophy of care in caregiving should be the notion of social and community integration. Assisted living which emphasises independence, autonomy, and privacy should be encouraged, with integrated care and support services rooted within the wider community. Loneliness and social isolation are a serious health risk for the elderly. While writing this piece, I recalled that when I was studying in Edinburgh I had volunteered as a part-time home help to a bedbound Scottish lady living alone. Back then, I always wondered why she talked so much instead of giving me actual chores to do. I have now come to realise that it was due to her loneliness.

In discussing caregiving in Singapore, we need to think about our current heavy reliance on overseas domestic workers. They may be hired for a caregiving role, but live-in domestic helpers are usually not certified caregivers who can provide specialised care. Even if they are, there are real risks involved in our heavy reliance on overseas workers. What if our neighbouring countries suddenly restrict their citizens from being deployed in Singapore as live-in help? Or if Singapore loses its economic competitiveness in the future and is no longer a choice destination for these workers? It is therefore timely to explore expanding the local pool of caregivers. One way to do this is to expand mandatory National Service to include women.

The notion of women performing national service through community work, including eldercare, is not a new one. It is something worth considering. The enlistment of women should not be on the basis of gender equality but to address a practical gap in social services. The eldercare community work option should not be restricted to women only, since men are increasingly taking up family caregiving duties, too.

The knowledge and skills acquired during this period, ranging from preventive care to performing home help services such as feeding and medicating to managing the elderly with mental illness and physical disabilities to supporting people with special needs, will continue to be relevant after national service, given the universal nature of caregiving. Those who are interested in developing their careers in this sector can then have the option to continue through public and private care providers.

I believe that this type of engagement will help combat negative stereotypes and ageism, nurture a culture of caregiving, facilitate intergenerational bonding, and ultimately draw our nation closer together. Caregiving is also relevant in times of war and should be regarded through the lens of Total Defence. After all, when the army fights in the frontline, skilled carers are needed in the rear to look after the sick, injured, disabled, and the elderly.

Euthanasia

Third, following the repeal of Section 377A which criminalised sex between men, I think our society is mature enough now to open discussion on another taboo subject — euthanasia, also known as assisted dying. Here, I am referring to very sick people having the option of ending their life before their suffering becomes too great.

There are complex moral, ethical, religious, and legal issues associated with this topic. A lot has been written on this so I will not repeat the for-and-against arguments here. What I note (and applaud) is that Singapore already has the Advance Medical Directive which, according to the Ministry of Health, "is a legal document that one signs in advance to inform the doctor treating oneself (in the event of terminal illness and unconsciousness) that one does not want any extraordinary life-sustaining treatment to be used to prolong one's life".

Personally, I would like my options to go one step further. Should I have a terminal illness, I want to be able to decide when to take my leave with dignity rather than have to suffer through the ravages of the disease.

Conclusion

It was only when I started looking after my mother as her primary caregiver that I realised the implications of our greying society. Ageing and the role of caregiving are pivotal issues that require comprehensive and bold solutions. Faced with a rapidly ageing population and changing family dynamics, Singapore needs to address the issue of adequate healthcare and social services support while ensuring that they are sustainable in the long term. This is to enhance the quality of life for Singapore's ageing population and their caregivers alike.

DR CHRISTOPHER LEN obtained his PhD from the Centre for Energy, Petroleum and Mineral Law and Policy (CEPMLP) at the University of Dundee in Scotland where he was awarded the Dean's Medal for Research. He also has degrees from the University of Edinburgh, Scotland and Uppsala University, Sweden. He was awarded the Commendation Medal (Pingat Kepujian) by the President of the Republic of Singapore at the 2021 National Day Awards for his work at the National University of Singapore.

"Place-making and place management includes a vision about how people use a place. Don't forget the people."

~ Urban planner Cheong Koon Hean, speaking to Challenge, Public Service Division, January 2012

CHAPTER 35

When I'm Sixty-Four: A Love Letter to the Future

Emma Goh

A t the tender age of 15, Paul McCartney of The Beatles wrote and composed "When I'm Sixty-Four", a song that captures the sentiments of a young man looking towards the future with anxious anticipation, wondering if his lover would still be there for him in his old age. Taking a leaf out of McCartney's book, this essay represents my love letter to the future, as I wonder if there might still be a home for me in the Singapore of my old age.

In my letter, penned from the point of a view of 24-year-old cynical idealist, I write about my anxieties about ageing in Singapore that have occupied my thoughts of late. I then, rather boldly, depict the Singapore of the future that I hope I can grow old in. As an aspiring urbanist, I envisage how the built environment can be re-fashioned to create a more empowering and sustaining environment where older adults can truly bask in their sunset years.

When I am sixty-four, I hope to see more spaces of empowerment for older adults in our neighbourhoods. Declines in physical and cognitive functioning inevitably result in lower mobility among older adults and a shrinking of their life-space. Yet, life-space mobility is vital to support autonomous participation in social life and the exploration of meaningful outlets of engagement.

These are critical in contributing to a greater sense of visibility, connectedness and purpose among older adults, aspects of life that might get diminished as one ages. Since we cannot drastically reverse diminishing mobility among older adults, what can be done to improve the quality of their life-spaces? I would like to envision creating more diverse and denser spaces of empowerment for older adults in our neighbourhoods, even if their life spaces are perceived to be more restricted.

At present, we have observed the expanding network of Active Aging Centres (AACs) all over Singapore (typically located in void decks) which aims to help older adults stay engaged and socially active. Established by the Agency for Integrated Care (AIC), AACs function as drop-in recreational centres for seniors living in the neighbourhood and go-to points for them to strengthen social connections, take part in recreational activities and contribute to the community.

Undoubtedly, AACs play an important role in enabling older adults to age in place. However, their set-up reproduces a sense of environmental determinism by designating the types of activities that can take place in a particular area. Seniors, upon the nudging of grassroot volunteers or their neighbours or at times on their own accord, gather at AACs to take part in karaoke, arts and craft, cooking and exercise programmes provided by the centre management. Seniors are occupied, entertained and at best stimulated, but I would venture to ask if such a backdrop is most conducive for empowered aging, where empowerment is defined by the building of capacities and connections?

Recently, the phenomenon of "seniors for seniors" has started to gain steam in AACs and we have seen an increase in the number of seniors organising and running activities and outreach initiatives among themselves. This is an encouraging step towards more empowered forms of active aging. But looking into the future, how else can the built environment be enhanced to facilitate more empowered forms of active aging? Can we imagine a landscape where the more structured and deterministic environments of AACs are complemented with more fluid and dynamic spaces of recreation where older adults have a freer rein to enact active aging on their own terms?

A dream comes to life

In 2022, five retirees opened Dakota Dreams, a little bookshop nestled between clothing and hardware stores on the second floor of Old Airport Road Hawker Centre. It sells children's books and comics by Singapore authors, pre-loved titles and crafts made by seniors (Ho 2022). The books might be the bookshop's mainstay, but it does so much more than just sell books. The founders intended for the bookshop to serve as a cozy nook for seniors to hang out, especially those who were seeking more social connection.

A year on, it has lived up to its founders' aspirations and more. Despite its unassuming façade, the bookshop has grown to become a collaborative space for pop-up events and a platform to spur conversations between and weave diverse perspectives across different communities. Dakota Dreams represents a pioneering example of placemaking, community organising and active ageing in a more independent and empowered form. It speaks volumes to me because it provides a glimpse of a future where seniors are more than just beneficiaries of existing structures of ageing in place but are the vanguard of a movement to shape the conversation around active ageing and extend it across generations.

In the Singapore I want to grow old in, I see the proliferation of such catalytic spaces within neighbourhoods or the life-spaces of older adults. This is not to mean that I am diminishing the role of top-down active-ageing programmes, like AACs. Instead, I hope that we can diversify the present active ageing ecosystem and give seniors the opportunity to pilot new initiatives that speak to a wider spectrum of lifestyles, skills and aspirations.

To translate this vision into reality, however, we need to start by pondering how we can foster more collaborative networks among older adults. Some might say that the stars aligned for the founders of Dakota Dreams since they were already friends and had some prior connection to the book industry. How do we get current and future cohorts of older adults to converse, ideate and collaborate? What kinds of resources are necessary to kickstart such ground-up initiatives without compromising the retirement financial adequacy of our seniors?

For example, the National Youth Council provides the Young ChangeMakers Grant to support youth-initiated projects that aim to benefit the community. Can there be an equivalent grant for senior-initiated community projects? Finally, what does it take to create more sustaining environments where pioneering active ageing projects like Dakota Dreams are more than just one hit wonders but are, instead, affirmed and nurtured by the wider community?

Caring spaces for caregivers

When I am sixty-four, I hope that we live in neighbourhoods where caregivers will also be cared for. So much of ageing in place is reliant on the work done by informal or family caregivers. Choosing to live and age in one's place of residence for as long as they can is often not only dependent on the choice of the individual. So much invisible labour, everyday recalibrations and psycho-emotional toil is needed on the part of caregivers to sustain the care recipient's choice to age in place, which remains the preferred option for most Singaporeans.

In 2018, the National Council of Social Service (NCSS) conducted a study to understand the quality of life of informal or family caregivers. The study sought to examine the well-being of caregivers and to provide a holistic view of the aspects of life deemed important to them. The study found that more than half of the caregivers reported being "burdened" or "barely coping" and having lower self-efficacy scores, especially caregivers who lived with their care recipients (National Council of Social Service 2022). Caregivers reported lowest quality of life scores in recreation and leisure, financial adequacy, sleep and rest, and positive feelings (National Council of Social Service 2022).

Even though caregiving arrangements have compromised the quality of life of caregivers, the study noted that less than 3 in 10 caregivers made use of external caregiving services. Understandably, 44 per cent of caregivers cited "cost of service" as a perceived barrier to utilising care services. More than a third, or 37 per cent, of caregivers had to provide care on their own, and an overwhelming majority of caregivers were female (69.6 per cent) (National Council of Social Services 2022).

This brief snapshot of the state of caregiver well-being points towards the need to channel more resources towards supporting caregivers. At present, the caregiver service landscape in Singapore does seek to fill the gaps by offering a range of social services in the areas of psychosocial, caregiver, respite care, financial and workplace support. However, the built environment and in particular, the neighbourhood, remain under-explored avenues in which more caregiver support can stem from.

In the Singapore where I want to grow old, I see the neighbourhood, as the predominant life space of caregivers and care recipients, being the first line of support for caregivers. I remember a caregiver recounting to me how participating in a caregiver support group was the first time she experienced a cathartic release since taking on the role of caregiver to her mother who was living with dementia. However, this moment of catharsis had been delayed many times over because she could not spare the opportunity cost of leaving her mother alone for a while and commuting to the venue where the support group was being held. Since caregivers often find it hard to carve out space, time and resources to care for themselves, can we instead bring care services directly to caregivers, within the comfort of their neighbourhoods?

Learning from Bogota

We can turn to Bogota for inspiration. Over there, Care Blocks, funded by the municipal government, provide a range of free offerings for female caregivers including community laundry facilities, physical wellness activities, health services, psycho-social support, legal aid, upskilling courses, cultural activities and opportunities for socialiding, whilst also offering care assistance by professional staff (Khosla 2023). Care Blocks are strategically located in areas of the city with existing municipal services and within walking distance from residential estates to render essential caregiving services and wellness resources for caregivers.

As part of their efforts to reframe caregiving as a less gendered activity, Care Blocks have a Care School catered towards men, where caregiving and homemaking training are provided. Care assistance by the state is costly to sustain in the long run and remains, at best, a temporary measure to the care gap. It is hence imperative for men to be included in the unpaid care work equation to alleviate the caregiving burden disproportionately borne by women and allow for more sustainable modes of caregiving.

Care Blocks are just one example of how our neighbourhoods can be transformed to better support the needs of informal caregivers. While Care Blocks would require heftier financial investment, greater institutional buy-in and might take longer to implement, we can pilot micro-level interventions in the short run. These interventions do not have to be radical ideas and can build upon existing spaces, initiatives and momentums. Why not include sensory gardens, designed to reduce stress, as part of our community gardening initiatives or have void decks function as active aging centres by day and women-friendly bars or cafes at night as an outlet for caregivers to decompress.

The well-being of caregivers is not only negatively impacted at present (whilst caring for their relatives) but might also be compromised in the future. Given Singapore's sub-replacement fertility rates, the caregivers of today will find themselves with a smaller or non-existent next generation of caregivers to depend on. Present caregivers are also less able to independently provide for themselves in their old-age due to reduced retirement adequacy, since their careers were disrupted when they supported their relatives to age in place earlier in life. Hence, caregivers need to be uplifted and empowered in more ways. The built environment, and in particular the neighbourhood, is one avenue in which more can be done.

Not just all in the family

When I am sixty-four, I hope to live in a Singapore that is more amenable towards living with friends in our twilight years. There is a growing phenomenon of older Singaporeans living alone. In 2020, 10.per cent of Singaporean adults aged 65 years and above lived alone. This figure was 8.2 per cent and 6.6 per cent in 2010 and 2000 respectively (Wong, Wong, and Feng 2022). There are also significantly more women than men who live alone, which is likely due to women's longer life expectancy and higher chances of remaining single and being widowed. This is a sobering reality, and its implications are concerning — without a household nucleus to fall back on, who will seniors turn to for economic, socio-emotional and caregiving support? How will changing household compositions affect seniors' well-being?

The Singapore social compact continues to uphold the family as the first line of support for older adults. At present, family members do play an integral role in providing finances, resources, and housing for older adults. But is this a tenable prospect for the future? Shrinking family sizes caused by falling fertility rates, later marriages, increasing non-marriage rates, and increasing rates of divorce point towards a reduction in the number of family members available to provide support to older Singaporeans. This is why I think we need to do more to normalise and scale up senior co-housing options where older adults can live alongside their friends.

Senior co-housing, or the concept of a group of active seniors living in a residential community and being able to access opportunities for socialisation, mutual support and agieng in place, is not a recent invention. In fact, it is one of the fastest growing forms of senior housing models in the world. In our local context, seniors have the option of living with their friends through the Community Care Apartments (CCA) scheme that offers assisted living in Housing and Development Board (HDB) flats. CCAs are about 32 sqm in size and sold on shorter leases (Housing and Development Board n.d.).

However, as Chua Mui Hoong posits in her op-ed "Senior Housing: Why not assisted living in every HDB block?", we need more than just dispersed CCAs across different HDB estates (Chua 2023). Instead, a cluster of CCAs within each precinct (a few blocks of flats) is needed to provide a critical mass to generate a sense of care and connectedness. Chua also suggests that this critical mass should be undergirded by a swell of friendship, human connection and community participation amongst seniors living in the same neighbourhood. Hence, the gap in senior housing might not only be one of a lack of physical infrastructure but also a lack of social infrastructure.

I echo Chua's sentiments that stronger bonds of friendship are needed to sustain the physical infrastructure design to enable older adults to age in place. However, public housing in Singapore has repeatedly been used to signify and institutionalise the hetero-normative family nucleus as an ideal (Teo 2013), as argued by Teo You Yenn (another contributor in this volume). The pro-family policies, as reified and articulated through our public housing policies, have created a situation where the nuclear family has become the dominant currency used to navigate public systems.

We need to change this if we want our senior co-housing model to truly be sustained by a critical mass of friendship and bonds beyond the nuclear family. Our housing policies need to be pro-friend and not just pro-family.

For example, the HDB can consider allowing young adults to experience a co-living environment with their friends at a subsidized rate before they decide to purchase their own flats to set up their own family nuclei. Another suggestion can be to lower the qualifying age of CCAs from 65 years to 60 or even 55 years to give the young-old a shot at co-living earlier on in their lives.

These policy changes will help to normalise the idea of building a home with our friends and allow older adults to make that transition more naturally when the time comes. When I think of my retirement, I see not just one supposed soulmate but the faces of those whom I would call my platonic life partners. I hope to grow old in a Singapore that allows me to enjoy a continuum of care from our public housing system and that lets friends build a home together in their twilight years.

In this love letter to the future, I have put forth three ways in which the built environment can be enlivened and reinvigorated to better empower older adults, provide care for caregivers, and support senior co-housing models with friendship as its bedrock.

Is this just a pipe dream? Not at all. As an urbanist, I know it can be done. And as a young Singaporean, I want it to be done so that I can look towards my older years with hope, whether it be 64 or 84 or 104.

EMMA GOH is a Master of City Planning candidate at the University of California, Berkeley. Prior to graduate school, she worked as a Research Assistant at the Lee Kuan Yew Centre for Innovative Cities where she critically explored issues relating to ageing urbanism and urban innovation. When she is not mulling over rabbit-hole-like questions such as how to make cities more just and inclusive places, she can be found engaging in existential escapades at East Coast Park. She graduated with a Bachelor of Arts (Urban Studies) from Yale-NUS College in 2022.

References

Agency for Integrated Care. n.d. "Active Ageing Centres and Active Ageing Centres (Care)". Agency for Integrated Care. Accessed 13 October 2023. https://www.aic.sg:443/care-services/active-ageing-centre.

Chua Mui Hoong. 2023. "Senior Housing: Why Not Assisted Living Units in Every HDB Block?" *The Straits Times*, 19 May 2023.

Ho, Olivia. 2022. "Retirees Open Bookstore at Old Airport Road Hawker Centre". *The Straits Times*, 2 January 2022. https://www.straitstimes.com/life/arts/retirees-open-bookstore-at-old-airport-road-hawker-centre.

Housing and Development Board. n.d. "HDB | Community Care Apartments". Accessed 13 October 2023. https://www.hdb.gov.sg/residential/buying-a-flat/finding-a-flat/types-of-flats/community-care-apartments.

Khosla, Prabha. 2023. "Bogota: Centring Women's Care Work as a Core Municipal Function". *Urbanet*. 18 July 2023. https://www.urbanet.info/centering-womens-care-work-bogota/.

National Council of Social Service. 2022. "Understanding the Quality of Life of Caregivers". National Council of Social Service. https://www.ncss.gov.sg/docs/default-source/ncss-publications-doc/pdfdocument/qol-caregiver-report.pdf.

Teo, Youyenn. 2013. *Neoliberal Morality in Singapore: How Family Policies Make State and Society*. Oxford: Routledge.

Wong Kwok Wing, Wong Wei Lin, and Feng Huimin. 2022. "Demographic Profile of Seniors in Singapore". *Statistics Singapore Newsletter* (1). https://www.singstat.gov.sg/-/media/files/publications/population/ssn122-pg6-9.ashx.

"Retirement should not mean being put out to pasture. It is the time to build another, useful life of quality. After all, we are special. In our retirement, we are neither parasites nor pests!"

~ Champion of farming Ivy Singh-Lim, writing for Social Space, Singapore Management University, 2009

CHAPTER 36

Aged to Imperfection?
Stop Worrying about Our
Ageing Society: What We Need
is an Age-integrated Longevity Society

Kanwaljit Soin and Margaret Thomas

Are you sexist? Since you are reading this book, probably not. Might you be racist? Again, probably not, though we all need to be alert to the possibility of unconscious bias creeping into our thoughts and actions.

The odds are very high, however, that you are ageist.

Ageism is everywhere — in our institutions, in the media, in national and corporate policies, in our relationships. And in ourselves.

Consider this: If you are middle-aged or older, have you not sometimes ruefully said 'senior moment' when you have been confused or forgotten something? Why do we do this? Young people also get confused or forget things, but they don't apologetically say 'junior moment'. So why are we playing into the narrative that being 'senior' turns us into bumbling old fools?

Because we are continuously exposed to negative images, stories, and messages about older people, and our brains get wired to believe that getting old means going downhill both cognitively and physically. The media plays a big role in perpetuating these stereotypes. Older people are, all too often, portrayed as frail, sickly, dependent, cranky, confused, ill-informed, fearful of technology, less adaptable, resistant to change, unable to learn new skills.

It doesn't help that policymakers and pundits tend to point in horror to the impending 'silver tsunami' and how ageing baby boomers riddled with chronic ailments and declining mental faculties will flood hospitals and care facilities and soak up public funds and become a fiscal burden that will have to be borne by the shrinking pool of income-earning and tax-paying younger people.

So ageing has got this really bad reputation, and this is fuelling ageism and making so many of us ageists. Like the sexist and the racist, the ageist has fallen into the trap of 'othering' — looking at a group of people as being distinct from us, as being markedly different from us. This is what leads to bias and prejudice.

Gerontologist and author Dr Robert Butler, who coined the term 'ageism' in 1971, identified three aspects of ageism: Prejudicial attitudes towards older people and the ageing process; discriminatory practices against older people; institutional practices and policies that perpetuate stereotypes about the elderly.

Ageism can, of course, also affect young people. Their job opportunities and career progression can be affected if employers have set ideas about who they want to hire and promote. Job advertisements may specify a minimum number of years of experience, for example. And a young person with the skills and maturity to manage a team may not be considered for a leadership position because the employer thinks they do not have enough experience or that the other workers may not accept a young team leader.

Like the other 'isms', ageism separates and divides society, and it is harmful at both the individual and the collective level. For individuals, ageism can contribute to poverty or financial insecurity in older age if they are unable to continue working and earning an income. At the societal level it can cost billions of dollars in terms of health and social services, and lost productivity.

Global campaign

Ageism is so entrenched that, according to the World Health Organization (WHO), one of two people in the world has ageist attitudes.

In 2021 WHO launched a global campaign to combat ageism because of the serious and far-reaching consequences for people's health, well-being, and human rights. Its Global Report on Ageism[1] looks at the impact of ageism and offers policymakers, civil society, and the public at large an action plan to reduce ageism and 'create a world for all ages'.

The WHO report says that for older people, ageism is associated with a shorter lifespan, poorer physical and mental health, slower recovery from disability, and cognitive decline. It reduces older people's quality of life, increases their social isolation and loneliness (both of which are associated with serious health problems), and

---

[1] https://www.who.int/publications/i/item/9789240016866

restricts their ability to express their sexuality. Ageism may increase the risk of violence and abuse against older people while for younger people, it can reduce commitment to the organisation they work for.

Importantly, the WHO report refutes many misconceptions about ageing. There is, for instance, no 'typical' older person as there is great diversity amongst old people. The physical and mental capacity of some 80-year-olds is comparable to that of many 30- or 40-year-olds.

People age very differently, and age is not a reliable indicator of someone's potential productivity or employability. Chronological age does not equate with function, and it does not equate with cognition. And yet it is chronological age that determines when most people leave the workforce.

Ageism at the workplace

In Singapore, the retirement age is now 63 and the re-employment age is 68, which means that workers can, in theory, continue in their jobs for up to five more years. The government plans to raise these to 65 and 70 by 2030. Surveys have shown that the majority of workers in Singapore welcome the higher retirement ages, but many older workers are concerned about age discrimination at the workplace.

A survey[2] conducted by the PAP Seniors Group and National Trades Union Congress (NTUC) in August 2023 asked some 1,500 workers aged 50 and above what were the top challenges and barriers they faced at work. Nearly two-thirds (63.4%) said negative employer attitudes and age discrimination, while almost as many (59.6%) pointed to inflexible working arrangements or long working hours.

---

[2] https://www.ntuc.org.sg/uportal/news/NTUC-and-PAP-Seniors-Group-push-for-age-inclusive-initiatives-and-champion-employment-rights/

Half of them were concerned about suitable job opportunities being available.

Another survey[3] done by NTUC at the end of 2022 of workers aged 20 years and above found a decline in the training participation rate as a worker got older. Employers have 'certain prejudices and assumptions' about older workers' ability to pick up new skills or their willingness to learn.

Meanwhile, a survey[4] of 1,000 workers in 2022 by gender equality advocacy group the Association of Women for Action and Research (Aware) and consumer research company Milieu Insight found that one in two workers in Singapore said he or she had experienced workplace discrimination in the past five years. The top reason for the discrimination was race (41%), and age (35%) was the second most common reason.

Recognising the problem of ageism at the workplace, the Singapore government began some time ago to offer incentives such as wage subsidies to encourage employers to retain or engage older workers. The workplace fairness legislation due to come into effect in 2024 will include protection against age discrimination, but much more is needed if we are to shift the assumptions and attitudes that are keeping businesses from making better use of Singapore's mature workforce.

When a significant proportion of older and middle-aged people are unemployed, especially those in the lowest income groups, they will become more dependent on informal family assistance, government transfers, or charity. This will increase social stratification and social division in the country.

---

[3] https://www.ntuc.org.sg/uportal/news/NTUC-Calls-For-Employers-To-Accord-Older-Workers-Equal-Training-Participation-Media-Release/

[4] https://www.aware.org.sg/2022/09/1-in-2-experienced-workplace-discrimination-aware-milieu-survey/

Ageism and health

Singapore is ageing so fast that by 2030 a quarter of the population will be 65 years and older. To try to ensure that Singaporeans will be as healthy as possible as they age, the government has launched Healthier SG, a visionary system of health care to promote health and prevent disease while continuing to treat chronic disease and injuries.

For Healthier SG to be fully effective, ageism has to be addressed. One of the biggest disruptors of healthy longevity is ageism.

The WHO Global Report on Ageing made this point:

> "*Age-based stereotypes influence behaviours, policy development and even research. Addressing these by combating ageism must lie at the core of any public health response to population ageing. Although this will be challenging, experiences combating other widespread forms of discrimination, such as sexism and racism, show that attitudes and norms can be changed.*"

There is growing evidence that negative and positive self-perceptions of ageing can have profound effects on health and longevity. One study by Yale professor of psychology Dr Becca Levy found that older people with more positive self-perceptions of ageing, measured up to 23 years earlier, lived 7.5 years longer than those with less positive self-perceptions of ageing. This advantage remained after age, gender, socioeconomic status, loneliness, and functional health were included as covariates.

Dr Levy and her group at the Yale School of Public Health have researched ageism for 20 years and she is the leader of the WHO-sponsored review of studies of ageism and health consequences. She has found evidence that older people who see ageing in positive terms are much more likely to recover from disability[5] than those who have a negative view of ageing. They are also more likely to practice preventive health measures[6] such as eating well and exercising. They experience less depression and anxiety.[7] They live longer.[8]

On the other hand, a negative view of ageing will become a self-fulfilling prophecy. The older person who believes that frailty and disease are inevitable consequences of ageing may not see any point in trying to age actively. Their fatalistic outlook will keep them from going for routine health screenings and from a healthy lifestyle.

It is crucial that we consider the effects of ageism as we implement the Healthier SG policies and programmes to keep older people healthy physically and mentally. The evidence is there that positive self-perceptions of ageing trump other social determinants of health; it should be an integral part of our health and social policies.

Ageism and dementia

A study[9] done by Dr Levy and her associates in 2018 suggests that positive age beliefs can act as a protective factor against dementia, even for older individuals at high risk of the disease. This is the first study to link the brain changes related to Alzheimer's disease to a culturally based psychosocial risk factor, that is, ageism.

With negative stereotypes, older people have a higher risk of dementia, the study report said. They have greater accumulations of plaques and tangles in the brain, the biomarkers of Alzheimer's

---

[5] https://jamanetwork.com/journals/jama/fullarticle/1392557
[6] https://pubmed.ncbi.nlm.nih.gov/15313104/
[7] https://www.sciencedirect.com/science/article/abs/pii/S027795361930108X
[8] https://pubmed.ncbi.nlm.nih.gov/12150226/
[9] https://www.ncbi.nlm.nih.gov/pmc/articles/PMC7489069/

disease, and a reduced size of the hippocampus, which is the part of the brain associated with memory.

We have yet to find reliable treatments for Alzheimer's disease, which is the most prevalent cause of dementia. The Singapore statistics for dementia are worrying: one in 10 people over the age of 60 and one in two over the age of 85 have dementia. More than 100,000 people are estimated to have dementia in Singapore. Women have twice the rate of dementia compared to men, and only part of this increased incidence is due to the longer life span of women.

If combatting negative beliefs about ageing offers us a potential way to reduce the rapidly rising rate of Alzheimer's disease, we should seize it and use it to try and reduce the incidence of this personal tragedy and public health issue.

Ageism and women

The gender dimension of ageism is a double blow for women in our modern society that continues to prize youth and 'beauty'. Ageism and sexism join hands at midlife and older women are judged more harshly than men of the same age for their looks and behaviour.

Grey hair and wrinkles are seen as making men look distinguished and experienced, whereas they make women look 'old'. Old age can make women invisible, and many women try to avoid looking old in order to remain socially and professionally engaged. In doing so, they are playing into the ageing narrative.

As Ashton Applewhite, a writer and anti-ageism advocate, points out, "As it is now, women 'compete' to stay young, but all that does is reinforce ageism and sexism."

So what should we do about ageism?

Singapore is one of the fastest ageing countries in the world. We have more people over 65 years old than people under 15 years. If we are to cope effectively with this demographic challenge, we need to convert our ageing society into a longevity society.

A Lancet article[10] offers this wisdom:

"An ageing society focuses on changes in the age structure of the population, whereas a longevity society seeks to exploit the advantages of longer lives through changes in how we age. Achieving a longevity society requires substantial changes in the life course and social norms and involves an epidemiological transition towards a focus on delaying the negative effects of ageing."

Ageism is a major barrier to achieving a longevity society. Dr Becca Levy and her colleagues estimate that age discrimination, negative age stereotypes, and negative self-perceptions of ageing lead to billions of dollars in excess annual spending in the US on common health conditions like cardiovascular and respiratory disease, diabetes, and injuries.

We need data like this about Singapore to spur us to take action against ageism instead of wringing our hands about how the ageing population is pushing up health care costs.

How can we become an age-integrated longevity society?

An age-integrated society builds on the complementarity of qualities and skills of both younger and older people. There are elements of this in the refreshed Action Plan for Successful Ageing.

For example, the plan calls for discussion in schools of ageing related themes and the importance of developing empathy for older people. There is also the suggestion that opportunities be created for older people to offer career guidance to young people via the MySkillsFuture service. Meanwhile, SportsSG will trial an Active

---

[10] https://www.thelancet.com/journals/lanhl/article/PIIS2666-7568(21)00247-6/fulltext

Silver Hub for young and old to interact through sports-related activities.

These are a good start but so much more can be done.

What we must do

We must more vigorously create the conditions for the old and the young to study, work, and live together. Older people want to age and die in the community and not in old age homes.

Ashton Applewhite notes that friendships with people of all ages are a tool to combat ageism. She explains: "People you've known all your life are going to die, and that's why it's so important to have younger friends. We are olders and youngers simultaneously — being friends with older people also makes younger people less afraid of aging."

But in Singapore we have been developing age-separated rather than age-integrated spaces! Building 'active ageing centres' and 'senior living housing' is not the answer. These age-specific facilities accentuate the distancing and divisions in society. We should abandon these ageist policies and consider instead approaches such as the Aconchego[11] programme that was started in 2004 in Porto, the Portuguese city with a large ageing population.

Aconchego aims to increase intergenerational contact by arranging for older people to provide housing to university students. In exchange, the students help alleviate older people's loneliness and isolation.

In Singapore, we can adapt our built environment to create more spaces where old and young interact and support and learn from each other. For example, why not build senior care centres that are

---

[11] https://extranet.who.int/agefriendlyworld/afp/aconchego-program/

also student care centres, with opportunities for the different generations to bond over common interests?

Arguably the most ageist policy of all is the retirement age. Instead of slowly ratcheting up the retirement and re-employment ages, why not just do away with the notion that chronological age determines our employability and productivity? This might seem a radical idea, but we need to be open to radical ideas and to discuss and debate them vigorously if we are to turn our demographic reality into a boon rather than a bane.

If we make the appropriate adjustments, our ageing population could yield an incredible longevity dividend. But first we must get to grips with ageism.

Are our policymakers ready to review and revise their ageist policies? Can employers look beyond chronological age when hiring or retaining people? Will the media stop perpetuating age stereotypes? Can we as individuals stop playing into the narrative that age turns us into bumbling old fools?

We say, Why Not?

* * *

Kanwaljit Soin is an orthopaedic and hand surgeon who retired in 2022 after 56 years in medical practice. She was Singapore's first female Nominated Member of Parliament (1992–1996). She was inducted to the Singapore Women's Hall of Fame in 2014. A founding member of AWARE (Association of Women for Action and Research) in 1985, she was its president from 1991 to 1993. She was the founding chair of the Singapore chapter of the United Nations Development Fund for Women (UNIFEM) and the founding president of Women's Initiative for Ageing Successfully

(WINGS). She has received the Singapore Medical Association Merit Award, the International Women's Forum's Women Who Make a Difference Award, a UNIFEM Lifetime Achievement Award, and Singapore's Woman of the Year award. She is the author of Silver Shades of Grey: Memos for Successful Ageing in the 21st Century.

Margaret Thomas was a journalist for more than 25 years at The Business Times, The Singapore Monitor, SPH AsiaOne, and TODAY. She now works primarily on book projects and, in various voluntary roles, on the pursuit of gender equality and an open, informed, and inclusive society. She was a founder member of AWARE (Association of Women for Action and Research) in 1985 and its president from 2018 to 2022. She has also been involved in civil society organisations and initiatives such as TWC2, the Singapore Women's Hall of Fame, and the Singapore Advocacy Awards.

A Bit More About This Book

Cheng Puay Koon explains how she came up with the cover design:
When Margie and Kani told me our book title, I thought 'Yeah, why not!' They suggested a subtle illustration showing some people looking forward. My watercolours were right next to me, and I couldn't resist whipping up a wash of diverse characters, in different sizes and overlapping spaces. In red that's bold, heartfelt, passionate, and Singaporean. With faces that belong to anyone and everyone, in postures accentuated by emphatic gestures. All on white, where new thoughts often begin. The words found themselves a place too, questioning the need to stay within boundaries. And the little dot simply asked to be coloured red.

The proceeds from the sale of this book will be donated to these organisations:

AWARE (Association of Women for Action and Research)
AWARE is the leading women's rights and gender equality group in Singapore. Formed in 1985, AWARE's mission is to remove all gender-based barriers so as to allow individuals in Singapore to

develop their potential to the fullest and realise their personal visions and hopes. This is done via research and advocacy, education and training, and support services.

www.aware.org.sg

Singapore Women's Hall of Fame

Launched in 2014 by the Singapore Council of Women's Organisations, the Singapore Women's Hall of Fame is a celebration of the women who have made, or are making, an impact on Singapore's development. They are the pioneers and pathfinders, boundary breakers and record holders, risk-takers and change makers, role models and standard setters.

www.swhf.sg

WINGS (Women's Initiative for Ageing Successfully)

WINGS is the only non-profit in Singapore focused on helping older women. Established in 2007, it aims to empower women to age well by keeping healthy both mentally and physically, being financially secure, and staying socially engaged.

www.wings.sg